W9-AOD-838

A History of Austrian Literature 1918–2000

Studies in German Literature, Linguistics, and Culture

A History of Austrian Literature 1918–2000

Edited by
Katrin Kohl and Ritchie Robertson

CAMDEN HOUSE

First published 2006
by Camden House

Camden House is an imprint of Boydell & Brewer Inc.
668 Mt. Hope Avenue, Rochester, NY 14620, USA
www.camden-house.com
and of Boydell & Brewer Limited
PO Box 9, Woodbridge, Suffolk IP12 3DF, UK
www.boydellandbrewer.com

ISBN: 1–57113–276–7

Library of Congress Cataloging-in-Publication Data

A history of Austrian literature 1918–2000 / edited by Katrin Kohl and Ritchie
Robertson.
 p. cm. — (Studies in German literature, linguistics, and culture)
Includes bibliographical references and index.
ISBN 1–57113–276–7 (hardcover: alk. paper)
 1. Austrian literature—20th century—History and criticism. 2. Politics and
literature—Austria—History—20th century. 3. Popular culture—Austria—
History—20th century. 4. Publishers and publishing—Austria—History—20th
century. I. Kohl, Katrin M. (Katrin Maria), 1956– II. Robertson, Ritchie.
III. Title. IV. Series: Studies in German literature, linguistics, and culture
(Unnumbered)

PT3818.H57 2006
830.9'94360904—dc22

2006013223

A catalogue record for this title is available from the British Library.

This publication is printed on acid-free paper.
Printed in the United States of America.

Acknowledgments

W̶E SHOULD LIKE TO THANK all contributors for the enthusiastic commitment they brought to this project — their cooperative approach made it a pleasure to work on the volume. We are also most grateful to Jim Walker and James Hardin of Camden House for their meticulous editing, probing questions, and generosity in finding mutually satisfying solutions. Their robust criticism posed challenges that invariably proved fruitful. Thanks are further due to Jane Best for seeing the book through the production stage.

Thanks are due to the following persons and institutions for permission to reproduce illustrations: Erwin Schuh, CONTRAST Foto, Vienna; The Austrian National Library; Carl Hanser Verlag and the Heirs of Elias Canetti; DLA Marbach; Filmdokumenationszentrum - Filmarchiv Austria and Wiener Film KG Morawsky & Co.; Colin Davey and Camera Press, London; Frau Christine Basil; steirischer herbst Press Office; Bezirksmuseum Alsergrund; Dokumentationsstelle für neuere österreichische Literatur / Bildarchiv Wien and Garibaldi Schwarze; Isolde Ohlbaum; Matthias Horn; Ingrid Votava, Pressefoto Votava, Vienna; edition exil, Vienna.

Katrin Kohl and Ritchie Robertson
Oxford, July 2006

Note on the Dates and Translations

LIFE DATES OF AUSTRIAN AUTHORS are provided in the index, and additionally given in the text where there is extended discussion of an author's work. On the first mention, the titles of German works are given in the original, with the translation in parentheses, normally followed by the date of first publication. Titles of published translations (in italics) are given where the translation is discussed. Quotations from the German are normally provided in the original with a translation in parentheses. Unless otherwise indicated, translations of titles and quotations are by the author of the contribution and intended primarily to convey the meaning of the original.

Key Dates

1918   3 November: Austria signs armistice, ending its participation in the First World War.

   11 November: The Emperor Karl formally gives up participation in state affairs (he never formally abdicates).

   12 November: The Republic of Deutsch-Österreich (German Austria) is proclaimed, though the name "Deutsch-Österreich" is abandoned in 1919.

1927   15 July: after members of an ex-servicemen's organization are acquitted of killing an old man and a boy by shooting on a Socialist march, a crowd gathers in Vienna to protest against this miscarriage of justice and sets fire to the Palace of Justice; the police open fire on the crowd, and 89 people are killed (including four policemen).

1933   Engelbert Dollfuss, supported as Chancellor by the Christian Social Party and the right-wing paramilitary Heimwehr, suspends Parliament, orders the disbandment of the Socialist militia (the Schutzbund), declares the Austrian Nazi Party illegal, sets up the "non-partisan" Fatherland Front, and begins reorganizing the state along corporate lines inspired partly by Italian fascism.

1934   February: the Civil War begins when units of the now illegal Socialist Schutzbund in Linz forcibly resist a search for weapons by the police, and spreads to Vienna. Though no mass uprising occurs, fighting in industrial centers kills 193 civilians and 128 members of government forces. The Socialists are defeated and outlawed.

   25 July: a Nazi putsch in Vienna fails, but Dollfuss is assassinated.

1938   12 March: the German Army enters Austria, which undergoes annexation (*Anschluss*) to the Third Reich.

1943   1 November: the Moscow Declaration by the Allies identifies Austria as the first free country to fall victim to Hitler's policy of aggression.

1945 Austria liberated by the Allies and divided into four zones.

27 April: the provisional Austrian government is recognized by all four occupying powers, restoring the Constitution of 1920.

1955 15 May: the State Treaty restores Austrian sovereignty.

1986 Kurt Waldheim, a distinguished diplomat who was Secretary-General of the United Nations from 1971 to 1981, is elected president of Austria, despite revelations that he had been an officer in a German army unit responsible for war atrocities, and that he had given an inaccurate account of his war service.

2000 Governing coalition formed between the conservative People's Party (ÖVP) under Wolfgang Schüssel and the far-right (anti-immigration, anti-EU) Freedom Party (FPÖ) under Jörg Haider, its chairman since 1986. At the end of the year, however, Haider resigns as Party leader in order to concentrate on his role as Governor of Carinthia, since when the FPÖ's national popularity has severely declined.

Introduction

Katrin Kohl and Ritchie Robertson

GIBT ES EINE ÖSTERREICHISCHE LITERATUR?" — Is there such a thing as Austrian literature? This question, posed for a survey in 1936, was famously answered in the affirmative by Thomas Mann: "Die spezifische Besonderheit der österreichischen Literatur ist zwar nicht leicht zu bestimmen, aber jeder empfindet sie" (The specific particularity of Austrian literature is not easy to define, but everyone perceives it).[1] The vagueness of Mann's response was not designed to lay this question to rest, and it has become a standard point of departure for reflections on Austrian literary identity. In 1976, exile writer Hilde Spiel used Mann's answer as the starting point for a history of postwar Austrian literature, and in 1995 the novelist and poet Julian Schutting asked the question afresh in his contribution to a literary anthology on Austrian literature.[2] The parameters of the question are clear: at issue is the relationship between Austrian literature and the "German literature" that ambiguously refers both to the literature produced by the larger neighbor and to all literature written in the German language.

The question of Austrian literature's identity is of interest not because it promises a stable definition of the characteristics of the country's national literature by means of robustly defensible criteria, but because it casts the spotlight on interactions between the country's literature, its linguistic identity, its cultural constellations, and the political developments that shape a continuously changing public sphere. Moreover, the introduction to this volume ought to provide the reader with some discussion of the question even if it fails to deliver a definitive answer. For the essays in this book cover ground that has already received attention in Ingo R. Stoehr's *German Literature of the Twentieth Century: From Aestheticism to Postmodernism* (2001), the final part of the Camden House History of German Literature.[3] Stoehr examines literature written in the German language in Germany, Austria, and Switzerland. The present volume complements his wider perspective with a closer look at the continuities and tensions of a literature that has derived strength both from its integration in the community of German speakers, and from its specific national and cultural identity.

Throughout the twentieth century, Austrian literature was caught up in political tensions between the assertion of Austrian difference and potential assimilation to Germany. Austria has repeatedly had to reconfigure its identity since the loss of the Austro-Hungarian Empire in 1918 — the year that forms the starting point for this volume. The history of Austrian literature in the twentieth century is connected at every turn with the country's political history, and the question of the identity of Austrian literature cannot be considered without the context of political developments. An overview of the country's history between 1918 and 2000 will therefore serve to highlight the issues that shape the debate about literary identity, while at the same time providing historical reference points for the essays on the literature itself.

Austrian History from 1918 to 2000

The year 1918 marks the defeat of Austria-Hungary in the First World War and the dissolution of the empire. There was no single moment of military defeat. Indeed 1918 began encouragingly with negotiations between the Central Powers, dominated by Germany and Austria-Hungary, and Russia, which after the Bolshevik Revolution was prepared to make peace even on the harsh terms dictated by the Treaty of Brest-Litovsk (signed on 3 March 1918). Despite a further peace treaty with Romania, Austria failed to defeat its other neighboring enemy, Italy, and in September 1918, when the Western Allies forced the German Army to abandon its front-line position, it became clear, with shocking suddenness, that the Central Powers had no hope of victory. The sufferings of soldiers at the front — Austrian troops recorded proportionately heavier losses than those of any other combatant nation — and of civilians at home, increasingly afflicted by starvation and disease, had all been for nothing. On 4 October 1918 Germany and Austria requested an armistice, which Austria signed on 3 November.

The various nationalities that composed the empire had grown increasingly restive as the unpopular war dragged on. Their aspirations to autonomy, or even independence, were fostered by France and Britain, who announced in January 1917 that their victory would mean the liberation of the Slavs, Italians, and Romanians within the empire. After the United States entered the war in April 1917, President Woodrow Wilson on 8 January 1918 issued his peace program consisting of Fourteen Points, of which the tenth ran: "The peoples of Austria-Hungary, whose place among the nations we wish to see safeguarded and assured, should be accorded the freest opportunity to autonomous development." Late in 1918, as military and political authority broke down, Czech nationalists assumed power in Prague, Hungary proclaimed itself a republic, and the state of Croatia-Slavonia was set up in Zagreb. As the empire fragmented around them, the German speakers in and around Vienna began constructing their own state. On 21 October 1918, they set up a provisional national assembly of "German Austria" (*Deutsch-Österreich*), with a coalition government formed ten days later. Bowing to the inevitable, the Emperor Karl issued a proclamation on 11 November, declaring: "I renounce any participation in the business of the State."[4] Unlike his German counterpart, he never formally abdicated. (He moved abroad, dying of pneumonia in Madeira at the age of thirty-five in 1922.)

The problems of the new republic included fuzzy boundaries and an uncertainty about its identity. Speakers of Slovenian in Carinthia and of Hungarian in the Burgenland were eventually able to decide their future by plebiscites that assigned these territories to Austria; South Tyrol, however, became part of Italy. Many speakers of German were stranded outside the new state, especially in the area called the Sudetenland, which was annexed by the new state of Czechoslovakia. Moreover, was "German-Austria" still Austria? The moderate Socialist leader Karl Renner, who became its first chancellor, suggested calling it "Ostalpenlande," the Eastern Alpine Lands. The name "German-Austria" was favored especially by Social Democrats, who hoped for union with a Socialist Germany. Such a union was expressly forbidden in the peace treaty of St. Germain, published in July 1919, and to discourage the idea further, the name "German-Austria" was forbidden. Despite the mismatch with its recent imperial past, the new rump state called itself the Republic of Austria.

As in Germany, the new state emerged amid revolutionary upheavals, vividly recounted by Franz Werfel in his novel *Barbara oder die Frömmigkeit* (Barbara or Piety, 1929). The Social Democrats were prevented from swinging far to the left, however, by fear of intervention from the victorious Entente powers, by concern that any extensive nationalization program would simply mean "nationalizing debts,"[5] and by the warning example of the short-lived Soviet Republic in Munich, bloodily suppressed in May 1919, and its Hungarian counterpart under Béla Kun. They were also aware that the provinces were dominated by a politically literate farming class that supported right-wing parties, especially the Christian Socials, and whose political influence counterbalanced that of the industrial workers. The Social Democrats introduced some national reforms, including unemployment benefits and the eight-hour day (both in winter 1918). As the largest party in the Constituent Assembly, but without a majority, they formed a coalition with Christian Social and German nationalist parties under Chancellor Karl Renner (February 1919), but the elections of November 1920 sent the Socialists into opposition, and for the rest of its life the First Republic was governed by a succession of Christian Social chancellors. Outstanding among these was Ignaz Seipel, a Catholic priest and intellectual of working-class origins, formerly professor of moral theology at Vienna University, who held office in 1922–24 and 1926–29. His influence was crucial in gaining Catholic support for the new republic. Seipel firmly opposed Socialism and favored instead the paternalistic and conservative social policies (*Sozialpolitik*) that were eventually formulated in Pope Pius XI's encyclical *Quadragesimo anno* (1931).

The First Republic was divided politically between its solidly conservative provinces and its Socialist capital. From May 1921, the city government had a Social Democratic majority in every election. "Red Vienna" under its mayor Karl Seitz practiced redistributive taxation, with heavy taxes on luxuries such as cars, racehorses, and servants helping to fund outstanding hospitals, schools, and welfare services. The greatest achievement of "Red Vienna" was its subsidized housing. Between 1923 and 1933, 65,000 new apartments were built, including such famous housing schemes as the Karl-Marx-Hof. These projects drew in distinguished architects like Adolf Loos, who from 1921 to 1924 was director of the Gemeindebauamt (Office for the Construction of Settlements). More generally, enthusiastic intellectuals sought to bring art to the people by such institutions as the Social Democratic Agency for Art (Kunststelle) founded by David Josef Bach.

In the provinces, however, an increasingly important role was played by paramilitary organizations, often consisting of ex-soldiers. They originated amid the chaos immediately after the war, to protect local populations and repel attempts at territorial annexation by Yugoslavia, Hungary, and Italy. They were soon united under the name "Heimwehr," and were encouraged by Christian Social governments as a kind of auxiliary police. A Socialist counterpart, the Schutzbund, was formed in 1923.

The young republic managed to survive the threat of civil war and overcome the inflation, which reached its peak in 1922. In that year Seipel persuaded the League of Nations to stabilize the Austrian currency by a loan of 650 million gold crowns. A new unit of currency, the Schilling, was introduced. The mass unemployment of the immediate postwar years was reduced, but it never fell below ten percent of the working population.

A defining moment for the republic was the riot outside the Palace of Justice in Vienna on 15 July 1927. This riot was provoked by a politically motivated miscarriage of justice: some members of a right-wing paramilitary organization, accused of shooting a forty-year-old Socialist and an eight-year-old boy earlier that year during a political confrontation in the village of Schattendorf, near the Hungarian border, were tried and acquitted on 14 July by a slender majority of the jury. On the following morning, protest demonstrations were held in Vienna. The demonstrators were forced by mounted police away from Parliament into the square outside the Palace of Justice. The police fired from inside the building into the crowd, which eventually succeeded in forcing an entrance and setting fire to the building. Ordered by their chief, Johannes Schober (himself following instructions from Chancellor Seipel), to clear the square, the police continued to shoot into the crowd (thus also preventing firemen from saving the building, which burned to the ground). This incident, together with sporadic disturbances the next day, resulted in ninety deaths and over a thousand injuries. "In the annals of policing in the western world," writes Edward Timms, "there is no massacre of comparable magnitude."[6] Instead of resigning or being put on trial, however, Schober was praised and decorated for maintaining order. Popular confidence in the government was irreparably damaged.

In September 1929 Schober became chancellor, against the background of the renewed world economic crisis. Although Schober actually strengthened democracy, the next few years saw an increase in the power of the paramilitaries. The Heimwehr formed a political party, which denounced parliamentary democracy. In September 1929 they briefly formed a governing coalition with the Christian Socials under Schober's successor, Carl Vaugoin, with the Heimwehr leader Prince Ernst Rüdiger Starhemberg as Minister of the Interior, but were sent into opposition by the elections two months later, which produced a Christian Social and Pan-German government.

All this time the growth of National Socialism in Germany was being watched from Austria, with dread by some and sympathy by others. From 1926 on the small Austrian Nazi Party, previously divided and ineffectual, was placed under the direct control of Hitler. As the crises of the republic deepened, Nazis increased their support: in 1930 they obtained only 27,000 votes in the civic elections in Vienna, but by 1932 they received 201,000 votes.

Austria seemed to be becoming ungovernable. In May 1932, the conservative Catholic Engelbert Dollfuss, a politician in Seipel's mold, became chancellor. In March 1933, prompted by a breakdown in parliamentary procedure, Dollfuss suspended Parliament and the Constitutional Court. The Socialist paramilitary, the Schutzbund, was disbanded. Dollfuss set up the Fatherland Front (Vaterländische Front) as an organization to unite the population and supersede political parties and trade unions. At its first mass rally on 11 September 1933, Dollfuss proclaimed the corporatist reorganization of the state, putting forward a conservative and Catholic definition of Austrian identity, deploring the decline of feudal society, the rise of liberalism, soulless materialism, and unrestrained capitalism, and promising to roll back liberal democracy.[7]

In thus creating the *Ständestaat* (corporate state), Dollfuss was fulfilling his own convictions and carrying out a long-established Catholic and anti-Socialist program; he was also following instructions from Mussolini, who wished Austrian society to be remodeled along lines similar to Italian fascism, as his price for supporting Austria's independence from Germany. Dollfuss firmly opposed Nazism. When the Bavarian Minister of Justice, who had recently called for the Austrian government to be overthrown, arrived in Austria for a lecture tour in May 1933, the Deputy Police Chief met his plane and informed him that his visit was unwelcome. The Austrian

Nazis stepped up a campaign of terror, while Hitler attempted to cripple Austria's tourist industry by imposing a tax of one thousand marks on German visitors to Austria. By April 1934 some 50,000 Nazis had been convicted of political or criminal offenses in Austria. Many of them were confined in a special camp near Wiener Neustadt.

The Left, however, suspected that Dollfuss's prime aim was to crush Social Democracy, and responded with armed insurrection. Raids on illegal Schutzbund arms depots in Linz prompted the Social Democratic Party leadership to proclaim a general strike on 12 February 1934. There was fighting in the Viennese suburbs, Linz, Graz, and various industrial centers, but the Social Democrats were disorganized and poorly armed, and the general strike did not happen. Despite desperate resistance in housing estates such as the Karl-Marx-Hof, the insurrectionaries were defeated within two days by the army supported by the police and the Heimwehr. Some two hundred Socialists were killed, as were 138 of the government forces. Social Democracy was crushed, its party suppressed, the trade unions dissolved, and the leaders of the Left were exiled. In retrospect, Dollfuss's decision to destroy Socialism for fear of its revolutionary potential, instead of allying himself with moderate Socialists against the internal and external Nazi threat, looks like a fatal error. Indeed, as a contemporary journalist asserted, it was "political suicide" — even if it did secure support from Mussolini (with whom Dollfuss had conferred only four days before the Civil War).[8]

Austria's incorporation into Greater Germany could not be long postponed. On 25 July 1934 the Nazis attempted to seize power in Austria by a putsch. Nazis attacked the Chancellery on the Ballhausplatz in Vienna during a cabinet meeting and shot Dollfuss, leaving him to bleed to death. Thanks to the army and the Heimwehr, the putsch was defeated. For a while, Hitler adopted more conciliatory tactics. But Italy, committed to imperialist war in Africa and under increasing German influence, could no longer guarantee Austria's independence. On 12 February 1938, Hitler summoned Dollfuss's successor as chancellor, Kurt Schuschnigg, to his Bavarian mountain residence at Berchtesgaden. He subjected Schuschnigg to a long tirade and demanded that Nazi activity should be freely permitted in Austria and the Austrian Nazi Arthur Seyss-Inquart appointed Minister of the Interior. Back home, Schuschnigg tried to challenge Hitler by calling a referendum on union (*Anschluss*) with Germany, but Hitler forestalled him by ordering the German Army to enter Austria on the day planned for the referendum, 13 March. Mussolini promised Hitler his support. Schuschnigg resigned as chancellor. At midnight on 11 March, after a day of rioting by triumphant Nazis, Seyss-Inquart was appointed as chancellor. Although Seyss-Inquart tried to stop the invasion, it went ahead, and on the afternoon of 12 March Hitler entered Austria at his birthplace, Braunau am Inn, whence he proceeded to Linz along roads lined by cheering crowds. On 13 March Austria was formally annexed to the German Reich. The next day Hitler arrived in Vienna, where the Archbishop, Cardinal Innitzer, had ordered church bells to be rung and swastika banners hung from church steeples (for which Innitzer was soon reprimanded by Pope Pius XI). On March 15, Hitler addressed an enthusiastic crowd, a quarter of a million strong, on the Heldenplatz, assuring them that Austria, now referred to as the Ostmark, would be the Reich's bulwark against the storms coming from the (Communist) East.[9]

Immediately after the *Anschluss,* many outrages were committed against Austrian Jews. Jewish women were ordered to scrub pro-Schuschnigg slogans off sidewalks with their bare hands or with tooth-brushes; Jewish actresses from the Theater in der Josefstadt were compelled to clean the toilets of the Nazi Sturmabteilung (SA); Jews were insulted, robbed, had their apartments looted and their automobiles confiscated.[10] In March 1938 alone, 220 Jews committed suicide. Within three months, Jews had been removed from Austrian public life. Some 128,500 managed to emigrate. The pogrom of 9 November 1938, known as "Kristallnacht" (Night of Broken Glass), was at least as savage in Austria as in Germany: all but one of the twenty-four synagogues and seventy prayer houses in Vienna were burned down, and over four thousand Jewish-owned shops were looted. The subsequent treatment of "the Jewish problem in Austria" was initially entrusted to the notorious Adolf Eichmann, who proved so efficient at arranging the deportation of Jews that in October 1939 he was promoted to take charge of Jewish deportation for the entire German Reich. Austrians were disproportionately prominent in conducting the Holocaust. Odilo Globocnik, who was Gauleiter (District Chief) of Vienna in 1938, later supervised the death camps at Treblinka, Sobibor, and Belzec. In the death camps, Austrians formed forty percent of the staff. Austrians also made up some thirteen percent of the Schutzstaffel, or SS, although their share in the population of the Reich was only eight percent. There was an Austrian concentration camp at Mauthausen, near Linz, where prisoners were worked to death within a few months. By the end of the war, 65,459 Austrian Jews had been killed by various means.

After the war, Austria's first imperative was survival. It was divided into four zones of occupation, with Vienna split into four sectors. Its impoverishment was made worse by the French and Russian troops' policy of living off the land, and by the Russians' confiscation of machinery and raw materials to rebuild the yet more devastated Soviet economy. Austria benefited, however, from the European Recovery Program, also known as the Marshall Plan after the US Secretary of State George Marshall. By 1949, industrial production was higher than before the war. The elections of November 1945 brought a narrow victory for the conservative Austrian People's Party (Österreichische Volkspartei; ÖVP) over the Socialist Party of Austria (Sozialistische Partei Österreichs, later Sozialdemokratische Partei Österreichs, SPÖ), with the Communists far behind. Fears that Austria would follow other Eastern European states into the Communist bloc were finally dispelled when the Russians withdrew in 1955. The Russians were probably responding to the lack of popular support and also anxious, after Stalin's death, to display a change of policy from expansionism to coexistence. They cooperated with the other powers in signing the Austrian State Treaty, after years of negotiation, on 15 May 1955 in the Belvedere Palace. In the treaty, Austria pledged to become a neutral country, like Switzerland.

To heal the scars left by the conflicts of the 1930s, especially by the Civil War, postwar Austria was governed from 1945 to 1966 by the Grand Coalition of the two major parties, the conservative Austrian People's Party and the Socialist Party of Austria. Political offices and civil service posts, right down to schoolteaching and local administration, were systematically divided between adherents of the two parties in a system known as "Proporz." In 1970, after a move toward the political center had increased support for the SPÖ, Bruno Kreisky became the first Social Democratic chancellor, continuing in office until 1983, when the SPÖ lost its majority. The next three years saw an incongruous coalition government between the SPÖ and the small right-wing Freedom Party (Freiheitliche Partei Österreichs, FPÖ), led by Kreisky's former minister of education Fred Sinowatz. Another Grand Coalition between the SPÖ and the ÖVP was established in 1987 and endured, under Chancellor Franz Vranitzky and (from 1997) his successor Viktor Klima, until October 1999.

The question of Austrian complicity in the Third Reich was for a long time avoided. It was carefully glossed over in the Moscow Declaration, issued by the Allies on 1 November 1943, which described Austria as "the first free country to fall victim to Hitlerite aggression," although it also warned that Austria must accept responsibility for taking part in the war on the side of Nazi Germany.[11] The "responsibility clause" was duly quoted in the Declaration of Austrian Independence (27 April 1945), but was described as only a "postscript," and it did not appear at all in the Austrian State Treaty (1955), which established the Second Republic. This elision matched the dominance in postwar Austria of an interlinked series of narratives that tended, as the historian Robert Knight has argued, to gloss over the darker side of recent Austrian history by stressing what Austria had learned from the Nazi past, its narrow avoidance of Communism, and its progress toward sovereignty and neutrality.[12]

However, it presently became apparent that many Austrians had learned little from the past, and that denazification had been perfunctory compared with the corresponding processes in East and West Germany. The Nazi past reasserted itself in a series of scandals. In 1965 Taras Borodajkewycz, a professor at the Vienna Commercial Academy (Wiener

Handelsakademie), was obliged to take early retirement because in his lectures he had repeatedly expressed sympathy with Nazism. Ten years later
Simon Wiesenthal, director of the Jewish Documentation Center in
Vienna, produced evidence that during the war Friedrich Peter, leader of
the FPÖ, had served as an SS officer in a unit that had carried out mass
murders. Surprisingly, Kreisky — an unimpeachable liberal of Jewish
descent — defended Peter, and the basis of Wiesenthal's charges remained
controversial. The FPÖ again made headlines in 1985 when its Defense
Minister, Friedhelm Frischenschlager, went to the airport to welcome in
person Walter Reder, a former SS officer who had just been released from
over thirty years' imprisonment in Italy for war crimes.

None of these incidents, however, attracted remotely so much attention as the Waldheim affair. Kurt Waldheim, a distinguished diplomat who
had been Secretary-General of the United Nations from 1972 to 1981,
stood for the presidency of Austria in 1986. It emerged that in his recently
published autobiography he had misrepresented his war service, claiming
that he had been recovering from wounds in Vienna at a time when he had
in fact been serving with the SA stormtroopers (paramilitary units of the
Nazi Party) in the Balkans. Suspicions that Waldheim might have been
concealing war crimes were never confirmed. An investigatory commission
reported that he had passed on intelligence about suitable targets for military "cleansing actions." The campaign against him, spearheaded by the
World Jewish Congress, placed him under a cloud internationally; he was
declared *persona non grata* in many countries, including the USA. In Austria, however, it probably increased his popularity, for he was elected president with an impressive fifty-four percent of the vote, and continued in
office until 1992.

Austria's next dose of negative publicity came with the electoral surprise of October 1999. The national elections confirmed the importance of
the FPÖ under the youthful and athletic Jörg Haider, who had been worry-
ingly outspoken since the late 1980s. Himself the son of committed Nazi
Party members, he had publicly praised Hitler's employment policies and
congratulated SS veterans on their decency.[13] Haider opposed the stagna-
tion of the "Proporz" system and advocated nationalist policies that were
hostile to immigration and to Austrian membership in the European Union
(Austria joined the EU in 1995). In 2000 the FPÖ won twenty-seven percent of the national vote. After months of slow negotiations, in February
2000 it formed a governing coalition with the ÖVP under Chancellor Wolfgang Schüssel. The rise to power of an unacceptably illiberal far-right party
caused international alarm, which was only slightly alleviated when Haider
resigned from his party's leadership in 2000 to concentrate on his role as
governor of Carinthia, for he was thought still to be controlling his party
from behind the scenes. The FPÖ's style of government and broken promises
also left many of their former voters disillusioned. In the elections held on

24 November 2002, they suffered the biggest loss of votes in Austria's history, going down from twenty-seven percent to only ten percent. Most of these losses went to the more moderate ÖVP, whose share of the vote rose from twenty-six percent to forty-two percent, the highest level in decades. In 2005, Haider founded a new party, the Bündnis Zukunft Österreichs (Alliance for the Future of Austria), and was expelled from the FPÖ. His career is perhaps most noteworthy for his success in uniting against him writers, artists, and intellectuals, foremost among them the courageously outspoken novelist and playwright Elfriede Jelinek, who in 2004 became the first Austrian writer (unless one counts Elias Canetti) to receive the Nobel Prize for Literature.

It is, then, hardly surprising that in recent decades the exposure of pretense, the investigation of the past, and the reconstruction of memory should have been of increasing concern to Austrian intellectuals. A substantial body of critical historical research now exists revealing long-term continuities in Austrian anti-Semitism and traditions of intolerance toward Slav nations.[14] Alongside this may be set the work of writers since 1945 who have looked behind the schmaltzy image projected by Austrian tourism to reveal social and ecological decay in Alpine landscapes (notably Thomas Bernhard in *Frost*, 1963, and Jelinek in *Gier*, Greed, 2000) and the continuing presence of pro-Nazi intolerance amid large sectors of the population (Bernhard again in his longest novel, *Auslöschung*, Extinction, 1986, and in his provocative drama *Heldenplatz*, 1988). Austrian literature is interwoven with Austrian history, often providing trenchant critiques of government policies and evolving hard-hitting narratives of resistance.

A Distinct National Literature?

Austria's independent national status established in 1945 secured not only its political and geographical shape, but also its cultural identity, although connections with Germany remain strong. The two countries share the same written language, the name of which can subsume literature by Austrian writers indistinguishably into the larger body of "German literature." Such assimilation is supported by the fact that the most successful Austrian writers have participated fully in the literary life of Germany and have published their work with major German publishers: to take only a few examples, Hugo von Hofmannsthal published mainly with Fischer, Peter Handke and Friederike Mayröcker with Suhrkamp, and Ingeborg Bachmann with Piper. Moreover, there is a shared literary heritage: like their German colleagues, Austrian writers in the twentieth century looked to Johann Wolfgang Goethe, Friedrich Schiller and Friedrich Hölderlin as their "classics," notwithstanding special affinities with Austrian writers such as Franz Grillparzer, Johann Nestroy, or Adalbert Stifter.

Nevertheless, the focus on Austrian literature yields distinctive perspectives. Unlike Berlin, Vienna retained its central national role throughout the twentieth century, and continued to be shaped by its illustrious history as the capital of an empire encompassing many cultures and languages. Although it underwent heavy bombing during the Second World War, Vienna was not ravaged like its German counterpart, and it has seen a more gradual transition into the modern era. There is a productive tension in Austria between the cosmopolitan center and the provincial periphery, while regional identities are well developed with their own cultural centers in cities like Klagenfurt, Graz, and Salzburg. These centers are by no means parochial: long before the current boom in literary festivals, Klagenfurt developed a major literary event in 1977 focused on the award of the prestigious Ingeborg-Bachmann-Preis. The Tage der deutschsprachigen Literatur (Days of Literature in German) now attract writers from Germany and Switzerland as well as homegrown Austrian talent, providing a whole series of prizes as well as a course for young writers, and giving authors intensive media coverage across German-language television and radio channels. Many rural areas of Austria saw virtually nothing of the two wars, and there is a strong sense of a continuous Austrian tradition that was indeed deliberately fostered in the postwar period in order to eliminate National Socialism from the nation's cultural memory.

In the postwar era, the difference between the literature written in Austria and the literature written in the Federal Republic of Germany is one of distinctive constellations rather than clearly defined boundaries. Where writers in Germany have negotiated narratives of cultural discontinuity and supposed new beginnings while also facing the issues of political and ideological division, Austrian writers have contended with the pressures of traditionalism. Yet the conservative literary establishment has provided a context in which avant-garde movements have flourished and literary provocations have gained a high public profile — most prominently those by Bernhard and Jelinek.

A different linguistic heritage also plays an important part in giving Austrian literature a distinct identity. The disintegration of the Austro-Hungarian Empire left Austria with only vestigial ethnic minorities — notably the Slovenes — to recall its rich linguistic past. Yet even with respect to the German language, there are differences by comparison with Germany. Dialect and regional linguistic variants have higher status in Austria than in Germany, and can be subsumed under the broad category of "Austrian" if the aim is to identify a national language distinct from "German." As with the issue of cultural identity, the question of Austrian linguistic identity is one that is based less on empirical facts than on cultural needs.

The changing concepts of identity emerge in comments by writers responding to the cultural and political environment. A prominent voice between the wars was that of Hugo von Hofmannsthal, himself an icon of Austrian culture.[15] In an essay entitled "Österreich im Spiegel seiner Literatur" (Austria in the Mirror of its Literature), published in 1916, he posits that Austrians experience an emotional dualism: in terms of nationality, they identify with Austria, while culturally, they feel that they belong to a greater German whole, a German "Gesamtwesen."[16] He finds a synthesis in the destiny of a Greater Germany when he celebrates Austrians as the supreme embodiment of the German spirit and the German past; in that context there is need for a practical, radical, and immediate "Austriazismus" (Austriacism, 349). By 1927, Hofmannsthal's focus has changed: in a lecture delivered in Munich, "Das Schrifttum als geistiger Raum der Nation" (Literature as the Spiritual Space of the Nation), Austrian identity is subsumed in the German nation to the point of invisibility as Hofmannsthal evokes the unity of spiritual culture and politics within a new German reality in which Austrians and Germans can participate as a united nation.[17]

In the light of the atrocities perpetrated in the name of the Greater Germany, postwar Austrian writers were generally keen to follow the lead of the politicians and assume separation from the discredited neighbor. While contact and integration with the larger German language community have generally been vital to literary success, asserting difference has served as a strategy to avoid association with Germany's National Socialist past, and as a means of establishing independence and indeed superiority in the face of the more prominent literary culture. Ingeborg Bachmann, for example, availed herself of all the publishing and publicity opportunities offered by the German authors' association Gruppe 47, and argued in 1955 on pragmatic grounds that Austrian writers should be considered part of German literature, since "provincial" and "regional" literary products had no chance of long-term survival.[18] Yet a visit to Auschwitz in 1973 prompted her to assert difference with respect to the very factor that most obviously unites the countries — language. Alluding to Bernard Shaw's much-cited distinction between the British and the Americans, she comments: "Wir haben sehr viele Fehler gemeinsam, [. . .] nur eins haben wir nicht gemeinsam — und das ist die Sprache. Sprache heißt aber auch: Unser Denken ist anders, weil unsere Sprache anders ist" (We have many failings in common, [. . .] but there's one thing we don't have in common — and that's our language. However, language also means: our thinking is different, because our language is different, 132). The comment is not just revealing with respect to the question of political and cultural identity — it also indicates the high status of language in the self-perception of Austrian writers. While Bachmann here draws on cognitive linguistics to assert that "Austrian" writing differs from "German" writing even when Austrian writers use standard German, other writers such as the avant-garde poets H. C. Artmann and Ernst Jandl enriched the common German medium

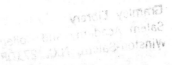

with a specifically Austrian idiom, bringing dialect into the domain of mainstream written German literature.

Following the end of the Cold War, the specter of National Socialism has receded as a factor contributing to national identity, but there has been a strengthening of regional identities across Europe. Tensions between cultures are no less evident today, as writers and cultural historians address issues of national identity in the face of far-right nationalist tendencies, multiculturalism, globalization, and the impact of American culture. For some, Austria's integration in the supranational context of a united Europe has justified a new confidence in its relation to Germany, as the country has gained a new "regional" identity on a par with that of other European cultures. Confidence in the specificity of Austrian culture underpins the historiographical projects undertaken by Herbert Zeman, who set out in the late 1970s to chart the course and identity of Austrian literature — producing the first Austrian literary history since Josef Nadler's history of 1948.[19] Zeman is not troubled about the existence or definition of his subject: for him, the distinct identity of Austrian literature is founded in an incontrovertible cultural truth, and it is in the service of that truth that he seeks to uncover Austria's enduring literary achievements.[20] His concern is to define the boundaries of the Austrian "Literaturraum" (literary territory) and gather proof of a distinctive consciousness of Austria as an entity — an "Österreichbewußtsein."[21] Writing from within Austria, he sees his ambitious historiographical project as a specifically Austrian contribution to the defense of regional identities in Europe.

The historiographical project presented with this volume is altogether more tentative and exploratory. When Mann affirmed the special quality of Austrian literature in 1936, he made little attempt to find criteria that might serve to secure it: subsequent generations have sought to identify an empirical basis for the "feeling" that Austrian literature has a distinct identity, and Zeman is currently seeking to provide scientifically robust evidence that will close the question once and for all. This volume will not add to these attempts. With its title it opts for the fuzzy boundaries of "Austrian literature" as opposed to the solution favored by Austrian literary historians, who generally define their subject as "literature written in Austria"; the choice of title is intended to signal the absence of clear-cut answers.[22] The editors did not prescribe boundaries that would definitively include or exclude specific writers based on cultural heritage, nationality at time of birth, or place of residence at the time of writing. Each essay will pursue connections on its own terms and be as inclusive as its author deems appropriate. Similarly, the temporal limits that mark out the subject of individual essays will be handled flexibly.

The essays follow a broadly chronological order, although the volume does not aim to provide a historical survey. Rather, it seeks to offer a network of approaches to twentieth-century Austrian literature in which the authors trace developments in the major literary genres, illuminate aspects of popular culture, investigate the role of cultural institutions, and consider the literary responses of writers to the most controversial issues of their time: the disintegration of the Habsburg Empire in 1918, National Socialism and the Holocaust in the middle of the century, and multiculturalism and migration at the turn of the millennium. The political and social caesura of National Socialism and the Second World War is reflected in Austrian culture, and most of the topics discussed are therefore dealt with in two essays, treating the prewar and postwar periods separately. Yet the discourse at the center of this volume is an uninterrupted one, and tradition provides important continuities that are as controversial as they are fruitful in the postwar period, so a number of essays bridge the divide in order to explore the ways in which the past is continually reconfigured in response to a fast-changing present. A number of essays on the major literary genres — two each on drama and prose fiction, one on poetry — focus on the writers and works that constitute the mainstream tradition of Austrian literature, giving a sense of their literary quality, highlighting experiments, and pursuing complex processes of reception. The specifically literary focus of these essays is complemented in other essays by a wide range of different perspectives that relate literature to its cultural, political, and institutional context. It should thereby emerge that throughout the twentieth century, Austrian literature is both highly self-reflexive and intensely responsive to other discourses, engaging with philosophical, linguistic, social, and political issues in ways that are seldom straightforward, often shocking, and at best linguistically vibrant and intensely thought-provoking.

In the changing fortunes of twentieth-century Austrian literature, drama occupied a particularly prominent place because of its dependence on public institutions and its contested role in forging the nation's cultural identity. It could build on a rich nineteenth-century tradition that ranged from the tragedies of Franz Grillparzer, which appealed to audiences across the German-speaking countries, to the *Volksstücke* by Ferdinand Raimund and Johann Nestroy, which were written in dialect and intended for a Viennese audience. In her chapter on Austrian drama in the first half of the twentieth century, Judith Beniston shows how this varied tradition is taken further. Going beyond such familiar names as Arthur Schnitzler, Hofmannsthal, Werfel, and Ödön von Horváth, she re-evaluates the work of Karl Schönherr, draws attention to Austria's contribution to Expressionist drama, and examines the efforts made, from various political directions, to express and explore the concept of Austrian identity. Juliane Vogel shows how theater was used in the postwar years to restore Austria's self-image in the spirit of the Habsburg era, while from the mid 1950s, new types of drama emerged that sought to counteract such myths of continuity. They do so less by overt political statement than by an experimental critique of language and by inventive use of the body as a performative medium, subverting the established order and foregrounding the violence of patriarchal structures. The chapter concludes with a discussion of the "new *Volksstück*," highlighting how postwar Austrian drama has built productively on tradition, using the sociocritical potential of this genre to give a grotesque view of the disintegration of urban and rural communities in the Alpine republic.

Austria has brought forth an impressive array of internationally established novelists in the twentieth century, and many others who are barely known outside the German-speaking world. Ritchie Robertson finds Austria's contribution to interwar prose fiction to lie not only in the "novel of totality" pioneered by Robert Musil and Hermann Broch, but also in the internationally-minded humanism of Joseph Roth and Stefan Zweig. He suggests a positive re-evaluation of the *Heimatroman*, whose association with conservative politics has caused critics to overlook the complexity and even the emancipatory thrust of some examples of the genre, and draws attention to the range of fiction by women, often anti-Nazi exiles, which has until recently been ignored. This chapter also looks ahead by discussing the work of Heimito von Doderer, who began writing in the 1920s, though his best-known novels appeared in the 1950s, and by considering how two novelists publishing after 1945, George Saiko and Albert Drach, offer searching retrospectives on the interwar period. In his chapter on prose fiction after 1945, Jonathan Long distinguishes two tendencies in the postwar years: conservative, stylistically traditional novels that support restorative values, and novels that draw on modernist techniques to confront the immediate Austrian past critically; the latter have generally been more successful in establishing themselves in the canon of literature in German. Like the *Volksstück*, the *Heimatroman* has continued to be a productive genre in the postwar era, with writers subverting its sentimental parochialism in order to articulate forceful critiques of contemporary society. The chapter discusses a wide range of novelists including a number of lesser-known women writers and Jewish writers, while looking in detail at the novels of Bernhard, Handke, Jelinek, and Bachmann, who are generally acknowledged to be among the most important postwar writers in German.

Poetry is treated in a single essay in order to trace the varied ways in which tradition contributed to a continuous dialogue beyond the ruptures of the war and provided an important stimulus for the rise of avant-garde movements in the postwar era. The chapter is permissive in its interpretation of "Austrian" literature, going beyond the borders established in 1918 to include poets such as Rainer Maria Rilke and Paul Celan, who were Austrian by cultural origin or nationality, but who lived and worked in other countries. In considering the poetic response to National Socialism, the chapter focuses on the complex role of the German poetic tradition both in the work of the Viennese Nazi poet Josef Weinheber and in the work of two Prague exile poets, Franz Baermann Steiner and H. G. Adler. The purpose of this juxtaposition is not to elide political and moral difference, but to demonstrate the diachronic and synchronic connectedness of a discourse that is all too often separated by means of political and geographical criteria. With respect to the postwar era, the chapter highlights the importance of Ludwig Wittgenstein's theory of "language games," which inspired ludic experiments with the linguistic elements of poetry and with dialect poetry. It concludes with a brief look at the trend toward diversification at the turn of the millennium, with the re-emergence of the "learned" poet, and the rise of performative, popular forms such as poetry slam.

Traditionally, Austrian culture is marked by a sharp distinction between "high" culture and "popular" or "entertainment" culture, although this is perhaps less extreme than in Germany, with the *Volksstück* and dialect poetry being examples of forms that refute such a division. The increasing importance of Anglo-American literature and the enhanced status of mass culture are tending to foster more integration at the turn of the millennium, and have also encouraged broader perspectives of historical study. Two essays focusing on prewar and postwar popular culture investigate how literature interacts with other media, in particular film, while also conveying the cultural context of the major literary genres. Janet Stewart traces the rise of mass commercial culture and evokes the vibrancy of cabaret and film in the prewar period. She explores the tension between culture and politics by showing how aspects of popular culture were mobilized first by the Social Democratic government of Vienna under the First Republic and then by the Catholic and conservative policies of the *Ständestaat*, while finally being subjected to totalitarian control under the Third Reich. This perspective indicates the powerful economic role of popular culture and highlights its significance as a political force — a force that intellectuals were slow to appreciate. Joseph McVeigh focuses on radio, television, film, and music in the Second Republic to trace the changing cultural role of these popular media. He considers the impact of the Allied radio networks on occupied Austria, discussing the clash between American concern with advocating responsiveness to public taste, and the aim of Austrian politicians to educate the public and provide it with "moral protection" through censorship. In all the media, he sees a tension between the popularity of foreign, especially American, media output, and a domestic policy of combating cultural "Überfremdung" (foreign domination). It is a tension he still finds evident at the turn of the millennium, especially in music, suggesting that popular culture in Austria is in no danger of losing touch with traditional forms.

The role of literature in the public arena cannot be fully appreciated without reference to the institutions that determine its dissemination, and two essays therefore investigate the means of publication and the institutional context of literature before and after the war. Murray Hall identifies the traditional importance of German publishing houses for Austrian literature, tracing this to a highly restrictive approach to literature in the Habsburg Monarchy: a multitude of regulations, the prevalence of censorship, and lack of copyright protection in Austria meant that throughout the nineteenth century, Austrian writers often preferred to publish with German publishers. Hall depicts the interwar years as a period of rapid change, with more favorable conditions encouraging the emergence of new publishing houses in Austria — though many were short-lived, and Germany remained the dominant market. He investigates the role of literary institutions in a period that was marked by political conflict, and shows how these institutions contributed to the debate about what literature is and how it should project itself in the public sphere. Anthony Bushell charts the political context of literature after the ravages of the war and traces the emergence of institutions that were to determine the publishing landscape of the postwar era. His essay investigates the divergence between those who sought to restore Austria on the basis of an earlier, uncontaminated era, and those who urged their contemporaries to build a new cultural world that would leave the past behind while addressing the questions it so urgently raised. He traces the role of exile writers in the emergence of the new institutions, but highlights the unwelcoming approach toward exile writers within Austria and the fact that most did not return, which meant a severe impoverishment of the literary life of the Second Republic. Literary journals are shown to be important for the postwar decades, as they provided authors with a medium of publication, although the conservative taste of most editors meant that the young avant-garde found it difficult to gain a foothold in the literary world. Bushell indicates the powerful influence of state-run institutions on literature, a notable example being the Vienna Burgtheater. More generally, the antagonism between state-sponsored and alternative literatures emerges as a distinctive feature of Austria's literary landscape.

Two essays focus specifically on the impact exerted by the all-encompassing force of National Socialism on Austrian literature. Andrew Barker traces the interaction between politics and literature in the years between 1927 and 1956. His essay takes as its starting point the year of the riot outside the Vienna Palace of Justice, which marked the end of the First Republic, and as its endpoint the year when Doderer published his novel *Die Dämonen* (The Demons, 1956), in which he pays tribute to the victims of 1927. Going beyond the traditional caesuras of the *Anschluss* in 1938 and the inauguration of the Second Republic in 1955, Bushell addresses the controversial question of writers' involvement with the conservatism of the *Ständestaat* and in some cases with Nazism, showing how more critical and left-wing writers were not just forced into exile but had their work recognized only gradually in a postwar Austria where conservative critics were still arbiters of taste. Dagmar Lorenz explores similar territory from a different angle by focusing on responses to National Socialism and the Holocaust, themes that came to the fore relatively late in Austria. In her essay, too, the quintessentially Austrian figure of Doderer is prominent, whose massive and engrossing Viennese novels display his talent while imperfectly concealing the right-wing sympathies that had led him in the 1930s to join the National Socialist Party. Lorenz's essay demonstrates the continuing importance of the past for Austrian writers, while also teasing out the ways in which politically aware writers engage with the changing threats to personal and social freedom in a society where new communication technologies are determining the individual's participation.

In the concluding essay, Allyson Fiddler examines responses in narrative prose, drama, poetry, and film to the shifts in a society where minority cultures are increasingly claiming a voice. While the end of the Habsburg era had reduced the country's identity to that of a German-speaking culture, and Nazism had driven out Jewish citizens, the assumptions of cultural homogeneity that characterized the postwar era have repeatedly been called into question as other ethnic groups have asserted themselves, and a defense of Austrian values became associated once again with nationalism and racism in the controversies around Jörg Haider. Fiddler's essay breaks new ground in showing how German-speaking Austrian writers, writers from indigenous ethnic minorities, and immigrant writers foreground processes of cultural interaction at the turn of the millennium. Fiddler considers works with black protagonists, written by white writers, in which skin color is used to expose Austrian cultural tolerance as part of the Habsburg myth, and she discusses films and installations that focus on xenophobic tendencies among Austrians. Documentary modes and techniques of reality TV reveal both subtle and overt mechanisms of cultural exclusion and highlight the nationalist prejudices that surround issues such as the expulsion of foreign workers and asylum seekers. Works by immigrant authors from Bosnia-Herzegovina are examined alongside works by the established writer Barbara Frischmuth, in which she treats Turkish-Austrian relationships. By demonstrating how Austrian literature has become a discursive space for the exploration of highly complex processes of cultural interaction, Fiddler also refutes the view that the emergence of literature in German by Austrians originating from non-German-speaking cultures weakens the identity of Austrian literature. She demonstrates rather that writers are reflecting current changes in Austrian society and challenging the German-language majority to expand its conception of Austrian culture.

The authors of the essays in this volume are from a variety of countries, and they are writing for an international readership. The purpose of the volume is to complement histories of German literature that subsume Austria into a larger whole by giving a more localized sense of the concerns and connections that were significant in literature written by Austrian writers and in Austria between the demise of the Austro-Hungarian Empire and the turn of the millennium. For there is no doubt that a focus on Austrian literature yields a specific sense of tradition as well as a special constellation of concerns and tensions. Yet the volume also differs from those stridently Austrian ventures that seek to press literary history into the service of cultural politics. It assumes that the question whether there is a distinct Austrian literature is most fruitful where it remains open-ended, exploring connections rather than defining essences and boundaries.

Notes

[1] Thomas Mann, "['Gibt es eine österreichische Literatur?']," in T. Mann, *Gesammelte Werke*, 12 vols. (Frankfurt: Fischer, 1960–74), vol. 10, 919.

[2] Hilde Spiel, "Die österreichische Literatur nach 1945. Eine Einführung," in *Die zeitgenössische Literatur Österreichs*, ed. H. Spiel, Kindlers Literaturgeschichte der Gegenwart. Autoren — Werke — Themen — Tendenzen seit 1945 (Zurich and Munich: Kindler, 1976), 11–127; here: 11. Julian Schutting, "Gibt es eine österreichische Literatur?" in *Literatur über Literatur: Eine österreichische Anthologie*, ed. Petra Nachbaur and Sigurd Paul Scheichl (Graz: Styria, 1995), 25–29.

[3] Ingo R. Stoehr, *German Literature of the Twentieth Century: From Aestheticism to Postmodernism*, vol. 10 of *The Camden House History of German Literature* (Rochester, NY: Camden House, 2001).

[4] Quoted from C. A. Macartney, *The Habsburg Empire 1790–1918* (New York: Macmillan, 1969), 833.

[5] Martin Kitchen, *The Coming of Austrian Fascism* (London: Croom Helm, 1980), 12.

[6] Edward Timms, *Karl Kraus, Apocalyptic Satirist*, vol. 2: *The Post-War Crisis and the Rise of the Swastika* (New Haven and London: Yale UP, 2005), 336.

[7] "Wir wollen das neue Österreich" in *Dollfuß an Österreich: Eines Mannes Wort und Ziel*, ed. by Hofrat Edmund Weber (Vienna: Reinhold, 1935), 31.

[8] See G. E. R. Gedye, *Fallen Bastions: The Central European Tragedy* (London: Gollancz, 1939), 91. Gedye's eyewitness account of events from 15 July 1927 to the *Anschluss* in March 1938 remains invaluable.

[9] This follows the detailed narrative in Ian Kershaw, *Hitler 1936–45: Nemesis* (London: Allen Lane, 2000), 70–82.

[10] Bruce F. Pauley, *From Prejudice to Persecution: A History of Austrian Anti-Semitism* (Chapel Hill, NC, and London: U of North Carolina P, 1992), 280.

[11] See Judith Beniston, "Introduction," *Austrian Studies* 11 (2003), 1–13; here: 2.

[12] Robert Knight, "Narratives in Post-War Austrian Historiography," in *Austria 1945–1955: Studies in Political and Cultural Re-emergence*, ed. by Anthony Bushell (Cardiff: U of Wales P, 1996), 11–36.

[13] See Hella Pick, *Guilty Victim: Austria from the Holocaust to Haider* (New York and London: Tauris, 2000), 183.

[14] For a conspectus, see *Das große Tabu: Österreichs Umgang mit seiner Vergangenheit,* ed. by Erika Weinzierl and Anton Pelinka ([Vienna]: Verlag der Österreichischen Staatsdruckerei, 1987).

[15] His essays serve as a point of reference for both Spiel, "Die österreichische Literatur," 14–16, and Schutting, "Gibt es eine österreichische Literatur?," 25.

[16] Hugo von Hofmannsthal, "Österreich im Spiegel seiner Dichtung," in Hofmannsthal, *Gesammelte Werke in Einzelausgaben,* ed. by Herbert Steiner (Stockholm: Bermann-Fischer, and Frankfurt am Main: S. Fischer, 1945–59), *Prosa III,* 333–49; here: 345.

[17] Hugo von Hofmannsthal, "Das Schrifttum als geistiger Raum der Nation," in Hofmannsthal, *Gesammelte Werke, Prosa IV,* 390–413; here: 413.

[18] Ingeborg Bachmann, *"Wir müssen wahre Sätze finden." Gespräche und Interviews,* ed. by Christine Koschel and Inge von Weidenbaum (Munich and Zurich: Piper, 1983), 12.

[19] Josef Nadler, *Literaturgeschichte Österreichs,* Linz 1948, [2]1952.

[20] Herbert Zeman, "Vorwort," in *Literaturgeschichte Österreichs von den Anfängen im Mittelalter bis zur Gegenwart,* ed. by H. Zeman (Graz: Akademische Druck- und Verlagsanstalt, 1996), vii–viii.

[21] Zeman delivers a systematic definition of the specific characteristics of Austrian literature as part of a mammoth seven-volume project: "Die Geschichte des Begriffs einer Literatur Österreichs. Literaturraum und Österreichbewußtsein," in *Geschichte der Literatur in Österreich von den Anfängen bis zur Gegenwart,* ed. by Herbert Zeman, vols. 1- (Graz: Akademische Druck- und Verlagsanstalt, 1994–), vol. 7, 639–84.

[22] See Josef Nadler, *Literaturgeschichte Österreichs* (Linz: Österreichischer Verlag für Belletristik und Wissenschaft, 1948). See also the titles of Zeman's volumes, cited above, who uses geographical and political boundaries to define his subject as well as seeking to identify special characteristics. We are grateful to Sigurd Paul Scheichl for giving us access to his lecture notes entitled "Abriss der Literaturgeschichte Österreichs" (University of Innsbruck, winter semester 2002/2003), in which he discusses the issue of terminology: he rejects use of the term "österreichische Literatur" not out of any nationalist or regionalist impulse, but because of its implied essentialism, and its problematic implication that Austrian literature differs in essence from that of the Federal Republic of Germany. While at first sight the designation "Literary history of Austria" is straightforward, it loses its clear boundaries if the coverage extends back beyond 1945. Even after 1945, both terms have often been used synonymously. This is evident from the volume edited by Spiel (see note 2, above), which specifies "literature of Austria" in its title but refers in the title of the introductory essay to "Austrian literature." Since literature is a cultural phenomenon, it is not unequivocally defined by political and geographical boundaries, as the importance of the German publishing context for Austrian writers demonstrates.

1: Drama in Austria, 1918–45

Judith Beniston

Political and Institutional Factors

T HE POLITICAL UPHEAVALS OF 1918–19 — the collapse of the Habsburg
Empire, the declaration of the First Austrian Republic and the associated threat of Bolshevik Revolution — were accompanied not only by economic crisis and grave material privations but also by widespread
sociocultural and psychological disturbance. Austrian identity became
problematic for many: deprived of the cohesion provided by the dynastic
factor, the rump Republic had little to unite its largely conservative and
rural Alpine provinces with an over-large, now geographically peripheral
capital city that had long been famed for its cosmopolitanism and for the
modernist culture of its predominantly Jewish intellectual elite. As elsewhere in Europe, the aftermath of war saw a destabilization of traditional
authority structures and of relations between the sexes, reflected in a relax-
ation of public morality and of censorship regulations. In the theater,
where censorship was immediately reduced and then abolished altogether
in 1926, this destabilization allowed many taboos to be broken but also
called forth hostile reactions that were all too frequently underpinned by
anti-Semitic prejudice. Furthermore, as the rival political camps grew ever
more implacable in their opposition to each other, dramatists found it
increasingly difficult to stand aloof from the competing ideologies.

The politics of the newly democratic republic had major institutional
repercussions for the Austrian, and especially Viennese, theater. Most
directly affected were the former court theaters (the Burgtheater and
Opera House), which came under state control and as such became the
subject of ongoing economic and ideological wrangling between the state
government, which was dominated from 1920 on by the Christian Social
Party, and, from 1919 until 1934, a Social Democratic municipal authority. While the perceived representative function of the Burgtheater as Austria's national stage meant that its future, which remained uncertain until
1922, was the subject of intense public debate, it became commonplace for
private theaters in the capital to change management with disturbing frequency,
experience periods of closure (sometimes permanent) due to bankruptcy

or be converted into cinemas.[1] This tendency was particularly marked during the early postwar years, which saw not only a shortage of material resources, rampant inflation, and the resultant impoverishment of the middle classes but also, and illogically, an expansion of the entertainment sector that was untenable given a decrease in the overall population of Vienna and ever greater competition from film, radio, and spectator sports.

The situation was rendered even more complex, both economically and ideologically, by the ambitious (and ambiguous) cultural politics of "Red Vienna." On the one hand, the introduction in 1918 of an entertainment tax (*Lustbarkeitsabgabe*) exacerbated the financial difficulties, even though drama, opera, and classical music were taxed at far lower levels than, for example, cinema, wrestling, and horse-racing. On the other hand, the creation of *Kunststellen*, cut-price ticket agencies making theater, opera, and classical music available to people who could not otherwise afford such entertainments, offered a lifeline to the theater industry by increasing the potential audience. However, this support came at an ideological price as two of these agencies, the Kunststelle der sozialdemokratischen Arbeiterzentrale (Cultural Agency of the Social Democratic Workers' Central Office) and the Kunststelle für christliche Volksbildung (Cultural Agency for the Promotion of Christian [i.e. non-Jewish] Community), functioned as the cultural arm of the major political parties (the Social Democrats and Christian Socials respectively) and aimed to influence both the cultural tastes of party members and, by force of numbers, the repertoire of the city's professional theaters. Until around 1926, the Social Democratic organization, and its president David Josef Bach, enjoyed considerable success, and many contemporary commentators note that, collectively, the *Kunststellen* brought about a marked change in the social composition of the theater-going public.

This opening up of the theater to new and more democratic influences did not, however, extend to women dramatists. Around the turn of the century, and coinciding with the beginnings of the women's movement, Marie von Ebner-Eschenbach, Else Bernstein (writing under the pseudonym Ernst Rosmer) and Marie Eugenie delle Grazie had all made tentative inroads into this traditionally male-dominated institution, and by the 1920s women were prominent in other areas of Austrian literature and intellectual life — for example, Enrica von Handel-Mazzetti, Paula Grogger, Vicki Baum, Helene Deutsch, and Rosa Mayreder. Between the wars, Austrian women continued to write drama, but no female playwright is conventionally present in literary histories of the First Republic, and analysis of the repertoire reveals that only a tiny number of plays written by women were performed in the major theaters.[2] In this respect, Vienna was more conservative than Berlin, where the politically leftist and artistically innovative circles around Bertolt Brecht and Erwin Piscator included not only Marieluise Fleisser and Elisabeth Hauptmann but also Anna Gmeyner

(1902–91), an Austrian who worked as Piscator's *Dramaturgin* for several years, and Galician-born Communist Berta Lask (1878–1967), both of whom will be discussed below.

War and Its Aftermath

During the First World War it had been observed repeatedly that Viennese audiences remained shamefully escapist in their predilection for comedy and operetta; but recent events did find a variety of responses in the work of Austrian writers, with the appearance of several powerful anti-war dramas. Alongside *Antigone* (1917) by Walter Hasenclever, *Jeremias* (Jeremiah, 1917) by Stefan Zweig (1881–1942) dresses up the modern conflict in mythical garb in order to plead for universal brotherhood, while the Euripedes adaptation by Franz Werfel (1890–1945), *Die Troerinnen* (The Trojan Women), completed in 1914 and staged in Vienna in 1920, uses similar techniques to dignify the sufferings of the defeated populace. Austria's most remarkable literary reckoning with the First World War and the mentalities it fostered was, however, produced by Karl Kraus (1874–1936) in his vast satirical panorama, *Die letzten Tage der Menschheit* (The Last Days of Mankind). Written largely between 1915 and 1917, it was serialized in Kraus's magazine *Die Fackel* (The Torch) in 1919, with the full revised text appearing in 1922. Structured as a five-act tragedy with prologue and epilogue, and comprising more than two hundred scenes of varying length, it has little traditional dramatic development and conveys only a limited sense of the progress of the war. Rather, the dominant principle is that of dramatic montage. As Kraus observes in his introduction, tragic events are played out by a cast more suited to operetta; consequently, cabaret, puppet theater, and carnivalesque moments repeatedly intrude. Another formal model on which he draws is that of "cosmic" drama, of a *theatrum mundi* observed, and ultimately judged, from an extraterrestrial standpoint. Whereas the traditional Christian view is that all human activity has value and meaning if considered aright, for Kraus war is senseless, however one views it, and demonstrates only the moral bankruptcy of society. Rather than expressing satisfaction with the world, as the Lord was to do at the close of Hugo von Hofmannsthal's *Das Salzburger große Welttheater* (The Salzburg Great Theater of the World, 1922), *Die letzten Tage* ends with a Voice from Above summoning a meteor shower to destroy the earth.

Historians have often asserted that the First World War was the first major conflict in which the media exerted substantial influence. Kraus, for whom the journalistic degradation of language had long been a prime satirical target, perceived from the outset that the military conflict was accompanied by a war of words: much of the text (even, according to

Kraus, the most improbable sections) is derived from documentary sources, and the vast majority of the named characters are based on real people. War correspondents, politicians, and creative writers turned propagandists are all condemned out of their own mouths. That such influences penetrated public discourse is suggested as each act opens with a Viennese street scene in which newspaper sellers tout their wares and as Kraus uses his ear for dialect to eavesdrop on the language and opinions of representative passers-by — juxtaposing his observations with those of newspaper reporters sampling the public mood in more partial fashion.

Carrying on its original frontispiece the notorious photograph of the execution of Cesare Battisti — an Irredentist whom the Austrians hanged for treason in 1916 — *Die letzten Tage der Menschheit* is a pioneering intermedial work. Several scenes are inspired by photographs, some of which, such as a line of nurses in gas masks looking like giant insects, were included in the published text. Propaganda posters provide a frequent topic of conversation for the Grumbler ("Der Nörgler") and the Optimist ("Der Optimist"), whose commentaries punctuate the play in a manner that anticipates Brechtian techniques, while cinematic projections are called for at several points. Although individual scenes are intensely theatrical — in both auditory and visual terms — *Die letzten Tage* has rarely been staged and Kraus himself deemed it fit only for a Martian theater ("Marstheater"). The sole exception to this lack of production, during his lifetime, was the Epilogue, "Die letzte Nacht" (The Final Night), which was performed in Vienna as a charity event in 1923. Here, the text shifts into verse, as Expressionist drama is prone to do at its climax; humanity is reduced to grotesque stylizations — Dying Soldier, Male Gas Mask, Female Gas Mask, Hussar of the "Skull-and-Crossbones" Regiment, the Lord of the Hyenas — and dialogue gives way to monologue and spoken oratorio.

While *Die letzten Tage der Menschheit* affords glimpses of how conditions on the home front deteriorated as the war dragged on, a grim picture of Vienna in its aftermath is offered by two of Austria's most important but neglected writers of the early twentieth century, Karl Schönherr (1867–1943) and Max Mell (1882–1971), each of whom published in a Viennese newspaper a dramatic poem that gives a voice to typical victims of war and poverty — women scavenging for food and fuel, mothers whose children are starving or dead, discharged officers waiting to die from their wounds, amputees, the homeless, the hungry and the unemployed. In *Das Wiener Kripperl von 1919* (A Viennese Nativity Play for 1919), excerpts from which appeared in the *Wiener Mittag* on Christmas Eve of that year, Mell offers these victims the solace of Christianity, as their number 52 tram takes them on an unexpected trip to Bethlehem, with God in the driving seat and Archangel Gabriel collecting tickets. In Schönherr's *Die Ballade vom Untergehen* (Ballad of Ruin), published in the *Neues Wiener Tagblatt* on 16 January 1921, there is no such comfort; the impression is rather of a *deus absconditus*, challenged in the final lines of the text to reveal his presence, but remaining ominously silent:

ERSTE KEHRFRAU *reckt die abgezehrten Arme gen Himmel:*
Herrgott,
Wenn bist:
Laß Schießpulver
Regnen.
Blitz drein.
Kehrfrauen verschwinden.

GROSSER SCHIEBER *springt auf. Mit Messer und Gabel in Händen.*
Reckt sich in wildem Übermut nach oben:
Da.
Straf mich.
Gott.
Blitz nieder:
Hunger schrein
Ist mir
Tafelmusik.

(FIRST WOMAN STREET-SWEEPER *stretches her scrawny arms heavenwards:* Lord God, if You are there, let it rain gunpowder. Strike him down with a lightning bolt. *The street-sweepers disappear.*
    BIG-TIME PROFITEER *jumps up. Brandishing his knife and fork. Stretches out his arms in a gesture of ferocious arrogance:* Go on. Punish me. God. Smite me down. For me, cries of hunger are music to dine to.)

In juxtaposing the plight of the victims with the selfish hedonism of the profiteer, Schönherr focuses attention firmly on the socio-economic rather than spiritual dimension of poverty. And, just as, most famously in Remarque's *Im Westen nichts Neues* (All Quiet on the Western Front, 1929), attention later turned back to the war in an attempt to understand the roots of present troubles, so in 1925 Schönherr returned to *Die Ballade vom Untergehen*, expanding it into a full-length play that he repeatedly revised in subsequent years, most evocatively under the title *Hungerblockade 1919*. Austria also provided a companion piece to Paul Reynal's *Le Tombeau sous l'Arc de Triomphe* (The Unknown Warrior, 1924) and R. C. Sherriff's *Journey's End* (1931) — the powerful *Wunder um Verdun* (Miracle at Verdun, 1931) by Hans Chlumberg (1897–1938), in which the war dead briefly rise from the grave and return to their former lives, only to discover how little their sacrifice has wrought.

Established Reputations:
Hofmannsthal, Schnitzler, Schönherr

Of the two Austrian dramatists who had enjoyed international renown in the prewar period — Arthur Schnitzler (1862–1931) and Hugo von Hofmannsthal (1874–1929) — only the latter continued to enhance his reputation as a dramatist and to develop new areas of activity. The fortunes of Karl Schönherr, who had enjoyed considerable success within the German-speaking countries since the early years of the century, were in certain respects comparable to those of Schnitzler.

The concern to define and defend his understanding of Austrian identity that dominates Hofmannsthal's wartime lectures and journalistic essays, culminating in "Die österreichische Idee" (The Idea of Austria, 1917), also underpins his work for the theater in the early years of the Republic. Indeed, in creative and ideological terms the collapse of the Monarchy appears not to have been a major caesura for Hofmannsthal: the comedy *Der Schwierige* (The Difficult Man) was substantially written between 1917 and 1919, while the Salzburg Festival, plans for which go back to 1916, was inaugurated in 1920 with a production on the cathedral square of his *Jedermann* (Everyman, 1911), and the Festival's ideology of rooted cosmopolitanism — at once showcasing local traditions of folk drama and celebrating a broader European heritage — had needed little revision in 1918.

Undoubtedly one of the best German-language comedies of the twentieth century, *Der Schwierige* combines irony and nostalgia in equal measure, inviting the spectator to laugh at and with the title figure but nonetheless allowing him and his values to prevail over an aggressive, unlovely modernity. Bringing to life the lists of contrasting characteristics set out in "Preuße und Österreicher" (Prussian and Austrian, 1917), the Prussian Baron Neuhoff spouts the rhetoric of the Nietzschean *Übermensch* and campaigns vigorously for affection and admiration, while the Austrian aristocrat Hans Karl Bühl blunders his way through the play in clownlike fashion, endlessly procrastinating, struggling to make himself understood, and feeling socially awkward. However, despite or because of this gaucheness he becomes the heart of the play in every sense and the repository of its civilized values. Historically, Neuhoff may be in the ascendant, but in this Molièresque comic allegory, it is the Austrian who triumphs, not in politics but in love. What is more, beneath the sparkling surface of the dialogue lies a philosophical questioning of language itself that makes *Der Schwierige* unmistakably a product of Wittgenstein's Vienna.

Its companion piece, *Der Unbestechliche* (The Incorruptible One, 1923), is even more programmatically backward-looking, rehearsing in miniature the "conservative revolution" that was to be the great cultural hope of Hofmannsthal's last years (as set out in the speech "Das Schrifttum als geistiger Raum der Nation" [Literature as the Nation's Spiritual Space, 1927]). The traditional comic intrigue, in which the servant Theodor restores order to the aristocratic household, provides an excellent vehicle for a comic actor, but the play has far less depth than *Der Schwierige* and leaves frustratingly open the significance of the fact that the philandering husband is also a second-rate novelist. However, with ingenious use of irony, Hofmannsthal contrives, as in *Der Schwierige*, simultaneously to advocate marriage as the ethical and mystical foundation of social order and to handle erotic dalliance with a remarkable lightness of touch. That he maintained a sentimental attachment to the multinational empire to the end of his life is demonstrated by *Arabella*, his last opera libretto for Richard Strauss, premièred posthumously in 1933.

Although Hofmannsthal thought of his comedies as continuing the Viennese tradition of the "conversation play" (*Konversationsstück*), long associated with the Burgtheater, his failure to establish his work there was one of several factors that led him in the First Republic to turn away from the capital and toward Salzburg. No less significant was his fascination, from 1918 on, with Josef Nadler's ethnographic approach to literary history. This allowed Hofmannsthal to explain his creativity in terms of a myth of cultural continuity tied in with the unchanging Alpine landscape and to view the Salzburg Festival as realizing "der eigentliche Kunstgedanke des bayrisch-österreichischen Stammes" (the original artistic vision of the Austro-Bavarian tribe). In so doing, he not only helped to deepen the cultural rift between capital and provinces but also laid himself open to the charge of pandering to anti-Semitic prejudice. Nadler's argument that the Austro-Bavarian "tribe" had a special talent for theater, first manifested in medieval folk drama and reaching its high point in the Baroque era, underpins Hofmannsthal's Salzburg promotional material; it also provides programmatic justification for the centrality of *Jedermann* in the Festival repertoire and for the Baroque allegory *Das Salzburger große Welttheater*. While *Jedermann* celebrates the overcoming of modern materialism, Hofmannsthal's *Welttheater* is one of numerous Austrian dramas of the interwar period to conjure up the spectre of Bolshevism. In this adaptation, the Beggar of Calderón's *El gran teatro del mundo* (The Great Theater of the World) becomes a representative of the defiant proletariat that demanded its rights in the revolutions of 1919. He desists from bringing down the social order represented by King, Rich Man, Beauty, Faith and Peasant ("Bauer") after an unexplained change of heart, of the kind typical of both miracle plays and Expressionist drama.

Characterized by a masterful handling of disparate verse forms, both of Hofmannsthal's festival plays also benefited enormously from the visual style of production that was director Max Reinhardt's hallmark. While the banquet scene interrupted by Death is the theatrical high point of *Jedermann*, the *Welttheater* culminates in a wordless pantomime representing the passing of time. The ultimately conciliatory message of *Jedermann*, reminding the rich man of his social and metaphysical duties but having Faith rescue him from the devil's clutches, is another reason why that work has established an enduring performance tradition. In the *Welttheater*, by contrast, there is neither salvation for the Rich Man nor sympathy for the Beggar. The latter's description of his wife and children dying is strikingly reminiscent of Schönherr's representations of 1919, but Hofmannsthal's response — that their suffering is a metaphysical rather than a social evil and that the poor should draw on their spiritual resources — lacks even the compassion of Mell's *Wiener Kripperl von 1919*.

Modern socio-political upheavals are presented with greater subtlety in *Der Turm* (The Tower), an adaptation of Calderón's *La vida es sueño* (Life is a Dream) that diverges much further from its archetype than the *Welttheater* had done: the story of Prince Sigismund, imprisoned by his father in response to a prophecy of parricide that is all but fulfilled in its central scene, is set against the backdrop of a moribund monarchy, paralyzed by war, inflation and class hatred. Especially in Hofmannsthal's first version, completed in 1924, the exploration of ideas has primacy over dramatic considerations, and the play ends with a fantastical conjuring scene in which Sigismund is killed by a gypsy woman. This text is, however, underpinned by a faith in spiritual and political renewal, manifested both in Sigismund's generational revolt and in the messianic figure of the "Children's King" who concludes the final scene. The shorter final version of *Der Turm*, performed in 1928, is much darker, as palace revolution is rapidly overtaken by peasants' revolt and Sigismund, who refuses to be harnessed to either cause, is murdered by the brutal peasant leader Olivier, a figure who, in the course of revisions, came to embody for Hofmannsthal the evils of revolution.

The two other major Austrian dramatists of the immediate prewar period, Arthur Schnitzler and Karl Schönherr, both made more muted impact after 1918, neither succeeding in emancipating himself from a reductive image of his prewar oeuvre. Even if the scandal provoked by productions of Schnitzler's *Reigen* (Round Dance, 1900) in Berlin (1920) and Vienna (1921) demonstrated that some of his work remained provocative, by the 1920s much of his prewar theater, with its focus on social strata that had changed utterly by 1918, was regarded as dated. Although late prose works such as *Fräulein Else* (1924) and *Traumnovelle* (Dream Story, 1926) and are undoubtedly among Schnitzler's best — technically innovative and informed by a complex, modern view of sociopsychological disturbance — none of the four plays completed after 1918 can compete in terms of originality and formal innovation with the best of his earlier work. However, unlike in the novellas, where the idea of mapping postwar concerns onto prewar society has been readily accepted, the fact that none of Schnitzler's postwar dramas is set after 1914 has led to some very harsh judgements. These are particularly undeserved in the case of *Komödie der Verführung* (Comedy of Seduction), the Burgtheater première of which was one of the high points of the Musik- und Theaterfest der Stadt Wien (Vienna Festival of Music and Theater) organized by the Socialist municipality in Autumn 1924. Set in summer 1914, *Komödie der Verführung* offers a panorama of the upper echelons of Austrian society on the eve of their dissolution. Certainly, there are shades of *Reigen* in the numerous projected and actual couplings, and the reassembling of the partygoers in the final act is contrived, but Schnitzler's depiction of relations between the sexes is more in line with Alfred Pfoser's image of the 1920s as a time of "verstörte Männer und emanzipierte Frauen" (confused men and emancipated women) than with earlier social models.[3]

By 1918 it had become commonplace among Austrian commentators to play off Schnitzler's work against that of Schönherr, ironically, a fellow doctor and personal friend.[4] The presumed decadence of the Jewish writer and his predilection for middle-class, urban milieus were contrasted with the supposedly more wholesome values of the Tyrolean peasant world favored by Schönherr. However, in the 1920s, Schönherr, unlike Schnitzler, did engage directly with contemporary social issues, focusing his attention on doctor figures working in urban environments. As well as drawing attention, in his representations of 1919, to the enormous personal sacrifices demanded by their profession, to long hours and often poor remuneration, he lays bare in plays such as *Narrenspiel des Lebens* (Fool's Game of Life, 1919) and *Vivat academia* (1922) the hierarchical career structures and mix of idealism and cynicism that he sees as characterizing the medical profession. There are some deftly drawn characters, but none is as memorable as the indestructible Grutz in *Erde* (Earth, 1907), and the depiction of the milieu is nowhere as complex or compelling as in Schnitzler's *Professor Bernhardi* (1912). The fact that Schönherr repeatedly reworked this material throughout the 1920s is suggestive of his own dissatisfaction with it.

Schönherr's prewar peasant plays had been conceived in a spirit of Liberal opposition to the clerical conservatism of Alt-Tirol; in the 1920s he attempted to distance himself from the more reactionary definitions of regional literature (*Heimatkunst*) that increasingly came to the fore and from the idealizations of Austria's Catholic Baroque heritage that tended to accompany them. This is reflected in his most successful postwar play, *Der Judas von Tirol* (The Tyrolean Judas, 1927), a substantial revision of his first completed work (staged briefly in Vienna in 1897) and one of only two texts from this period to be set in the Tyrol. Taking place in Passeier in January 1810, *Der Judas von Tirol* deals with the betrayal of Andreas Hofer to the occupying French but focuses not on the Tyrolean leader, who appears only in the final tableau, but on Raffl, the farmhand who betrays him.

Remarkably, Schönherr contrives to arouse sympathy for the traitor by painting an extremely unflattering picture of the community that belittles and ultimately excludes him. In the first two acts a passion play is rehearsed and then performed offstage. This is not a cherished folk custom but an empty tradition that the villagers are paid to uphold; the only performer for whom it has religious significance is Raffl, who dreams of playing Christ and has studied the role with a devotion that is as much spiritual as thespian. His ambition is out of the question because tradition demands that Christ is played by a landowner's son ("ein erbgsessner Bauernsohn"); Raffl is expected to play Judas. Conjuring up the Baroque topos of the *theatrum mundi* in unmistakably critical fashion, Schönherr maps onto the passion play a rigid social hierarchy based on property: "Wer Geld hat, hat auch den Heiligenschein" (If you have money, you can have a halo to go with it). The exchanges in which Raffl rejects the costume of Judas and the social injustice it represents strongly recall the recalcitrance of the Beggar in Hofmannsthal's *Das Salzburger große Welttheater*.

The idea of the actor converted to Christianity by playing the part of a Christian is another familiar Baroque motif. Schönherr inverts it: by playing Judas, Raffl gradually becomes him, losing the ability to distinguish between play and reality in a process of onstage transformation that is psychologically and theatrically enthralling. After hearing of the price on Hofer's head, Raffl's acting undergoes an uncanny improvement, and in betraying him to the French he repeats Judas's lines, counting the ducats into his bag as he had done the thirty pieces of silver.

Alongside *Das Salzburger große Welttheater*, another valuable point of comparison with this play is the work of Max Mell, a friend and protégé of Hofmannsthal who made his name with a trilogy of festival plays, *Das Schutzengelspiel* (The Guardian Angel Play, 1923), *Das Apostelspiel* (The Apostle Play, 1923), and *Das Nachfolge-Christi-Spiel* (The Play of the Imitation of Christ, 1927). The best of these, which was widely staged throughout the German-speaking world, is *Das Apostelspiel*. Here, as in *Der Judas von Tirol*, psychological transformation results from theatrical role-play. In a more flattering portrayal of the Alpine peasantry, two returning soldiers, converted to Communism as a result of their experiences on the Eastern Front, arrive with murderous intent at an isolated croft that is home to fifteen-year-old Magdalen and her grandfather but desist as a result of playing along with Magdalen's naïve belief that they are two of Christ's apostles. The intruders' creed founded on hatred is swept aside by the unshakable love and trust in humanity that flow from the girl's Christian faith. *Das Apostelspiel* is a humorous, actorly little play written in a folksy verse reminiscent of Hans Sachs; just as strident in its condemnation of Communism as Hofmannsthal's Calderón adaptations, it continued to be popular in Austria during the Cold War.

Responses to Expressionism

While Mell drew on the folk traditions of his native Styria, much Austrian drama of the early postwar years was influenced, at least to some extent, by Expressionism. *Mörder, Hoffnung der Frauen* (Murderer, Hope of Womankind) by Oskar Kokoschka (1886–1980) had been staged at the Kunstschau garden theater in 1909, but aside from that and possibly *Die Verführung* (The Seduction, 1916) by Paul Kornfeld (1889–1942), Austrian writers produced none of the movement's defining dramatic works. Although Expressionist staging techniques were gradually introduced, audiences and theaters alike remained wary of radical innovation, with the result that the Berlin theater scene was widely perceived to be more vibrant. The maverick Arnolt Bronnen (1895–1959), author of *Vatermord* (Parricide, 1920), moved there in 1920, for several years working closely with Brecht, and there was certainly no Austrian equivalent to the Brecht–Piscator dynamic. The avant-garde theater designer Friedrich Kiesler (1890–1965), who was born in Czernowitz and studied in Vienna, likewise made his career in Berlin. When he returned to Vienna in 1924 to curate an International Exhibition of New Theater Techniques ("Internationale Ausstellung neuer Theatertechnik") that was part of the Musik- und Theaterfest der Stadt Wien, his work elicited very mixed responses.[5] Furthermore, some of Vienna's most inventive theater productions of the 1920s — making full use of spotlights and of the revolving stage, and influenced in part by Kiesler's work — were created at the Raimundtheater by the Berlin-based director Karlheinz Martin. There was also nothing homegrown to match the visionary radicalism of Georg Kaiser and Ernst Toller: neither Berta Lask's depictions of proletarian revolts past and present in *Thomas Münzer* (1925) and *Leuna 1921* (1927) nor Anna Gmeyner's *Heer ohne Helden* (Army without Heroes, 1929), a chronicle of the 1926 Scottish miners' strike that takes its cue from *Die Weber* (The Weavers, 1893) by Gerhart Hauptmann, made any impact in Vienna, and the Russian Revolution merely furnishes the backdrop for the melodramatic prostitution tragedy *Tanja* (1919) by Ernst Weiss (1882–1940). Instead, the work of Anton Wildgans, Hans Kaltneker, Franz Theodor Csokor and Franz Werfel, the Austrian dramatists most readily identified with Expressionism, is characterized by a more abstract humanism.

The dramatic oeuvre of Anton Wildgans (1881–1932), which spans the period 1913 to 1920, combines realism with a dreamy mysticism, sympathizing with the poor and oppressed in plays such as *Armut* (Poverty, 1914) but stopping well short of political agitation. Derided by such prominent contemporaries as Kraus and Musil, Wildgans nevertheless won broad institutional support, with the result that he twice served briefly as Director of the Burgtheater (in 1921–22 and in 1930–31). His most Expressionist play is *Dies irae* (1918), which deals with the suicide of a son who realizes that each of his parents sees in him only the hated characteristics of the other. Wildgans's sympathy is unmistakably with the school-leaver as he rejects both his father's bourgeois cultural legacy (*Bildung*) and his mother's more mercantile values, with the play ultimately pleading against selfish and thoughtless procreation. Like Moritz in Frank Wedekind's *Frühlings Erwachen* (Spring Awakening, 1891), the son is offered a final chance to embrace life in the form of sexual experience, but his beloved Rosl has more in common with Goethe's Gretchen than with the good-time-girl Ilse and suicide ensues. As in the final acts of *Armut* and of *Liebe* (Love, 1916), prose gives way to verse in the love scene, with the final act of *Dies irae*, "Actus quintus phantasticus," universalizing the family drama by means of a quasi-Goethean finale sung by a "Chorus puerorum et adolescentium" and suggesting that every child's first action at birth is a Munch-like scream of despair.

Less grandiose in its pathos is *Das Bergwerk* (The Mine) by Hans Kaltneker (1895–1919), which was premièred posthumously in 1923 as the thousandth performance under the aegis of the Social Democratic Kunststelle (*Arbeitervorstellung*). Although Kaltneker shows workers planning a general strike in the aftermath of a mining disaster that could have been avoided, and his play can be interestingly compared with both Gmeyner's *Heer ohne Helden* and delle Grazie's *Schlagende Wetter* (Firedamp, 1898), the workers' uprising is ultimately a side-issue in this *Verkündigungsdrama* (drama of annunciation). Whilst trapped in the mine in the first act, the central figure, Michael, has undergone a mystical experience of the goodness of all living things that overturns twenty years as a revolutionary Socialist; as class hatred evaporates, he refuses to lead the workers against their oppressors and is ultimately shot by a younger man, in whom the experience of immolation prompted an epiphany of the opposite kind. Whereas in *Heer ohne Helden* the women of the mining community are strongly characterized and carry much of that play's political message, in *Das Bergwerk* the anxiety of the crowds gathered at the pithead tends to hysteria rather than rage, followed by the pathos of the trapped miners and the agonized debates on the eve of the strike which, in typical Expressionist fashion, are interrupted by the birth of Michael's first child. In contrast to Gmeyner's final scene, which owes more to agitprop than to Naturalism, in *Das Bergwerk* the tension between social and spiritual renewal is upheld to the last, with Michael torn between the desire to pass on an unsullied moral creed and to provide his son with "Bett und Haus, Wiese und Himmel" (a roof and a bed, meadow and sky).

In the case of Franz Theodor Csokor (1885–1969), a dramatic career extending well into the Second Republic continued until the late 1920s to betray its Expressionist roots. The starting-point is *Die rote Straße* (The Red Road, 1918), a balladesque *Stationendrama* that is strongly influenced by Strindberg and Kaiser and follows the relationship of an archetypal couple — identified only as "He" and "She" — as their love is gradually destroyed, from within by compulsive behaviors neither is able to overcome and from without by oppressive social forces, first and foremost the power of money. This is personified in the grotesque non-verbal figure of "der gelbe Mann" (the Yellow Man) who wordlessly seduces the woman by burying her in a pile of gold and symbolically placing the last pieces on her heart and womb. The play is strikingly innovative in theatrical terms: the setting repeatedly shifts from the social to the surreal, as when, in the third scene, the houses of the Lästergasse (literally "Malicious Street"), each with its own voice and architectural style, provide a moralizing commentary on the couple's relationship. Of related interest is the undeservedly neglected intermedial work *Ballade von der Stadt* (Ballad of the City, 1922), inspired by the work of the artist and stage-designer Carry Hauser (1895–1985).

Csokor had a longstanding fascination with the life and work of the revolutionary German playwright Georg Büchner, producing an adaptation of *Woyzeck* that was staged in 1926 and, in 1929, *Gesellschaft der Menschenrechte* (Society for the Rights of Man), a historical drama depicting the radical circles in which Büchner moved in the last three years of his life (1834–37). Although nowadays one smiles at stage directions such as "Wirft sie auf das Sofa. Orgie" (Hurls her onto the sofa. Orgy), the exclamatory diction so typical of Expressionist drama provides a plausible literary idiom for the feverish revolutionaries grouped around Pastor Weidig, and by drawing on Büchner's correspondence and occasionally pastiching the visionary language of his dramas, Csokor makes a good fist of imagining how a great playwright might speak. Csokor's fundamentally humanist stance acquires a political edge as his *Woyzeck* ends with Andres shaving the Captain and barely restraining the desire to slit his throat, and *Gesellschaft der Menschenrechte* offers a deferred hope of revolution in the figure of Wilhelm Liebknecht, Weidig's nephew, who was to become one of the founders of the Social Democratic movement.

The dramatic career of Franz Werfel likewise spans the whole interwar period, ending with his death, in American exile, in 1945. With a couple of exceptions, his plays have not been his most enduring work, even though he established an international reputation with *Bocksgesang* (Goat Song, 1921) and was financially very successful. As lyric poet, Werfel is the most strongly represented in numerical terms in Kurt Pinthus's Expressionist anthology *Menschheitsdämmerung* (Twilight of Humanity, 1920); but by the time he published his "Magical Trilogy" *Spiegelmensch* (Mirror Man) in 1920 he was highly critical of the movement. There is much about the work that is characteristically Expressionistic — it is a *Stationendrama* in which the central figure, Thamal, undergoes a mystical journey of self-development and discovery; in so doing he embroils himself in conflict with his father, develops messianic pretensions, betrays friend and beloved in a manner reminiscent of

Claudio in Hofmannsthal's *Der Tor und der Tod* (Death and the Fool, 1893), and liberates Spiegelmensch, a repressed *alter ego* that is conceived in Freudian rather than Faustian terms, despite many verbal and structural echoes of Goethe's work. Although the relationship between the two figures is not fully developed, the seriousness with which Thamal engages in these activities is repeatedly undermined by the more satirical and worldly commentaries of Spiegelmensch and a protean trio labeled "Die drei Bewunderer" (The Three Admirers). Full of intertextual and topical references, including an escalation of Werfel's feud with Karl Kraus that prompted the latter to respond in satirical kind in *Literatur oder Man wird doch da sehn* (Literature or You Ain't Seen Nothing Yet, 1921), *Spiegelmensch* now appears very dated.

More interesting as drama rather than cultural document is Werfel's next work, *Bocksgesang*. Once again there is an Expressionist *Aufbruch* and a potential for Freudian readings as a couple hide their deformed, goat-like elder son, only for him to escape and become the cultic figurehead for a violent uprising of those socially marginal figures (symbolically including a Jew, a returned émigré and an actor) whose existence their community likewise attempts to deny by refusing them land. Having briefly participated in the revolutions of 1918–19 as a member of Vienna's Red Guard, Werfel repeatedly includes in his dramatic work a critical reckoning with the phenomenon of proletarian revolt and with the nature of political leadership. In *Bocksgesang* revolution is depicted as a Kafkaesque eruption of repressed demonic drives into a world that is dominated by a culture of shame, and the play even has a scene in which, like the Samsas in *Die Verwandlung* (Metamorphosis, 1915), the parents rediscover a loving relationship liberated from the tyranny of their dead son.

Werfel's extremely diverse dramatic oeuvre registers and contributes to several key trends of the interwar period. This includes the revival of interest among Austrian-Jewish intellectuals in Jewish history and traditions that was precipitated by the severe crisis of identity and upsurge of anti-Semitism that they faced following the collapse of the Monarchy.[6] Whereas a sympathetic attitude towards conversion is implicit in Werfel's depiction of the historical emergence of Christianity in *Paulus unter den Juden* (Paul among the Jews, 1926), as it is in *Die Judastragödie* (The Tragedy of Judas, 1920) by Egon Friedell (1878–1938), Werfel's mammoth Jewish festival play *Der Weg der Verheißung* (1935; staged in America as *The Eternal Road*) can be seen as part of a subsequent wave of dissimilation that was largely a response to the Nazi threat. Old Testament history likewise provides the starting-point for the theological drama by Richard Beer-Hofmann (1866–1945), *Jaákobs Traum* (Jacob's Dream, 1918), the prelude to a planned trilogy, of which one further part was completed in 1933, and for Stefan Zweig's *Jeremias* (1917), which he presents in his autobiography, *Die Welt von Gestern* (The World of Yesterday, 1943), as vital for the

development of both his pacifism and his Jewish identity. It is also no coincidence that the Jüdische Bühne (Jewish Theater), which was part of the
Viennese theatrical landscape from 1908 to 1938, enjoyed its most successful year in 1921, despite competing from 1919 until the mid-1920s
with a Freie Jüdische Volksbühne (Free Jewish Popular Theater) that
focused more narrowly on modern Yiddish drama.[7]

Developments in Popular Dialect Drama

It was an irony not lost on right-wing commentators that, while Yiddish
drama flourished, by the 1920s the Viennese tradition of popular dialect
drama (the *Wiener Volksstück*) had all but died out, with hardly any new
works of note having appeared since the 1890s. Furthermore, the legacy of
that tradition was contested territory, with the Catholic camp yoking
together cultural and political conservatism, German nationalists harness-
ing dialect drama to an often anti-Semitic *völkisch* ideology and Karl Kraus
attempting to protect the satirical heritage from being overwhelmed by
Biedermeier quietism, not only in the essay "Nestroy und die Nachwelt"
(Nestroy and Posterity, 1912), but also by regularly including the plays of
Johann Nestroy (1801–62) in the public readings that he had been giving
since 1910. Polemically conceived as the antithesis of Max Reinhardt's
intensely visual style of direction, this text-centered theater of literature
("Theater der Dichtung") was, until 1925, included in the program of the
Social Democratic Kunststelle.

During the interwar period, traditional Viennese dialect drama was
overtaken by two ideologically opposed developments — by the greater
prominence in theater repertoires of regional, especially Alpine dialect
drama, the tenor of which was increasingly anti-modern, anti-Semitic and
anti-urban, and by the emergence of the "kritisches Volksstück," a genre
most notably associated with Ödön von Horváth (1901–38) and Jura
Soyfer (1912–39). Interestingly, both developments draw on the Viennese
tradition, exemplified in the work of Ferdinand Raimund, of the *Zauber-*
and *Besserungsstück*, in which a character with a fault is cured of it by means
of magic or of a magically induced dream.

The Tyrolean peasant play had established itself in Vienna and elsewhere
in the early years of the twentieth century, thanks both to Karl Schönherr
and to the Exl-Bühne, a family-run theater company from Innsbruck who
had been coming to the capital since 1905 and, from the late 1920s on,
often performed there for much of the theater season. While the Liberal
tradition spearheaded by Ludwig Anzengruber and by Schönherr was not
entirely submerged, the potential for erosion of it in works such as Schönherr's *Erde* was increasingly realized, with an emphasis on irrationalism and
on the supposed existence of a religious or mystical bond between the land

and those who traditionally worked it, between *Blut* and *Boden*. Typical of this trend, but not without literary merit, is Max Mell's *Das Spiel von den deutschen Ahnen* (The Play of the German Ancestors, 1935), which begins as a quasi-naturalistic study of the postwar crisis in the rural way of life, as embodied in the dysfunctional Hüttenbrenner family: a family farm bankrupted by mismanagement and wartime neglect; the farmer's flighty wife and her good-for-nothing brother urging him to sell up and turn innkeeper; and his two brothers, one a former pilot horribly disfigured and deracinated as a result of a crash, the other an artist endlessly painting self-portraits in order to find out who he is. Mell's treatment of these problems draws on the tradition of the *Zauberstück*, as the family is suddenly faced with Thomas and Gertraud Hüttenbrenner, their eighteenth-century ancestors. With much of the gentle humor and naivety that are Mell's trademark, even when writing in prose, the revenants confront aspects of modernity (including the bicycle), at the same time reminding successive family members of their duty to the land and to the heritage symbolized by the family Bible. The play's ending is, however, anything but gentle as the impenitent wife, childless by choice, and her wastrel brother are ruthlessly expelled from the family circle.

The writer whose name is most closely associated with the revival of provincial dialect drama at this period is, however, the Upper Austrian Richard Billinger (1890–1965). Initially known as a lyric poet, and promoted by Hofmannsthal and Mell, he occupies an ambiguous position in both political and aesthetic terms. Despite being imprisoned in Germany for three months in 1935, after the *Anschluss* he publicly expressed loyalty to the new regime; and although his work continued to be performed under the Nazis, several of his plays are far less compatible with fascist cultural ideologies than the peasant tragedies *Rosse* (Horses, 1931) and *Der Gigant* (The Giant, 1936).[8] Whereas Mell never loses sight of the Catholic heritage, in Billinger's plays this is invariably in conflict with and theatrically subordinate to pagan myths and folk traditions — which are, in turn, infused with a strikingly modern eroticism. In *Das Perchtenspiel*, written for the 1928 Salzburg Festival, a misguided farmer puts his faith not in the "vierzehn Nothelfer" (fourteen helpers of the needy) but in the eroticized spirit world of the "Perchten"; and in *Rauhnacht* (1931), the celebration of Christmas is overshadowed by the Dionysian excesses that precede it. Like Mell's *Spiel von den deutschen Ahnen*, *Das Perchtenspiel* draws on the tradition of the *Zauberstück* and is uncompromising in its resolution; but Billinger distinguishes far less cleanly between the everyday and the spirit realm, thereby incorporating a pagan mysticism into the presentation of the peasant milieu. While the uninhibited *Ausdruckstanz* and scanty costumes of the "Perchten" led to the play's rapid removal from the Salzburg program, Billinger's best work, *Rauhnacht*, goes even further, demonizing and eroticizing the peasant world in a claustrophobic manner that is reminiscent of Strindberg and Wedekind and culminates in sexual murder (*Lustmord*).

While Austrian audiences in the 1920s and 30s had plenty of opportunity to experience various forms of provincial dialect drama, Horváth's work had only limited exposure, with his dramatic masterpiece, *Geschichten aus dem Wiener Wald* (Tales from the Vienna Woods, 1931), even causing a scandal when it was first performed in the capital in 1948. Jura Soyfer's five surviving *Mittelstücke*, satirical mini-dramas that in 1936–38 formed the centerpiece of left-wing cabaret programs, were seen in the lifetime of their author by only a tiny number of Viennese intellectuals. Drawing on both cabaret techniques and the mechanisms of the *Zauberstück*, Soyfer's theater is unashamedly primitive and political, but nevertheless addresses the burning issues of the day — unemployment, the relationship between technological and social progress, and the threat of fascism — with an energy and artfulness that take it far beyond mere agitprop. In texts such as *Der Lechner Edi schaut ins Paradies* (Edi Lechner's Trip to Paradise; first performed 1936), with its interpolated songs and homely dialect idiom, Soyfer builds on the satirical tradition of Nestroy and Kraus, making it relevant and entertaining for a modern, politicized audience.

Horváth, less aligned with party politics than the Socialist-turned-Communist Soyfer, focuses attention on the social psychology of a petty bourgeoisie that has abandoned dialect in favor of what he calls "Bildungs-jargon," an inauthentic linguistic idiom that condemns them to be at once victims and abusers of language. The ethical core of Horváth's plays invariably lies in sympathetically presented female characters, but the mood is darker than in either Soyfer or Brecht, as no character has the intellect or articulacy to identify the real causes of their oppression and most are prone to take refuge in a vicious, instinct-driven irrationality. While the resultant atmosphere was compared by contemporaries to the work of George Grosz, the recurring stage direction "Stille" (silence) calls for a staccato, non-naturalistic style of acting that draws attention to the gap between conscious speech and subconscious thought and impulse, whether that be attributable to the inherently flawed nature of human language or to specific deceptions and illusions. Above all in *Geschichten*, the inclusion of popular music as ironic counterpoint to the dialogue effects a rapprochement between the legacy of the *Wiener Volkstheater* and Brechtian alienation techniques — as well as attracting the charge of *Nestbeschmutzung* (denigrating his own country).

Catholicism, History, and Constructions of Austrian Identity

In his history of the Burgtheater, published in 1934, Rudolph Lothar suggests that 1927, the year in which political and civil unrest culminated in the burning down of Vienna's Palace of Justice and precipitated a shift towards a more authoritarian style of government, also saw the emergence of "eine ganz neue, großzügige, ernste Wiener Kunst" (a completely new, ambitious and serious Viennese art). On the one hand, this draws inspiration from Catholic traditions; on the other, it has evolved "aus einem nationalen Bewußtsein, das erst im Erwachen, Erstehen und Erstarken ist" (out of a national consciousness that is only now awakening, rising up and growing in strength).[9] What these remarks suggest, especially given the year of publication and the endorsement in the volume's foreword by then education minister and later Austrian Chancellor Kurt Schuschnigg, is that the cultural policy of the Austrian *Ständestaat* (corporate state), declared by Chancellor Dollfuss in May 1934, following the suspension of parliamentary democracy in 1933 and the brief Civil War of February 1934, drew on what were already established trends. The dramatists whose works were to be promoted by the Austro-fascist regime had already enjoyed considerable success in the period Lothar identifies.

For Lothar the Catholic dimension was epitomized by Max Mell. The third of his trilogy of festival plays, *Das Nachfolge-Christi-Spiel*, was indeed premièred at the Burgtheater in January 1928. Much larger in scope than the *Apostelspiel*, it nevertheless reprises several of the key themes, combining a graphic depiction of the breakdown and restoration of traditional order in the aftermath of hostilities (this time the Turkish wars) with an illustration of the redeeming power of lived Christianity. The play's strength as theater is that its outcome, like that of the *Apostelspiel*, can be explained in terms of the Catholic doctrine of mystical substitution (*Stellvertretung*) but is also psychologically plausible: as the central character asserts, "Ich bin ein Mensch, kann nur wie ein Mensch erlösen" (I am a man, I can only redeem as a man). However, as the theater critic Raoul Auernheimer noted in his review, the message of Christian love and forgiveness is accompanied by an unpleasant stereotyping of the play's Jewish characters.[10]

It was Mell's brand of *völkisch* Catholicism, rather than Hofmannsthal's, that attracted imitation. By the author's own admission, *Das Wächterspiel* (The Play of the Guards, 1931) by Rudolf Henz (1897–1987) is modeled on the *Apostelspiel*: "Nur ist es realistischer, dabei ein im Grunde sakramentales Karsamstagspiel, brutal katholisch" (It is just more realistic, basically a sacramental drama for Easter Saturday, brutal in its Catholicism).[11] Although this work was professionally staged, Henz's primary attachment was to the Catholic tradition of amateur dramatics (the *Laienspiel* movement) that had existed alongside Vienna's professional theaters ever since the Christian Social Party had come to power in the late 1890s and had been increasingly active during the First Republic. As the president from 1936 on of the leisure organization Neues Leben (New Life) and author of *St Michael, führe uns!* (Lead Us, St Michael!), a massive sacramental work experienced by a crowd of 50,000 at Vienna's sports stadium in September 1933, he was instrumental in creating the Catholic festival culture of the *Ständestaat* and was also to be a prominent cultural politician in the early years of the Second Republic.[12]

The charmingly naïve, *völkisch* atmosphere of Mell's *Apostelspiel* and *Schutzengelspiel*, in particular, likewise invited imitation, the most commercially successful product being *Tobias Wunderlich* (1929) by Hermann Heinz Ortner (1895–1956). Labeled a "Dramatic Legend," it tells the story of a fifteenth-century altarpiece that is saved from being sold to America by a simple shoemaker (Wunderlich) who is the only villager to value it not merely in monetary terms but as an artwork that was inspired by faith and is part of the local folk heritage. Lacking the sophistication of the *Apostelspiel*, Ortner's play demands an acceptance of the miraculous, at least as theatrical motif, with St Barbara returning to life in the shape of Elisabeth Velbacher, the young woman who had modeled for the original statue. Her evolving relationship with Wunderlich produces much gentle humor and there are heart-warming instances of Christian charity but the religious dimension is ultimately subordinated to an aggressively *völkisch* one — as one reviewer pointed out, this church appears to be without a priest. What matters more is that the art dealers are Jewish and the village worthies ready to sell their own cultural heritage are seen consorting with showgirls and enjoying a sleazy jazz cabaret, complete with Negro compère — thus pandering to *Feindbilder* to which large sectors of the political and cultural Right could assent.

Returning to Lothar's comments on the emergence of "eine ganz neue, großzügige, ernste Wiener Kunst," the second source he identifies for this is a heightened national consciousness. In the theater this manifested itself above all in historical drama, and Lothar claims the *Österreich-Trilogie* (Austrian Trilogy) by Hanns Sassmann (1892–1944), comprising *Metternich* (1929), *Haus Rothschild* (House of Rothschild, 1930) and *1848* (1932), as "der erste Versuch, ein national österreichisches Drama zu schaffen" (the first attempt to create an Austrian national drama).[13] Covering the period between July 1809 and the Battle of Leipzig in October 1813, the first play attempts to rehabilitate Metternich as the statesman who liberated Europe from Napoleon and ensured the survival of Habsburg Austria, thereby providing conservatively minded Austrians with a version of their history to be proud of; the second and third plays, set in 1830–31 and 1848 respectively, show Metternich defeated first by Jewish capitalism and then by revolutionary liberalism. Sassmann, who was the theater critic for the *Neues Wiener Journal*, shared that paper's reactionary stance, with *1848* not only offering an extremely unflattering portrait of the revolutionaries but also endeavoring to win sympathy for Prince Alfred Windischgrätz, the man who brutally suppressed the insurrections in Prague and Vienna.

Sassmann's plays are theatrically dull. He tends to produce character portraits rather than intense dramatic conflicts, invariably fails to integrate private and public aspects, and dodges potentially climactic confrontation scenes, for example having the famous nine-hour meeting between Metternich and Napoleon reported all too briefly by eavesdroppers in an antechamber. It is symptomatic of unconcern with rigorous causality that many costume dramas published at around this time (including Sassmann's) are divided into *Bilder* as well as or instead of Acts, suggesting that picture-book history is to be produced by means of illustrative tableaux. Although the printed texts of Sassmann's history plays (and two commissioned pieces followed the "Austrian Trilogy") give little indication of a strongly theatrical imagination at work, Lothar clearly relates them to the tradition of intensely visual, Baroque theater that was particularly associated with the Burgtheater; historical plays that involved large, often predominantly male casts, had elaborate crowd scenes and drew on the theater's vast resources of historical costumes and weapons (not to mention, in the case of Sassmann's *1848*, the imperial furniture store, *Hofmobiliendepot*) were produced with consummate skill and perennially popular with audiences, almost irrespective of their literary value.

Somewhat surprisingly, Sassmann is not mentioned in Claudio Magris's *Der habsburgische Mythos in der modernen österreichischen Literatur* (The Habsburg Myth in Modern Austrian Literature, 1966); but such elements as his depiction in *Metternich* of the court of Emperor Franz I are clearly part of that myth-making process. Indeed, as John Warren has wryly observed, practically every Habsburg Emperor, Empress and Archduke found their way onto the Viennese stage at some point in the interwar period.[14] This includes everything from Benatzky and Stolz's operetta version of *Im Weißen Rößl* (White Horse Inn, 1930) — the spoken drama by Oskar Blumenthal and Gustav Kadelburg had been a sentimental favorite since 1898 — to *Kaiser Karl der Fünfte* (Emperor Charles V, 1936), a rare theatrical success for Felix Braun, and Rudolf Henz's deeply earnest *Kaiser Joseph II.* (Emperor Joseph II, 1937), the central scene of which depicts Pope Pius VI's meeting with him in 1782, when he came to Vienna to protest against Joseph's religious reforms. In drama as in other media, particular attention was paid to the reign and person of Emperor Franz Joseph.[15] While Sassmann's *1848*, which originally bore the title "Franz Josef I," presents a hopeful image of the young Emperor, Richard Duschinsky's *Kaiser Franz Josef I. von Österreich* (Emperor Franz Josef I of Austria, 1932) focuses on the turbulent period between 1897 and 1914. Beginning as the insult "Sie schamloses Arschgesicht!" is hurled across the parliament chamber during the Badeni Crisis, it notably resists the temptation to caricature any of the key players.

Whereas Duschinsky is relatively sympathetic to the ageing Emperor, other works create a dialectic between an idealized "Österreichische Idee"

(Idea of Austria) and a flawed reality presided over by Franz Joseph I. This is most evident in Friedrich Schreyvogl's *Johann Orth* (1928; reworked as *Habsburgerlegende*, Habsburg Legend, 1933). Archduke Johann Salvator, who gave up his title in 1889 to marry his mistress Milly Stubl, and in *Habsburgerlegende* also Crown Prince Rudolf, who was to take his life at Mayerling in the same year, become the spokesmen for an idealized vision of Austria, which for the Catholic Schreyvogl (1899–1976) was founded on the notion of Christendom and preserved the legacy of the Holy Roman Empire. The designation "Legende" signals a fanciful approach to history as Orth, instead of dying in a shipwreck in 1890, returns to Austria in the early years of the Republic. These plays are heavily freighted with ideas (conveyed using far too many extended similes) and too thin on characterization to make good theater. Indeed *Habsburgerlegende* literally ends with talking heads, as a waxwork model of Orth asserts in surreal fashion: "Der Traum von Johann Orth lebt, nicht er" (Johann Orth is dead, but his dream lives on).

The central scene in both versions of Schreyvogl's play has Orth intending to confront Franz Joseph but desisting after encountering in an antechamber Hofrat Dürrmoser, an elderly gentleman who bears an uncanny resemblance to Franz Grillparzer, and debating with him the nature and survival chances of the "Österreichische Idee." This ersatz dialogue underlines that Austria's greatest historical dramatist not only cast a very long shadow in theatrical terms but had also come to be viewed as a symbol of Austrian patriotism. Indeed it is no coincidence that *König Ottokars Glück und Ende* (Rise and Fall of King Ottokar, 1825), replete with Ottokar von Hornek's eulogy to the good land "inmitten / Dem Kind Italien und dem Manne Deutschland" (between the child Italy and the man Germany), was staged in grandiose fashion at the Burgtheater in 1933.

Notwithstanding the conscious traditionalism of Schreyvogl's work, one can hardly disagree with Magris when he writes: "Das historische Drama ist in der modernen österreichischen Literatur recht häufig vertreten und ist, wenn es dem Andenken Habsburgs gewidmet ist, selten mehr als eine literarische Übung" (In modern Austrian literature there is plenty of historical drama, but whenever it commemorates the Habsburgs, it is rarely more than a literary practice piece).[16] It is only with certain reservations that I would exempt from that verdict Franz Werfel's *Juarez und Maximilian* (1924), a dramatic account of Archduke Maximilian's brief reign as Emperor of Mexico (1864–67), while the two most innovative and interesting costume dramas of the period, Werfel's *Das Reich Gottes in Böhmen* (The Kingdom of God in Bohemia, 1930) and Ferdinand Bruckner's *Elisabeth von England* (1930), have no direct connection with the Austrian Habsburgs.

In *Juarez und Maximilian*, as in the earlier *Bocksgesang*, Werfel experiments with the device of the absent protagonist, with neither the Mexican

People's President Benito Juarez nor the Pan-like monster being seen on stage. This works well in *Bocksgesang*, where the absentee is a polyvalent symbol, but is potentially awkward in *Juarez und Maximilian*, insofar as one logically expects a personalization of both competing ideologies. Consequently, attention focuses on the well-meaning but humorless Maximilian and the power politics that ultimately destroy him, while his opponent retains an uncanny facelessness. As in Schreyvogl's *Habsburgerlegende*, an idealistic sense of mission is favorably contrasted with the reign of his brother Franz Joseph I — but Maximilian's stylization of himself as "der Stellvertreter der weltlichen Liebe Gottes" (the representative of God's love for the world) reveals a degree of self-absorption that serves him ill in view of his questionable legitimacy. In the 1920s and 30s, historical drama, like the historical novel, is repeatedly used not only to foster national identity but also as an indirect means of addressing topical issues. In *Juarez und Maximilian* Werfel characterizes the native Indian figures in terms of both class and ethnicity, thus suggesting an analogy with both Jewish dilemmas and recent political upheavals. While some assimilate to the lifestyle of the white colonists, others hold onto their old ways, and General Meha offers a textbook example of self-hatred. Since *Juarez und Maximilian* was published only a year after the death of Emperor Karl and premièred in 1925, one also wonders whether audiences saw contemporary parallels in Maximilian's refusal to abdicate.

As a historical dramatist, Werfel is strongly but productively indebted to his predecessors, especially Grillparzer: the uneasy pageantry of the scene in which Maximilian effectively presents himself with the crown of Montezuma is reminiscent of the opening act of *König Ottokar*, while in the final scenes a defeated Maximilian struggles, like Ottokar, to achieve self-knowledge. And, as in recent epic films (*The Lord of the Rings: The Return of the King* and *Troy*), the unexpected appearance of a hooded man provides the cue for a tense, dramatic encounter — even if the fact that it involves only a minister of Juarez makes it another of the ersatz dialogues so typical of costume drama at this time.

Juarez und Maximilian is, however, put in the shade by *Das Reich Gottes in Böhmen*, which charts the final phase of the fifteenth-century Hussite Wars and the fall of the rebel leader Prokop the Great. Here again is a reckoning with the ideals of Socialist revolution, combined with religious questioning. Although respected as a military tactician, the forbidding Prokop fails to realize his teetotal, collectivist vision of heaven on earth because he is from the outset unable to command love and out of touch with those around him. His wife betrays him with a renegade aristocrat, a gathering of his Taborite supporters turns violent despite his best efforts, his policy of land redistribution leaves peasants idle and troops starving, and his outlawing of camp prostitutes leads him to order the execution of his own sister. Here, unlike in *Juarez und Maximilian* and in programmatic contrast to Prokop's milk-drinking earnestness, Werfel does dare to introduce comedy, above all among the characters whom the Grillparzer-inspired villain Rosenberg manipulates in order to safeguard aristocratic interests — the Prague burghers Ach and Ichgereut, the garrulous parvenu Drahomira von Riesenburg and her sugar-daddy husband, and the frequently inebriated *bon viveur* Sternberg.

Das Reich Gottes in Böhmen is also theatrically adventurous: short intermezzos taking place at the front of the stage — usually street scenes involving only two or three characters — alternate with and provide commentary on the big setpieces. The central scenes dealing with the Council of Basel take place on a tripartite stage, simultaneously depicting the Council Room, its antechamber and the monastic cell of Prokop's main interlocutor, the papal legate Cardinal Julian. Werfel indeed heightens the moral and philosophical dimension at the expense of verisimilitude by having a disguised Julian repeatedly debate with Prokop in the first part of the play and appear to him in a fevered vision towards the end. *Das Reich Gottes in Böhmen* is also a very visual play: props such as the gold chain that Prokop's wife refuses to accept from him and the flowers she receives from her lover are important at key moments, and there are several striking crowd scenes and tableaux, such as that of the Taborite leaders silently circling the stage before each casts his vote for or against Basel by throwing a counter into the jug that will soon contain the adulterer's flowers.

While Jura Soyfer was to suggest mischievously (in *Broadway-Melodie 1492* (1937)) that Hanns Sassmann was a pseudonym under which the Burgtheater doorman published his literary endeavors, Ferdinand Bruckner (the Berlin-based theater director Theodor Tagger, 1891–1958) only revealed his identity following the runaway success of his historical drama *Elisabeth von England*. Drawing on Lytton Strachey's *Elizabeth and Essex. A Tragic History* (1928), it offers a complex portrait of the ageing Queen Bess that is rooted in psychoanalysis and, even more so than Werfel's *Das Reich Gottes in Böhmen*, makes striking use of the split stage. Bruckner deftly interweaves private and public strands by superimposing the build-up to the defeat of the Spanish Armada in 1588 onto Elizabeth I's dalliance with Robert Devereux, Earl of Essex, and his execution in 1601 following an abortive coup. In this work, a love-hate relationship with her father Henry VIII and a deeply disturbed attitude to the erotic underpin both Elisabeth's dalliance with the much younger Essex and her fixation with Philipp II of Spain, the former suitor whose political aggression she reads as that of the lover spurned, acknowledging at his death that he is both the ultimate focus of her erotic energies and the negative example against which she defines her own identity and ideal of kingship.

Building on Nestroy's use of the split stage in *Zu ebener Erde und erster Stock* (Upstairs and Downstairs, 1835) and *Das Haus der Temperamente* (The House of Humours, 1837), as well as on the overtly politicized

experiments with dramatic simultaneity that had been carried out by Piscator in Berlin since the mid-1920s, each of the last three acts of *Elisabeth
von England* includes a scene placing the English and Spanish courts side
by side: first, as the two monarchs resolve to go to war; then as each prays
for victory and is told of the outcome; and finally, as Philipp dies and
Elisabeth awaits confirmation of that death. By demanding that the spectator should actively interrogate differences and similarities between the
two courts — in world-view and in the processes of historical decision-
making — Bruckner also promotes reflection on the play's contemporary
relevance. Notwithstanding her personal fragility, Elisabeth's rationally
founded pragmatism and horror of war are contrasted powerfully with the
quasi-religious sense of mission and climate of political irrationalism that
prevail in Philipp's Spain, as they were increasingly to do in Hitler's
Germany.

Austro-fascism, *Anschluss,* and Exile

As parliamentary democracy in Austria was replaced by the authoritarian
one-party state, so the original pluralism of the Kunststelle system gave
way in 1934 to a single Österreichische Kunststelle, presided over by Hans
Brečka (1885–1954), formerly in charge of the Kunststelle für christliche
Volksbildung. Although the leisure organization Neues Leben, into which
this was incorporated in 1937, was too belated and improvised a creation
to bear detailed comparison with either the Nazi Kraft durch Freude
(Strength through Joy) or the Italian Dopolavoro, in the theater section
the infrastructure was already in place; Brečka had long pursued a
Catholic-patriotic agenda and was quick to exploit his monopoly on the
sale of cut-price tickets. Two projects can be singled out to illustrate the
climate of what, in 1937, Robert Musil disdainfully termed "Kulturpolitiks-
kultur" (culture generated by cultural politics).[17]

First, the play that the Österreichische Kunststelle publicized most
assiduously was Hans Naderer's *Lueger, der große Österreicher* (Lueger, the
Great Austrian), which had its première at the Deutsches Volkstheater in
November 1934.[18] It is an often sentimental, anecdote-driven portrayal of
"der schöne Karl," Vienna's famously handsome Christian Social mayor
who held power from 1897 to 1910 and, for example, explains his bache-
lor existence saying "Ich kann net Einer g'hörn, ich g'hör dem ganzen
Volk!" (I can't belong to one woman, I belong to everyone). It is also
highly tendentious: as well as stressing Lueger's role in bringing to light
Liberal corruption in the development of the city's tramway system and in
the provision of gas and water supplies, Naderer's play demonizes his Jewish opponent, Dr Singer, and effectively writes the achievements of "Red
Vienna" out of the city's history, instead presenting Lueger as the advocate

of the poor and oppressed and the originator of a programme of municipal Socialism that includes building roads and housing, schools, hospitals, orphanages, public parks and leisure facilities — all under the motto "Wo der Herr nicht mitbaut, da bauen wir Menschen vergebens" (Unless the Lord lends a hand, we mortals build in vain).

Second, and following the precedent established by the Kunststelle für christliche Volksbildung, which, throughout the 1920s, had supported the development of a Catholic performance tradition at local level, the Österreichische Kunststelle also promoted amateur dramatics. Brečka's showcase project was to stage *Der Spielmann* (The Minstrel), a dramatized legend by Rudolf Henz and Franz Krieg. The performances in June 1935 took place in the arcaded central courtyard of Vienna's Town Hall — a space that, ironically, had been used by Reinhardt in 1929 for a production of Büchner's *Dantons Tod* (Danton's Death) and had, until 1934, been the stronghold of the Social Democratic Party. Like Ortner's *Tobias Wunderlich, Der Spielmann* celebrates the principle that true art — here music rather than sculpture — is inspired by faith and rooted in autochthonous folk culture. Once again a statue (this time of the Virgin Mary) miraculously comes to life and, with a frankness about violence characteristic of Henz's work, saves the vagrant violinist of the title, falsely accused of stealing the statue's golden shoe, from torture and execution. This miraculous intervention points to the fallibility of human justice and the need for a spiritual dimension to civil institutions. Rather than merely being staged, *Der Spielmann* was celebrated, reputedly by 1000 amateur performers, including a choir of 600, while a further 2000 spectators participated in the hymn-singing that punctuated the theatrical action.

The most thought-provoking drama to appear during the time of the *Ständestaat* is, however, Franz Theodor Csokor's *3. November 1918* (1937). Like *Radetzkymarsch* (Radetzky March, 1932) by Joseph Roth and *Die Standarte* (The Standard, 1934) by Alexander Lernet-Holenia, *3. November 1918* presents the Austro-Hungarian army as the embodiment of Habsburg supra-nationalism. The play is set in an isolated officers' convalescent home just as hostilities end and the territorial dispute known as the "Kärntner Nachkrieg" is about to put former comrades on opposing sides; the residents enact the dissolution of the Empire, each rediscovering his national identity in a manner reminiscent of the infantry officers in *Radetzkymarsch* when the murder of Archduke Franz Ferdinand is announced. Whereas in Roth's novel Carl Joseph von Trotta is the only true "Austrian," Csokor splits that role between three characters: the senior officer, Colonel Radosin, who promptly commits suicide; the regiment's Jewish doctor, who is the only one to cast "Erde aus Österreich" (Austrian soil) into his grave; and their young nurse, Sister Christina, a military orphan who becomes Csokor's mouthpiece at the end of the play. The officers debate the distinction between *Vaterland* and *Heimat*, with Radosin vainly

arguing that, whereas the loyalty to the fatherland requires a conscious ethical commitment, local or regional patriotism is an instinctive emotional
attachment that leaves the individual little freedom of choice. Compulsive
behavior is seen not only as the play's representatives of Carinthia and
Carniola declare war on each other after years of brotherly coexistence but
also, echoing Grillparzer's adage about the descent via nationality to bestiality, mapped onto the sexual sphere, as animal imagery abounds and
instinctual behavior culminates in attempted rape. Although *3. November
1918* was welcomed by the *Ständestaat*, not least because it was perceived
as a requiem for the "old Austria," that regime's promotion of loyalty to
the *Heimat* is not exempted from Csokor's critique; and the lost Empire is
used above all as a means to concretize an otherwise nebulous humanist
vision of life "in einem Reich, das aus Menschen gebaut wird und nicht aus
Nationen und Grenzen" (in an empire made up of human beings and not
of nations and borders).

Although Csokor was staunchly opposed to Nazism and refused to set
foot in Germany after 1933, the political sympathies of several of the
dramatists lionized by the Austro-fascist regime were, to say the least,
ambiguous. As Klaus Amann has demonstrated, from 1936 onwards
writers of nationalist, potentially pro-Nazi sympathies came together in the
Bund der deutschen Schriftsteller Österreichs (Association of German
Writers in Austria). Its president was Max Mell, whose Catholic credentials
and links with Hofmannsthal allowed him to function as a "prominentes,
schwer angreifbares Aushängeschild" (prominent front-man who was not
easily criticized);[19] other members included Schreyvogl, whose Johann
Orth had in *Habsburgerlegende* been roused from amnesia by the politically ambiguous strains of Haydn's *Kaiserhymne,* used from 1930 on for
both the Austrian and the German national anthems; Ortner, whose ruthless ambition and political opportunism have been amply demonstrated by
Julia Danielczyk;[20] Mirko Jelusich (1886–1969), who was briefly to act as
director of the Burgtheater in 1938; and the South Tyrolean dramatist
Josef Wenter (1880–1947), who had been a member of the Nazi Party
since 1933.[21] Exploiting the fact that, as a result of attempting to compete
with rather than oppose Hitler's Germany, the Austrian *Ständestaat* shared
many of its *Feindbilder*, figures such as these were easily able to build
bridges between the two ideologies, thereby undermining its cultural institutions from within. In 1938, this grouping published the notorious
Bekenntnisbuch österreichischer Dichter (Austrian Writers Confess their
Faith), which includes contributions welcoming the *Anschluss* from all of
the above, as well as from Richard Billinger.

The *Anschluss* had an immediate effect on Austrian theatrical life, as
the immense Jewish contribution was systematically wiped out, along with
that of all perceived opponents of the Nazi regime. Directors, performers
and backstage staff were sacked; repertoires were purged of plays by foreign,

Jewish or left-leaning writers, and by Austrian patriots such as Henz and Csokor; what little pluralism had remained among theater critics after 1934 gave way to ideologically conformist appreciations of the proffered fare; and legislation ordering the "Aryanization" of the theater-going public came into force in November 1938. Many of the individuals who have featured in this account only escaped persecution by going into exile; as in every other walk of life, careers were interrupted, lives changed utterly, and some were cut tragically short. To cite but a few examples, Ferdinand Bruckner left Berlin for Switzerland and then France as soon as Hitler came to power in 1933, moving on to America three years later; Stefan Zweig fled Austria following the civil unrest of February 1934 and spent seven years in London before emigrating to Brazil in 1941, where he and his wife committed suicide the following year. Werfel and Reinhardt, both abroad in March 1938, were never to return to Austria. Ödön von Horváth, who had left Berlin for Vienna in 1933, took refuge in Paris, dying there in a freak accident in June 1938; Franz Theodor Csokor began a perilous Balkan odyssey within days of the *Anschluss*. Among theater critics, David Josef Bach fled to London and died there in 1947; Raoul Auernheimer only escaped to America after six months' imprisonment in Dachau. Others fared even worse: Egon Friedell took his own life whilst attempting to escape arrest in 1938; Jura Soyfer died in Buchenwald concentration camp, at the age of only twenty-six.

Once war had broken out, the main purposes of the theater were to inspire, instruct and entertain. Relatively little new work was produced within Austria at this time, and what there was consisted mainly of light comedy and propaganda, with anything experimental being firmly outlawed.[22] Established names whose plays remained in the repertoire included Schreyvogl, Wenter, Ortner, Billinger and, at least initially, Mell; the Exl-Bühne still toured extensively, and Hans Brečka continued for a time to run a renamed "Deutschösterreichische Kunststelle." Since the early 1930s, the motif of the charismatic leader who re-establishes authority following revolutionary upheaval had been a popular subject. The young Emperor Franz Joseph is effectively cast in that role in Sassmann's *1848*, and the trend is epitomized by Mussolini and Forzano's Napoleon drama *Hundert Tage* (Napoleon: The Hundred Days), which Sassmann adapted for the Austrian stage in 1933. Although Jelusich's thinly veiled Hitler biography, *Cromwell* (1934), was banned in Austria until after the *Anschluss*, several works in this mould were politically ambiguous enough to find favor with both regimes, including Wenter's *Der Kanzler von Tirol* (The Chancellor of Tyrol: first performed 1934) and Schreyvogl's *Der Gott im Kreml* (The God in the Kremlin, 1937). However, to find challenging new work for the theater being produced by Austrian-born writers during the wartime period, one must look to the various countries of exile, and I want to close by highlighting three outstanding, if very different,

Austrian exile dramas — Fritz Hochwälder's *Das heilige Experiment* (The Holy Experiment / The Strong are Lonely, 1943), which stands at the beginning of a distinguished career; Ferdinand Bruckner's *Die Rassen* (The Races, 1934), which marks something of a mid-point in his trajectory; and Franz Werfel's final comic masterpiece *Jacobowsky und der Oberst* (Jacobowsky and the Colonel, 1944).

Bruckner's *Die Rassen*, written in 1933 under the immediate impact of Hitler's seizure of power but not performed in Austria until 1951, paints a disturbing picture of the crisis of Weimar Germany, of the political irrationalism and racial intolerance that had so quickly taken hold, even among the educated elite. Seduced by Nazi rhetoric, medical student Heinrich Karlanner abandons Helene Marx, the Jewish girlfriend who has supported him through his studies, and participates in acts of verbal and physical abuse against Jews, including the humiliation of a fellow student, graphically depicted on stage. *Die Rassen* has in common with *Professor Mamlock*, written by Friedrich Wolf in Russian exile and published in the same year, that it explores a range of Jewish responses to the Nazi threat: as Karlanner discovers his German identity, so Helene becomes conscious of her Jewishness, and one of the play's most moving scenes is an interview between Helene and her hyper-acculturated father, a wealthy industrialist who, like Wolf's title figure, believes in the possibility of working with the new regime. Bruckner's play ends with a glimmer of hope: in a final meeting with Helene (where the dialogue unfortunately starts to resemble an operatic aria) Karlanner rediscovers the humanist ideals of his intended profession. His last words, as he is arrested for betraying the Party, put faith in the resistance of a democratic "other" Germany: "In Ewigkeit: Deutschland. Mein Deutschland. Auch für mich: in Ewigkeit" (Forever: Germany. My Germany. For me too: forever). What are most memorable for the postwar reader are, however, the play's many darkly prescient moments.

Hochwälder's *Das heilige Experiment*, written during penniless exile in Switzerland and an international success in the early postwar years, is a tightly plotted but disconcertingly unresolved problem play dealing with the collapse, in 1767, of the Jesuit state in Paraguay, an experiment in social utopianism that, historically, lasted more than 150 years. The plot is, however, freely invented, and *Das heilige Experiment* is no epigonal Austrian historical drama. Despite the possibilities offered by the exotic Catholic setting, visual effects are sparingly used: the play is driven not by theatrical considerations but by the drama of ideas. For Hochwälder (1911–86) the crisis in eighteenth-century Paraguay is a means to address obliquely a range of contemporary moral and political issues. As in Werfel's *Das Reich Gottes in Böhmen*, these include but are not restricted to the rights and wrongs of the Austrian Socialist experiment. The presentation of the Jesuit order raises the question of Church–state relations alongside that of the relationship between conscience and authority — an issue with broad resonance in the early postwar years, attractively packaged by Hochwälder insofar as the Jesuit Fathers are depicted as fundamentally decent men, bound to obedience and yet realizing that they will incur guilt however they act. That *Das heilige Experiment* has gradually disappeared from the repertoire can be attributed in large measure to its conventional, non-Brechtian dramaturgy, even though it prefigures the sort of moral dilemmas that were to become the trademark of Frisch and Dürrenmatt.

The Austrian exile drama that has proved most enduring in its appeal is Werfel's *Jacobowsky und der Oberst.* An immense hit on Broadway and filmed as *Me and the Colonel* in 1958, it is set during the fall of France in 1940. Drawing on Werfel's own experiences of that time, it follows the adventures of the Jewish refugee Jacobowsky, an incorrigible optimist despite four previous forced emigrations, as he attempts to evade the advancing German forces in company with the anti-Semitic Colonel Stjerbinsky, a Pole, his batman Szabuniewicz and French mistress Marianne Deloupe. The play's subtitle, "Komödie einer Tragödie in drei Akten" (The Comedy of a Tragedy, in Three Acts), indicates the delicate balancing act that Werfel undertakes. Its first two acts are a theatrical delight, full of sparkling wit, dramatic cliffhangers and comic business with unwieldy props (including a clapped-out car). Jacobowsky is an unreservedly engaging character and, like Brecht's Schweyk, seemingly inexhaustible in his imagination and resourcefulness, to which traits the group repeatedly owe their survival. However, the tragedy behind the comedy — for France and for European Jewry — is repeatedly called to mind and dominates the anxious café scene of the final act, in which one despairing refugee takes his life and all but the quick-thinking Jacobowsky are arbitrarily rounded up by the Gestapo. Central to Werfel's message — and necessary to answer the frequently leveled charge that he reproduces and condones racial stereotypes — is a brief scene in which St Francis and the Wandering Jew appear together riding a tandem. Coming just after the inebriated Colonel has declared that "Hitler hat recht" (Hitler is right) with respect to the Jews, this surreal pairing not only embodies Werfel's hopes for the tolerant co-existence of Christian and Jew, but also marks the point after which the Colonel begins to develop respect for the traveling companion to whom he owes his life several times over. There is further hope in the final farewell scene, reminiscent of *Casablanca,* in which Marianne, who has gradually grown into the allegorical role of "Madame la France," resolves to stay and resist the occupation, leaving Jacobowsky to depart for England with her lover.

If one were to underline by way of conclusion some of the most striking features of Austrian drama between the wars, an obvious starting-point would be the quite remarkable contrast between this period and the *fin de siècle*. Whereas, around 1900, emphasis had tended to focus on universal questions such as the nature of the human psyche, on social interactions primarily in the domestic sphere, on sexual rather than party politics, and on individual rather than national identity, the events of 1914–18 brought collective and political concerns strongly to the fore, while the privations and instabilities of the following decades ensured that they remained there, not necessarily replacing previous emphases but certainly recontextualizing them. While some kept alive the hope of social revolution, either in abstract, visionary terms or by memorializing past insurgency, for writers of a conservative bent — most obviously Hofmannsthal, Mell and Werfel — the upheavals of 1918–19 were little short of traumatic. For a decade or more the fear of renewed unrest reverberates through their work with a sometimes startling intensity. Hofmannsthal is, however, the only dramatist to have made substantial impact under both Empire and Republic; there are far more established names who provide continuity between the First and the Second Republics — not only Csokor, who returned to Austria in 1946, but also Mell, Henz and Schreyvogl, all of whom were to be instrumental in ensuring that the conservative antimodernism of the 1930s enjoyed a substantial afterlife in postwar Austria.[23]

Some of the dramatic production of the interwar years is nowadays of interest only to cultural historians, and rightly so, but even in the 1930s one finds plenty of works for the theater that are of considerable artistic merit and ought not to be dismissed, as Jura Soyfer recommended in 1937, "mit ein paar bedauernden Worten" (with a few words of regret).[24] A significant number of texts, most obviously regional dialect dramas, that stand in complex relation to literary tradition and to politicized definitions of *Heimatkunst* deserve to be re-evaluated independently of their contemporary reception or of their authors' subsequent biographies. Especially if one focuses on Austrian-born writers rather than merely on what was happening within the Austrian theater, one finds, alongside the bridge-builders and fellow-travelers of fascist regimes, a good many compassionate, warning voices, expressing profound unease at the climate of irrationalism and intolerance increasingly taking hold, and doing so in innovative and entertaining plays that deservedly continue to be read, performed and enjoyed.

Notes

[1] For these reasons, the institutional history of Viennese theater in the interwar period is particularly difficult to track. A brief overview is given in W. E. Yates, *Theatre in Vienna: A Critical History, 1776–1995* (Cambridge: Cambridge UP, 1996), 199–227. For a more detailed account, see Heidemarie Brückl-Zehetner, "Theater in der Krise: Sozialgeschichtliche Untersuchungen zum Wiener Theater der ersten Republik" (Diss., U of Vienna, 1988).

[2] Valuable information on writers, texts and performance is assembled in Anne Stürzer, *Dramatikerinnen und Zeitstücke: Ein vergessenes Kapitel der Theatergeschichte von der Weimarer Republik bis zur Nachkriegszeit* (Stuttgart and Weimar: Metzler, 1993). However, no study attempts to distinguish between Austria and Germany.

[3] Alfred Pfoser, "Verstörte Männer und emanzipierte Frauen" in Franz Kadrnoska, ed. *Aufbruch und Untergang: Österreichische Kultur zwischen 1918 und 1938* (Vienna, Munich, and Zurich: Europaverlag, 1981), 205–22.

[4] See Konstanze Fliedl, "Künstliche Konkurrenzen: Schnitzler und Schönherr" in Arno Dusini and Karl Wagner, eds. *Metropole und Provinz in der österreichischen Literatur des 19. und 20. Jahrhunderts* (Vienna: Dokumentationsstelle für Neuere Österreichische Literatur, 1994), 115–27.

[5] See John Warren, "Friedrich Kiesler and Theatrical Modernism in Vienna," *Austrian Studies*, 4: *Theatre and Performance in Austria* (1993), 81–92.

[6] See Michael Brenner, *The Renaissance of Jewish Culture in Weimar Germany* (New Haven and London: Yale UP, 1996), especially chapter 5.

[7] See Brigitte Dalinger, *"Verloschene Sterne": Geschichte des jüdischen Theaters in Wien* (Vienna: Picus, 1998), 46–84.

[8] Several of Billinger's works were also made into films during the Nazi period, including *Der Gigant*, which formed the basis of Veit Harlan's *Die goldene Stadt* (The Golden City, 1942).

[9] Rudolph Lothar, *Das Wiener Burgtheater: Ein Wahrzeichen österreichischer Kunst und Kultur* (Vienna: Augartenverlag, 1934), 483.

[10] Raoul Auernheimer, "Max Mell im Burgtheater" in *Neue Freie Presse*, 22 January 1928, 1–3.

[11] Rudolf Henz, *Fügung und Widerstand*, 2nd edition (Graz, Vienna, and Cologne: Styria, 1981), 139.

[12] On Henz's involvement with the corporate state, see Friedbert Aspetsberger, *Literarisches Leben im Austrofaschismus: Der Staatspreis* (Königstein/Ts.: Hain, 1980), especially 93–95; on his postwar role, see Evelyn Deutsch-Schreiner, *Theater im "Wiederaufbau": Zur Kulturpolitik im österreichischen Parteien- und Verbändestaat* (Vienna: Sonderzahl, 2001), 185–89.

[13] Lothar, *Das Wiener Burgtheater*, 485.

[14] John Warren, "Werfel's Historical Drama: Continuity and Change," in Lothar Huber, ed. *Franz Werfel: An Austrian Writer Reassessed* (Oxford: Berg, 1989), 153–73; here: 163.

[15] See Leopold R. G. Decloedt, *Imago Imperatoris: Franz Joseph I. in der österreichischen Belletristik der Zwischenkriegszeit* (Vienna, Cologne and Weimar: Böhlau, 1995).

[16] Claudio Magris, *Der habsburgische Mythos in der modernen österreichischen Literatur*, revised edition (Vienna: Zsolnay, 2000), 295.

[17] Robert Musil, *Tagebücher*, ed. Adolf Frisé (Reinbek bei Hamburg: Rowohlt, 1983), 885.

[18] A copy of the typescript is available in the Wienbibliothek im Rathaus. Excerpts from the play, simply referred to as *Lueger*, can be found in *Hans Naderer. Ein österreichischer Volksdichter. Dem Dichter zum 70. Geburtstag gewidmet*, ed. Eine Arbeitsgemeinschaft von Freunden des Dichters (Vienna and Munich: Wedl, 1961), 30–44.

[19] Klaus Amann, *Der Anschluß österreichischer Dichter an das dritte Reich* (Frankfurt am Main: Athenäum, 1988), 157.

[20] Julia Danielczyk, *Selbstinszenierung: Vermarktungsstrategien des österreichischen Erfolgsdramatikers Hermann Heinz Ortner* (Vienna: Braumüller, 2003).

[21] See the case-study on Wenter in Aspetsberger, *Literarisches Leben im Austrofaschismus*, 116–50.

[22] On the institutional organization of the Viennese theater under Nazism, see Evelyn Deutsch-Schreiner, "Nationalsozialistische Kulturpolitik in Wien 1938–1945 unter spezieller Berücksichtigung der Wiener Theaterszene" (Diss., U of Vienna, 1980).

[23] There are case-studies on Mell and Schreyvogl in Karl Müller, *Zäsuren ohne Folgen: Das lange Leben der literarischen Antimoderne Österreichs seit den 30er Jahren* (Salzburg: Otto Müller, 1990), 200–56 and 287–312.

[24] Jura Soyfer, "Die Unbekannte von Arras" in *Der Wiener Tag, Beilage "Der Sonntag,"* 21 February 1937, in *Werkausgabe*, vol. 3: *So starb eine Partei: Prosa*, ed. Horst Jarka (Vienna: Deuticke, 2002), 307–11; here: 310.

2: Austrian Prose Fiction, 1918–45

Ritchie Robertson

A USTRIAN FICTION BETWEEN THE WARS is marked by the trauma of the Habsburg Empire's dissolution. It left a former Imperial capital incongruously stranded in a small, largely Alpine republic. The progressive Socialism of "Red Vienna" was at odds with the conservatism of the provinces. Inflation, unemployment, and threats from opposing paramilitary forces culminated in the Civil War of February 1934, the suspension of parliament, and the installation of the clerical authoritarian *Ständestaat* (corporate state), which was nevertheless a bulwark against Nazi Germany. The *Anschluss* in March 1938 drove some writers to suicide and sent many into exile. Of those who remained in Austria, some adjusted to the new regime in ways that have only been uncovered by recent research. Politics and literature are therefore inextricable, yet historical distance has not only disclosed political allegiances but shown that their relation to the value of literary texts is a complex one.

"Austria" is a contested term, and the spatial and temporal boundaries of this chapter cannot be firm. Writers born in the former Habsburg Empire who thematized Austria will be discussed, even if they led much of their lives abroad. Writers from Prague will otherwise be excluded, despite the injustice to the many talented German-language writers of the generation after Kafka who lived in the First Czechoslovak Republic.[1] And some novels will be discussed which, though published after the Second World War, deal with events of the 1920s and 1930s.

"Young Vienna" after 1918

The writers who emerged in the 1890s as members of the "Young Vienna" circle — Arthur Schnitzler (1862–1931), Hugo von Hofmannsthal (1874–1929), Hermann Bahr (1863–1934) — were still active in the uncomfortable new postwar world, though their fiction was still set amid the relative stability of the Habsburg Empire before the war or even earlier. Hofmannsthal's unfinished novel *Andreas oder die Vereinigten* (translated as *Andreas, or The United*), begun in 1907 and written mainly in 1912 and 1913, was published only posthumously in 1932. Although

Hofmannsthal set it, like his play *Der Rosenkavalier* (The Chevalier of the Rose, 1911), in the eighteenth century, this modernist Bildungsroman anticipates many concerns of interwar fiction. It begins with the arrival of the twenty-two-year-old Andreas, a member of the minor Viennese nobility whose parents have sent him on an educational tour, in Venice in 1778. Soon, however, we have a lengthy flashback to Andreas's experiences on his journey, especially at a Carinthian farmstead, and within this retrospect there are remoter recollections of traumatic childhood experiences. The contrast between city and country — pitting the heartless formality of Vienna and the labyrinthine intricacy of Venice against the quasi-feudal idyll of Castell Finazzer — recurs constantly in Austrian fiction between the wars. So does the figure of the lower-class criminal, embodied here by Andreas's sadistic servant Gotthelf, who anticipates Musil's sex-murderer Moosbrugger, Broch's cynical Huguenau, and Doderer's gangster Meisgeier. Gotthelf and his antithesis, the pure but thoroughly corporeal Romana, externalize aspects of Andreas, who suffers from self-division. If Hofmannsthal had completed the novel, Andreas would have reunited his personality by unifying that of his lover, who herself is split into two antithetical personalities, the pious Maria and the playful Mariquita. This complex psychological narrative remains a tantalizing, fragmentary masterpiece.

Schnitzler, previously best known as a dramatist, built on his earlier fictional oeuvre after the war with a series of major novellas and the underrated novel *Therese: Chronik eines Frauenlebens* (Therese: Chronicle of a Woman's Life, 1928). All set before the war, they are innovative in both form and content. The stream-of-consciousness narrative which Schnitzler had pioneered in the brief satire *Leutnant Gustl* (1900) is developed in *Fräulein Else* (1924) to recount the last hours of a young woman whose sheltered life is disrupted by a series of emotional shocks which she ends by taking an overdose. *Traumnovelle* (Dream Novella, 1926) explores how a man and wife descend separately into the unconscious: the wife in dreams full of violent and sexual content, her husband by an inexplicable adventure with a secret society that appears to practice orgies, and by a series of confrontations with death. *Flucht in die Finsternis* (Flight into Darkness, 1931) uses *erlebte Rede* (free indirect speech) to adopt the perspective of a man sliding into paranoid delusions and burdened by his overcharged relationship with his brother; the latter, a doctor, has promised to administer euthanasia if the protagonist should become incurably insane, and this foreboding proves self-fulfilling. Not only does Schnitzler let us glimpse the consciousness of the mentally disturbed, he explores specifically female experiences with considerable sensitivity, both in *Fräulein Else* and in *Therese*. The latter, told in the third person, is a somewhat grey portrayal of a frustrating and all-too-plausible life centering on humiliating employment as a governess, unsatisfactory dealings with men, and a difficult relationship between Therese and her illegitimate son, a violent criminal who finally murders her.

Hermann Bahr, a hugely prolific author of dramas, stories, and essays, also produced a series of novels intended as a panorama of Austrian society. The most ambitious and controversial, *Die Rotte Korahs* (Korah's Rabble, 1919), tries to reconstruct Austria as a multiracial polity whose unity is spiritual, based on allegiance to the Catholic Church. It consists of a series of conversations arising from the situation of its protagonist, Ferdinand, a Catholic Austrian diplomat who discovers that he is the natural son of a Jewish financier. His interlocutors include a racist anti-Semite; a Jew, Dr. Adolf Beer, who claims that Jews are guilty of killing Christ and of creating a modernity dominated by commerce; and the Canon, a prominent cleric representing Catholic Austria, who agrees that the Jews are under God's curse. Bahr's arguments, though indefensible, are less anti-Semitic than they may sound: his spokesmen define Jewishness not as a racial but as a spiritual quality that finds expression in the cynical materialism characteristic of the present, so that Ferdinand, despite his ancestry, being free from such materialism, retains a firm spiritual identity as an Austrian Catholic.

The Novel of Totality

A number of novelists, however, aspired to confront the age in which they lived, and to press beneath the surface of contemporary life to understand the historical and intellectual forces which had dissolved traditional values and created a modernity in which everything seemed unstable and relative. The novelist, argued the young Elias Canetti in 1936, must grasp his age as a whole, driven by "der ernste Wille zur Zusammenfassung seiner Zeit, ein Drang zur Universalität" (the serious resolve to sum up his age, an urge for universality).[2]

Robert Musil (1880–1942) seemed equipped for such an attempt by virtue of the breadth of his education and interests. He attended a military academy, then trained as an engineer, then studied philosophy and psychology in Berlin under Carl Stumpf, an exponent of Gestalt psychology, and wrote a doctoral thesis on Ernst Mach (1838–1916), whose *Die Analyse der Empfindungen* (The Analysis of Sensations, 1886) provided a theoretical counterpart to the literary practice of Impressionism. Musil's academic study of consciousness accompanied his early experiments in its literary representation in *Die Verwirrungen des Zöglings Törleß* (The Confusions of Young Törless, 1906) and *Vereinigungen* (Unions, 1911). After his war service he lived precariously as a freelance writer in Vienna. Though he wrote many substantial essays and theater reviews, besides two plays, Musil concentrated increasingly on his vast novel project, *Der Mann ohne Eigenschaften* (The Man Without Qualities), of which the first volume appeared in 1930, the second in 1933. Poverty, ill-health, writer's block, and from 1938 the hardships of Swiss exile prevented him from completing the novel.

Musil, a supreme intellectual novelist, was committed to rationality. But he discriminated subtly among its varieties.[3] Instead of crudely opposing the rational to the irrational, he defined the "ratioïdes Gebiet" (ratio-like domain), best represented by solid, quantifiable scientific facts resting ultimately on mathematics, and distinguished it from the "nicht-ratioïdes Gebiet," represented by the unquantifiable, ethereal subtleties of the moral life. Both, however, should be approached rationally. Morality and emotion were the territory of the poet, who should neither reduce them to scientific data, nor feign an impossible and ultimately self-centered empathy, but explore them, using imagery as a precise cognitive instrument. Musil conducts such an exploration in *Drei Frauen* (Three Women, 1924), a set of three stories whose male protagonists have their intellectual and emotional capacity tested by involvement with women they find enigmatic, and takes his inquiry into consciousness further in *Der Mann ohne Eigenschaften*.

In this great novel, Musil renounces narrative order in favor of a leisurely satirical portrayal of social life in prewar Vienna, interspersed with essayistic reflections. The novel's unity comes from the figure of Ulrich, who in August 1913 resolves to take a year's holiday from life and passively observe. He is drawn into the preparations for a "Parallelaktion" which plans to celebrate in 1918 the seventieth anniversary of the Emperor Franz Joseph's accession to the throne (parallel to the simultaneous thirtieth anniversary of the accession of the relative upstart Wilhelm II of Germany). Unlike the reader, the characters cannot know that their plans are futile, so the progress of history is ironized from the outset. An alternative dimension is introduced by Ulrich's "Möglichkeitssinn" (sense of possibility), which he fosters to counteract the much-praised, normal "Wirklichkeitssinn" (sense of reality); it allows him to envisage that things might always be different, and helps him to be suspicious of established constructions of reality.

Ulrich and Musil are responding to the dissolution of the old anthropocentric cosmos. Not only is humanity no longer the center of the universe; the "self" is no longer the center that organizes subjective experience:

> Es ist eine Welt von Eigenschaften ohne Mann entstanden, von Erlebnissen ohne den, der sie erlebt, und es sieht beinahe aus, als ob im Idealfall der Mensch überhaupt nichts mehr privat erleben werde und die freundliche Schwere der persönlichen Verantwortung sich in ein Formelsystem von möglichen Bedeutungen auflösen solle. Wahrscheinlich ist die Auflösung des anthropozentrischen Verhaltens, das den Menschen so lange Zeit für den Mittelpunkt des Weltalls gehalten hat, aber nun schon

seit Jahrhunderten im Schwinden ist, endlich beim Ich selbst angelangt [. . .].[4]

[A world of qualities without a man has arisen, of experiences without the person who experiences them, and it almost looks as though ideally private experience is a thing of the past, and that the friendly burden of personal responsibility is to dissolve into a system of formulas of possible meanings. Probably the dissolution of the anthropocentric point of view, which for such a long time considered man to be at the centre of the universe, but which has been fading away for centuries, has finally arrived at the "I" itself [. . .].][5]

What does now organize experience? Ulrich concludes that experience can only be ordered by narrative, by telling a story, by saying "first this happened and then that happened." Such an order does not correspond to reality, except as a useful simplification:

Es ist die einfache Reihenfolge, die Abbildung der überwältigenden Mannigfaltigkeit des Lebens in einer eindimensionalen, wie ein Mathematiker sagen würde, was uns beruhigt; die Aufreihung alles dessen, was in Raum und Zeit geschehen ist, auf einen Faden, eben jenen berühmten "Faden der Erzählung," aus dem nun also auch der Lebensfaden besteht. (*Der Mann ohne Eigenschaften*, 1: 650)

[It is the simple sequence of events in which the overwhelmingly manifold nature of things is represented, in a unidimensional order, as a mathematician would say, stringing all that has occurred in space and time on a single thread, which calms us; that celebrated "thread of the story," which is, it seems, the thread of life itself. (*The Man Without Qualities*, 708–9)]

In practice, Musil had to strike a compromise between subjectivity and narrative sequence. He retains enough narrative to serve as a basis for the exploration of different consciousnesses: the mind of the sex-murderer Moosbrugger; the Dionysiac ecstasy sought by Clarisse, an enthusiast for Nietzsche; the soulful emotionalism of Ulrich's cousin Diotima; and the "anderer Zustand" (other state) sought as Ulrich in Book Two develops an increasingly intimate relationship with his long-lost sister Agathe. Musil did not sympathize with modern anti-rationalism, which is satirized in Diotima's pseudo-empathetic verbiage, more sharply in Clarisse's desire to bear Ulrich a child who will redeem the world, and in the Christian-Germanic group around Hans Sepp and Gerda, who solemnly read the poet-priest Stefan George. Musil is examining sham mysticism alongside the real thing. Instead of feigning an empathy that could only be spurious, Musil's reflective, essayistic style allows us to approach other psycho-physical states in a provisional, hypothetical manner, which combines feeling and understanding. In keeping with the dethronement of the self from the centre of consciousness, these states are not presented primarily as events in the biography of the people who experience them, but as relatively free-floating.

That applies, for example, to the evocation of absorption in music (144), a near-mystical state of heightened experience (155), drunken anger (157), and even the presumed consciousness of Graf Leinsdorf's horses (175–76). Yet this exploration of consciousness is not actually an alternative to story-telling. The novel does have a narrative drive, which comes from the gradual build-up of erotic attraction among the characters — the attraction between Diotima and the German poseur Arnheim, Clarisse's and Gerda's desire for Ulrich, and above all the attraction between Ulrich and Agathe.

Another polymath, Hermann Broch (1886–1951), reluctantly studied engineering in order to run his father's textile business from 1915 to 1927, but preferred philosophy and mathematics. Dissatisfied with the value-free logical positivism that was dominant in Vienna, Broch sought through fiction to convey a deeper sense of humanity's spiritual needs. His first novel, *Die Schlafwandler* (The Sleepwalkers), seeks in its three parts — *1888. Pasenow oder die Romantik* (Pasenow or Romanticism, 1931); *1903. Esch oder die Anarchie* (Esch or Anarchy, 1931); and *1918. Huguenau oder die Sachlichkeit* (Huguenau or Sobriety, 1932) — to chart a cultural decline: from the naive illusions of the Prussian officer Joachim von Pasenow, via the confused quasi-religious aspirations of the book-keeper August Esch, to the shallow, calculating, egoistic outlook of the war profit-eer Huguenau. In order to include intellectual content without composing artificial conversations, as in Thomas Mann's *Der Zauberberg* (The Magic Mountain, 1924), Broch developed the "polyhistorischer Roman" (poly-mathic novel).[6] He juxtaposed fiction and reflection by including in *Huguenau* an essay on the fragmentation of values into self-contained, self-justifying domains (signalized by slogans like "art for art's sake" and "business is business"), and illustrating this process with several narrative strands unconnected to the Huguenau action. Imagery of death, resurrection, and salvation becomes prominent; *Huguenau* ends with an appeal for human solidarity taken from Acts 16: 28 (Broch had converted from Judaism to Catholicism in 1909).

In a lecture, *James Joyce und die Gegenwart* (Joyce and the Present, delivered in Vienna 1932, published 1936), Broch praised Joyce for countering modern fragmentation by finding a way of grasping the totality of modern life in the focus of a single day. Broch attempted something analogous in the novel now known as *Die Verzauberung* (The Spell), where a remote Alpine village focuses contemporary political and social conflicts; working titles of the novel, which was never published in Broch's lifetime, included *Bergroman* (Mountain Novel) and *Der Versucher* (The Tempter). Through the eyes of the doctor, a scientifically-minded immigrant from Vienna, we see how the villagers, whose traditional way of life is already being eroded by capitalism (embodied in Wetchy, an insurance agent), succumb to the spell of a wandering prophet called Marius Ratti. Ratti exercises power because his charisma appeals exploitatively to genuine religious impulses that the Church no longer satisfies. Under his spell, the villagers assault the convenient scapegoat Wetchy (as a Protestant, he represents other outsiders, the Jews) and conduct a human sacrifice of a young woman amid mass hysteria which draws in even the normally cool-headed narrator. At its close, the novel moves from political allegory to myth: the wise old Mutter Gisson (an anagram of *gnosis*, knowledge) appears as Demeter, while the sacrificial victim appears as Persephone and hence capable of symbolic rebirth.

In his Joyce lecture, Broch also noted how, in *Ulysses* and still more in the published portions of *Finnegans Wake*, Joyce relied on the variation of quasi-musical motifs. Myth and musicality combine in *Der Tod des Vergil* (The Death of Virgil, 1945), the major product of Broch's American exile. The novel presents the last eighteen hours of Virgil's life. Death confronts him with the ethical problem of whether his lifelong devotion to literature was all a huge mistake, for which he should atone by destroying the *Aeneid*. It confronts him also with the personification of worldly power, the Emperor Augustus. And it brings him to the final frontier, death, whose approach Broch conveys by a pattern of archetypal images (the novel's four sections are headed "Wasser," "Feuer," "Erde," and "Äther" (water, fire, earth, and air), by labyrinthine sentences developing musical motifs, and by a bold attempt in the fourth section to present the dissolution of the poet's consciousness into a realm beyond language.

In exile, Broch dedicated himself also to extensive writings on mass delusion, human rights, and internationalism. His ethical concerns feature in his last fictional work, *Die Schuldlosen* (The Guiltless, 1950), eleven interlinked stories exploring how so many people have been able to commit criminal acts with an easy conscience. At one extreme we have the German proto-Nazi schoolteacher Zacharias, at the other the moral authority of the blind old beekeeper who makes the protagonist, Andreas, suddenly aware that he himself, through indifference to his fellow-beings, has been complicit in wrong-doing all his life.

To the younger novelist Elias Canetti (1905–94), Broch was an important mentor and model, against whom he had to define his own territory. The third volume of Canetti's autobiography, *Das Augenspiel* (The Play of the Eyes, 1985), includes a (doubtless largely fictional) conversation between the two, in which Canetti, with immense self-assurance, rejects Broch's view that the novelist living in the age of Freud and Joyce must take account of modern psychology. No subsequent novel, says Canetti, has surpassed *Don Quixote*, which presents not a rounded human being but a sharply outlined figure ("Figur") whose distinctive traits emerge in clear, almost caricatural relief. Moreover, modern psychology is helpless before the phenomenon of the crowd or mass ("Masse"), to which, in Canetti's belief, individual psychology cannot be applied. From another early hero, Karl Kraus, Canetti derived the technique which he called "das akustische Zitat" (acoustic quotation), the spoken utterance which, reproduced in print or on stage, captures the essence, not so much of an individual, as of a social attitude.[7]

All these techniques combine in Canetti's novel *Die Blendung* (translated as *Auto da Fé*, 1935), the only product of his resolve to become a twentieth-century Balzac by writing a "Comédie Humaine an Irren" (a Human Comedy of Madmen).[8] Not only the fanatical scholar Peter Kien, who has drawn up a rigid daily schedule so that he can devote his entire waking time to studying Oriental languages in his book-lined flat, but all the characters are obsessed. Kien's housekeeper Therese, who tricks him into a sexless marriage and converses entirely in set phrases expressing petty-bourgeois resentment; the Jewish rogue Fischerle, who dreams of becoming a chess grandmaster; the brutal porter Benedikt Pfaff, who has abused and murdered his daughter; and even Peter's brother, the seemingly more worldly and supple psychiatrist Georges Kien, are in their various ways monomaniacs. Expelled from his library, Kien, accompanied by Fischerle, like Don Quixote with Sancho Panza, roams through a hideous urban underworld where acts of violence, evoked with shocking understatement, are normal, and finally releases his own pent-up violence by an auto-da-fé in which he burns himself alive among his books.

Behind the novel lies Canetti's experience of crowd violence, not only at the burning of the Viennese Palace of Justice in July 1927 but earlier, at food riots in Frankfurt, though it only occasionally surfaces explicitly in *Die Blendung*. Georges Kien prophesies that throughout the world individuals will merge into a single mass organism, forebodings which Canetti himself used to utter, inspired by collectivism in the Soviet Union. After Canetti and his wife Veza had left Vienna in November 1938, settling in London, he devoted himself for many years to a study of crowd phenomena in anthropology and mythology. His answer to Freud's contentious paper "Massenpsychologie und Ich-Analyse" (Crowd Psychology and the Analysis of the Ego, 1921) and Broch's writings on mass psychology was the highly original social treatise, *Masse und Macht* (Crowds and Power, 1960), which views the crowd ambivalently: as invading the private space of the individual, but also as releasing the individual from solitude. Alongside plays, essays, aphorisms, and travel sketches, Canetti also gained a wide readership with his autobiography, which covers his youth in *Die gerettete Zunge* (The Tongue Set Free, 1977) and early manhood in *Die Fackel im Ohr* (The Torch in My Ear, 1980), while his life in Vienna from 1931 to 1937 is recounted in *Das Augenspiel*. However fictionalized it may be, the autobiography is arresting both by its vivid detail and by its honest treatment of Canetti's difficult relationship with his domineering, early-widowed mother, whose death in 1937 brings this life-story to an end.

Both the fiction and the life of Heimito von Doderer (1896–1966) have a particularly complex relation to the ideologies of his time. After the breakdown of his marriage to Gusti Hasterlik, whose Jewish descent supplied him with a convenient pretext for anti-Semitism, he joined the National Socialist Party in 1933, not long before it was banned in Austria. Dissatisfied with the Viennese literary scene, he moved to Germany and settled in the town of Dachau, apparently unconcerned about the nearby concentration camp. Disillusioned with Nazism, though without leaving the Party, he converted in 1940 to Catholicism. While his major novels appeared in the 1950s, their conception goes back to the late 1920s, and his reflections on fiction take issue with that of Musil, so they may suitably be treated here. Doderer did, however, publish novels in the 1930s that anticipate later concerns. *Ein Mord den jeder begeht* (A Murder Everyone Commits, 1938) introduces his favorite theme of obsession. An obsessed person is trapped in a "zweite Wirklichkeit" (second reality), an impoverished version of reality, and needs to develop the "Apperzeptionsfähigkeit" (perceptive ability) required to respond freshly to experience. The protagonist of *Ein Mord*, Conrad Castiletz, is trapped in an obsession with order from which he is finally released by the discovery that he inadvertently caused his sister-in-law's death. Doderer's interest in fate, and his belief that it takes a circuitous, not a linear path, structures his next novel *Ein Umweg* (A Detour, 1940), set in seventeenth-century Austria.

The major novels of the 1950s, *Die Strudlhofstiege* (The Strudlhof Steps, 1951) and *Die Dämonen* (The Demons, 1956), are intended, like Broch's *Die Schlafwandler*, to preserve in fiction the Goethean universality which has broken down under the modern fragmentation of knowledge into specialisms, and to take fiction beyond the dead end of Musil's overly cerebral "Zerdenken" (thinking to pieces).[9] But Doderer's "total novel" did not seek, like Broch and Musil, to incorporate diverse intellectual materials. Its mission was rather to draw on memory, to present people and events concretely and vividly, and to resist ideologies, especially totalitarianism, with their seductively simplified "second realities," by fostering our apperception of the solid reality around us. The novelist is the opposite of an idealist; he does not see earthly reality as a mere imitation of Platonic ideas:

> Er hat von vornherein innig die Erkennbarkeit der Schöpfung aus dem, was sie uns in wechselndem Flusse darbietet, umarmt, und meint fest, daß die Sachen, wie sie sich als Konkretionen zeigen, durchaus sie selbst sind, ja, mehr noch — daß sie durchaus auch wir selbst sind (Doderer, "Grundlagen," 166–67).

> [From the outset he has warmly embraced the principle that creation, as it presents itself in flux, is knowable, and he is convinced that things, showing themselves as concrete phenomena, are absolutely themselves — moreover, that they are also ourselves.]

Rather than a Platonist, the novelist may unwittingly be a Thomist. The convert Doderer eagerly absorbed St. Thomas Aquinas's doctrine of the *analogia entis*, the analogy of being, whereby earthly things, in their solid reality, correspond to the divine plan.

To keep the reader's eye fixed on the object, Doderer avoids any simple exposition or linear narration. The reader of his two huge Viennese novels, which are linked by sharing many characters, must navigate among a bewildering array of incidents and life-stories, from which patterns gradually emerge. Memory provides both theme and structure, as in the subtitle of *Die Strudlhofstiege, Melzer und die Tiefe der Jahre* (Melzer and the Depth of the Years); the consciousness of the very unintellectual hero, Major Melzer, links two narrative levels, one pre-1914, and the other set in the early 1920s. Obsession is also common: in *Die Dämonen* it ranges from Kajetan von Schlaggenberg's obsession with fat ladies to the fascism of a sinister group of smugglers. Their positive counterpart is the working man Leonhard Kakabsa whose firm grasp of reality shields him from the allure of Socialism. Commitment to reality, Doderer asserts, can save the novelist from slipping into Romanticism (meaning the quasi-religious dreams Broch criticized in *Pasenow*) or into ideology. Here we may be skeptical: Doderer's late humanism, however attractive, is of course an ideology, and in opposing ideology he is not only covertly disavowing his earlier Nazism but explicitly rejecting Communism and thus assisting his popularity during the Cold War. However, it would be a shame if skepticism about Doderer's politics were to prevent anyone from enjoying his major novels, which, with their idiosyncratic narrative voice, their wealth of characters, and their minutely registered setting, afford pleasures more often associated with English fiction — as though Anthony Powell had been reading *Tristram Shandy*. Doderer himself says that the vivid, concrete storytelling he likes is an English speciality. Of an American character with a gift for narrative, he says: "er verfiel nie seinem Gegenstande, die Sprache wuchs ihm nie daran fest, möchte man sagen, eine Tugend, die allerdings dem Englischen überhaupt innewohnt, das mehr Sprech-Sprache ist, als alle anderen" (he never succumbed to his subject, his language never got stuck to it, as one might say; a virtue inherent in English, which is more of a speaking language than any other).[10]

The *Heimatroman*

Between the wars, and especially after the advent of the *Ständestaat*, special popularity and official recognition went to novels dealing with rural Austria which can very loosely be classified as *Heimatromane*. As a genre depicting the hardships of rural life under pressure of urbanization, the *Heimatroman* can be found throughout Europe, from Hardy's Wessex to Knut Hamsun's Norway. Its Austrian variant looked back partly to German naturalist fiction, partly to the celebrations of rural life by the once hugely popular Styrian novelist Peter Rosegger (1843–1918), who also recorded rural decline in his novel *Jakob der Letzte* (Jakob the Last, 1889). The sentimental conservatism associated with the concept of "Heimat" has often provoked skepticism. Thus Musil's Ulrich returns home remembering ironically "daß man der Heimat die geheimnisvolle Fähigkeit zuschreibe, das Sinnen wurzelständig und bodenecht zu machen" (that home is credited with the mysterious ability to make thought authentic by rooting it in the soil; *Der Mann ohne Eigenschaften*, 1: 19). Since 1945 the *Heimatroman* has fallen into disrepute for its conservative, often fascist politics and its sometimes clichéd style. Such condemnations might well apply to the work of Karl Heinrich Waggerl (1897–1973), who, under the *Ständestaat*, received the first Austrian "Staatspreis für Literatur" in 1934, and who in 1938 welcomed the *Anschluss* and joined the Nazi party. His novel *Schweres Blut* (Heavy Blood, 1931) illustrates basic features of the genre. Timeless, dogged peasant virtues are celebrated in simple language, linking human life to organic growth in a present tense that aims to deny historical change:

> Der Bauer ist ewig wie die Erde selbst, denn er lebt durch sein Geschlecht. Er kommt nicht von ungefähr in die Welt, von irgendwo her, sondern, wenn das neugeborene Kind in der Wiege liegt, dann blüht draußen schon der Weizen, dann wachsen die jungen Fichten im Walde mit ihm auf, und wenn der alte Jakob stirbt, so hat er vorher noch das Korn gesät, hat den Wald aufgeforstet, und er hat dem jungen Jakob alles gesagt, was er selbst weiß und was zu wissen nötig ist. Der Sohn drückt die Pflugschar auf die gleiche Art und mit der gleichen Kraft in die Erde wie er. Das Leben des Bauern ist ruhmlos, nichts bleibt von ihm zurück als sein Name und sein schweres Blut.[11]

> [The farmer is everlasting like the earth itself, for he lives through his kindred. He does not come into the world at random, from just anywhere; no, when the newborn child lies in the cradle, the wheat is already flourishing outside, the young spruce-trees in the forest grow up with him, and when old Jakob dies, he has first sown the corn, replenished the forest, and told young Jakob everything that he himself knows and that needs to be known. His son thrusts the ploughshare into the soil in the same way and with the same strength as he did. The farmer's life is not glorious: nothing remains of him but his name and his heavy blood.]

The central figure, Blas, has abandoned farming for manufacture: he owns a sawmill, and is determined to build a weir. His obsession with machinery and progress is gendered as male and contrasted with the female belief in continuity and organic life embodied in the main woman character, Elis. Machinery introduces the malign influence of the city-based money economy which replaces quasi-feudal relations of service with the impersonal cash nexus. Blas's disaffected workers, egged on by trade unionists, call a strike, to which he responds by summoning strike-breakers from the city. Eventually nature takes a hand; a spring flood sweeps away the weir, and Blas, seeing his project destroyed — like Hauke Haien in Storm's *Der Schimmelreiter* (The Rider on the White Horse, 1888) — returns to farming.

Yet even *Schweres Blut* has redeeming features. Focusing on a community rather than an individual, it presents numerous viewpoints, including those of women, and acknowledges dissension, frustration, malice, even violence, even though all conflicting forces are again harmonized by the homogeneous, simple style. Other *Heimatromane* escape further from the limitations conventionally ascribed to the genre. Its dismissal as "trivial" may be due partly to its popularity with women writers. A fresh look is required, such as the German *Heimatroman* has recently received.[12] Thus, the much-read novel *Das Grimmingtor* (The Grimming Gate, 1926) by Paula Grogger (1892–1984) makes creative use of the supernatural. A legendary gateway in a Styrian mountain may conceal vast treasures or the souls of the damned. The uncanny wooer of the respectable heroine vanishes through it when rebuffed, and it exercises a mysterious attraction over her son, who becomes a wastrel and eventually meets his death outside it. The story suggests much about the conflict between piety and passion in rural culture.

Still less conventional was another winner of the Staatspreis, *Philomena Ellenhub* (1937) by Johannes Freumbichler (1881–1949), the grandfather of Thomas Bernhard, recounting the hard life of a farm servant in the mid nineteenth century. Writing in an old-fashioned, confidential, chatty style, Freumbichler far surpasses Waggerl and Grogger in his circumstantial detail and emotional range, including a discreetly frank treatment of sex: his intelligent and capable heroine, who copes with becoming an unmarried mother at the age of sixteen, is in confident control of her own sexuality. Politically, the novel supports the moderate reforms associated with the "Volkskaiser" Joseph II and treats with skepticism the slogans uttered by the heroine's brother, a revolutionary engaged in the events of 1848.

Even the Carinthian novelist Josef Perkonig (1890–1959) proves on examination to be a complex case: though a strong supporter of Nazism, he was denied Party membership because he had been a Freemason, and his novel *Mensch wie du und ich* (Human like You and Me, 1932), awarded the Staatspreis in 1935, was banned in 1942 for its overly sympathetic portrayal of Russian prisoners of war in a Carinthian camp. Yet another mythmaker, Alexander Lernet-Holenia (real name Alexander Marie Norbert Lernet, 1897–1976), who wrote about the Austrian army, implausibly claimed to have chosen "inner emigration" by spending most of the war as "Chefdramaturg zur Heeresfilmstelle" (Army film director) in Berlin, the German army having rejected him as an officer. Although his novel *Mars im Widder* (Mars in the Ram, 1941), set in the Poland campaign of 1939, was banned immediately on publication, this was not owing to any anti-Nazi content, but presumably because the supernatural destruction of a regiment did not suit the exalted militarism of the time.

The work of Franz Nabl (1883–1974) urgently deserves revaluation. An important provincial writer, he remained a powerful literary presence, though his novels were written at or before the beginning of our period. *Ödhof* (1911) was long misread as a celebration of rural vitality by people who failed to appreciate that its headstrong central figure destroys himself and his family. *Das Grab des Lebendigen: Eine Studie aus dem kleinbürgerlichen Leben* (The Grave of the Living: A Study in Petty-Bourgeois Life, 1917), reissued in 1936 as *Die Ortliebschen Frauen* (The Ortlieb Women), uses omniscient but unobtrusive narration to describe a family which, under the influence of the dead father, tries to lead an absolutely unchanging, isolated life but ends in a chilling catastrophe. Subtly and without explicit judgements, Nabl shows family affection being perverted into insane possessiveness. *Die Galgenfrist* (A Short Time to Live, 1921) raises existential questions and modernizes the theme of Hofmannsthal's *Jedermann* (Everyman, 1911) by showing how a man, told by doctors that his death is imminent, searches for meaning in life. Disclaiming any interest in politics, Nabl did not join the National Socialist Party nor support it by political statements. His passive conformism under the Third Reich has, however, damaged a reputation that deserves new scrutiny.

International Humanism

Writers committed to nationalist and, latterly, racial ideals contrast ever more sharply with liberal writers who espouse a humane internationalism. Increasingly, the latter saw politics within a religious framework.

Franz Werfel (1890–1945) was brought up in Prague, where he was a close friend of Kafka and the novelist and journalist Max Brod. He made his name initially as an Expressionist poet and dramatist, but established himself as a novelist after the war, starting with his short novel about a father–son confrontation, *Nicht der Mörder, der Ermordete ist schuldig* (Not the Murderer but the Victim is Guilty, 1920). Of his many novels, the most widely read, especially in English translation, is probably *Das Lied von Bernadette* (The Song of Bernadette, 1941; filmed in 1943), written during his Californian exile, about the visionary of Lourdes, which encouraged the belief that Werfel — married since 1929 to the Catholic Alma Mahler — had converted from Judaism to Catholicism. In fact, he always maintained an ambiguous position between Judaism and Christianity, regarding both Abrahamic religions as intimately linked, but inclined to believe in the Messianic status of Jesus. Religion in his major fiction appears as a respect for simple piety and a cautious allegiance to divine providence.

Two of Werfel's novels stand out. In *Barbara oder die Frömmigkeit* (Barbara or Piety, 1929), the devout old nursemaid of Dr Ferdinand R., the central figure, represents a stable point in his life and enables him to return to religious belief after experiencing the dissolution of traditional values during and after the First World War. Ferdinand is contrasted with Alfred Engländer, a Jew unable to reconcile his loyalty to Judaism with his deep attraction to Christianity, and, like Bahr's Dr. Beer, sharply aware of the disintegrative effects of modernity. Werfel frames their relationship in a lively and circumstantial narrative of the revolutionary upheavals in Vienna in 1918–19. This part of the novel, for many readers the most interesting, is a transparent *roman à clef*, in which Gebhardt represents the radical psychoanalyst Otto Gross (1877–1920), Weiss the left-wing journalist Egon Erwin Kisch (1885–1948), while on a deeper level Ferdinand and Engländer embody conflicting aspects of Werfel himself.

Soon afterward, Werfel learnt about a much graver modern catastrophe, the genocide of the Armenians by the "Young Turk" regime during the First World War. From the narratives of survivors and written sources, he composed *Die vierzig Tage des Musa Dagh* (The Forty Days of Musa Dagh, 1933), based on an actual incident in which a small Armenian community took refuge on a mountain by the sea and held out against Turkish besiegers for some six weeks before being rescued by a French ship. In Werfel's novel, an exciting and engaging adventure story is the vehicle not only for a protest against mass murder but also for an exploration of the relation between the intellectual and the national community. The central figure, Gabriel Bagradian, after studying in Paris, has returned to his ancestral home with his French wife and half-French son. As a member of the traditional elite, he assumes leadership in the crisis, and exercises it, in a difficult learning process, together with the Armenian Orthodox priest. Both are contrasted with such false leaders as the money-obsessed local mayor, the demagogic schoolteacher, and the ineffectual Protestant clergyman (embodying respectively the capitalist, the intellectual, and the sectarian), while Gabriel's need to belong to the "Blutsheimat" (blood-home) contrasts with his Parisian existence as an abstract human being and with the empty cosmopolitanism of the Franco-Greek adventurer who seduces his wife. Such vocabulary has brought Werfel under suspicion of opportunistically adopting the *Blut und Boden* language of the Nazis, and it is true that in March 1933 he unwisely signed a declaration of loyalty to Germany's new rulers, who soon afterwards burnt his books. However, *Musa Dagh* expresses a differentiated conservatism, as remote from fascism as it is from the inhuman modernizing nationalism of the Young Turks, whose leaders are vividly portrayed in the novel. Ultimately, like *Barbara*, it frames politics within religion, culminating in a faint, tentative affirmation directed toward "Dem Unerklärlichen in uns und über uns" (The Inexplicable within us and above us).[13]

Though born in the town of Brody in the remote province of Galicia, Joseph Roth (1894–1939) spent only a small part of his adult life in Austria, yet he is remembered especially as an ambivalent elegist for the declining Habsburg Empire. In the early 1920s he established himself as a successful journalist on the liberal *Frankfurter Zeitung*, and in 1933 he left Germany for exile in Paris, where he was plagued by poverty, alcoholism, and despair at European politics. Yet despite his troubles, exacerbated by the insanity of his wife Friederike ("Friedl") Reichler, Roth maintained the self-discipline to produce a large quantity of polished, perceptive, witty and arresting journalism, and a body of fiction written in a simple, understated, sometimes formulaic style that owes much to Stendhal and Flaubert.[14]

Roth's novels of the 1920s give a critical portrayal of modernity, especially as experienced by discharged soldiers ("Heimkehrer") whose stable pasts vanished in 1918. Thus, Franz Tunda in *Die Flucht ohne Ende* (The Flight Without End, 1927) moves from Siberian imprisonment through revolutionary Russia and the sham culture of Western Europe and returns, disillusioned, to Siberia. An exploration of family relationships begins with *Zipper und sein Vater* (Zipper and His Father, 1928), where an unsuccessful, somewhat absurd businessman, a "sad clown," invests extravagant hope in his son, who suffers professional and emotional failure: unable to rise beyond a low civil service grade, he devotes himself to his actress wife, and when she discards him, makes his living as a literal clown. The family theme continues in *Hiob* (Job, 1930), the first of many novels in which Roth returns to the world of the Eastern European *shtetl*. The dissolution of traditional Jewish life devastates the family of the devout Jew Mendel Singer, the modern Job who loses his faith in God, until it is restored by an apparent miracle: the appearance of his youngest son, left behind in Galicia as hopelessly disabled, now cured and a successful orchestra conductor.

In *Radetzkymarsch* (The Radetzky March, 1932) Roth interweaves imperial decline with a narrative of family tensions and personal failure. Carl Joseph is a mediocrity who only gets through military school thanks to his family connections. His upbringing by his widowed father, a conscientious Habsburg administrator (*Bezirkshauptmann*), displays a rigid discipline amounting to paralysis. Only at rare, and correspondingly moving, moments do father and son manage to break through their emotional armor-plating and exchange tight-lipped expressions of affection. The same paralysis afflicts the declining Empire. Both the Emperor and his near-double, the *Bezirkshauptmann*, maintain a dogged, conscientious devotion to tradition; but the Emperor feels fatalistically that the Empire's disintegration is inevitable, while the novel searingly conveys how much the "Habsburg myth" depends on falsifying history.

Although he described himself as "a Catholic with a Jewish brain,"[15] Roth never converted, and much of his later fiction mingles Jewish and Christian motifs. Increasingly, Roth not only explores failure, but suggests possibilities of redemption. *Tarabas* (1934) evokes the millennial suffering of the Jews but centers on a Russian soldier who, having assaulted a Jew, does penance by becoming a beggar, eventually dying in a monastery. The misfortunes undergone by Baron Taittinger in *Die Geschichte von der 1002. Nacht* (The Tale of the 1,002nd Night, 1939) initiate a kind of spiritual growth. Allegory enters with the devil-figure who instigates murder and betrayal in *Beichte eines Mörders* (A Murderer's Confession, 1936), and who reappears, embodying corrupt modernity, in *Der Leviathan* (The Leviathan, 1940), while *Das falsche Gewicht* (The False Weight, 1937) is a subtle parable about the relations between law and love. The Novelle *Die Legende vom heiligen Trinker* (The Legend of the Holy Drinker, 1939) adopts the genre of the saint's legend with an unstable, humorous, teasing irony. Roth's sympathy for the poor attains perhaps its finest expression in this story of a Polish tramp in Paris for whom the gift of 200 francs by a generous Christian initiates a series of improbable strokes of good fortune, reawakening him from drunken oblivion to moral awareness, convincing him of divine grace and enabling him to die peacefully.

Stefan Zweig (1881–1942), a more secular writer, shared the conviction that Jewish allegiance was a basis for an international humanism. Well traveled and widely read in several languages, he deplored the First World War for wrecking the ideal of Europe, and conveyed in an outstanding Novelle, *Buchmendel* (Book-Mendel, 1929), how the war devastates the life of a harmless Jewish bookseller once famous for his prodigious memory. Zweig's many best-selling novellas turn especially on unexpected erotic experiences which disrupt people's comfortable though often boring lives. Thus, we have sexual obsession in *Der Amokläufer* (Running Amok, 1922); homosexual attraction, culminating in a passionate kiss, in *Verwirrung der Gefühle* (Confusion of Emotions, 1927); a forty-year-old woman's passion for a young Polish gambler in *Vierundzwanzig Stunden aus dem Leben einer Frau* (Twenty-Four Hours in the Life of a Woman, 1927). In *Phantastische Nacht* (Fantastic Night, 1922), a nobleman, shaken out of his boring routine by the sight of a beautiful woman at a race-course and by inadvertently stealing her winnings, feels for the first time "die heißen Ströme des Lebens" (the hot streams of life) and strays into the proletarian underworld of the Prater, where he narrowly escapes from a dangerous encounter with a prostitute and her accomplices. His brush with "life" makes him feel rejuvenated. But a comparison with Fridolin's similar adventures in Schnitzler's *Traumnovelle* would show the limitations of Zweig's excitable, verbose style. His only novel, *Ungeduld des Herzens* (Impatience of the Heart, 1939), is an over-long but acute psychological study, showing how a young officer is drawn into a relationship with a paralysed girl by pity, which for a long time blinds him to the fact that she is in love with him. Instead of his compassion, she wants the love that he does not feel, and his emotional dishonesty drives her to suicide. His best-known story, *Schachnovelle* (Chess Novella, 1941), turns, like *Buchmendel*, on a psychological oddity: this time, the abstract monomania of chess champions. But it also has political overtones, for the culminating chess match pits Dr B., a Habsburg monarchist who was imprisoned after the *Anschluss*, against Mirko Czentovic, a Slav from a Transylvanian village of the former Empire, and the crude proletarian is too much for the sensitive, damaged patrician.

A surer touch appears in some novelists who take the authoritarian school system as the focus for a wider criticism of society. In Werfel's *Der Abiturientag* (translated as *Class Reunion*, 1928) the protagonist, Sebastian, recalls how he wrongly incriminated a fellow-schoolboy whom he envied; but since Sebastian, twenty-five years on, is now a judge, the story raises questions about the corruptibility of all institutions, not only the school. Friedrich Torberg (1908–79), who adopted a pseudonym combining his father's name Kantor and his mother's name Berg, showed in *Der Schüler Gerber hat absolviert* (Gerber Has Left School, 1930) a sensitive schoolboy being driven to suicide by a sadistic teacher. Torberg, as a Jew, spent 1938–51 in exile, mostly in the USA, returning to Vienna in 1951 as a firmly anti-Communist writer and editor. Ödön von Horváth (1901–38), best known for his critical "Volksstücke," used a school setting in *Jugend ohne Gott* (Young People without God, 1938) to expose the creeping inhumanity with which Nazism deliberately infected children; the teacher, as the last representative of humanity and justice, finally resolves to emigrate to Africa. His other exile novel, *Ein Kind unserer Zeit* (A Child of our Time, 1938), conveys the death of human sympathy under Nazism by using a self-betraying first-person narrator, a soldier who ends up buried in snow.

Women Writers

Women writers can easily seem marginal in this period. Conservative social attitudes, the male dominance of coffeehouse society, the critical disposition to stigmatize women's writing as "trivial," and some women's own self-abnegation, can all be blamed. The veteran Catholic novelist Enrica von Handel-Mazzetti (1871–1955) was still at work, but by common consent her best fiction (e.g. *Jesse und Maria*, 1906) came before the First World War, and her unrealistic commitment to a Catholic monarchy led her into gestures of sympathy with Nazism. Another Catholic writer, Paula von Preradović (1887–1951), primarily a lyric poet, published one novel, *Pave und Pero* (1940), based on the life of her grandfather, a noted Croatian poet. Her son's involvement in the Austrian resistance led to her own arrest by the Gestapo late in the War. Martina Wied (1882–1957), a Catholic convert who combined a nostalgia for a provincial Christian Austria — for example in *Rauch über Sanct Florian* (Smoke over St. Florian, 1937) — with an admiration for Georg Lukács, went into exile in Scotland. Her exile novels *Das Einhorn* (The Unicorn, published 1948) and the massive *Die Geschichte des reichen Jünglings* (The History of the Rich Young Man, written 1928–43, published 1952) center on the difficult theological theme of vicarious sacrifice. She awaits rediscovery along with other Catholic novelists (notably the German Gertrud von le Fort) who, as is being gradually recognized, created a German-language equivalent to the French *renouveau catholique*.

A far worse fate awaited Alma Johanna Koenig (1887–1942), who, born in Prague to a prosperous Jewish family, acquired fame as a historical novelist in the 1920s. After the *Anschluss* she suffered persecution and forced labor because of her ancestry. She wrote a work about Emperor Nero, *Der jugendliche Gott* (The Youthful God, written 1942, published posthumously 1947), wrapped in blankets in an unheated room. Soon after completing it she was deported and gassed in a concentration camp at Minsk. Unlike other historical novels of the time — *Der falsche Nero* (The False Nero, 1936) by Lion Feuchtwanger, for example — it is not a direct allegory about Hitler; it explores Nero's deprived emotional life, particularly his relationship with his mother, sometimes using modern political clichés to suggest analogies between ancient and modern dictatorship. Her emperor figure recalls Hitler particularly through his aestheticism, seen in his ambitious building plans for Rome after the Great Fire (similar to the building projects devised by Hitler and Albert Speer).

A number of feminist and Socialist writers have recently received overdue attention. Lili Körber (1897–1982) was brought up in Moscow, where her father was an Austrian buisnessman. She attracted wide attention with her journalistic fictions, *Eine Frau erlebt den roten Alltag* (A Woman's Experience of Red Daily Life, 1932), based on her work in a Soviet car assembly plant, and *Eine Jüdin erlebt das neue Deutschland* (A Jewish Woman's Experience of the New Germany, 1934; reissued as *Die Ehe der Ruth Gompertz*, Ruth Gompertz's Marriage, 1984), in which a Jewish woman's marriage to an ambitious German collapses under political pressure. Exile in Paris and later in the USA provided material for further factual fictions which were both anti-Nazi and anti-Stalinist. Hermynia Zur Mühlen (1883–1951), born in Vienna as the daughter of a diplomat in the Habsburg Empire's service, and briefly and unhappily married to a minor Baltic aristocrat, lived in Frankfurt from 1919 to 1933 as a member of the Communist Party of Germany and author of politically engaged novels and children's books. From April 1933 until the *Anschluss* she lived in Vienna, and from June 1939 to her death in British exile. Perhaps her most noteworthy novel is *Unsere Töchter, die Nazinen* (Our Daughters, the Nazi Women, 1935), which presents the voices of three mothers — a working-class Socialist, an aristocrat, and an ambitious middle-class woman — whose daughters all join the NSDAP, respectively from misguided idealism, desire for a purpose in life, and social conformism. For them, Zur Mühlen coins the strange word "Nazine." Beyond that, we gain a broad picture of how a small German town capitulates before Nazism. The ex-Socialist daughter repents and works with her mother in the resistance. Though, like Körber's work, the novel does not disguise its didactic purpose, it breaks new literary ground in presenting women's viewpoints with no controlling narrative authority, and is accessible and appealing in its portrayal of political uncertainties.

Recently there have been major rediscoveries. One is Anna Gmeyner (1902–91), who published *Manja: Ein Roman um fünf Kinder* (Manja: A Novel about Five Children) under the pseudonym Anna Reiner with the exile publisher Querido of Amsterdam in 1938. As a realist novel, it intertwines the history of five families who represent different social groups within the Weimar Republic and whose children are born on five successive nights. It also has mystical overtones: Manja, the child of Eastern Jewish parents, has a spiritual aura that unites the group under the recurrent symbol of the star. Though she becomes the victim of Nazi violence, the redemptive suggestions around her form a counterpoint to the historical pessimism voiced by her friend the liberal physician Ernst Heidemann, who sees in Nazism "die Rache, die das zwanzigste Jahrhundert am neunzehnten nimmt. Die Reaktion auf die Überschätzung der Menschheits- und Freiheitsidee, die zur Schablone geworden war" (the revenge taken by the nineteenth century on the twentieth. The reaction to the overestimation of the idea of humanity and freedom which had become a cliché).[16] There is similar pessimism in the work of Venetiana (Veza) Taubner-Calderon (1897–1963), who, as the first wife of Elias Canetti, appears to have sacrificed her literary ambitions to his, and to have indicated her self-abnegation by using the pseudonym Veza Magd for the few stories she published during her lifetime. A series of linked narratives, originally published in the Socialist *Arbeiter-Zeitung* in 1932–33, appeared in book form as *Die Gelbe Straße* (Yellow Street) only in 1990. A challenging, painful and courageous book, it quietly compels the reader to confront the desperation of a cripple ("Der Unhold") and the horror of domestic violence ("Der Oger"), against a hard and loveless background. Her exile novel, *Die Schildkröten* (The Tortoises, written 1939, published 1999), uses understatement and symbolism to evoke the atmosphere of mounting terror surrounding an Austrian Jewish family awaiting their exit visas and obliged to share their house with an SA man. The central symbol of the tortoise suggests both the tendency to ignore danger by retreating into one's shell, and also the stubborn tenacity of the Jewish people.

Retrospections

In *Der Mann im Schilf* (The Man in the Reeds, 1955), George Saiko (1892–1962), an art historian whom the Nazis regarded with suspicion and forbade to publish, took a retrospective look at the failed Nazi putsch of 1934. He dramatizes the city-country antithesis by setting his novel mainly in a village in the Salzkammergut, where pro-Nazi undercover and paramilitary activity forms part of a pervasive, unsettling climate of violence. The action is punctuated by moments of brutality, as when the Viennese visitor, Robert, is suddenly beaten up on a street in Salzburg; in political assassinations; in a hideous scene of gang rape; and in a flashback to an outburst of sexually charged violence on an archaeological expedition on Crete. The novel, basically a thriller, uses modernist techniques of interweaving past and present, exploring memory, and adhering to the perspective of puzzled or unreliable figures to create an appropriately tense, uncertain atmosphere. Beyond that, it probes the roots of political violence in male bonding, antagonism toward women, rural superstition, and (in the Cretan interlude) the remote, mythical past; its insights anticipate those set out by Klaus Theweleit in his study of German fiction about soldierly violence *Männerphantasien* (Male Fantasies, 1977–78).

Albert Drach (1902–95), a Jewish lawyer, established himself as a poet and dramatist in the 1920s, but after fleeing Austria in 1938, and narrowly surviving in occupied France, he reflected on his experiences above all in the autobiographical novel *"Z.Z." das ist die Zwischenzeit* ("Z.Z.," the Interval, 1968). Drach's specialty is a peculiar, bureaucratic, circumlocutory, seemingly unemotional style he uses in this work to recount both the protagonist's erotic adventures and the political catastrophes culminating in the *Anschluss* and in desperate efforts to obtain an exit visa. A sentence early in the novel illustrates how Drach's style reveals human baseness in the shadow of the Holocaust. It refers to guests at his father's funeral:

> Einige von ihnen, und gerade solche, welche des nunmehrigen Leichnams vorheriges Dasein zu glorifizieren beitrugen, hatten in viel späterer Zeit andere Aufgaben zu erfüllen, die etwa mit der Einäscherung des Judentempels begannen und mit der von dessen fallweisen Besuchern endigen sollten, nachdem dieselben rechtzeitig vorher in die horizontale Dauerlage gebracht waren.[17]

> [Some of them, the very ones who were now assisting in eulogizing the prior existence of the current corpse, had at a much later date to fulfill other tasks, beginning with the reduction to ashes of the Jewish temple and ending with that of its occasional visitors, the latter having previously been duly brought to a permanently horizontal position.]

By making it difficult for the reader to respond to such a passage, Drach forces us to confront the dehumanizing potential of language. While his monological style anticipates Thomas Bernhard, his critique of language looks back to Karl Kraus, to whom he pays tribute later in the novel (198). Although in the postwar period Drach has seemed an eccentric, unclassifiable writer, he fits into a longer Austrian tradition of political, linguistic, and moral skepticism. His fictional retrospective on the interwar years, like Saiko's, places them in a larger, more universal context. While Saiko ponders the roots of violence, Drach considers the degradation of language. Though post-1918 Austria is a small, landlocked country, its best writers have found in universal themes and ambitious fictional projects an intellectual substitute for the vanished Empire.

Notes

[1] On these writers, see Jürgen Serke, *Böhmische Dörfer: Wanderungen durch eine verlassene literarische Landschaft* (Vienna and Hamburg: Zsolnay, 1987).

[2] Elias Canetti, "Hermann Broch. Rede zum 50. Geburtstag. Wien, November 1936," in E. Canetti, *Das Gewissen der Worte* (Munich and Vienna: Hanser, 1975), 9–22; here: 13.

[3] See Robert Musil, "Skizze zur Erkenntnis des Dichters" (1918), in R. Musil, *Gesammelte Werke*, ed. Adolf Frisé, 9 vols. (Reinbek: Rowohlt, 1978), 3: 1025–30.

[4] Robert Musil, *Der Mann ohne Eigenschaften*, in Musil, *Gesammelte Werke*, 1: 150.

[5] Robert Musil, *The Man Without Qualities*, tr. Sophie Wilkins, 2 vols. (London: Picador, 1995), 1: 158–59.

[6] See Broch's letter to Daniel Brody, 5 August 1931, in Hermann Broch, *Briefe I (1913–1938),* ed. Paul Michael Lützeler (Frankfurt am Main: Suhrkamp, 1981), 150–52.

[7] Elias Canetti, "Karl Kraus: Schule des Widerstands," in *Das Gewissen der Worte*, 39–49; here: 42.

[8] Elias Canetti, "Das erste Buch: *Die Blendung*," in *Das Gewissen der Worte*, 222–33; here: 225.

[9] Heimito von Doderer, "Grundlagen und Funktion des Romans," in H. v. Doderer, *Die Wiederkehr der Drachen. Aufsätze, Traktate, Reden*, ed. Wendelin Schmidt-Dengler (Munich: Biederstein, 1970), 166.

[10] Heimito von Doderer, *Die Dämonen* (Munich: Biederstein, 1956), 44.

[11] Karl Heinrich Waggerl, *Schweres Blut* ([1931] Salzburg: Müller, n.d.), 11–12.

[12] See Elizabeth Boa and Rachel Palfreyman, *Heimat: A German Dream* (Oxford: Oxford UP, 2000).

[13] Franz Werfel, *Die vierzig Tage des Musa Dagh*, 2 vols. (Berlin, Vienna, Leipzig: Zsolnay, 1933), 1: 56; 2: 557.

[14] Most of Roth's fiction is now available in English versions by the well-known translator Michael Hofmann.

[15] Joseph Roth, *Briefe*, ed. Hermann Kesten (Cologne: Kiepenheuer & Witsch, 1970), 9.

[16] Anna Gmeyner, *Manja. Ein Roman um fünf Kinder.* Mit einem Vorwort von Heike Klapdor-Kops (Mannheim: Persona-Verlag, 1984), 168.

[17] Albert Drach, *"Z.Z." das ist die Zwischenzeit* (Hamburg: Claassen, 1968), 19.

3: Publishers and Institutions in Austria, 1918–45

Murray G. Hall

The World of Publishing

IN 1921, JUST THREE YEARS AFTER the founding of the First Austrian Republic, a Viennese observer of the book trade by the name of Carl Junker lamented that there were no *literary* publishing houses worthy of mention ("[kein] namhafter belletristischer Verlag") in Austria.[1] There is some truth in this statement, for a glance at the publishing world at the time reveals that the popular literature of the turn of the century, which is today considered by literary historians to be representative of the period and of Austrian literature in general, appeared in publishing houses in Berlin or Leipzig. The works of the modern writers of Jung-Wien, for example, appeared primarily in the publishing house of Samuel Fischer in Berlin. Those of the equally popular pan-German or nationalistic writers were published by the L. Staackmann Verlag in Leipzig, whence the term "Staackmänner." Developments between 1918 and 1945 have to be viewed in light of the circumstances under which publishing was possible in the Habsburg Monarchy. Indeed, from the eighteenth century on, the many "Buchhändlerordnungen" — the official rules and regulations of the book trade — and general restrictions from above give the impression that printing and selling books was something to be tolerated rather than welcomed. The official attitude toward the book trade over the decades explains why Germany, not only because of the larger German-speaking population, was able to persuade so many Austrian writers to publish there, and why the book and publishing trades were so dependent on the German market. It is important to note that the major feature which distinguished the "Austrian" book trade from the "German" book trade in the nineteenth century and on up until the end of the First World War was greater commercial freedom and better copyright protection.

The fact that many nineteenth-century Austrian writers, among them Franz Grillparzer or Marie von Ebner-Eschenbach, also published a good part of their works in Germany raises the question as to the characteristics of the nineteenth century publishing landscape in Austria(-Hungary), a landscape which was to change dramatically after the First World War. Traditionally, Vienna, as the capital of the vast Habsburg Monarchy, was the main book selling and publishing center. Prague and Budapest were a distant second and third and the publishing trade in Austria-Hungary differed from that in Germany in being multiethnic, multicultural and multilingual, although scholars today tend to focus on the German-language book trade.

Throughout the nineteenth century, the trades of book publisher and bookseller were combined, this being one of the ways to restrict the number of bookselling outlets. It was not until 1899 with the founding of the Wiener Verlag that the situation began to change. The vast majority of the companies were publishing houses that specialized in certain fields, and the proprietors of most of the new firms established in the course of the nineteenth century were North German Protestants. The fields of specialization included medicine (partly because of the fame of the Vienna School of Medicine), veterinary medicine, natural and social sciences, agriculture, and law, with a wide array of relevant scholarly journals, schoolbooks and cartography. Among the companies we find the k.k. Schulbücherverlag, which long held a monopoly on the publication of schoolbooks in all the languages of the monarchy, Manz (legal texts), Hölder-Pichler-Tempsky (medicine, school textbooks), Franz Deuticke (the publisher of Freud's *Traumdeutung*), Anton Schroll & Co. (art books), Universal-Edition (contemporary music), Urban & Schwarzenberg (medicine), Moritz Perles (medicine, veterinary medicine, geography, agriculture, etc.), Halm & Goldmann (art books and lexica), Verlag der Wiener Volksbuchhandlung (Social Democrat publications), Wilhelm Frick (agriculture), Wilhelm Braumüller (law, social and political science, medicine, veterinary medicine), Carl Fromme (court printers; calendars, scientific works), and L. Rosner (dramatic works).

Despite the number of specialized publishers in Vienna who also operated bookshops, it would be incorrect to assume that the literary publishing landscape was completely barren. One example of a publisher with a mixed program is the Carl Konegen Verlag. Still, except for the Wiener Verlag, there were no exclusive publishers of belles lettres, and thus Austria-Hungary exported literary manuscripts to Berlin or Leipzig and imported the published books.

Although the Austrian book trade was fully integrated into the German book trade and many booksellers and publishers were members of the Börsenverein der deutschen Buchhändler, the umbrella organization of German booksellers and publishers established in 1825, the book publishing trade in Austria-Hungary took a different route because of the heavy-handed bureaucracy. It was not until 1859 that the Verein der österreichischen (later: österreichisch-ungarischen) Buchhändler was established, its statutes modeled on those of the Börsenverein. The association's official publication, the *Buchhändler-Correspondenz*, appeared from 1860 on. Whereas in Germany various factors led to the emergence of a new type of publisher, the so-called "Kulturverleger" — such as Samuel Fischer, Eugen Diederichs, Anton Kippenberg of the Insel Verlag, and later Kurt Wolff and Ernst Rowohlt — and restrictions were removed on the publication of the works of classical German literature, there was no such pioneering atmosphere at the time in the Habsburg Monarchy. Access to the trade was restricted by an antiquated and often corrupt system of granting licenses ("Konzessionen"), and the strict censorship laws made literary publishing, especially, a risky business. Another major factor preventing Vienna, despite the obvious literary talent, from becoming an important center for literary publishing was copyright protection. Despite intensive lobbying by publishers and others, Austria-Hungary did not join the Bern Convention of the late 1880s, relying instead on reciprocal agreements with some, but not all key countries. Indeed, Austria was not to join the Convention until forced to do so by the Treaty of St. Germain (1919). Although the membership issue was brought before parliament in Vienna before the collapse of the monarchy, the non-German-speaking nationalities in the monarchy were adamantly opposed. As book piracy was rampant and writers and composers were often victims, they chose to publish in the German Reich, where their works enjoyed full copyright protection. There, as today, they also had a larger market. This lack of legal protection was, in the words of the contemporary book historian Carl Junker, a "catastrophe." From a legal standpoint, the writers were "fair game," as he put it. The proclamation of the First Austrian Republic in November 1918 improved the situation for both writers and local publishers.

The first exclusively literary publisher in Vienna was the Wiener Verlag (successor to the firm founded in 1874 by the Viennese actor, later bookseller and publisher Leopold Rosner, and which specialized in theatrical works), established in 1899 by the brother of Egon Friedell, Oskar Friedmann, and later taken over by a businessman named Fritz Freund. Until its demise and bankruptcy in 1908, newspaper articles about the Wiener Verlag were to be found just as often in the court section of the papers as on the culture pages. The Jugendstil publisher attracted turn-of-the-century literary talents such as Hugo von Hofmannsthal and Arthur Schnitzler, and the debut novel *Die Verwirrungen des Zöglings Törleß* (The Confusions of Young Törless, 1906) by Robert Musil, also appeared in the Wiener Verlag. Fritz Freund not only attracted authors and artists with healthy royalties, he was also active in the business of book piracy, exploiting the fact that Scandinavian and Russian writers, for example, were not copyright protected under Austrian law.

The end of the First World War, the collapse of the Monarchy, the loss of the vast industrial hinterland and natural resources, unemployment, high inflation, lack of fuel and suitable paper for printing, not to mention the political rivalry between "Red Vienna," the bastion of the Social Democrats, and the "Black" federal government of the Christian Socials, all influenced the publishing trade in Austria in the 1920s. Paradoxically, these times were a "Gründerzeit" (period of rapid economic expansion) or, as one observer put it, there existed a "mushroom atmosphere."[2] For the first time, new companies argued — in a brief expression of a newly-found Austrian cultural identity — there was a need to "repatriate" Austrian literature.

The first half of the 1920s saw the rise and fall of many new publishing houses. Only a very few of the newcomers, however, were still around in 1938, when Austria was annexed by Nazi Germany. While the many specialized firms of the nineteenth century continued to exist despite losing some markets, it was now time for literary publishers to try their hand, and Austrian writers were actually attracted to them, although later figures showed that roughly nine-tenths of Austrian literature was published in Germany. All the newcomers had ambitious programs, but several were undone by managerial incompetence and the ambition to run a publishing company as a stock-holding company. Richard Kola, for example, a banker with a passion for books, founded the Rikola Verlag in 1920, aiming to produce good quality literature at an affordable price, but his appetite for acquiring other companies — publishers, printers, paper mills — coupled with bank scandals, inflation, and poor sales put an end to the company by the mid-1920s. WILA, the Wiener Literarische Anstalt, was another promising literary publisher, focusing on young and contemporary Austrian authors, but, short of capital during the inflation period, it also made the mistake of becoming a stock-holding company and getting involved with dubious banking houses. The years immediately following the war were also a time of experiment. In Germany, "socialization" had become a buzzword and the process was also extended to the publishing trade. Disgruntled writers, annoyed at what they saw as exploitation by their capitalist publishers, set about "socializing" literary creativity and founded a writers' co-operative called the Genossenschaftsverlag in Vienna in 1919. The venture brought together a group of strange bedfellows, among them the poets Albert Ehrenstein, Fritz Lampl, and Hugo Sonnenschein, the versatile writer Franz Werfel, the psychoanalyst Alfred Adler and the psychotherapist Jakob Moreno Levy. Profits from the sale of the works of German classical writers should fall to them and not to publishers, they argued. The co-operative experiment, which brought forth periodical publications such as *Daimon, Der neue Daimon* and *Gefährten* and works by Oskar Kokoschka, Ernst Weiss, Heinrich Mann, and others, was short-lived. By 1922 it had disappeared. Another interesting publisher in Vienna around this time was the Ed. Strache Verlag, which consciously promoted the "young generation" of Austrian writers.

One early success story, however, was the E. P. Tal & Co. Verlag, established in 1919 by Ernst Peter Tal, who had earlier worked for S. Fischer in Berlin. Despite financial difficulties in the early 1920s. the Tal company, operated after his death in 1936 by his wife Lucy Tal, remained in business until March 1938, whereupon it was taken over by an "Aryan" employee and renamed Alfred Ibach Verlag. The Paul Zsolnay Verlag, founded at the end of 1923, was the most successful Austrian publisher of the interwar years, both from a literary and financial standpoint. Although a lover of books without experience in the trade, Paul Zsolnay had other advantages: he had financial backing from a wealthy family; he established the company at a time when the economy was gradually emerging from inflation; he had an experienced literary director at his side; he was able to offer disgruntled writers in inflation-ridden Germany royalties no German publisher could come close to matching; and he was able to purchase the rights to the works of the British author and later Nobel Prize laureate John Galsworthy, who proved to be phenomenally successful and Zsolnay's "cash cow." Zsolnay was also the German-language publisher of H. G. Wells, Pearl S. Buck and A. J. Cronin, to name but a few of the writers in his "international" program. More importantly, unlike other publishers in interwar Austria, he was a respected player on the German book market, and the renowned German publishing houses were his peers. Although Zsolnay's "mission" was not specifically the promotion of Austrian writers, and he saw himself as a "German publisher," he published dozens of Austrian writers, among them Franz Werfel, Felix Salten, Robert Neumann, Roda Roda (nom de plume of Sándor Friedrich Rosenfeld), Hilde Spiel, Ernst Lothar, Hans Kaltneker, Friedrich Torberg, and Leo Perutz. Zsolnay was also the publisher of German writers such as Heinrich Mann, Kasimir Edschmid, Carl Sternheim, Emil Ludwig, Walter von Molo, and Frank Thiess, to name but a few. Hitler's accession to power in Germany, where Zsolnay sold roughly three-quarters of his books, dealt a severe blow to both production and program. Around twenty Zsolnay authors fell victim to the official and unofficial lists of proscribed books. Their books could no longer be sold or distributed in Germany and some of the writers, among them Max Brod, went on to publish in exile publishing houses in Holland. But others, facing the prospect of trying to live off the sale of books on the Austrian or Swiss market, turned their backs on Zsolnay altogether.

To keep his company going under these difficult circumstances, Zsolnay entered into a compromise with Austrian Nazi writers in 1934, this being the price he was willing to pay for continuing access for his other books on the German market. Financially and politically speaking the venture proved to be a flop, and Zsolnay was still regarded in Germany as a "Jewish" publisher. His days were numbered when the Nazis took over Austria in March 1938. By engaging an "Aryan" front man immediately after the annexation Zsolnay managed for a time to trick the Nazi authorities into believing the Paul Zsolnay Verlag was now an "Aryan" company. When the company's "Aryan" nature was questioned, the Gestapo closed it in April of 1939. Meanwhile, in November 1938, Zsolnay had left for England, ostensibly to carry out business there for the firm in Vienna. He was not to return until 1946. After months and years of wrangling, the Paul Zsolnay Verlag was taken over by the bookseller Karl H. Bischoff, who had worked for the Reichsschrifttumskammer in Berlin and was responsible for overseeing the closing of Jewish-owned publishing houses in Vienna. Unlike other publishing firms which had survived despite the war and were then forced to close in 1943, the Karl H. Bischoff Verlag remained in business until the end of the Second World War, continuing with an "international" program, but focusing on the literature of southeastern Europe.

Another company worthy of mention on account of its literary program and its ideological affinity to the Social Democrats is the Anzengruber Verlag Brüder Suschitzky, established in 1901 in Favoriten as the first bookstore in that working-class district. The Anzengruber Verlag published fiction and non-fiction on topics of the day, including abortion. After the *Anschluss,* and despite attempts by a potential new "Aryan" proprietor, the Reichsschrifttumskammer ordered the company to be closed because of its Jewish-Marxist tendencies. Also on the proscription list was the Phaidon Verlag, owned by Bela Horowitz. Phaidon was a key player on the German market in the field of inexpensive high-quality art books, and because it was considered "Jewish," the company was a thorn in the flesh of those in Germany who wanted to eradicate the supposed Jewish domination of the book trade.

Hitler's accession to power heralded the politicization of art and literature, and Austrian publishers soon began to feel the effects as lists of banned books were circulated in Germany. The publishing trade in Austria was virtually dependent on the German authorities, who achieved their "literary" aims through a series of political moves that were ostensibly of a commercial nature. Not only were Austrian publishing houses unable to sell the books of banned writers in Germany, imports into Germany were also restricted as were transfers from sales of books in Germany back to Austria. In 1935, Germany, in an effort to increase the inflow of foreign currency into the country to back its armaments industry, introduced a 25% discount on the sale of German books in Austria, thus harming not only the publishing trade, but also the printing industry. "National Socialism at dumping prices" was the reaction of some of the critical newspapers. Despite the many and varied difficulties with the German book market, a number of new literary publishers did enter the market in the 1930s. Perhaps the most famous is Gottfried Bermann Fischer, the son-in-law of the Berlin publisher Samuel Fischer. In an effort to save part of the S. Fischer program — successful writers whose works could no longer be published or sold in Germany — Bermann Fischer first wanted to establish a firm in Switzerland, but the narrow-mindedness of the writers' and publishers' organization prevented it. In 1936, Bermann Fischer set up shop in Vienna after the German authorities allowed him to transport about three quarters of a million S. Fischer books to Vienna. Among the most celebrated writers in his program were Thomas Mann and Robert Musil. Immediately after the *Anschluss,* the publishing house was closed and Bermann Fischer was able to flee to Switzerland.

Other publishing companies and bookshops in Vienna became targets after the *Anschluss.* Some, such as the E. P. Tal Verlag, were allowed to be "aryanized," but many others, such as the Herbert Reichner Verlag, which published the works of Stefan Zweig, were simply eliminated.

Throughout the interwar years, Austrian booksellers were highly dependent on book imports from Germany, Austria being Germany's most important foreign market. At the same time, with only minor exceptions as in the case of school textbook publishers, Austria's literary publishers sold between fifty and ninety percent of their books on the German market and were thus perpetually at the mercy of the German authorities. For the period 1938 to 1945, it is just as difficult to speak of an Austrian publishing establishment as to speak of the continuance of an Austrian literature. So many of the writers associated today with that literature were either murdered or had fled into exile, and along with them often their publishers as well.

Literary Institutions

Although literary historians today tend to perceive only works belonging to a literary canon (and in the search for a positive cultural identity after the Second World War Austria was eager to regard authors such as Robert Musil, Joseph Roth, Franz Kafka, or Hermann Broch as *the* representatives of Austrian literature in the interwar years), twentieth-century Austrian literature can actually be seen as the sum of a number of different "literatures" ("Binnenliteraturen") co-existing parallel to one another. The history of Austrian writers' organizations from the mid nineteenth century on mirrors these parallel literary currents, and there is much to support the thesis put forward by Ernst Fischer that Austrian literary life was ideologically and politically segmented.[3] As Fischer notes, this "stratification" is not only to be found where ideologically like-minded writers band together, but, in the Austrian context, at other levels as well. Distribution and consumption of literature are two examples. Thus we find Catholic, Social Democrat, German nationalist and liberal publishing houses and book clubs, lending libraries and literary journals existing side by side, albeit with some crossovers. Accordingly, there were highly successful Austrian writers in the

1910s and 1920s who published their works in the L. Staackmann Verlag in Leipzig (Robert Hohlbaum, Karl Hans Strobl, and many others) because of the ideological affinity. In Austria itself, the publisher most closely associated with anti-Republican and anti-Semitic sentiment was the Leopold Stocker Verlag in Graz, established in 1917. It would be completely unthinkable for writers such as those mentioned to ever be published or want to be published by the likes of S. Fischer, Kurt Wolff, Ernst Rowohlt or the Insel Verlag. Similarly, one could not expect to find liberal or Jewish writers among the "Staackmänner."

Although they shared such concerns as the social well-being of their members, pension and health benefits, the common characteristic of writers' organizations in Austria from their inception in the late 1850s was the explicit affiliation to a political or ideological camp. Essentially, this was a reflection of the political landscape.

It was in the Schiller centenary year, 1859, that the first "writers' organization," the Journalisten- und Schriftstellerverein Concordia, was established as an association. Among the founders were journalists-cum-writers from the 1848 generation, as opposed to strictly book authors. Concordia's public presence and close ties to the newspaper business are evidenced by one of the big events on Vienna's social calendar, namely the Concordia Ball, which was staged annually from 1863. Concordia, too, developed plans to provide its members with a retirement pension and health care insurance. Poetry readings and lectures were also an essential part of the association's public image. All in all, Concordia, whose members included writers and editors of Vienna's most powerful newspapers, was labeled "liberal" and pretentious.

It is not surprising then that anti-liberal forces soon gained strength. The first counter movement to Concordia, the Wiener Schriftstellergenossenschaft (Vienna Writers' Cooperative), applied in 1896 for legal status and its founding members came from Iduna, the free German society for literature (established 1891), a grouping of pan-German, conservative writers. In the following year, the association revised its statutes and became the Deutschösterreichische Schriftstellergenossenschaft (DÖSG). The prime mover was Adam Müller-Guttenbrunn (1852–1923), a known anti-Semite who had the backing of a number of anti-Semitic and/or pan-German newspapers and periodicals and felt spurned by Concordia, which presented itself as primus inter pares. During the four decades it existed, the DÖSG failed to become the anti-liberal counterpart to Concordia and did little to care for the professional needs of its writing members. Instead, it mainly functioned as an ideological platform.

A further ideological differentiation from the liberal Concordia and the pan-German DÖSG came in the year 1895 with the founding of the Verband katholischer Schriftstellerinnen Österreichs (Society of Austrian Catholic Women Writers) against a background of growing political

Catholicism. It derived its *raison d'etre* in part from the dominant public role played by the liberal and Jewish Concordia.

The last witness to the segmentation of Austrian literary life was the Schutzverband deutscher Schriftsteller (Protective Society of German Writers). Founded in Germany in 1909 as a type of trade union for writers, the SDS first tried to establish a Vienna branch in 1916 with Engelbert Pernerstorfer as chairman. Among the members of the board at the time were Hugo von Hofmannsthal, Raoul Auernheimer, Franz Karl Ginzkey, Karl Glossy, and Anton Wildgans. But the association did not get off the ground and it was re-established in early 1920 as the Schutzverband deutscher Schriftsteller in Österreich (SDSÖ), albeit without links to prominent Social Democrats. When more conservative elements had been eliminated from the association, the SDSÖ, although decried as leftist, became a force to reckon with and managed to bring into its fold, as a champion of the economic interests of its members, Austrian authors who, for ideological reasons, would not otherwise want to be seen together. The SDSÖ sought equal opportunities for writers under the country's social insurance legislation, fought for authors' royalties for the publication of their works in the new medium of radio, offered members free legal advice, and so on. One writers' organization that seemed to surmount the political and ideological barriers separating Austrian authors was the "apolitical" PEN Club, established in 1923 in Vienna by the writer Grete von Urban-itzky. Its first president was none other than Arthur Schnitzler. But another well-known literary figure of the time, the satirist Karl Kraus, refused to become a member because "the afternoon get-togethers and joint sup-pers" were anathema to him. Although politics officially had no place in the PEN Club, that was to change in May 1933 in Dubrovnik at its first international conference after Hitler's rise to power and the book-burnings across Germany earlier that month. The issue of what position the PEN Club should take toward Nazi Germany split both delegates and the ranks of the club in Vienna down the middle. The debate in which the chief Aus-trian delegates, Felix Salten and Grete von Urbanitzky, refused to support measures against Nazi Germany for the first time made Austrian writers, for whatever motive, distinguishable as friend or foe in Berlin. The dispute led many long-standing members to leave the PEN Club for political or pragmatic reasons. At this time, other efforts were being made to "orga-nize" writers in Austria. Following the creation of the Reichsschrifttums-kammer (RSK), one of seven chambers of the Reichskulturkammer established by propaganda minister Joseph Goebbels in the fall of 1933 to bring all creative activity under the control of a central body, the ability to publish hinged on membership of the RSK and thus a declaration of loyalty to the Führer. It goes without saying that those writers who were deemed "unreliable" were simply excluded from the book market. Meanwhile, other noteworthy attempts to organize writers were underway in Austria.

The Schutzverband deutscher Schriftsteller in Germany had undergone what is known as "Gleichschaltung" and been replaced, under Goebbels' aegis, by the Reichsverband deutscher Schriftsteller (RDS). Soon afterwards, the Salzburg writer Franz Löser began to canvas his colleagues in Austria about becoming members of an Austrian branch of the RDS. And he garnished his "invitation" with a warning that, in future, membership of the RDS would be a deciding factor in whether a writer would be able to publish his works in Germany. Anyone who was not a member of the RDS, he argued, would simply not be "heard" in Germany any longer. Response from writers in Austria was low and only about 30 of the 100 who had received Löser's newsletter bothered to apply. But in the fall of 1933, the RDS was incorporated into the RSK and in December it was announced that Austrian writers were under no obligation to seek membership in the RSK, although German publishers, newspaper and journal editors and the like continued to demand a declaration of loyalty to the German government from Austrian authors.

Even before the so-called July Agreement between Austria and Germany in 1936, which led the government in Vienna to pardon some 16,000 members of the illegal Nazi Party and further opened the floodgates to ongoing cultural domination, there had been a number of National Socialist writers' organizations in the widest sense in Austria. In 1931, for example, the Kampfbund für deutsche Kultur (German Fighting Union) established an Austrian branch to promote the ideals of a German culture, based on race, blood and *Volk*. The list of its members reveals the *völkisch* canon and includes the names of countless writers whose careers were to take off during the Nazi period in Austria from 1938 and who seemed to believe their political persuasion ("Gesinnung") was worth more in terms of public and party recognition than their literary talent. After Chancellor Dollfuss's government banned the Nazi Party, the Kampfbund was forced to dissolve in November 1933, although it still led an illegal existence. Writers closely associated with the Kampfbund were Hermann Graedener, Mirko Jelusich, and Josef Weinheber. Earlier, Austrian sympathizers with German "renewal" had used the Kampfbund, that is one of its sections, the "Fachschaft Schrifttum" under Josef Weinheber, as the platform to establish another National Socialist association, namely the Ring nationaler Schriftsteller. Following the banning of the Nazi Party in November 1933, the Ring disappeared from sight. In 1934 another offshoot of a Nazi German organization, this time the Nationalsozialistische Kulturgemeinde (National Socialist Cultural Community), was established underground. Planned as strict party organization, membership of the NSDAP was a prerequisite, although the illegal association likely only played a minor role in literary affairs. The two most prominent figures in the NSKG were Rudolf Haybach, the first publisher of Heimito von Doderer, and Anton Haasbauer.

The most conspicuous writers' organization established between 1933 and 1938 is the strictly "Aryan" Bund der deutschen Schriftsteller Österreichs (BdSÖ; League of German Writers in Austria). It was founded in November 1936 at the initiative of the *Landeskulturamtsleiter* of the illegal NSDAP, Hermann Stuppäck, in what was the third attempt to create a National Socialist authors' association by writers such as Friedrich Schreyvogl, Max Mell, Wladimir Hartlieb, Hermann Heinz Ortner, Hermann Graedener, Mirko Jelusich, Franz Spunda, and Josef Wenter, in other words, the literary stalwarts among Nazi or conservative-nationalistic writers in Austria. Indeed, the BdSÖ saw itself as the focal point of National Socialist writing in Austria and its members are, needless to say, absent from any literary canon today. Shortly before Christmas 1936, the BdSÖ held its constituent meeting and chose, for the sake of appearances, a non-party member affiliated with exponents of the *Ständestaat* (corporate state), the conservative writer Max Mell, as chairman. However, the state or secret police spoke out against giving legal status to the association, arguing that it appeared to be a front for previous, now banned Nazi organizations and nothing more than a grouping of Nazi-minded writers. The Federal Chancellery, for its part, dismissed the arguments and sided with the Vienna police department which could offer no reason *not* to allow the BdSÖ to become a legally sanctioned association. The Bund's statutes could not, of course, include the "Arierparagraph" (a regulation restricting membership to "Aryans"), but in practice non-Aryans were not admitted. In earlier decades, other writers' organizations had followed the principle of not allowing non-Aryans to become members. Although the Bund was very soon to outlive its usefulness, in that its members were all required after March 1938 to seek admission to the Reichsschrifttumskammer, its short existence is significant nonetheless. For the authorities making literary policy in Nazi Germany, to whom the names of most Austrian writers meant little or nothing, the estimated one hundred members of the Bund were not only distinguishable from Jewish, liberal or otherwise undesirable writers in Austria; they were considered the true representatives of Austrian writing. And last, but not least, the main exponents of the Bund facilitated the smooth transition in Austria after March 1938 to the rule of the Reichsschrifttumskammer. Several weeks later, Austria's nationalistic writers celebrated the "liberation" of their homeland (and their role in it) in the form of an expression of political and ideological conviction, in the *Bekenntnisbuch österreichischer Dichter* (Austrian Writers Confess Their Faith). Published by the Bund der deutschen Schriftsteller Österreichs itself, seventy-one of the 100 contributors were actual members who could now give free rein to their innermost feelings about the "savior" Adolf Hitler. With the *Anschluss,* the segmentation of literary life ended, and literary history has all but forgotten the gravediggers.

Notes

[1] Carl Junker, "Der Verlagsbuchhandel in der Republik Österreich. Betrachtungen anläßlich der ersten Wiener Buchmesse," in *Deutsche Verlegerzeitung* 2 (1921), Nr. 22, 406–13. The following essay is based to a considerable extent on the author's two-volume history of literary publishing in Austria in the interwar years: *Österreichische Verlagsgeschichte 1918–1938*. Volume I: *Geschichte des österreichischen Verlagswesens;* Volume II: *Lexikon der belletristischen Verlage*. Vienna: Böhlau Verlag 1985. (= Literatur und Leben. Neue Folge, volume 28/I–II.)

[2] "in der Pilzatmosphäre der ewigen Krisenschwüle schossen die neuen Verlage auf." Carl Julius Haidvogel, "Wir jungen Österreicher," in *Österreichische Monatshefte* (Vienna), 5. Jahrgang, November/December 1929, 554–59; here: 555.

[3] Ernst Fischer, "Literatur und Ideologie in Österreich 1918–1938. Forschungsstand und Forschungsperspektiven," *Internationales Archiv für Sozialgeschichte der deutschen Literatur. 1. Sonderheft Forschungsreferate* (1985): 183–255. N.B.: the Ernst Fischer cited here is *not* the writer and politician Ernst Fischer (1875–1954).

4: Popular Culture in Austria: Cabaret and Film, 1918–45

Janet Stewart

IN 1895, THE MUSEUM DER VOLKSKUNDE (Museum of Folklore) was established in Vienna, a year after the constitution of the Verein für Volkskunde (Association for Folklore), which sought to understand a particular form of popular culture — traditional folk culture — from the vantage point of historical anthropology. Programmatically, the first issue of the association's journal, *Die österreichische Zeitschrift für Volkskunde* (The Austrian Journal of Folklore), included articles by Richard von Kralik titled "Zur österreichischen Sagenkunde" (The Study of Austrian Legend and Myth") and Alois Riegl titled "Das Volksmäßige und die Gegenwart" (The Folkish and the Present).[1] The whole undertaking was essentially an exercise in documenting the traditional folk culture of the Habsburg Monarchy, but it was being carried out in a period that was witnessing significant sociocultural change as industrialization brought about large-scale migration from the countryside, the location and object of these ethnographical studies, to the city. While academics devoted their attention to one form of popular culture, a different manifestation of that culture was gaining in importance. The twin processes of industrialization and urbanization brought in their wake a new form of popular culture, mass commercial culture, which developed as a result of new technological possibilities coupled with the people's experience of living in rapidly expanding cities. The First World War and the subsequent dissolution of the Habsburg Monarchy served merely to intensify this dynamic; after 1918, particularly in Vienna, mass commercial culture appeared as the dominant form of popular culture. This development was, however, not without its critics and challengers.

Old and New Cultural Forms

The roots of mass commercial culture in Austria extend back into the nineteenth century and can be found in popular theater and variety theater, as well as in the "illusory world" of the Prater.[2] The latter, in particular, often appears in Austrian literature of the first decades of the twentieth century, functioning as an alternative to the bourgeois world of high culture.[3] After the First World War into the 1930s, the Prater remained a prime location of popular culture, home to a permanent amusement park, as well as a large number of circuses and variety theaters. The 1920s, however, also saw new developments in mass commercial culture, as radio and film gained in importance. This development, in turn, had an effect on existing forms of popular culture; in the 1920s circuses and variety theaters were increasingly forced to work together in their efforts to modernize and remain attractive in the changed commercial environment, with circuses diversifying to include boxing matches as part of their performances and variety theaters making use of so-called "living photographs" and short films. In addition, variety theaters sought to remain competitive by attracting high-profile international acts, such as the American cabaret artist Josephine Baker, or the British dance troupe, the Tiller Girls, to Vienna.[4] They also increasingly used the promise of partial nudity to generate audiences, as satirized by Ödön von Horváth in *Geschichten aus dem Wiener Wald* (Tales from the Vienna Woods, 1931). Despite all these efforts, however, which saw a number of variety theaters continue to flourish, by 1933, many prominent variety theaters had fallen prey to technological innovation and had been converted into cinemas.

In terms of mass commercial culture, film was undeniably the major player in Austria in the period 1918 to 1945. By the early 1920s, Vienna had become a prominent center of film production, although as with the rise of mass commercial culture, itself, the history of film-making in Austria predates the First Republic. It can be traced back to 1906, when a company named Saturn began producing "Gentlemen's Films" (*Herrenabendfilme*). These soon found a global market, and enjoyed considerable success until production was halted by the police in 1910. Around the same time, a number of film studios (*Filmfabriken*) were established in Vienna, but most struggled due to a lack of capital. It was not until the final two years of the First World War that adequate capital began flowing into the industry. This, coupled with a ban on the import of films from enemy foreign countries, brought about an upturn in its fortunes, and by 1918, Vienna housed more than 200 firms involved in aspects of film production and distribution.[5] Immediately after the war, restrictions on trade were lifted and Viennese studios embarked on an ambitious program of film-making, which has led some commentators to describe Vienna in the period 1919 to 1924 as a veritable "Film-Mecca."[6] During this time, the most successful films produced in Vienna were monumental silent films, such as *Sodom und Gomorrha* (1922) or *Der junge Medardus* (1923), an adaptation of Arthur Schnitzler's historical drama set in 1809, as Vienna was defending itself against Napoleon. These internationally acclaimed films were the work of multinational creative teams, with much of the personnel drawn from the successor states to the Habsburg

Monarchy. In other words, the history of film in the early 1920s suggests that in the field of popular culture, 1918 did not represent a complete break with the past. The boom in Austrian film production seen immediately after 1918 was fueled by postwar inflation, and as such, was a short-lived phenomenon. In 1922, this period of inflation, which had allowed Austrian companies to sell films at cut price to the global market, came to an end and many studios and production companies went bankrupt. Although during 1921–22, 138 full-length feature films had been made in Vienna, in 1924 only fifteen were produced, and in 1925, the figure dropped again to five.[7] The late 1920s saw a brief upturn in Austrian film production, but this was then dealt a blow by the advent of sound film, which limited the market for German-language productions.[8] Austrian film did, however, continue to enjoy limited success with the genre of the so-called "Vienna film."

While Austrian film production in the 1920s underwent a series of ups and downs, film distribution was a straightforward commercial success story.[9] Film-going, as a number of commentators have pointed out, was becoming an increasingly popular pastime, with 400 to 500 different films showing in Viennese cinemas each year in the 1920s. Helmut Gruber argues that cinema's popularity can be attributed not only to its status as a relatively cheap leisure activity, but also to the way in which the cinema's darkened auditoria offered consumers both light escapism and real erotic opportunities.[10] These reasons, however, also formed the cornerstone of the widespread critique of cinema as popular culture being voiced in the 1920s. Often, the critique centered on moral judgments; connections were made between criminality and the cinema, and between alcoholism and cinema-going. Across the political spectrum, cinema was viewed as something both threatening and unpredictable, as nothing less than the "symbol of a collapsing order, as a symptom of cultural nihilism and the loss of power."[11] Writers and other intellectuals, even if not openly hostile to the cinema as a form of popular culture that posed an active threat to the hegemony of bourgeois culture, still voiced an ambivalent attitude toward popular film. The novelist Robert Musil, for example, noted in his diary after one of his first visits to the cinema: "Was nun? Ich verleugnete mein Leben und ging ins Lichtspiel" (What now? I denied my life and went to the cinema).[12] Musil and others were not immune to the fascination of film, but also perceived commercial mass entertainment, including film, to harbor certain dangers. As the German sociologist Siegfried Kracauer pointed out in his programmatic essay on popular culture, "Das Ornament der Masse" (The Mass Ornament) intellectuals often sought to express these dangers by arguing that mass popular culture served as a form of "Zerstreuung" (distraction) for the masses.[13] This, of course, is similar to the critical stance towards the "culture industry" that later came to dominate Frankfurt School thinking on popular culture.[14]

Kracauer's position, however, diverges from the orthodox Frankfurt School view of popular culture. In "Das Ornament der Masse," he claimed:

> Der Ort, den eine Epoche im Geschichtsprozeß einnimmt, ist aus der Analyse ihrer unscheinbaren Oberflächenäußerungen schlagender zu bestimmen als aus den Urteilen der Epoche über sich selbst. [. . .] Der Grundgehalt einer Epoche und ihre unbeachteten Regungen erhellen sich wechselseitig.[15]

> [The position that an epoch occupies in the historical process can be determined more strikingly from an analysis of its inconspicuous surface-level expressions than from that epoch's judgments about itself. [. . .] The fundamental substance of an epoch and its unheeded impulses illuminate each other reciprocally.]

Taking its impetus from Kracauer, this chapter will demonstrate connections between popular culture and politics in Austria in the period 1918 to 1945, a time in which popular culture was a highly contested phenomenon, characterized by ongoing political struggles to gain control over it and to define its nature. Much of the evidence discussed in this chapter relates specifically to Vienna. This is because of the close links between urbanization and new forms of popular culture and because it is in the urban environment that tensions between different understandings of "popular culture" are at their most palpable. The period saw attempts to provide alternatives to mass commercial culture, as well as efforts to appropriate and influence mass commercial culture, often through gaining political control over the means of production of popular culture. It also witnessed folk culture being heralded as an alternative to mass commercial culture, sometimes while simultaneously being transformed into mass culture. The resulting tale of the popular, the commercial, and the political during the period under consideration is one of conflict, compromise, and resistance.

"Red Vienna": Culture for the People

While widespread criticism of mass commercial culture dominated the political and intellectual climate of the early 1920s, it was above all from the political left that attempts to counter this kind of culture through the creation of an alternative, "truly Socialist" popular culture were to be found. This form of cultural politics was a key strand of Austro-Marxist thought, which was itself influenced by neo-Kantianism and the pedagogical idealism of Kant and Schiller. The ideal of Socialist popular culture was given its most visible and lasting form in the architecture of Red Vienna, and in the symbolic "Ringstrasse of the Proletariat," as the new municipal housing complexes (*Gemeindebauten*) on the Margarethengürtel were dubbed in 1930.[16] As Eve Blau has argued, such *Gemeindebauten* appropriated "the formal typologies of the historical city [and so] took possession of the cultural symbols of Vienna," thereby pressing high culture into the service of popular culture.[17] Vienna's ambitious building program was the most visible of a large number of cultural initiatives connected to the Social Democratic Party (SDAP) during this period. By 1931–32, around 400,000 members belonged to the forty or so cultural organizations allied to the SDAP in Vienna. Although these groupings were by no means all subject to centralized control, two main organizations were instrumental in the drive to create Socialist popular culture — the Sozialistische Bildungszentrale (Socialist Cultural Center), which dated back to about 1908 and focused on education, and the Sozialdemokratische Kunststelle (Socialist Art Center), which was set up in 1919 to provide access to the arts. Together these organizations set out to elevate the tastes of the working classes, so that workers would be in a position to consume high culture.[18] In the early 1920s, neither film nor architecture but the printed word was accorded central importance in the cultural education of the working class; the Socialist Cultural Center oversaw the creation and maintenance of workers' libraries, organized lecture series and public readings, and published newspapers, such as *Die Arbeiter-Zeitung* and *Das kleine Blatt*, and journals, such as *Der Kampf* (the party's main theoretical publication) and *Die Unzufriedene* (which targeted a female readership). Historians, however, have questioned how popular the kind of culture promoted by the Socialist Cultural Center really was. Gruber notes that the number of people attending lectures in a year was probably only equivalent to the numbers attending a soccer match or going to the cinema in a week.[19] Meanwhile Alfred Pfoser has examined the workers' lending libraries, highlighting gaps between policy and popularity. He argues that the libraries' acquisition policies demonstrated a clear preference for scientific and educational books above literature, and contained an imperative to offer alternatives to the scourge of "Schund- und Kitschliteratur" (the "penny dreadful").[20] Policy makers were, however, also obliged to take into account popular tastes, particularly in the field of adventure novels, and compromised by being selective in terms of the authors they stocked, approving classic novels by authors such as Charles Sealsfield, Alexandre Dumas, Joseph Conrad, and Robert Louis Stevenson, while characterizing Karl May and others as the "enemy." Calls to stock only "revolutionary art" were, meanwhile, rejected by the Socialist Cultural Center as attempts to limit the aspirations of the working class. Why, asked Franz Trescher, writing in the *Arbeiter-Zeitung* in 1929, should workers have the opportunity to read Upton Sinclair, Alfons Petzold, and Emile Zola, but be denied access to Thomas Mann, Hofmannsthal and Rilke?[21]

In his article, Trescher outlines a position that approaches Walter Benjamin's description of the "historical materialist," whose task it was to unlock the revolutionary potential of great works of art for the working class.[22] This view also formed the basis of the cultural policy pursued by the Socialist Art Center under the direction of David Josef Bach, who drew on Enlightenment thought, and in particular, on Kant and Schiller, to argue "that all art, to the extent that it is art at all, is revolutionary and has a revolutionary effect."[23] The main task of the Socialist Art Center, which drew on earlier initiatives such as the Freie Volksbühne (Free People's Stage) established in Berlin in 1890, or the "Arbeiter-Sinfonie-Konzerte" (workers' concerts) organized by Bach in Vienna in 1905, was to encourage the working class to become consumers of bourgeois art by "bringing music, theater, and the arts to workers, employees, and students."[24] Bach set out to achieve this aim by securing cheap theater tickets for members of the Socialist Art Center. This exercise allowed him to exert influence on theater programs. Particularly in staging new modern plays, Viennese theaters in the early to mid 1920s were dependent on the ticket sales to the Socialist Art Center. Although the majority of tickets sold through the Socialist Art Center were for performances of Naturalist or classical plays, its financial support was instrumental in bringing works by Bernard Shaw, Georg Kaiser, Ernst Toller, Bertolt Brecht, and Henrik Ibsen to the Viennese stage. Bach's aim, however, was not merely to influence the programs of existing theaters, but also to set up a new Socialist popular theater. This aim was partly realized in 1928, when the Socialist Art Center experimented with running its own program in the Carltheater, beginning with a performance of *Lenin* by Ernst Fischer. However, financial problems caused the venture to fail and left the Socialist Art Center open to criticism and hostility from within the SDAP. It was argued, for example, that the cultural politics of the Socialist Art Center were tailored to the tastes of the coffeehouse intellectual rather than the workers of Favoriten. Bach found himself at the center of a tension in the SDAP between a belief in the right of workers to partake of culture that had previously been denied them, and attempts to create a new proletarian culture. Although Oscar Pollock, writing in the SDAP journal, *Der Kampf*, criticized Bach for producing a program more suited to the liberal middle classes than the workers of Favoriten, Pfoser argues that Bach's position was genuinely liberal and that his main aim was to avoid the divisions that characterized the development of Socialist art and literature in Germany.[25] In other words, Bach was attempting to steer a clear course through the polarity between Brecht and Lukács that characterized cultural politics in Germany in the late 1920s.[26]

The Socialist Art Center did not limit itself to "serious" drama, but also distributed discounted tickets for popular bourgeois culture, such as operetta. This nod toward commercial culture was lampooned by Karl Kraus in his *Nachträgliche Republikfeier* of 1925, and his criticisms were then taken up by the "Politisches Kabarett," formed by a group of young people from the left wing of the SDAP.[27] The irony of their position is that cabaret itself belonged to popular bourgeois culture, and indeed, as we have seen, to mass commercial culture. The origins of cabaret in Vienna lie in the first decade of the twentieth century, with ventures such as Nachtlicht and the Cabaret Fledermaus. The immediate postwar period saw cabaret begin to flourish once more, as new entertainment establishments opened in Vienna, to complement those already in existence. In these early years of the First Republic, critical voices from within the cabaret scene objected to the commercialization of cabaret and to its proximity to high bourgeois culture. Bela Laszky, for example, who was associated with the group "Brettl," bemoaned the fact that cabaret's role was to offer the audience "eine möglichst wenig störende Zugabe zum Sekt, Kalbsbraten und schwarzen Kaffee" (an accompaniment which provides the least possible disruption to their champagne, veal fillet and coffee).[28] This did not mean, however, that all cabaret in this period was apolitical. The celebrated compére, Fritz Grünbaum, regularly used his position to articulate an anti-Christian-Social stance, although it appears that his views were not well received, even by the *Arbeiter-Zeitung*.[29] Meanwhile, from 1922 on, Karl Kraus enhanced his celebrated readings of Nestroy and Offenbach with "Zusatzcouplets," satirical political and social commentaries delivered in cabaret style.[30] In 1927, Kraus directed his criticism at Johann Schober, Chief of Police in Vienna from 1918 to 1932, who was responsible for the bloody repression of the riot at the fire of the Palace of Justice in July 1927. At this point, Kraus combined cabaret — "Das Schoberlied," in which he satirized Schober's tendency to excuse his actions by claiming to be performing his duty[31] — with direct action: he plastered Vienna with posters calling for Schober's resignation. This was in the same year, 1927, that saw Oscar Teller establish the "Jüdisch-Politische Cabaret." Its programs were based on aggressive satire and played only to local Zionist groups; premieres were held in the Porrhaus on Karlsplatz. The successful first program, "Juden hinaus" (Jews Out), was followed by a further four, and the group continued to function until 1938.

In the early 1920s, commercial cabaret was located almost exclusively in Vienna's city center and in the Prater. Later in the decade, those concerned to exploit the political aspects of cabaret also sought to extend its reach from the center to the city's suburbs. The "Jüdisch-Politische Cabaret," as we have seen, took its performances from the Karlsplatz to local Zionist groups throughout the city. Meanwhile, Karl Kraus performed before working-class audiences in Viennese locations such as the Volksheim (community center) in Ottakring, the Arbeiterheim (workers' center) in Favoriten, and the Bildungsheim (education center) in Hietzing.[32] And in 1926, Fritz Grünbaum undertook to bring cabaret to the working-class suburbs of the city, performing together with Ludwig Stärk in the Arbeiterheim in Favoriten.[33] Although Grünbaum and Stärk were well received in Favoriten, this was an isolated excursion into the suburbs;

mainstream cabaret artists preferred to celebrate their popularity in the city center. This being the case, in 1925 young members of the SDAP, led by Ludwig Wagner and Paul Lazarsfeld, banded together as the "Sozialistische Veranstaltungsgruppe" (socialist performance group) and set out to create their own cabaret, the "Politisches Kabarett."[34] As was the case with the "Jüdisch-Politische Cabaret," the first performances of the "Politisches Kabarett" took place in Vienna's city center, in the former Pan-Künstlerspiele, but subsequent performances, of which there were over 400 in total, took place throughout the city. Initially, the "Politisches Kabarett" consisted in a "colorful potpourri of short sketches and songs," with texts written mainly by Robert Ehrenzweig and Karl Bittmann. Others involved with the program included Jura Soyfer, Viktor Grünbaum and Fritz Jahoda. The work, which became known internationally, was influenced by ideas coming out of the Soviet Union, and the "Politische Kabarett" understood its role in terms of "agitprop theater." This was recognized by the leadership of the SDAP, who, with the help of the Sozialistische Veranstaltungsgruppe, set out to create a set of "agitprop theater groups" throughout Austria, which would provide political popular entertainment to accompany election speeches and enliven party events.[35]

By the late 1920s, the SDAP had appropriated cabaret, initially a form of bourgeois popular culture and mass commercial culture, for its own political purposes. Seeing the advantages in appropriating commercial culture, it also turned its attentions to film. Discussions about how to tame what the SDAP saw as the rampant commercialism of film had been taking place from as early as 1919, when Paul Wengraf argued in the *Arbeiter-Zeitung* for the nationalization of the film industry; indeed, such ideas had their roots in the prewar cinema reform movement. At this time, the position of the Social Democrats on film was close to the general bourgeois view of the moral dangers of the cinema, and in the early years of the Republic, the consensus was strong enough to establish a national Filmstelle (film council), which was set up in 1918, and, until its demise in 1923, was charged with producing educational films, as well as propaganda films for the various ministries. Its role was not to enter into competition with the film industry, but to provide alternative projects that would silence cinema's most vociferous opponents. In 1924, the adult education association, Urania, attempted to resuscitate the state-run film council. Among other initiatives, it organized a conference on cinema reform, which was held in Vienna that year, without representation from the film industry. According to Schwarz, only two contributors to the conference spoke on points that were of lasting interest and influence: the German film director Fritz Lang argued for film's importance as the "herald of German identity," while Béla Balázs, who provided the Viennese newspaper *Der Tag* with film reviews in 1922–24, suggested that the cultivation of film criticism could bring about a general cinema reform.[36] Meanwhile, the

SDAP in Vienna began to turn its attention to film's potential, setting up its own film council as part of the Socialist Cultural Center in 1923, and using film as a party political tool in the 1923 elections. This film council functioned above all as a film distributor, initially focusing on documentary and propaganda films, but increasingly devoting space to feature films, particularly Soviet films, on which the Socialist Cultural Center had a virtual monopoly. Finding commercial cinemas reluctant to screen Socialist films, the Social Democrats then turned their attention to building its own cinemas in Vienna, which it accomplished by establishing its own distribution network (Kinobetriebsgesellschaft or Kiba) in 1926. By 1931, there were twelve Kiba cinemas in Vienna.[37] The relationship between the Socialist Cultural Center and the Kiba was, however, strained, with Fritz Rosenfeld, the director of the Center, arguing that the program on offer in Kiba cinemas was no different to what was on offer elsewhere; they too, he claimed, screened only the "üblichen Schund" (usual trash).[38]

Rosenfeld's critique of the films on offer in Vienna's mainstream and Socialist cinemas alike found an echo in the work of other left-wing intellectuals at the time. Writing in the *Frankfurter Zeitung* in 1928, Kracauer outlined the aesthetic and thematic deficiency of popular film in that year, singling out the "Vienna film" for special disparagement.[39] Kracauer, however, like Walter Benjamin in his programmatic essay, "The Work of Art in an Age of Mechanical Reproduction" of 1935–39, also recognized and argued for the emancipatory potential of film.[40] One work that demonstrated the incendiary, if not the emancipatory potential of film in the early 1930s, was Lewis Milestone's film of Remarque's *Im Westen nichts Neues* (All Quiet on the Western Front). The film had already been banned in the Weimar Republic after Nazi protests when, in December 1930, just before its planned Austrian premiere, calls came for it to be banned there too. The issue was debated in parliament, which resulted in a recommendation that each individual federal state, with whom responsibility for the cinema lay, should disallow performances of the film on the grounds of "national solidarity." In many provinces, a ban quickly followed, but not in Vienna. This led to a situation that Pfoser has described as a brief civil war, with anti-film demonstrators — National Socialists and members of the Christian Social paramilitary organization, the Heimwehr — engaging in violent protests and clashing with Social Democrats protesting against the idea of a ban.[41] Although the Socialist art center had already sold 30,000 tickets for the film, in early January 1931 parliament moved to ban any further performances, citing public safety as the reason. Like H. K. Breslauer's film version of *Die Stadt ohne Juden* (City without Jews, 1924) by Hugo Bettauer, *Im Westen nichts Neues* had fallen victim to the so-called "censorship of the street." The Social Democrats then organized special trips to Bratislava for those who wanted to see the film, but did not effectively challenge the parliamentary decision, thereby, as Pfoser argues, losing control of the cinema as an important means of production of popular culture. The year 1930, however, also saw the Social Democrats commissioning a full-length feature film as part of their election campaign, providing further evidence for their belief in the political impact of fictional film. The result was Frank Ward Rossak's *Das Notizbuch des Mr. Pim* (Mr. Pim's Notebook, 1930), a film in which, as was also the case with Brecht's *Kuhle Wampe* (1932), the subject is not the individual, but the masses: "The masses dominate the image, the street and delivers the grand promise for the future."[42] This work constitutes a filmic portrayal of life in Red Vienna concentrating on the cultural politics pursued by the Social Democrats in their attempts to provide an alternative form of popular culture to commercial mass culture.

Das Notizbuch des Mr. Pim ends with a montage of documentary footage of May Day celebrations, and other similar Socialist holidays. In so doing, it calls attention to other kinds of popular culture against which the Social Democrats were seeking to define their program. Carefully organized and choreographed May Day celebrations, along with flagship events such as the Festival for the Masses (*Massenfestspiele*), held to celebrate the opening of the Wiener Stadion, a new public sports stadium, in 1931, were constructed to provide a Socialist alternative to pre-existing forms of folk culture and the rituals of Catholic culture.[43] As with other forms of mass culture, the Socialist May Day celebrations predated the First Republic, having their roots in the late nineteenth century. According to Friedrich Engels, in 1890 the Viennese workers, under the direction of the leading Austro-Marxist and founder of the *Arbeiter-Zeitung*, Victor Adler, first demonstrated to the world "how proletarian festivals should be celebrated."[44] Other symbolic dates were adopted later as times of celebration, including a day of remembrance for those who fell in the March Revolution of 1848, and a requiem for the victims of 15 July 1927. Despite Engels's perception of the first May Day celebration as a paradigmatically proletarian festival, the Social Democrats' festival culture was based, as Pfoser argues, on a perceived need to appropriate the bourgeois-feudal symbolism of the dominant culture of the time and to utilize its "heritage value" within their own movement. Certainly the *Massenfestspiele* of 1931, written by Robert Ehrenzweig and directed by Max Reinhardt's pupil, Stephan Hock, which centered on the symbolic fall of the idol of capital, were seen as a left-wing alternative to the Salzburg Festival, something that Ernst Fischer had been calling for since he witnessed a performance of *Jedermann* in 1921.[45]

The Social Democrats' appropriation of those aspects of bourgeois and feudal culture that formed the cornerstone of ritualized Catholic culture was satirized by commentators such as Kraus, who parodied the poems and songs written by the likes of Luitpold Stern for such occasions. It was, however, taken seriously by their political opponents who, particularly in

Germany of the 1920s and early 1930s, adopted and adapted the forms of representation developed by the Workers' Movement in the first decades of the twentieth century. In Austria, this takeover did not take place, and the power of the political spectacle belonged, in the early 1930s, to the Social Democrats. Their mistake, however, was to confuse the aesthetic strength of demonstrations and festivals, the creation of an alternative form of mass popular culture, with real political power. The political struggles of 1933, culminating in the so-called "self-elimination" of the National Council following the resignation of all three presiding officers, and the Civil War of 1934 then served as a stark wake-up call, making it clear that, in the words of the defeated Socialist paramilitaries, the Schutzbündler, "We may have the knowledge, but the others have the power."[46]

Conservative Counter-Attack

After the Civil War of February 1934, Vienna experienced a significant change in the dominant ideological form of popular culture, with a shift from Austro-Marxist thought to the conservative cultural values of the *Ständestaat* (corporate state), based on belief in the Fatherland, in universal Catholicism, in German nationalism, and in old Austrian culture. Just as, in the early 1920s, architecture had served as perhaps the most visible symbol of attempts to create a truly Socialist popular culture, so in 1934 it again adopted the mantle of medium of mass communication, as the prominent housing projects of Red Vienna were renamed. In the best known example, the Karl-Marx-Hof, depicted in 1934 on the cover of a publication entitled "The Fall of the Red Fortress," was re-christened Heiligenstädter-Hof.[47] As the conflict surrounding the screening of *Im Westen Nichts Neues* demonstrated, however, Christian Social attempts to impose their vision of popular culture on the capital city could be seen well before 1934. In fact, the events of July 1927 heralded the beginning of a conservative *Kulturkampf*, which was a concerted attempt to gain control of culture in the capital. At the level of popular culture, the Christian-Conservative Youth Movement championed folk culture as an alternative to what they denigrated as "Negerkultur," and traditional hairstyles and clothing as an alternative to the short hair and dresses fashionable in the capital. Such criticism of the popular culture of the urban center was accompanied by a sustained move to counter any influence that the Social Democrats might have over the city's cultural institutions.

One important site of the struggle to impose a particular ideological form of popular culture on Vienna was radio, a mass medium organized not according to commercial interests, but based on the perceived interests of the nation. In 1924, RAVAG (Österreichische Radio-Verkehrs A.G.) was constituted, heralding the beginning of radio broadcasting in Austria. The initiative was the product of co-operation between the national government, the Viennese municipal council, a bank, and industrial companies. From the outset, it was agreed that RAVAG should not be dominated by any one political party, and during the first years of its existence, a policy of neutrality was followed in terms of program scheduling, with the emphasis on "bland information (crime, weather, stock market, sports)."[48] After 1927, however, there was a change in emphasis, as neither the Social Democrats nor the Christian Socials were happy with the status quo and agreed instead to move toward a position of political pluralism in the program schedules. The Social Democrats, supported by the Workers' Radio Club, pursued a policy of programs specifically created for the working classes, but were forced to compromise in their demands. Up till 1931, the administration did find space for programs covering workers' interests and activities, but always insisted that they were balanced by equal time being devoted to Catholic and conservative interests. The major interest pursued by Christian Social politicians, however, was not programming as such, but control over radio broadcasting. While the Social Democrats focused their efforts on creating culturally enriching programs, the Christian Socials, their hand strengthened by new recruits to the Catholic Radio Club from the early 1930s on, were striving for, and gaining, political control of Ravag itself.

By the early 1930s, the Christian Socials were seeking to gain political control over film as well as radio. The dissolution of parliament in 1933 enabled them to impose state control on film distribution. This was the beginning of an aggressive film policy undertaken by the party, which argued that the state should take the film economy "under its protection."[49] The first move toward asserting control over the industry was through the imposition of so-called "Telegraph Laws" in 1933, which meant that cinemas were now dependent on permission to operate from the Telegraph Authority. After the SDAP was banned in 1934, a large number of cinemas, including those previously belonging to Kiba, besides others, came under state control. Cinemas located in the Arbeiterheime (workers' centers) in Ottakring and Favoriten had been prime locations of Socialist resistance in the Civil War of February 1934, and after the defeat of the Social Democrats, they were either too badly damaged to be reused or simply remained shut anyway. However, control was not exercised without some resistance. The cinema in the Eisenbahnerheim (railway workers' center), for example, which had been taken over by new owners, was the site of disruptive political agitation, carried out during the compulsory showing of so-called "vaterländische Filme."[50]

As part of its strategy to exert control over the cinema industry, the Corporatist government set up a company, the Vaterländische Tongesellschaft, specifically to produce "vaterländische Filme." Modeling its policies on Italian fascism, the Austrian government compelled all cinemas to screen these short films as part of their regular program. These films were designed to present newsworthy events in a way that conformed to the government line, as well as serving to widen knowledge about cultural and economic life in Austria. Films such as *Der freiwillige Arbeitsdienst* (Voluntary Work, 1935) or *Das Kinderferienwerk der vaterländischen Front* (The Children's Holiday Program of the Fatherland Front, 1937) were conceived not merely as internal propaganda films, but also as instruments that would encourage tourism by demonstrating the achievements of the "New Austria" to the wider world. As the 1930s progressed, further legislation was enacted with the aim of binding the Austrian film industry ever more closely to the aims of the Corporatist government. A key step in this program was the founding of the Austrian Filmkonferenz in 1935. This body, which was to supersede the film industry's pre-existing interest groups, was conceived as the equivalent of the Film Rings that had been set up in both National Socialist Germany and fascist Italy, but in pre-*Anschluss* Austria, the new body's influence did not extend beyond the creation of a number of new laws and statutes.

While there were limits to the direct political control that the Corporatist government was able to impose on the Austrian film industry in the period 1933–38, external political forces, particularly from National Socialist Germany, were able to influence considerably the nature of the industry. A gradual but inexorable process of emptying the Austrian film industry of its Jewish protagonists began as early as 1933, as National Socialist Germany began to exert pressure on Austrian film production through the mechanism of import regulations.[51] In 1933, for example, the German authorities refused to approve the import of *Abenteuer am Lido* (Adventures on the Lido) and *Wenn du jung bist, gehört dir die Welt* (When You're Young, the World Belongs to You), both directed by Richard Oswald, an "enemy" and critic of National Socialism.[52] In 1935 an agreement was reached between the German authorities and representatives of the Austrian film industry which allowed Austria to export twelve films per year to Germany, while not placing any limits on the number of films that could be exported from Germany to Austria. Austrian films could, however, be considered German, as long as they could provide documentary evidence that they were "Aryan" products. In other words, those negotiating on behalf of the Austrian film industry undertook to apply the same anti-Semitic restrictions on film production that were already being applied in Germany, which meant that the Aryan credentials of Austrian film-makers were being systematically checked from 1935, albeit illegally.

This form of commercial pressure also affected Austria's independent film-makers in the pre-*Anschluss* period. After the National Socialists came to power in Germany in 1933, Austria was the first destination for many critical filmmakers, the majority of whom were Jewish.[53] Since the established Austrian film industry was primarily oriented toward the German market, these filmmakers were, in the main, unable to establish themselves in existing companies, but were forced to found their own independent film companies, such as Wien-Film KG, Morawsky & Co. This company produced the first independent film, *Salto in die Seligkeit* (Leap into Bliss, 1934), a light comedy in the "Vienna film" tradition, which enjoyed moderate box office success. During the next three years, a number of independent films were produced in Austria, but, by 1936, production had declined sharply due to the further emigration of key figures in the independent scene, such as Joe Pasternak and his circle, as well as the effect of German import restrictions. Although these restrictions only applied to films destined for the German market, independent films could be sabotaged by labeling them "anti-German."[54] This meant that stars such as Hans Moser and Leo Slezak then refused to appear in such films, for fear of damaging their own careers.

The history of the Austrian film industry from the early 1930s onwards, then, can be understood in terms of an increasing orientation towards the German film industry. This primarily commercially driven phenomenon meant that popular culture, rather than politics, played a leading role in Austria's move toward National Socialism. As Loacker points out, by 1936 agreements were in place to bring together the Austrian and German film economies, and to exclude Jewish citizens from the Austrian film industry, which went far beyond the terms of the political agreement between the two countries signed on 11 July 1936, the so-called July Agreement.[55] Indeed, full economic parity between the two countries was not agreed until the Berchtesgaden Agreement of 12 February 1938, while the general exclusion of Jewish citizens did not come about until after the *Anschluss* had taken place. Loacker is not alone in identifying popular culture as a prime site of convergence between the Austrian *Ständestaat* and National Socialist Germany. Pfoser also devotes some attention to this phenomenon, naming specifically "Neues Leben" (New Life), an organization led by Guido Zernatto and brought into being in July 1936 as the Vaterländische Front's equivalent to the National Socialist movement, "Kraft durch Freude" (Strength Through Joy). Like the Social Democratic cultural organizations of the 1920s, "Neues Leben" was an attempt to provide an ideologically-motivated alternative to mass commercial culture, and encompassed writing, visual arts, music, theater, film radio, lectures, travel and festivals, and sport.[56]

Despite the commercially driven orientation towards National Socialist Germany that characterized Austrian popular culture in the 1930s, there was, arguably, also resistance to the German way. This came, first, from the government, which, at least until the July Agreement of 1936, banned not only National Socialist short propaganda films, but also feature films such as *Sturmtage 1919* (Days of Unrest 1919, 1935). Until 1937, independent films also resisted the effects of National Socialist ideology, but it is the genre of the "Vienna film" that, after the end of the Second World War, was posited as a site of resistance to National Socialism until and after the *Anschluss*.[57] This genre, which enjoyed considerable international success, following Max Ophüls's German production of Schnitzler's *Liebelei* (Flirtation, 1932), was essentially apolitical, aiming at distraction from the contemporary socio-political climate. The key figure in the production of the "Vienna film" was Willi Forst, director of *Leise flehen meine Lieder* (Softly Plead my Songs, 1933), which told the story of Schubert's *Unfinished Symphony*, and *Maskerade* (1933). Forst continued to make timeless "Vienna films" after 1938, including *Wiener Blut* (Viennese Blood, 1942) and *Wiener Mädeln* (Viennese Girls, 1943), and at the end of the war, claimed that his emphasis on the Austrian dimension and a specific Austrian, rather than pan-German, history in these films had been a form of protest against National Socialism. Tillner argues, however, that it is only possible to give credence to Forst's claim when subscribing to the myth of Austria as Hitler's "first victim." While Forst himself may have concentrated on directing apolitical Vienna films, he also served on the Advisory Council of the nationalized film production company, Wien Film, created after the German government took possession of the Austrian company Tobis-Sascha in the aftermath of the *Anschluss*. Other important directors involved in the company included Gustav Ucicky, who made a number of propagandistic films following the National Socialist line on women returning to their traditional domestic role, including *Mutterliebe* (Mother-Love, 1939), *Ein Leben lang* (A Whole Life Long, 1940) and *Späte Liebe* (Late Love, 1943), and also E. W. Emo, director of the strongly anti-Semitic film, *Wien 1910* (1943), which tells of the last three days in the life of Mayor Karl Lueger. The film was made to legitimize the annexation of Austria, but even after a number of cuts and changes, it was never actually released in Austria.[58]

A more convincing case for popular culture's ability to provide a site of resistance to the dominant political structures can be made by considering the role of cabaret in the 1930s, although its room for maneuver was limited by the authoritarian government. The aftermath of the Civil War of February 1934 caused many leading Social Democrats to leave Austria, but the influence of popular cultural movements associated with the party continued. In the field of cabaret, for example, although the "Politisches Kabarett" was banned in 1934, individual contributors still appeared in a variety of Viennese venues such as the "Literatur am Naschmarkt" (Literature in the Naschmarkt) or the "ABC," home of the "Alsergrundbrettl," to which, according to reports in the Viennese press, Egon Friedell and Alfred Polgar, stalwarts of the Viennese cabaret scene in the first decade of the twentieth century, were also contributors.[59] These groups, however, were limited in their ability to provide political critique since their programs were subject to increased censorship, meaning that police officers sat in the audience solemnly comparing the approved script with the actual perform-ance.[60] After the *Anschluss,* cabaret retained its critical role, with figures such as Robert Ehrenzweig appearing in exile in London, and Viktor Grünbaum in the USA.[61] Meanwhile, at Christmas 1938, shortly before his death from typhus in early 1939, Jura Soyfer wrote and performed political cabaret sketches while interned in Buchenwald. Cabaret also con-tinued to exist in Vienna after the *Anschluss,* although already in the Spring of 1938, many cabarets were either closed down or, as with "Simpl," Aryanized.[62] Those that survived, such as the "Wiener Werkl," did so by adapting themselves to the new National Socialist regime.

The National Socialist regime exerted a great deal of control on popu-lar culture in Austria, as elsewhere in the Third Reich, by employing so-called *Blockwarte* (caretakers) to report on the activities of their neighbors, and by strongly encouraging people to join organizations such as "Kraft durch Freude" (Strength Through Joy), the "Deutsche Arbeitsfront" (German Labor Front) and the Hitler Youth. However, the regime's con-trol was not total. Traditional Catholic culture, for example, provided some young activists with an alternative to officially sanctioned popular culture. Early resistance to the National Socialist regime found expression in the Rosary Festival of October 1938, which saw between 6,000 and 8,000 youngsters take part in a mass in St. Stephen's Cathedral in Vienna, which then turned into an anti-Nazi rally. The outcome of this protest was, however, a week of anti-clerical rioting and a rally attended by 200,000 on the Heldenplatz. This was then followed, less than a month later, by the carefully orchestrated savagery of Kristallnacht (Night of Broken Glass), which, in Vienna, met with general approval and encouragement. The Catholics, meanwhile, experienced increasing alienation in both Bavaria and Austria, and this led to protest demonstrations being staged, and the creation of a loose network of anti-Nazi Catholic activists.[63]

During the early years of the National Socialist regime in Austria, resis-tance to dominant ideology in the form of popular culture remained rela-tively rare. After Hitler's defeat at Stalingrad in 1943, however, a change could be discerned in the political climate. A certain "springtime stupor" could be observed in Austria, as in the rest of the Third Reich. This mani-fested itself in a number of "political offences," including listening to for-eign radio broadcasts, as well as in the creation of a sub-culture of youth gangs increasingly alienated from Nazi associations such as the Hitler Youth. In Vienna, the most prominent youth gang was the "Schlurfs," which had been in existence since before the beginning of the war. The "Schlurfs" were marked by their apolitical outlook and their orientation towards "the casual elegance of Hollywood." Their home was the Prater, where they "strummed guitars, and aped the manners of Viennese dandies," but they also took part in more aggressive actions, disrupting a

Hitler Youth concert held in the Sofiensaal, for example.[64] Meanwhile, as suggested in *Die größere Hoffnung* (The Greater Hope, 1948), Ilse Aichinger's fictional account of the life of a half-Jewish girl in National Socialist Vienna, other young people who were excluded from public life defined a culture of their own in opposition to the hegemonic position of the Hitler Youth.

Popular culture, then, encompasses both the hegemonic and the counter-cultural. It manifests itself in a number of forms, from "new media" such as film and radio, to festivals that draw on the experience of traditional folk culture, and acts of defiant self-representation on street corners. Individually, and in juxtaposition with one another, these forms function as sites of tension; the history of popular culture is the history of attempts to define and gain control over popular culture. To consider the period 1918–45 through the lens of popular culture is to gain insight into the power of the popular, as a political, economic, and cultural force. Functioning simultaneously as a site of conflict and compromise, popular culture, in all its many guises, is a phenomenon that, as Kracauer noted in "The Mass Ornament," intellectuals ignore at their own peril.

Notes

[1] Richard von Kralik, "Zur österreichischen Sagenkunde I–III," *Österreichische Zeitschrift für Volkskunde* 1 (1895), 7–9, 111–17, 204–16; in the same volume, Alois Riegl, "Das Volksmäßige und die Gegenwart," 4–9.

[2] For further detail see H. C. Ehalt, Gernot Heiss and Hanns Stekl, ed., *Glücklich ist, wer vergißt . . . ? Das andere Wien um 1900* (Vienna: Böhlau, 1986). For insight into the "illusory world" of the Prater see Felix Salten, *Wurstelprater* (Vienna and Leipzig: Graphische Kunstanstalt Brüder Rosenbaum, 1911).

[3] For example, Alfred Pfoser points out how often Arthur Schnitzler sends his characters into the Prater. See "Schnitzler gegen Lueger. Schnitzlers Stadtansichten — Von den Vorzügen und Grenzen seines Werkes beim Studium des Wien um 1900," in Roman Horak, ed., *Metropole Wien: Texturen der Moderne*, 1 (Vienna: WUV-Universitäts-Verlag, 2000), 214–83; here: 268.

[4] Helmut Gruber, *Red Vienna: Experiment in Working-Class Culture 1919–1934* (Oxford: OUP, 1991), 119.

[5] See Armin Loacker, "Werkstätten der Seh(n)sucht: Produktionsgeschichte und Produktionsstrukturen des monumentalen Antikfilms in Österreich" in Armin Loacker and Innes Steiner, eds., *Imaginierte Antike: Österreichische Monumental-Stummfilme. Historienbilder und Geschichtskonstruktion in "Sodom und Gomorrha," "Samson und Delila," "Die Sklavenkönigin" und "Salammbô"* (Vienna: Filmarchiv, 2002), 21–62; here: 21.

[6] Loacker, "Werkstätten," 62.

[7] Loacker, "Werkstätten," 26.

[8] Armin Loacker, *Anschluß im 3/4 Takt: Filmproduktion und Filmpolitik in Österreich 1930–38* (Trier: Wissenschaftlicher Verlag, 1999), 2.

[9] Loacker, "Werkstätten," 26.

[10] Gruber, *Red Vienna*, 128–29.

[11] Werner Michael Schwarz, *Kino und Kinos in Wien: Eine Entwicklungsgeschichte bis 1934* (Vienna: Turia & Kant, 1992), 42.

[12] Robert Musil, *Tagebücher*, 2 vols. (Reinbek: Rowohlt, 1976), 1: 699.

[13] Siegfried Kracauer, "Das Ornament der Masse," in *Das Ornament der Masse. Essays (1920–1931)* (Frankfurt am Main: Suhrkamp, 1963), 50–63.

[14] See Theodor W. Adorno, *The Culture Industry: Selected Essays on Mass Culture* (London: Routledge, 1991).

[15] Kracauer, "Ornament," 50.

[16] "Ringstrasse des Proletariats" in *Die Unzufriedene*, 30 August 1930: 1. Cited in Eve Blau, *The Architecture of Red Vienna 1919–1934* (Cambridge, MA: MIT Press, 1999), 260.

[17] Blau, *The Architecture of Red Vienna*, 400.

[18] Gruber, *Red Vienna*, 85.

[19] Gruber, *Red Vienna*, 92.

[20] Pfoser, *Literatur und Austromarxismus* (Vienna: Löcker, 1980), 117–50.

[21] Franz Trescher, "Probleme der Arbeiterbibliotheken" in *Arbeiter-Zeitung*, 15 September 1927, 17.

[22] Walter Benjamin, "Eduard Fuchs, der Sammler und der Historiker" in *Gesammelte Schriften* (Frankfurt am Main: Suhrkamp, 1972–), II.2 [1991], 465–505.

[23] David Josef Bach, "Die Kunststelle der Arbeiterschaft" in *Arbeiter-Zeitung*, 30 October 1921, 7.

[24] Pfoser, *Literatur*, 59.

[25] See Pfoser, *Literatur*, 62–64; Gruber, *Red Vienna*, 84.

[26] On this debate and its consequences, see Ernst Bloch et al., *Aesthetics and Politics* (London: New Left Books, 1977).

[27] Pfoser, *Literatur*, 63.

[28] See Hans Veigl, *Lachen im Keller: Von den Budapestern zum Wiener Werkel: Kabarett und Kleinkust in Wien* (Vienna: Löcker, 1986), 78.

[29] Veigl, *Lachen im Keller*, 76.

[30] Veigl, *Lachen im Keller*, 159. For details of Kraus's Offenbach performances, see Georg Knepler, *Karl Kraus liest Offenbach* (Vienna: Löcker, 1984).

[31] Kraus, "Das Schoberlied / La Chanson de Schober" in *Die Fackel* 838–44 (1930), 138–39.

[32] See Hans Eberhard Goldschmidt, "Die Vorlesungen für Arbeiter: Eine Dokumentation" in Knepler, *Karl Kraus liest Offenbach*, 233–37.

[33] Veigl, *Lachen im Keller*, 88.

[34] Veigl, *Lachen im Keller*, 167.

[35] Pfoser, *Literatur*, 66–70.

[36] Schwarz, *Kino*, 47. See also Béla Balázs, *Der sichtbare Mensch oder die Kultur des Films* (Vienna: Deutsch-Österreichischer Verlag, 1924).

[37] Schwarz, *Kino*, 48–56.

[38] Cited in Schwarz, *Kino*, 55.

[39] Siegfried Kracauer, "Der heutige Film und sein Publikum" in *Frankfurter Zeitung*, 30 November 1928 and 1 December 1928.

[40] Walter Benjamin, "Das Kunstwerk im Zeitalter seiner technischen Reproduzierbarkeit" in *Gesammelte Schriften* (Frankfurt am Main: Suhrkamp, 1972–) I.2, 431–508.

[41] Pfoser, *Literatur*, 201; Schwarz, *Kino*, 63.

[42] Büttner and Dewald, eds., *Das tägliche Brennen*, 269.

[43] For details of the Social Democrats' festival culture, see Bela Rasky, "Arbeiterfesttage. Zur Fest- und Feiernkultur der österreichischen historischen Sozialdemokratie bis 1933" in: www.kakanien.ac.at/beitr/fallstudie/BRasky2. Accessed 1 April 2005.

[44] Quoted in Dietmar Fricke, "Die Maifeiertage in den Beziehungen zwischen August Bebel und der österreichischen Sozialdemokratie im ersten Jahrfünft nach Hainfeld" in *Die Bewegung: Hundert Jahre Sozialdemokratie in Österreich*, ed. Erich Fröschl et al. (Vienna: Passagenverlag, 1990), 278.

[45] Pfoser, *Literatur*, 274–87.

[46] Joseph Buttinger, quoted in Pfoser, *Literatur*, 290.

[47] Pfoser, *Literatur*, 251. See Josef Schneider and C. Zell, *Der Fall der roten Festung* (Vienna: Manz, 1934).

[48] Gruber, *Red Vienna*, 135–41; here: 136.

[49] Loacker, *Anschluß*, 31.

[50] Schwarz, *Kino*, 66.

[51] Georg Tillner, "Österreich, ein weiter Weg: Filmkultur zwischen Austrofaschismus und Wiederaufbau," in Ruth Beckermann and Christa Blümlinger, ed. *Ohne Untertitel: Fragmente einer Geschichte des österreichischen Kinos* (Vienna: Sonderzahl, 1996), 177. See also Loacker, *Anschluß*, 138–66.

[52] Loacker, *Anschluß*, 147.

[53] See Armin Loacker and Martin Prucha, ed. *Unerwünschtes Kino: Der deutschsprachige Emigrantenfilm 1934–1937* (Vienna: Filmarchiv, 2000), 14.

[54] Tillner, "Osterreich, ein weiter Weg," 177.

[55] Loacker, *Anschluß*, 187.

[56] Pfoser, *Literatur*, 233–34.

[57] Tillner, "Österreich, ein weiter Weg," 176.

[58] Tillner, "Österreich, ein weiter Weg," 176–77.

[59] Pfoser, *Literatur*, 70. See also "Kabarett A-B-C" in *Neues Wiener Abendblatt*, 19 April 1935, 4.

[60] Veigl, *Lachen im Keller*, 125.

[61] Pfoser, *Literatur*, 70.

[62] See Hans Veigl, ed. *Bombenstimmung: Das Wiener Werkl, Kabarett im Dritten Reich* (Vienna: Kremayr & Scheriau, 1994), 9.

[63] See Evan Burr Bukey, *Hitler's Austria: Popular Sentiment in the Nazi Era, 1938–1945* (Chapel Hill and London: U of North Carolina P, 2000), 102–3; 145.

[64] Bukey, *Hitler's Austria*, 194–96.

5: The Politics of Austrian Literature, 1927–56

Andrew Barker

1927: The Defeat of Austrian Freedom

ON 15 JULY 1927, A DEMONSTRATION outside the Vienna Palace of Justice ended with corpses on the street and the building gutted by fire. It was a decisive moment in the chain of events leading to the suspension of parliamentary government in March 1933, the Civil War of February 1934, the assassination of Chancellor Dollfuss in July 1934 and the instant demise of the "state that nobody wanted" when Hitler's German troops marched in on 12 March 1938.[1]

The effects of what Erich Fried dubbed "Bloody Friday"[2] went far beyond the political sphere, highlighting the extent to which literature in Austria reflected (and refracted) these turbulent times. Writing as late as 1975, Manès Sperber claimed that the experience of July 1927 had never ceased being felt.[3] Initially, the demonstration inspired Karl Kraus to a campaign against Johannes Schober, the Vienna police chief, whose men had fired on the crowd demonstrating against the acquittal of right-wing paramilitaries who had killed a child and a war veteran during a skirmish with Socialists. In *Die Fackel*, then in its twenty-eighth year, Kraus denounced the social system that made such atrocities possible, a religion that denied mercy and charity to the victims, a republic that pinned medals on the breast of murderers.[4]

For Kraus's ambivalent devotee, the later Nobel Prize winner Elias Canetti, the fire at the Palace of Justice was crucial in the conception of the novel *Die Blendung* (Auto-da-Fé), first published in Vienna in 1936; for Heimito von Doderer it represented the "Cannae of Austrian freedom" (recalling the devastating defeat of the Romans by Hannibal at the battle of Cannae in 216 B.C.), and inspired the vast panoramic novel he finally published as *Die Dämonen* (The Demons) in 1956.[5] Already completed in its first but unpublished draft in 1936, Doderer's novel is set largely in the Vienna of 1926–27 and culminates in a depiction of the chaos on 15 July. Shortly before publication of *Die Dämonen*, the State Treaty of 1955 had finalized the establishment of a Second Republic far more resilient than the

First, whose end could already be anticipated when the flames leapt from the roof of the burning law courts.

Die Dämonen erects a literary memorial to the victims who died there, but it also makes a political statement whose values chime perfectly with those of the new Second Republic: it is a political novel which "urges that 'ideology' [. . .] be replaced by a brave realism and a determined individualism."[6] It is a novel aimed at conservative 1950s Austria whose narrative breaks off in 1927, and is paradigmatic of what Robert Knight calls the "continuity narrative" in Austrian political and cultural self-understanding.[7] Continuity, that is, with a time before the embarrassment of the *Ständestaat* (corporate state) and the seven years when Austria became the "Ostmark" of the Third Reich. Born in April 1945 out of defeat and liberation, this new Austria would finally establish a sense of Austrian identity for which, crucially, use of the German language no longer meant identifying with the German state.[8] It would be an identity deliberately shaped to a considerable extent by cultural politicians and writers in the first decade after the war. It was directed from a Ministry of Education in the hands of the conservative ÖVP, the Austrian People's Party, whose cultural policies harked back in several respects to those of the *Ständestaat*'s Vaterländische Front (Fatherland Front). Above all, however, this reborn Austrian state would strive to make amends for the omissions and commissions of its predecessor by abandoning the ideological battles between Left and Right, Red and Black, which had helped seal the fate of the First Republic. Dominated until 1966 by a Grand Coalition of Social Democrats and Conservatives, its politics would be conciliatory and non-confrontational, but would also deny the recent past. As Klaus Amann has succinctly observed, looking to the future spared looking into the past.[9]

In this climate, it is no surprise that in the 1950s Doderer, who had joined the NSDAP on 1 April 1933, and whose postwar novels studiously avoid the period after 1927, became the "Staatsdichter" *par excellence*, and a novel like *Die Strudlhofstiege* (The Strudlhof Steps, 1951) one of the new republic's party pieces. This novel, which the author saw as a "ramp" leading to *Die Dämonen*, concerns itself chiefly with events in Vienna in 1911 and 1923–25, with barely a passing reference to the First World War and the ensuing loss of an empire. Far from being exceptional, however, Doderer's rehabilitation, which culminated in the award of the Großer Österreichischer Staatspreis in 1957, was entirely consistent with that of other former supporters of Austrofascism or the Nazis, such as Felix Braun, who won the prize in 1951, Rudolf Henz in 1953, Max Mell in 1954 and Franz Karl Ginzkey in 1957.

Literature in the 1930s

The sense of *déjà vu* accompanying the award of the State Prize was not a new phenomenon in twentieth-century Austrian letters. Writing in 1925, some three decades before the signing of the State Treaty, the Viennese Socialist poet Fritz Brügel reflected that after a few brief flirtations with Expressionism and Socialism, the Austrian literary world was beginning to resemble the years before the collapse of the Habsburg Empire: writers with reputations made before the First World War were continuing to recreate the world of the *ancien régime*, confronting "an ugly present with a beautiful past."[10] At the same time, however, Brügel had to confirm the growing presence of a German nationalist and *völkisch* literature, glorifying peasants and the soil, and railing in equal measure against the corrupt urban civilization of Vienna and the iniquities of Bolshevism and Judaism. Surveying Austrian lyric poetry written between the Civil War and the *Anschluss*, Wendelin Schmidt-Dengler has concluded that with the exception of Theodor Kramer, whose work bears the clear imprint of *Neue Sachlichkeit* (New Objectivity), the impression could arise that Austria was a country which had managed to change itself from an industrialized country back into an agrarian state.[11] In creating this impression, however, writing in Austria merely mirrored a more general trend in German writing as a whole around 1930, which saw a shift away from "Sachlichkeit" and towards "Innerlichkeit."[12]

The increasing politicization of literary life in Austria meant that artists, too, became caught up in the events being played out in the streets. A baleful result of this was the murder in 1925 of the Viennese Jewish writer Hugo Bettauer, author of the novel *Die Stadt ohne Juden* (The City without Jews, 1922), an event which pointed to the antinomies observable in Austrian letters for years to come. On the one hand, there were the survivors from Musil's "Kakanien," the old world of the Habsburg Empire, overwhelmingly Jewish in origin, skeptical, often nostalgic, but nevertheless open to the world, writers whom nowadays many would hold to represent the "true" Austrian literary canon: Hermann Broch, Egon Friedell, Karl Kraus, Robert Musil, Alfred Polgar, Joseph Roth, Arthur Schnitzler, Ernst Weiss, Franz Werfel, and Stefan Zweig. On the other hand, there were now mostly forgotten writers hell-bent on reflecting and encouraging the rise of pan-Germanism in its conservative, intolerant, anti-Communist and above all anti-Semitic mode.

Increasingly in the 1930s, German nationalist writers in Austria, reflecting the mood of the times, looked to Berlin rather than Vienna, yet they also basked in official renown in their homeland as the ever more desperate *Ständestaat* attempted to buy their loyalty. These writers first openly allied themselves with National Socialism in May 1933, when the German section walked out of a meeting of the International PEN Club in Dubrovnik after some muted criticism of the recent book-burnings. They were joined by a single Austrian representative, Grete von Urbanitzky, but soon afterwards a host of other Austrian writers also left the PEN Club, amongst then Bruno Brehm, Enrica von Handel-Mazzetti, Franz Nabl, and Karl Hans Strobl. What Klaus Amann has described as the "annexation of Austrian writers to the Third Reich" was completed in 1938 when dozens of like-minded writers such as Robert Hohlbaum, Mirko Jelusich, Erwin Guido Kolbenheyer, Hermann Stuppäck, Karl Heinz Waggerl, and Josef Weinheber signed the *Bekenntnisbuch österreichischer Dichter* (Austrian Writers Confess their Faith), pledging their allegiance to Hitler and National Socialism in an act which few would disagree represented "the nadir of twentieth-century Austrian literature."[13]

By the mid-1950s, however, when Doderer published *Die Dämonen*, the reality of Austrian literature as a literature written in German, in the same way that literature written in English in Ireland is Irish literature, had become widely accepted in Austria, if not in Germany. Many in that country have still not accepted it.[14] This growing recognition of the autonomy of Austrian literature, at least within Austria itself, is one of the greatest achievements of Austrian letters in the first decade after the rebirth of the Austrian Republic. That it was achieved at a time when conservative survivors of the 1930s continued to enjoy the greatest official esteem makes it nigh-on a miracle. As the Viennese-born Arnolt Bronnen trenchantly declared in 1955, having left the "reaktionärer Kleinstaat" (reactionary petty state) to take up residence in the GDR: "Of course there exists an Austrian literature. It exists in a much stronger form, much more consciously, than does Swiss-German literature. [. . .] Here — in the literary arena — we could vary a saying of Bernard Shaw's: Germany and Austria have two literatures divided by a common language."[15]

Doderer made little of his own roots in earlier Viennese modernism, though his earliest works include "Fortunatina und die Löwin" (Fortunatina and the Lioness), a recasting of one of Peter Altenberg's sketches from *Ashantee* (1897); but the inspiration for the notion of an Austrian literature which he epitomized and espoused after 1945 can be traced back to Hermann Bahr's propagandizing work at the turn of the century. Looking back in his autobiography at his work during the 1890s, Bahr notes that he had been merely articulating aloud, and rather brazenly, what writers such as Grillparzer and Stifter had known all along: that Austrian art exists *sui generis*, and not just as an appurtenance to German art.[16] Yet for all Bahr's efforts, including his underrated influence on the founding of the Salzburg Festival, his friend Hugo von Hofmannsthal still identified himself as a "deutscher Dichter" (German poet) in 1928.[17] This is particularly ironic because in essays like "Preuße und Österreicher" (Prussian and Austrian, 1917) or in his drama *Der Schwierige* (The Difficult Man, 1921), Hofmannsthal had contributed probably more than any of his contemporaries to the conscious literary demarcation of the Austrian from the German. There is no question that Hofmannsthal's death in 1929 palpably marked the end of something more than just a writer's career. An era itself had also passed.

The complex position of Austrian writers around 1930, torn between conflicting visions of history, society, religion and politics, is particularly well demonstrated in the figure of the same Arnolt Bronnen who by the 1950s had become convinced of Austria's literary autonomy: Berlin-based, of Jewish descent, sympathetic at different periods to Communism, Nazism, and again Communism.[18] Moreover, in the early 1930s, what are nowadays regarded as texts central to a modern understanding of Austrian literature were increasingly written by writers who, like Bronnen, no longer resided in Austria itself: Joseph Roth and Robert Musil, for example, were both now also based in Berlin. It is one of the neater ironies in the chronicle of Austrian writing in the twentieth century that two novels which have probably provided the most celebrated and enduring literary monuments to the last days of Imperial Vienna were composed within a few hundred yards of each other in Berlin in the early 1930s. As Roth completed *Radetzkymarsch* at his table in Mampe's Gute Stube at 15 Kurfürstendamm, Musil was laboring with *Der Mann ohne Eigenschaften* (The Man without Qualities) in his apartment at 217.[19] (Musil polemically ascribed his decision to leave Vienna in 1931 to the agreement by both Left and Right that Anton Wildgans was a great poet.[20]) Similarly, Ödön von Horváth, whose *Volksstück* entitled *Geschichten aus dem Wiener Wald* (Tales from the Vienna Woods, 1931) has become a key text in any understanding of the interwar years, was primarily a German-based writer until forced into exile after 1933. Even then he chose not to make Austria his long-term domicile, and was famously killed by a falling branch in Paris on 1 June 1938 when sheltering under a tree in the Champs Elysées. The *Volksstück* was clearly important to the cultural politics of the *Ständestaat*, but rather than the sort of critically ironic drama written by Horváth, the state encouraged unproblematic dramas reflecting the hearty common sense of everyday folk in everyday situations.[21] Indeed, *Geschichten aus dem Wiener Wald*, a flop at its Viennese première in 1948, still offended conservative audiences when Horváth's works were revived in the 1970s.[22]

It is a further irony of this period that whilst writers like Roth, Musil and Horváth lived outside Austria, others like Oskar Maria Graf and the Vienna-born Stefan Grossmann arrived there from Germany after 1933 to begin life as writers in exile.[23] There they were able to contact writers in the Vereinigung sozialistischer Schriftsteller (Association of Socialist Writers), founded in Vienna on 22 January 1933 in response to the provocation of Nazi literary organizations such as the Ring nationaler Schriftsteller (League of National Writers) established by Mirko Jelusich and Robert Hohlbaum.[24] Musil himself left Germany for Vienna in 1934, where he was able to complete his *Nachlass zu Lebzeiten* (Posthumous Papers of a Living Writer) in 1936. He was supported until 1938 by the Wiener Musil Gesellschaft, after which he departed for his final exile in Switzerland. Another by-product of Hitler's coming to power was the return to Austria (at least until 1938) of a host of German-based critics and cabaret artists (many of Austrian origin), leading to a short-lived renaissance of Viennese "Kleinkunst" featuring such writers as Anton Kuh, Alfred Polgar, Oskar Karlweis, Fritz Grünbaum, and Peter Hammerschlag.[25]

Inevitably, many of the generation of Jewish-Austrian writers who had come to prominence in the 1890s died in the 1930s and hence were spared the consequences of the *Anschluss*. Arthur Schnitzler died in 1931, his work still anchored in a world which had ended in 1914, Hermann Bahr died in 1934, Stefan Grossmann in 1935. Karl Kraus, the implacable enemy of both Grossmann and Bahr, died in 1936. Egon Friedell, whose *Kulturgeschichte der Neuzeit* (A Cultural History of the Modern Age, 1927) is one of the greatest intellectual achievements of the First Republic, was not so fortunate: he jumped to his death from his flat in Vienna shortly after the *Anschluss*.

The *Ständestaat*

After the 1934 Civil War Schnitzler's work was banned from the Vienna Burgtheater, though as late as 1936 an adaptation of the novella *Fräulein Else* was staged at the private Theater in der Josefstadt. His exclusion from the Burgtheater was, however, symptomatic of the official cultural politics of the *Ständestaat*. Instead of Schnitzler, the theater now hosted plays by writers such as the anti-pacifist German Nationalist Hanns Sassmann, whose historical drama *Metternich* met with enormous success. The descent into provincialism at the Burgtheater is thrown into still starker relief by the return of Max Reinhardt to the Theater in der Josefstadt in 1933, having turned down the Nazis' offer of becoming an "honorary Aryan." He remained at work for four years in Vienna, the premiere of Franz Werfel's *In einer Nacht* (In One Night), in the presence of Chancellor Schuschnigg in October 1937, being his last European production before emigration to the USA. (There in 1935 he had made his only film, a version of *A Midsummer Night's Dream* with a score by the exiled Viennese composer Erich Wolfgang Korngold.) Reinhardt died in Californian exile in 1943, Werfel in 1945.

In 1933 Werfel had completed *Die vierzig Tage des Musa Dagh* (The Forty Days of Musa Dagh), the first novel to thematize genocide in its depiction of the Turkish-Armenian conflict in 1915, but, like his adversary Kraus, Werfel became reconciled to the Dollfuss-Schuschnigg regime. This was because he felt it provided a bulwark against National Socialism, and because anti-Semitism was not part of the official program of the *Ständestaat* (the reality was, of course, very different, Jews being excluded from the civil service, police, army, railway, postal service, national bank). Looking back at the 1930s, the composer Ernst Křenek noted how he soon discovered that the Dollfuss and Schuschnigg regimes were honest in their anti-Nazi sentiments, but in matters of culture were as reactionary as the Nazis themselves.[26] But this fact did not deter Werfel, who thanks to his wife Alma's friendship with Schuschnigg, moved close to the center of power. He even became "a kind of poet laureate, receiving in 1937 the Verdienstkreuz für Kunst und Wissenschaft. This he treasured so much that he wished it to be buried with him and was to make his hero F.W. wear it in his last novel, *Stern der Ungeborenen* ([Star of the Unborn,] 1946)."[27]

Kraus made no such accommodation with the leadership of the *Ständestaat*, but even so, his problematically taciturn response first to Hitler's accession to power in January 1933, and then to the failed Social Democratic rebellion of February 1934, alienated many previously staunch supporters. *Die Fackel* failed to appear between December 1932 and October 1933, when the shortest edition of all (number 888) was issued in response to the death of Adolf Loos. The only other contribution apart from Loos's obituary is the enigmatically lyrical ten-line response to Hitler's accession to power beginning "Man frage nicht, was all die Zeit ich machte. / Ich bleibe stumm; / und sage nicht, warum" (Don't ask me what I was doing all this time. / I shall stay silent; / and shall not say why).[28] It ends with one of Kraus's most poignantly memorable formulations: "Das Wort entschlief, als jene Welt erwachte" (The word fell asleep when that world awoke). Kraus's apparent sleep remained unbroken until July 1934, when he ironically acknowledged the despair his silence had caused so many of his supporters. These "Nachrufe auf Karl Kraus" (Obituaries for Karl Kraus, *Die Fackel*, no. 889) were followed by the longest single issue of *Die Fackel*, "Warum die Fackel nicht erscheint" (Why the *Fackel* doesn't appear), where Kraus attacked the defeated Social Democrats, admitting his total agreement with Dollfuss: once Wotan was resurrected, parliamentary debate was futile and democracy failed when faced with the mysteries of blood and soil.[29]

What both Kraus and Werfel were able to overlook was that the *Ständestaat* was inherently authoritarian and repressive, both politically and culturally. Unsurprisingly, with the possible exception of Werfel, it produced little of lasting literary value. Understandably too, apart from some short poems, the impact of 1934 Civil War was best recorded in literature created outside Austria itself.[30] When Stefan Grossmann published his powerful and prescient analysis "Unabhängiges Österreich" (Independent Austria) in Klaus Mann's Amsterdam-based journal *Die Sammlung*, it was promptly banned in Austria.[31] Two of the most powerful evocations of those dark February days came from exiled German Communist writers: Anna Seghers in her novel *Der Weg durch den Februar* (The Way through February, 1935) and Friedrich Wolf in his drama *Floridsdorf: Ein Schauspiel von den Februarkämpfen der Wiener Arbeiter* (Floridsdorf: A Play about the February Struggles of the Viennese Workers, 1936).[32] In fact, the subject soon became a taboo in Austrian writing, and it was only with the novel *Das Himmelreich der Lügner* (The Heavenly Kingdom of Liars, 1959) by Reinhard Federmann, and subsequently *Schlagschatten* (1977; tr. *Refractions*, 1995) by Alois Vogel, that the "Februartage" received a suitable literary monument from Austrian writers.

In contrast, the 1930s saw a string of works in various genres written within and beyond Austria which correspond to Claudio Magris's later formulation of the "Habsburg Myth," in which writers perceived and idealized an underlying harmony between the apparently dichotomous constituent peoples of the Empire under the tolerant rule of the now defunct House of Habsburg.[33] This was a line encouraged by the *Ständestaat*, which strove to promote its own view of Austrianness — "free, independent, Christian, German, hierarchical and authoritarian"[34] — through a celebration of the Habsburg past as part of its strategy to combat the twin enemies of atheistic Communism and heathen National Socialism. For Guido Zernatto, the differences between Hitler's Germany and the *Ständestaat* could be reduced to a pithy antithesis between blood and soil: "For the National Socialist there is the law of blood, for the Austrian the law of the landscape."[35] Thus the *Ständestaat* could recommend such diverse historical works, by writers differing widely in temperament, ethnicity and talent, as Joseph Roth's *Radetzkymarsch* (1932); *Florian, das Pferd des Kaisers* (Florian, the Emperor's Horse, 1933) by Felix Salten; *Die Standarte* (The Standard, 1934) by Alexander Lernet-Holenia; *Elisabeth, die seltsame Frau* (Elisabeth, the Strange Woman, 1934) by Egon Caesar Conte Corti; *Kaiser Karl der Fünfte* (Charles V, 1936) by Felix Braun; Kurt Hildebrand Matzak's *Der Sieger Prinz Eugen* (Prince Eugen, the Victor, 1936); Rudolf Henz's *Kaiser Joseph II.* (1937); and *3. November 1918* (1937) by Franz Theodor Csokor. That some of these works were written by Jews confirms Horst Jarka's laconic observation that the *de facto* anti-Semitism which rejected Schnitzler and Kraus after 1934, when their works were removed from public libraries along with those of the pacifist Berta von Suttner and the leftist Heinrich Mann, was proof of a stereotypically Austrian "dictatorship softened by carelessness" in which one set of conservatives did not know what another set of conservatives was up to.[36]

The support for the production of historical novels in the *Ständestaat* further illustrated how literature in Austria mirrored the wider tendency in German letters in the 1930s to move away from the representation of contemporary reality. As with the vogue for nature poetry, it was a trend followed by émigré writers as well as those still working within the German-speaking world, by writers living in "Innere Emigration," and by those who supported National Socialism.[37] Literary policy in the *Ständestaat* thus mirrored and encouraged pre-existent literary trends — agrarian, provincial, religious, anti-Semitic — that is, those roots that had given birth to the state itself. Hence the state made no secret that encouraging literature to be unpolitical was in itself a political act, for like other dictatorships it perceived itself as fulfilling and protecting everything beautiful and sacred which the *Volk* had hitherto produced.

The mid-1930s witnessed not only the demise of the "Old Guard" of writers exemplified by Schnitzler and Kraus and the exile of major talents like Roth and Horváth, but also the continuing development of one of the most problematically gifted Austrian writers of this era: the lyric poet Josef Weinheber, whose *Wien wörtlich* (Vienna at Its Word, 1935) provides a counter to the otherwise overwhelming provincialism of so much Austrian writing at the time.[38] Yet despite having paid homage to Kraus as a guardian of language, Weinheber happily sank into Nazi panegyrics, exclaiming in his contribution to the *Bekenntnisbuch* in 1938: "Deutschland, ewig und groß, / Deutschland, wir grüßen dich! / Führer, heilig und stark, / Führer wir grüßen dich! / Heimat, glücklich und frei, / Heimat, wir grüßen dich!"[39] (Germany, eternal and great, / Germany, we greet thee! / Führer, sacred and strong, / Führer we greet thee! / Homeland, happy and free, / Homeland we greet thee!).

Such lyric effusions were, however, symptomatic of the times, and not just in the *Bekenntnisbuch*. Verse in a similar vein came from the writer and artist Albert Paris Gütersloh, who sent his friend Doderer his poem "13. März 1938 zur Befreiung Österreichs und Südtyrols" (On the 13th of March 1938, to the Liberation of Austria and the South Tyrol).[40] This was, however, the same author who in 1918 had edited a weekly journal whose first run ended with the cry "Long live Communism and the Catholic Church!"[41] and who subsequently had the good fortune to be declared degenerate by the Nazis, thus enabling him after the war to find renown as a leader of the "Fantastic Realist" movement and achieve high academic office in the Academy of Art in Vienna. Weinheber, however, chose suicide as the Red Army advanced in April 1945.

The parochialism of so much Austrian writing in the 1930s was underlined by the popularity of the *Heimatroman* (novel of the homeland), itself a counter to the popular genre of the urban "Wienroman" (Vienna novel) of the early 1920s. It culminated in the unlikely figure of Hermann Broch, whose multi-versioned "Bergroman" ("mountain novel," eventually published as *Der Versucher* (The Tempter) in 1953) represents one of the most problematic products of the period under discussion. Although a first version was completed in 1935, it remained unfinished at the time of its author's death in his Connecticut exile in 1951. Not even the title had been decided upon. In writing an anti-urban novel which claims that cities are the world's misfortune,[42] Broch thus found himself in the company of Guido Zernatto, Schuschnigg's Secretary of State from 1936 to 1938 and General Secretary of the Fatherland Front. Zernatto's *Sinnlose Stadt: Roman eines einfachen Menschen* (Senseless City: Novel of a Simple Man) appeared in 1934, and as Wendelin

Schmidt-Dengler points out, there are passages in it which could just as easily have been found in Broch's novel.[43]

Under the guise of an Alpine *Heimatroman*, however, with a setting recalling the popular "Bergfilme" (mountain films) of 1930s cinema, Broch also broached the burning issue of dictatorship, the nature of the dictator, and a community's responses. Not surprisingly, in the 1930s this theme exercised Austrian authors of such different persuasions as Jelusich and Roth (not to mention Thomas Mann and Brecht further afield). However, two of the weightiest Austrian contributions from this decade to the examination both of the specific personality of Hitler himself and of the wider phenomenon of fascism remained unpublished until long after the collapse of the Third Reich: Kraus's *Dritte Walpurgisnacht* (Third Walpurgis Night, 1933) remained unpublished until 1952; Ernst Weiss's novel *Der Augenzeuge* (The Eyewitness), completed in Parisian exile in 1938, was not published until 1963.

Nevertheless, just as the politics of the Right came to dominate officially sanctioned literature of the period in both pre-1938 Austria and Germany, there was also the continuance of literature produced from a left-wing perspective, even though the literary Left did not exist in Austria to the same extent as in Weimar Germany. In Austria, the most notable figure is Jura Soyfer, both in his journalism, his cabaret writing, and his unfinished novel of the decline of Austrian Social Democracy, *So starb eine Partei* (How a Party Died), set in 1932–34. The narrative breaks off just before the events of February 1934, leading Rolf Schneider to remark that, had it been completed, Soyfer's novel would have constituted the most important political novel in the German language.[44] Soyfer died in Buchenwald in 1939, having been interned on several occasions between 1933 and 1938. Avoiding the fate of Soyfer, some Socialists went into exile — Fritz Brügel, Ernst Fischer, Luitpold Stern — and others into "internal emigration."

After the Socialists' defeat in 1934, the ensuing closure of the *Arbeiterzeitung*, especially its feuilleton, shut off an important avenue of literary enlightenment, as did also the "cleansing" of the workers' libraries which had played such a central role in the Social Democrats' cultural policies. The authors banned were the predictable galaxy of Socialists and Jews, some of whose work has taken decades to re-emerge. A salient example of this neglect, and of progressive women's writing in the 1930s in Austria, is Veza Canetti, wife of Elias: her works have only been widely received, and in some cases only published, from the 1990s on.

The practical exclusion of most Jewish writers (with the exception of Werfel) from the official literary life of the *Ständestaat* is evident from the list of writers who were awarded the Großer Österreichischer Staatspreis für Literatur in the years 1934–37. As Franz Kadrnoska has observed, it appears barely credible that Ernst Scheibelreiter was nominated for his lyric poetry at a time when Theodor Kramer and Ernst Waldinger were already well-known figures, and that Josef Perkonig and Karl Heinrich Waggerl were honored when Broch and Canetti had already published great novels.[45] In determining aesthetic values, *völkisch*-Catholic literary ideology favored unchallenging, conservative texts.

The continued denial of official prizes after 1945 to writers as eligible and deserving as Broch, Canetti, Fried, Kramer, Polgar, in favor of writers groomed and grounded in the sectarianism of the 1930s, illustrates the unavoidable conclusion that in some aspects of cultural politics at least, the *Ständestaat* and the Second Republic formed a seamless continuum. That this went beyond the world of literature is exemplified by the exiled composer Egon Wellesz, resident in England after 1938, who like Werfel was both Jewish and a supporter of the *Ständestaat*. He was awarded the Großer Österreichischer Staatspreis in 1961.

After 1938, the systematic exclusion of Jews from all aspects of public existence became the order of the day, with literary life in the new Ostmark rapidly assimilated into the Third Reich as a whole. Thus Waggerl, already successful in the *Ständestaat*, continued to flourish in the Third Reich. He then effortlessly maintained that success until his death in 1973, thanks to the conciliatory cultural and political climate of the Second Republic (at least where writers of the Right were concerned; for those of the Left things were less easy). The determining factor in the ease with which a writer with Waggerl's history accommodated political change after 1945 was, of course, the 1943 Moscow Declaration, which for tactical and strategic reasons accepted Austria not as a willing collaborator in the Third Reich, but as Hitler's first victim.

Virtually by definition, however, after 1938 most *Austrian* literature became exile literature. Some very notable figures committed suicide abroad: Joseph Roth and Ernst Weiss in Paris, Stefan Zweig in Brazil. Zweig in particular had enjoyed a world-wide reputation, but found it impossible to adapt to a life where he could no longer function in a European context. Yet the exile which proved so uncongenial was at the same time the spur to a work which has assumed talismanic status in modern attempts to understand the Austrian spirit and artistic temperament in the earlier part of the twentieth century: his autobiographical study *Die Welt von Gestern* (The World of Yesterday, 1942). Especially after the fall of France, many Austrian writers grouped together in exile, most notably in the USA (particularly California and New York / New England) and in the United Kingdom, where Viennese theater life, especially that of the "Kleinbühne," was kept alive in the Laterndl theater founded in London in March 1939.[46]

The Second Republic

Many exiles, especially those of Jewish extraction, never returned home, thus setting up a postwar constellation of Austrian writers abroad, for example, the novelists Hermann Broch and Robert Neumann in Connecticut and Locarno, the poet Erich Fried in London, and the dramatist Fritz Hochwälder in Switzerland. Some, such as the poet Stella Rotenberg in Leeds, who has devoted her work to the Holocaust and the experience of exile, are still active at the time of writing (2004). Others such as Paul Celan and Jean Améry, having spent decades trying to reconcile past and present, took their own lives.

As Ulrike Längle points out, many exiled authors avoided using the Third Reich as material for their writings in their new and often exotically strange surroundings.[47] This could have been because they doubted their ability to write about things they had not known directly, and could not trust their imagination to make up the gap in experience. In particular, the experience of the concentration camps does not figure prominently, and hence the Holocaust is largely absent from exile novels and plays. However, it is certainly not absent from lyric poetry, where Celan's "Todesfuge" (1952) has proved to be one of the twentieth century's most memorable poems, one which flies in the face of Adorno's famous assertion (which in any case he soon revised) that after Auschwitz writing lyric poetry was barbaric.

The "Habsburg myth," which had proved so alluring to Joseph Roth and Ernst Weiss in their prewar exile in France, also provided a safe refuge for Alexander Lernet-Holenia, a writer who did not go into emigration, but whose example loomed so large in the postwar restoration of Austrian literary life that in 1948 the returnee Hans Weigel declared in exasperation that contemporary Austrian literature consisted of just two writers: Lernet and Holenia. In his polemical eagerness Weigel overlooked Georg Saiko's debut novel *Auf dem Floß* (On the Raft, 1948), whose references to Habsburg times make it very much a work of the day, but whose indebtedness to Freud and Joyce marks it out as a work pointing to the future. Given the uncritical credence the newly reconciled leaders of the Second Republic gave to the Moscow Declaration, there was, however, no equivalent to the West German "Stunde Null" (zero hour) in Austrian letters, no attempt to wipe clean the Nazi slate and start again from scratch, although writers like Doderer with a direct Nazi connection were banned from publishing their works throughout most of the 1940s. Instead, Austrian literature took on a many-headed form, with survivors from the *Ständestaat* like Lernet-Holenia and Mell reasserting their claims to attention; they and similar figures such as Rudolf Felmayer, Oskar Maurus Fontana, Ginzkey, and Henz continued to figure prominently in literary life through the 1950s and even into the 1960s.[48] In the face of official indifference and even hostility, a small number of Jewish émigrés like Hans Weigel and Friedrich Torberg returned to Austria to become powerful, often conservative arbiters of taste in the young Second Republic. Others still, writers living abroad such as Canetti and Celan, whose roots were broadly "Old Austrian" rather than Viennese, were nevertheless eventually subsumed into the canon of Austrian literature. Finally, soon after the war, there began to emerge a group of gifted women writers such as Ilse Aichinger and Ingeborg Bachmann, who also chose mostly not to live in Austria. Significantly, while former Nazi sympathizers were being showered with honors in Austria, Aichinger and Bachmann achieved early prominence not at home but in West Germany, where they were awarded the "Preis der Gruppe 47" in 1952 and 1953 respectively.

It fell to two women authors in particular to thematize early in the literary life of the fledgling republic the horrors of the recent past. Echoing the "call for mistrust" issued in her 1946 essay "Aufruf zum Mißtrauen," Ilse Aichinger's novel *Die größere Hoffnung* (The Greater Hope, 1948) draws upon her own mixed-race childhood in Vienna, the symbolism of her suggestive but non-specific prose helping to establish her enduring reputation across the German-speaking world. In *Der graue Mann* (The Gray Man, 1949) the returning Jewish emigrée Marie Frischauf (née Pappenheim), a survivor from the culture of "Vienna 1900" and author of the libretto for Arnold Schoenberg's revolutionary musical monodrama *Erwartung* (Expectation, 1909), examines the growth of anti-Semitic fascism in Vienna in the 1930s. Frischauf's conventionally realistic novel, with its undisguised Communist ideology, appeared at the height of Cold War sentiment in Austria, and inevitably it sank without trace.[49]

It was, of course, the rapid spread of anti-Communism in Austria, encouraged both by the experience of Soviet occupation and the events in neighboring countries such as Czechoslovakia, which lent further weight to the conservative tenor of so much literature in Austria in the immediate postwar period. This tenor was encouraged both by survivors from the prewar period like Henz, who held powerful positions with Austrian Radio both before and after the war, and by Jewish returnees such as Weigel and Torberg. Perhaps surprisingly, however, Lernet-Holenia, though he seemed to epitomize the amnesia of the times, also produced work which grappled with issues of Austrian self-understanding in the context of the recent Nazi past, first in the elegy "Germanien" (1946) and then in the novels *Der Graf von Saint-Germain* (The Count of St. Germain, 1948) and *Der Graf Luna* (The Count Luna, 1955).

Of particular importance for the emergence of a new literary culture in Austria after 1945 were short-lived progressive periodicals such as *PLAN* (1945–48), *Die literarische Welt* (1946–47) and *das silberboot* (1946–52), which introduced readers to modern writing of the kind which had been forbidden in the Third Reich (Joyce, Pound, Eliot, Virginia Woolf) but which all too often fell on to the stony ground of Austrian conservatism and a reading public which now preferred travelogues and utopian fictions to conventional *belles lettres*.[50] In the early 1950s the literary monthly

Freude an Büchern (1951–54), edited by the literary historians Heinz Kindermann and Margret Dietrich, also explained the newest trends in international modernism such as Existentialism and Surrealism, but from a most unexpected quarter, given Kindermann's long and enthusiastic involvement with National Socialism. Undeniably important were also Hans Weigel's *Stimmen der Gegenwart* and *Neue Wege*, but taking stock today it appears that the most significant of these journals was Otto Basil's *PLAN* which, invoking the critical spirit of Karl Kraus, introduced the ideas of Surrealism into Austria.[51] In this Basil was aided by Gütersloh's presidency of the Vienna Art Club, which he used to make effective propaganda for both abstract art and the artist's right to experiment. Around 1949–50 a "Surrealists' Group" was founded which in turn led to the appearance in 1951 of the *publikationen einer wiener gruppe junger autoren*. This was the work of, among others, Andreas Okopenko, H. C. Artmann, Gerhard Fritsch, and Friederike Mayröcker and paved the way for the Wiener Gruppe of the later 1950s, marking the belated appearance of the European avant-garde in Austria.

The early stirrings of the Wiener Gruppe should not, however, conceal the unambitious nature of much literary production in Austria in the immediate postwar period. Lyric poetry after the restoration of statehood may have witnessed the emergence of three major poets in Erich Fried, Paul Celan, and Ernst Jandl, but of these only Jandl lived in Austria; Fried had settled in London, and after a brief spell in Vienna in 1947–48 Celan's wanderings brought him finally to France. Otherwise, the production of lyric poetry after 1945 within Austria itself broadly followed lines already set down in the *Ständestaat*, underlining once more Klaus Amann's observations on the often astonishing continuity between Austrian literature from the 1930s through to the 1950s.[52]

As the city of Vienna had always perceived itself as a theater city *par excellence*, it was no surprise that theatrical life was quickly re-established there in 1945, abetted by the occupying Russians and Americans who saw it as both a return to normality, and as an educational tool. Among new plays, there were premieres by Franz Theodor Csokor, Ferdinand Bruckner and Fritz Hochwälder, all three Austrian-born writers of high repute, and all three representatives of the liberal, humane tradition in Austrian writing which the authorities clearly now wished to foster. Yet these three outstanding contemporary dramatists, with a total of six new plays between them, enjoyed barely more performances than Hofmannsthal's *Jedermann*, which was put on no fewer than 106 times between 1945 and 1951.[53] Moreover, one of the most influential figures in the newly-restored Burgtheater was its Deputy Director Friedrich Schreyvogl, a man with an infamous record in the conscious subversion of Austrian culture by the Nazis.

With so many artists who are ascribed to the Austrian literary tradition continuing to live outside Austria's borders after 1945, the relationship between place of domicile, literary taxonomy and literary history, already complex before 1938, remained equally so in the new Second Republic. For example, is Hermann Broch's *Der Tod des Vergil* (The Death of Virgil), published in the USA in 1945, an Austrian novel? The interaction between Austrian culture and the wider world is nowhere more complex than in the case of Bertolt Brecht, who was quietly granted Austrian citizenship in 1950. Not even the most ardent champion of the independent status of Austrian literature would claim him for Austrian letters on the basis of his new passport, but Brecht is nevertheless an important figure for an understanding of Austrian literature in the first decades after the restoration of statehood because of his unwitting involvement in the boycott of his works in Austria. Thanks to the relentless anti-Communism of Torberg and Weigel, there were no Brecht performances at any of the established theaters in Vienna between February 1952, when *Die Dreigroschenoper* (The Threepenny Opera) was staged at the Volkstheater, and 1963, when *Mutter Courage* was put on in both Vienna and Linz.[54] There could be few better illustrations than this of the similarities in practical cultural politics between the Catholic conservatism of the *Ständestaat*, where it goes without saying that Brecht's works were not performed, and the almost hysterical anti-Communism in the early years of the Second Republic.

And it was, of course, in this climate, amidst the euphoria and relief of the State Treaty which rid the country of its Russian occupiers/liberators, that the most impressive of all postwar Austrian novels appeared, Doderer's *Die Dämonen*. The novel as it finally emerged represented the fruits of Doderer's long struggle to free himself from the obsessions of ideology and to present a work which transcended its early, unpublished version. This had been completed in Dachau (the town, not the concentration camp) in 1936 with the title *Die Dämonen der Ostmark*, the demons of the Ostmark being the Jews. As a Western-style democracy, Austria in the mid 1950s was fundamentally different from how it had been in the 1930s, and Doderer's published novel was a far cry indeed from its earlier version, when he had labored in vain to produce a work in the true Nazi spirit. Nevertheless, on closer examination it becomes clear that just as in wider Austrian culture and society, something from those times remains in the recast novel — for example, a villain named Levielle whose birth name is the unmistakably Jewish Levi. Thus, as with Brecht's boycott at the Burgtheater and beyond, there are aspects of Doderer's novel, and not just its evocation of the *Justizpalastbrand*, which provided a tangible sense of continuity between two very different eras, a link which only finally began to be severed three decades later when, in the aftermath of the Waldheim affair, Austria belatedly but openly confronted the uncomfortable truths of its dim but not very distant past.[55]

Notes

[1] See Hellmut Andics, *Der Staat, den keiner wollte: Österreich von der Gründung der Republik bis zur Moskauer Deklaration* (Munich: Goldmann, 1981).

[2] Quoted in Ulrich Weinzierl, ed. *Februar 1934: Schriftsteller erzählen* (Vienna and Munich: Jugend & Volk, 1984), 130.

[3] Quoted in Erika Weinzierl and Kurt Skalnik, *Österreich 1918–1938: Geschichte der ersten Republik* (Graz: Styria, 1983), 641.

[4] Karl Kraus, "Der Hort der Republik" in *Die Fackel* 766–77, October 1927, 63–64.

[5] See Heimito von Doderer, *Die Dämonen* (Munich: Biederstein, 1956), 1328.

[6] C. E. Williams, *The Broken Eagle: The Politics of Austrian Literature from Empire to Anschluss* (London: Elek, 1974), 137–38.

[7] See Robert Knight, "Narratives in Post-war Austrian Historiography" in Anthony Bushell, ed., *Austria 1945–1955: Studies in Political and Cultural Re-emergence* (Cardiff: U of Wales P, 1996), 11–36.

[8] See Hans Wolfschütz, "The Emergence and Development of the Second Republic" in Alan Best and Hans Wolfschütz, eds., *Modern Austrian Writing* (London: Oswald Wolff, 1980), 1–22.

[9] Klaus Amann, *Der Anschluß österreichischer Schriftsteller an das Dritte Reich* (Frankfurt am Main: Athenäum, 1988), 17.

[10] Amann, *Der Anschluß österreichischer Schriftsteller an das Dritte Reich*, 15.

[11] Weinzierl and Skalnik, *Österreich 1918–1938*, 642.

[12] See Frank Trommler, "Emigration und Nachkriegsliteratur: Zum Problem der geschichtlichen Kontinuität" in Reinhold Grimm and Jost Hermand, eds., *Exil und innere Emigration: Third Wisconsin Workshop* (Frankfurt am Main: Athenäum, 1972), 173–97. Most recently, see Stephen Parker, Peter Davies, and Matthew Philpotts, *The Modern Restoration: Rethinking German Literary History 1930–1960* (Berlin: de Gruyter, 2004).

[13] Donald G. Daviau, ed., *Major Figures of Austrian Literature: The Interwar Years 1918–1938* (Riverside, CA: Ariadne, 1995), 74. See now the second, enlarged edition of Amann's important study, *Zahltag: Der Anschluß österreichischer Schriftsteller an das Dritte Reich* (Bodenheim: Philo, 1996).

[14] See Klaus Zeyringer, *Österreichische Literaturgeschichte seit 1945* (Innsbruck: Haymon, 2001), 25–59.

[15] Arnolt Bronnen, "Neutralien oder Klösterreich? Anmerkungen zur Lage der österreichischen Literatur nach dem Staatsvertrag" in *Sonntag: Eine Wochenzeitung für Kulturpolitik, Kunst und Unterhaltung*, 30, July 24, 1955, 9, quoted in Friedbert Aspetsberger, Norbert Frei, and Hubert Lengauer, eds., *Literatur der Nachkriegszeit und der 50er Jahre in Österreich* (Vienna: Österreichischer Bundesverlag, 1984), 263.

[16] Hermann Bahr, *Selbstbildnis* (Berlin: Fischer, 1923), 277.

[17] Zeyringer, *Österreichische Literaturgeschichte seit 1945*, 47.

[18] See Friedbert Aspetsberger, "Die Polemiken um Arnolt Bronnens Roman *O.S.*" in Wendelin Schmidt-Dengler, Johann Sonnleitner, and Klaus Zeyringer, eds. *Konflikte — Skandale — Dichterfehden in der österreichischen Literatur* (Berlin: Erich Schmidt, 1995), 163–90.

[19] See Michael Bienert, ed., *Joseph Roth in Berlin: Ein Lesebuch für Spaziergänger* (Cologne: Kiepenheuer & Witsch, 1999), 32–33.

[20] Weinzierl and Skalnik, *Österreich 1918–1938*, 644.

[21] See Franz Kadrnoska, ed. *Aufbruch und Untergang: Österreichische Kultur zwischen 1918 und 1938* (Vienna: Europaverlag, 1981), 516–18.

[22] See Traugott Krischke, ed., *Materialien zu Ödön von Horváths "Geschichten aus dem Wiener Wald"* (Frankfurt am Main: Suhrkamp, 1978), 8.

[23] See Ursula Seeber, ed., *Asyl wider Willen: Exil in Österreich 1933 bis 1938* (Vienna: Picus, 2003).

[24] See Gerhard Renner, "Österreichische Schriftsteller und der Nationalsozialismus. Der 'Bund der deutschen Schriftsteller Österreichs' und der Aufbau der Reichsschrifttumskammer in der Ostmark," Vienna, Phil. Diss. 1981, 16.

[25] See Regina Thumser, " 'Kümmere dich nicht um ihren Hass, denn ihr Heil sind Kot und Würmer. Fahre in die Stadt Wien, welche einst dich Liebling nannte.' Kabarett und Kleinkunst in Österreich 1933 bis 1938" in Seeber, ed., *Asyl wider Willen*, 56–65.

[26] Quoted in Wendelin Schmidt-Dengler, *Ohne Nostalgie: Zur österreichischen Literatur der Zwischenkriegszeit* (Vienna: Böhlau, 2002), 166.

[27] Lothar Huber, ed., *Franz Werfel: An Austrian Writer Reassessed* (Oxford: Berg, 1989), 8. Werfel left Vienna for the USA after the *Anschluss*. Reinhardt had hoped to continue working with him there, having produced his Jewish epic *Der Weg der Verheißung*, now entitled *The Eternal Road*, in New York in 1937. Reinhardt also proposed a dramatization of the novel *Das Lied von Bernadette* (1941) but it was eventually made into a film without his involvement and won three Oscars as *The Song of Bernadette* (1943).

[28] For a decoding of these lines, see Klaus Weissenberger, "Zum Rhythmus der Lyrik von Karl Kraus. Das schöpferische Prinzip eines 'Epigonen,' " in Joseph P. Strelka, ed., *Karl Kraus: Diener der Sprache, Meister des Ethos* (Bern: Francke, 1990), 19–37.

[29] Karl Kraus, *Die Fackel*, 890–905 (1934), 276–77.

[30] See Walter Göhring, ed., *Roter Feber: Gedichte zum Februar '34* (Eisenstadt and Vienna: Roetzer, 1984).

[31] Stefan Grossmann, *Die Schultern der Mizzi Palme*, ed. Traugott Krischke (Vienna: Kremayr & Scheriau, 1995), 182–96. See Bernhard Fetz and Hermann Schlösser, eds., *Wien-Berlin: Mit einem Dossier zu Stefan Großmann* (Vienna: Paul Zsolnay, 2001).

[32] See Andrew Barker, "Anna Seghers, Friedrich Wolf, and the Austrian Civil War of 1934" in *Modern Language Review* 95 (2000): 144–53.

[33] Claudio Magris, *Der habsburgische Mythos in der österreichischen Literatur* (Salzburg: Otto Müller, 1966).

[34] Guido Zernatto, *Die Wahrheit über Österreich* (New York and Toronto: Longmans, Green & Co, 1938), 79.

[35] Zernatto, *Die Wahrheit über Österreich,* 19.

[36] Kadrnoska, ed. *Aufbruch und Untergang,* 502.

[37] See Annette Schmollinger, *"Intra muros et extra": Deutsche Literatur im Exil und in der Inneren Emigration* (Heidelberg: Winter, 1999), 82–86.

[38] See Albert Berger, *Josef Weinheber (1892–1945): Leben und Werk — Leben im Werk* (Salzburg: Otto Müller, 1999).

[39] Josef Weinheber, "Hymnus auf die Heimkehr" in *Bekenntnisbuch österreichischer Dichter* (Vienna, 1938), 116.

[40] Doderer and Gütersloh, *Briefwechsel, 1928–1962,* ed. Reinhold Treml (Munich: Biederstein, 1987), 133.

[41] Grossmann, *Die Schultern der Mizzi Palme,* 205.

[42] Hermann Broch, *Der Versucher* (Zurich: Rhein-Verlag, 1953), 342.

[43] Schmidt-Dengler, *Ohne Nostalgie,* 1.

[44] Quoted in Jura Soyfer, *Das Gesamtwerk: Prosa,* ed. Horst Jarka (Vienna: Europaverlag, 1984), 14.

[45] See Kadrnoska, ed., *Aufbruch und Untergang,* 522; Daniela Strigl, *"Wo niemand zuhaus ist, dort bin ich zuhaus": Theodor Kramer — Heimatdichter und Sozialdemokrat zwischen den Fronten* (Vienna: Böhlau, 1993).

[46] See Charmian Brinson, "Eva Kolmer and the Austrian Emigration in Britain" in Anthony Grenville, ed., *German-Speaking Exiles in Great Britain* (Amsterdam: Rodopi, 2000), 143–69; Franz Bönsch, "Das österreichische Exiltheater 'Laterndl' in London" in *Österreicher im Exil 1934 bis 1945* (Vienna: Dokumentationsarchiv des Österreichischen Widerstandes und Dokumentationsstelle für neuere österreichische Literatur, 1977), 441–50.

[47] Ulrike Längle, *Ernst Weiß, Vatermythos und Zeitkritik: Die Exilromane am Beispiel des "Armen Verschwenders"* (Innsbruck: Institut für Germanistik der Universität Innsbruck, 1981), 68.

[48] Zeyringer, *Österreichische Literaturgeschichte seit 1945,* 33.

[49] See Andrew Barker, "Marie Frischauf's *Der graue Mann:* National Socialism and the Austrian Novel" in Judith Beniston and Robert Vilain, eds., *"Hitler's First Victim"? Memory and Representation in Post-War Austria,* Austrian Studies 11 (Leeds: Maney, 2003), 33–44.

[50] See Heinz Lunzer, "Der literarische Markt 1945 bis 1955" in Aspetsberger et al., eds., *Literatur der Nachkriegszeit,* 41.

[51] See Volker Kaukoreit and Wendelin Schmidt-Dengler, eds., *Otto Basil und die Literatur um 1945: Tradition — Kontinuität — Neubeginn* (Vienna: Zsolnay, 1998).

[52] Klaus Amann, "Vorgeschichten: Kontinuitäten in der österreichischen Literatur von den dreißiger zu den fünfziger Jahren," in Aspetsberger et al., eds. *Literatur der Nachkriegszeit,* 46–58.

[53] Friedbert Aspetsberger, "Versuchte Korrekturen. Ideologie und Politik im Drama um 1945" in Aspetsberger et al., eds. *Literatur der Nachkriegszeit*, 242.

[54] See Kurt Palm, "Brecht und Österreich" in Aspetsberger et al., eds. *Literatur der Nachkriegszeit*, 134.

[55] I am much indebted to Leo A. Lensing (Middletown, CT) and Wendelin Schmidt-Dengler (Vienna) for their wise and generous comments on the penultimate draft of this essay.

6: Austrian Poetry, 1918–2000

Katrin Kohl

O F ALL THE LITERARY GENRES, poetry is perhaps most strongly shaped by the language in which it is written, and least determined by political territory. Poems often have no culturally and nationally distinctive setting; they are seldom peopled by characters with an obvious national identity; and reception of the poetic forms that were dominant in the twentieth century is rarely dependent on performance in a public space. Nevertheless, all poetry is specific to language communities and therefore to cultural and political communities. The complexity of those communities in Austria, and their changing identities in the political contexts of the Austro-Hungarian Empire, First Republic, Third Reich, and Second Republic, have given poets a keen awareness of language and its possibilities. This is enhanced by the daily encounter with the difference between High German and dialect, between the regionally neutral "German" *Schriftsprache* (written language) and the regionally specific "Austrian" language of oral communication. Throughout the twentieth century, the Austrian lyric has reached out across national boundaries to the point of obscuring its cultural origins, appealing to the entire German language community. Simultaneously, it has served to articulate and strengthen local identities. The purpose of this chapter is to explore connections and continuities in Austrian poetry from the perspective of Austria as a changing political and cultural entity that is defined as much by its tensions, fissures, and dispersals as by its cohesiveness.

The Legacy of Rilke

While the poetry of Hugo von Hofmannsthal continued to resonate in the work of younger poets, and the visionary imagery and sonorous diction of Georg Trakl provided an important stimulus for many poets between the wars and after, it was above all Rainer Maria Rilke (1875–1926) who constituted the benchmark for younger Austrian poets. He was born in Prague, far from the territory that was to define Austria from 1918 onward, but in a cultural center within the Austrian Empire that contributed vitally to the now established canon of German modernist literature.

Much of Rilke's poetry was written, or at least commenced, before the First World War, but the works that gave him his supreme status were completed in 1922: *Duineser Elegien* (Duino Elegies, 1923) and *Die Sonette an Orpheus* (The Sonnets to Orpheus, 1923). In his cycle of ten free-verse elegies — begun in 1912 in Castle Duino in (then) Austria, and completed in Castle Muzot in Switzerland — Rilke achieved a major statement on the poet's role in modern times. His cycle responds to the epic *Der Messias* (The Messiah, 1748–71) by Friedrich Gottlieb Klopstock, who had set out to emulate Homer in German hexameters, and surpass Milton as a poet-prophet mediating between God and man. While Klopstock was both famed and ridiculed for sustaining his emotive, highly charged verse over twenty cantos with little external action, Rilke creates an intensely concentrated cycle that benefits from his work also with Goethe and Hölderlin, celebrating the traditional human themes of poetry: lovers, heroes, and the creatures and objects that make up man's earthly world. The angels that populated Klopstock's metaphysical realm here become symbolic addressees that enable the modern poet to make the transition from a futile attempt to recover a transcendental purpose to accepting a more modest role. The grand cosmos becomes a poetic landscape within — the "Weltinnenraum."[1] It offers refuge to spiritualized forms of the "Dinge" (things) created by nature and man, the poet's voice granting them a transformed existence beyond transience. Man, aware of life's boundary, is situated between the angels with their supreme consciousness, and the animals with their freedom from awareness of death. The poems celebrate human existence in its most intense forms, pursuing a personal myth that follows the path into the inner self opened up by the Romantics. However, unlike Novalis, whose cycle *Hymnen an die Nacht* (Hymns to the Night, 1800) moves away from life to celebrate mystical union with the beloved and the divine in death, Rilke evokes the reciprocity of life and death through the complementary poetic modes of praise and lament in a space that unites subject and object.

In his *Sonette an Orpheus*, a two-part cycle of fifty-five sonnets written in February 1922 and inspired by the premature death of a young dancer,[2] Rilke projects his voice through the figure of Orpheus, that most ancient and powerful of poets who was permitted to transgress the boundary to the underworld after the loss of his beloved Eurydice. Rilke's imagery shows an exquisite balance of tangible symbols and fanciful abstraction, fashioning a world that confounds physical laws, as in the aural metaphors of the two opening sonnets celebrating Orpheus and the dancer: "O Orpheus singt! O hoher Baum im Ohr!" (O Orpheus sings! O high tree in the ear!); "[sie] machte sich ein Bett in meinem Ohr. // Und schlief in mir" ([she] made her bed inside my ear // And slept in me) (241). Rilke's mastery of the sonnet form is evident in the exuberant development of its potential as he varies the meter, line-length, and rhyme scheme: "das Sonett abzuwandeln, es zu heben, ja gewissermaßen es im Laufen zu tragen, ohne es zu zerstören, war mir [. . .] eine eigentümliche Probe und Aufgabe" (The special challenge and my purpose was to modify the sonnet, to raise it, indeed to carry it while moving, as it were, without destroying it).[3] In his use of language, too, Rilke strives for a dynamic medium, pushing established modes of expression to their limits while seeking to preserve their essence. He eschews the radical neologisms and syntactic dislocations that characterized the work of avant-garde poets in the early decades of the twentieth century — for example the poetry of August Stramm — in order to experiment more subtly with the morphological and syntactic possibilities of the language, bringing out unexpected nuances and enhancing the sound quality of words in unusual rhymes. Expression is strengthened by omitting prefixes ("Sang" for "Gesang," song) and rejuvenating obsolescent words ("Genist," nest), by creating unusual compound words ("mädchenhändig," with the hands of a girl) and new adjectives ("höhlig," from "Höhle," cave) (241, 244, 262). Verbs attain surprising delicacy in unusual subjunctive forms ("göß," from "gießen," to pour; "entrönnen," from "entrinnen," to escape) and intensified force when used in unconventional transitive constructions ("Sie schlief die Welt," she slept the world; "Tanzt die Orange," Dance the orange) (253, 261, 241, 248). Rilke learned from the classical poets in the German language as well as other traditions, notably French Symbolism, and he is perceived in the international context as the greatest "German" poet writing in the first half of the twentieth century. In cultural terms, he is quintessentially a European poet: born in cosmopolitan Prague and attending school in Lower Austria, his poetry draws inspiration from Germany, Russia, France, Italy, Spain, and Switzerland. His avoidance of political themes, his non-confessional yet metaphysical visions, his celebration of universal "things," his focus on internationally significant locations in his *Neue Gedichte* (New Poems, 1907–8) and creation of symbolic rather than realistic landscapes in his later work, make his poetry infinitely appealing and culturally transferable.

Rilke's importance for the generations that followed is exemplified in the work of Alexander Lernet-Holenia (1897–1976), who paid homage to him in his dedication of the collection *Kanzonnair* (1923) and in other works.[4] Lernet-Holenia's verse epitomizes the high status poetry had gained in Vienna with Modernism. He published it in beautifully produced, limited editions in order to ensure that it would be read only by those able to appreciate its worth, an approach to the reading public reminiscent of Stefan George. Lernet-Holenia projects himself as a *poeta doctus*, displaying erudition in numerous poems on figures and events from the Old Testament. He uses elevated diction and attempts the most ambitious forms such as the Petrarchan sonnet, the classical ode, and hymnic free verse in the style of Hölderlin. The composition of his collections is designed to demonstrate mastery of form on a grand scale.

With characteristic venom, Karl Kraus labeled him "Sterilke" and "Puerilke" and commented on his verse as follows in his influential periodical *Die Fackel* (The Torch): "Gleich dem Vorbild reimt Herr Maria Lernet alles, Präfixe, Präpositionen, Silben, Artikel [. . .], hält Konstruktionen durch Strophen durch, [. . .] verdinglicht Ätherisches" (Like his model, Mr Maria Lernet rhymes everything with everything, prefixes, prepositions, syllables, articles [. . .], sustains constructions over stanzas, [. . .] turns ethereal concepts into things).[5] The similarity with Rilke's verse is indeed striking, but at times, high artifice lapses into the merely prosaic, while his strict treatment of syntax and form is closer to the poetic techniques of George and Gottfried Benn. His neologisms are less subtle than Rilke's, without having the dynamic adventurousness of Stramm's morphological experiments (for example, "seigneurile Landschaft," seigneurile landscape, 147; "in schwerem Geatme," in heavy breathing, 198; "die jünglingischen Engel," the youthful angels, 205).

For many young writers, Rilke was the center of the lyric universe, as is evident especially in the early work of Erika Mitterer (1906–2001). At the age of eighteen, in May 1924, she entered into a correspondence with him that took the form of poems, with Rilke picking up on her words and images and extolling her verse as a "Herzlandschaft" (landscape of the heart).[6] She celebrates the older writer much as the monastic poet in Rilke's *Das Stunden-Buch* (The Book of Hours, 1905) had celebrated God: "Laß mich Weihrauch sein in deinem Dom, / laß mich Rahmen sein an deinem Bild, / Laß mich Weg sein. Du bist Ziel" (Let me be incense in your cathedral, / let me be the frame for your painting, / let me be the path. You are the destination, 1/42). For Mitterer, Rilke's encouragement was enormously important: she was in effect receiving master classes in the art of poetry that strengthened her confidence to develop her career as a poet while posing the challenge of moving beyond Rilke's sentiment and style. With respect to Rilke, the correspondence at first sight has little to offer beyond its biographical interest. The discrepancy in the age, status, and technical accomplishment of the two poets, Rilke's identification of his ideal beloved with a real addressee, and his real-life references to the leukemia of which he was to die in December 1926, have prompted critics to dismiss this poetic correspondence as a somewhat embarrassing aberration by a poet who is generally held to epitomize the purity of poetry.[7] Yet it is a remarkable — and remarkably underrated — correspondence in terms of its sustained poetic form, the sheer quantity of poems, and the complex, dialogic mode of poetic interaction. Mitterer wrote around 117 poems to Rilke, which display a fascinating process of creative reception and increasing mastery. Alongside her inherent attractiveness for Rilke as an unattainable young woman enraptured by his person and work, it must have been her finely attuned response to his sensibilities that prompted him to answer with some fifty poems. They comprise one third of his poetic output in German in the last two-and-a-half years of his life (he also wrote poems in French), and range through widely varying modes of love poetry, from expressions of sublimated desire to a passionate celebration of the orgasm evoked by writing to his beloved.[8] He treated Mitterer's poems with the utmost respect, incorporating her utterances and transforming them into new poetic statements that are characteristic of his mature work. The inclusion of epistolary details about his life needs to be taken seriously in critical terms: it demonstrates not the failure of poetic power, but Rilke's conviction that poetry is integrated with life.

While Mitterer's collection *Dank des Lebens* (1930) includes poems from the Rilke correspondence and for the most part continues in the Rilkean vein, the collection *Gesang der Wandernden* (1935) tends toward a more realist mode that focuses on natural subjects, typically specifying a moment and perspective. Subjects of her poems include a descent on skis and an evening of deerstalking (2/16, 18), an evening view of a glacier and a small horse on a mountain (2/20, 21), generally in simple imagery and language. Like many of her contemporaries, Mitterer writes poems on classical topics such as Nausicaa, Sappho or Calypso (2/24, 25, 29), but unlike Lernet-Holenia or Josef Weinheber, she does not generally seek to emulate classical verse forms, preferring iambic, rhymed four-line stanzas. In the programmatic poem "Anrufung Apollons" (Invocation to Apollo, 2/42–44), however, the poet defines her task in dactyls and longer sections. The perspective is gendered along traditional lines, as she sets the gift of poetry against the demands of family life. Projecting herself as an "irdische Frau" (earthly woman) who refrains from writing heroic odes and needs no immortality, she lays claim to a life-oriented aesthetic and everyday happiness: "Einem Mann will ich sterbliche Kinder gebären, / die blühen und wachsen wie Blume und Tier" (I wish to bear mortal children for a man, / which blossom and grow like flowers and animals, 2/42–43). The author continued her writing career into old age, concentrating on more pronounced religious themes.[9] In the aftermath of the war, she addressed Austrians at home and abroad with *Zwölf Gedichte* (Twelve Poems, 1946), which show sympathy with those who were driven into exile while advocating Christian forgiveness. The poem "An Österreich" warns her compatriots: "Bevor du richtest, forsche in Geduld: / Wie viele unter uns sind ohne Schuld?" (Before you pass judgment, examine patiently: / How many of us are without guilt? 2/63).

Religion and War

Biblical motifs and religious themes are a feature of Austrian poetry in the interwar years: where Rilke and his followers tended to depict individual figures and episodes, the Expressionist trend was toward apocalyptic visions and images of all-encompassing dislocation. In the 1920s and 1930s, however, these give way to less extreme forms of dissolution, and the immediate localities of the Austrian *Heimat* gain prominence, as was already evident in the work of Mitterer. There is a trend toward depicting people in contemporary society without giving them timeless significance through myth, elevated language, or complex form.

The heritage of Expressionism can be traced in the postwar collections by Franz Werfel (1890–1945), whose dramas and novels gained wider acclaim but who also remained committed to poetry, the genre in which he had inspired his generation before the war. The volume *Der Gerichtstag* (The Day of Judgment, 1919) centers on the grand themes of transience, guilt, and death in apocalyptic visions and hymnic rhythms written for the most part during the war. The religious focus strengthens in later collections, but there is considerable variety of subject, language, and form. Werfel continues to advocate an anti-rational aesthetic, which finds its fulfillment in the divinely inspired moment of poetic creation, as exemplified in the poem "Gebet um Sprache" (Prayer for Speech) from the collection *Schlaf und Erwachen* (Sleep and Awakening, 1935).[10] In the final lines, the concept of inspiration is imbued with the power of the divine as the poet prays for a moment of revelation through language:

> Laß mich an überraschender Biegung
> Dir begegnen im Dornenbusch des Wortes,
> Im stotternd zerrissenen Strauch,
> Der mit der bläulichen Flamme
> Deines Gleichnisses brennt!

> [Let me meet you at a surprising bend / In the burning bush of the word, / In the stuttering torn shrub, / That burns with the blue flame / Of your parable!]

Like Rilke, Werfel seeks a poetic mode to counter transience: "Geschaffen ist die Welt, daß sie vergeh! / Doch ich, wenn ich ihr Bild in Sprache treibe, / Ich schaffe sie, verstört von ihrem Weh, / Damit im Wort sie bleibe, bleibe, bleibe . . ." (The world is created so that it may pass away! / But I, when I drive its image into language, / I create it, disturbed by its woe, / So in the word it may remain, remain, remain . . . , 481). In the work of this iconic poet of Expressionism, the task of poetry has its goal in eternity.

Alongside such trajectories toward timelessness, a rich variety of verse focuses on the immediate present. Karl Kraus (1874–1936) depicts the figurehead of the erstwhile Empire in the poem "Franz Joseph," published in 1920 in *Die Fackel*, posing a series of questions on the Kaiser's personality: "Wie war er? War er dumm? War er gescheit?" (What was he like? Was he

stupid? Was he clever?).[11] The poem culminates in questions on his motive
for the war that destroyed his Empire:

> Wollt' er den Krieg? Wollt' eigentlich er nur
> Soldaten und von diesen die Montur,
> von der den Knopf nur? Hatt' er eine Spur
> von Tod und Liebe und vom Menschenleid?
> Nie prägte mächtiger in ihre Zeit
> jemals ihr Bild die Unpersönlichkeit. (339)

> [Did he want war? Did he in fact just want / Soldiers, or rather
> their uniform, / indeed only the button? Did he have a trace / of
> death and love and human suffering? / Never did a lack of
> personality stamp its image / more powerfully on its age.]

Kraus deflates the ideal of the lost Empire by reducing the power of its
greatest representative to the whim of a nonentity.

The experience of the war itself, which Trakl and Stramm had evoked
so vividly in 1914–15, is conveyed by Theodor Kramer (1897–1958) in his
collection *Wir lagen in Wolhynien im Morast* . . . (We Lay in the Morass in
Volhynia . . . , 1931) — in poems written more than a decade after the war
had ended, indicating the time it took Kramer to find a mode for his
response. The effect is far removed from the Expressionist war poems: precisely observed details are shown dispassionately in straightforward language and rhymed, mainly alternating verse forms. The volume has been
compared to Remarque's *All Quiet on the Western Front*,[12] but while it
shows the perspective of the simple soldier and refrains from glorifying the
war, it is devoid of the political thrust of the novel and discourages emotional empathy. Kramer offers occasional shocking details — the stripping
of a wounded soldier by comrades (105) or the amputated leg of a whore
(126) — but also moments of pleasure as the soldiers relish an adventure
(117) or enjoy singing "tausend alte Lieder" (a thousand old songs, 128).

Kramer's treatment of the war is characteristic of his poetry: he creates
cameos that show contemporary everyday lives, set in realistically depicted
landscapes. His first collection, *Die Gaunerzinke* (The Secret Sign of the
Crook, 1929), impressed readers with its range of first-person perspectives
from underprivileged sections of society — laborer (59), bargeman on the
Danube (61), baker's boy (68), or tramp, as in the poem "Vagabund":
"Zerschunden kam ich von den Steinbruchklippen / — die Eichenhügel
brausen braun im Wind — und feuchte gierig die verstaubten Lippen /
mit Trauben, die im Frost verrunzelt sind" (With cuts and grazes I came
from the quarry cliffs / — the oak-covered hills are raging brown in the
wind — / and greedily moisten my dusty lips / with grapes that have
shriveled in the frost, 47). In the later collection *Mit der Ziehharmonika*

(With the Concertina, 1936), the poem "Altes Paar im Prater" (Old Couple in the Prater) shows the pleasures of the fairground from the point of view of an old man addressing his wife: "Hinterm Pfeiler kreist das Karussell, / die Tschinellen laden laut zu Gast; / komm, nicht geizig kann ich heute sein, / setz dich, gönn dir einen Tropfen Wein, / Lebzelt, Käs, worauf du Gusto hast" (Behind the pillar the roundabout is revolving, / the cymbals are loudly inviting us; / come, I can't be tight-fisted today, / sit down, treat yourself to a glass of wine, / gingerbread, cheese, whatever you fancy, 183). A local flavor is imparted not least by the local vocabulary: to help the non-Austrian reader, Kramer supplied glossaries for his volumes. However, his verse is designed above all for ordinary local people, and many of his poems were initially published in newspapers.

While some of Kramer's poems are written in the style of songs with refrains, and depict acts of violence, he does not write lurid street ballads in the style of the early Bertolt Brecht, and neither is his poetry specifically political, though a number of poems written in response to the rise of Hitler take on a strong political edge, for example, "Im Konzentrationslager" (In the Concentration Camp, 3/424), published on 9 April 1933 in the Viennese *Arbeiter-Zeitung*, the organ of the Social Democratic Party. By contrast, the verse of Jura Soyfer (1912–39) — much of which was published in the same newspaper — was consistently political and hard-hitting, designed to fight apathy and to unite readers in resisting the National Socialists. Written mainly between March 1932 and October 1933, the extant poems are generally in the form of songs and contain specific references to issues of the moment, as in "Krupps Morgenliedchen" (Krupp's Morning Song) of 6 March 1932, which comments on the Geneva Disarmament Conference convened on 2 February 1932:

> Die Hoffnungen schießen empor, froh und frisch,
> Gleich Flugzeugabwehrgeschützen!
> Hurra! Ich freue mich mörderisch,
> Die Hoffnung ist grün wie der grüne Tisch,
> An dem sie in Genf jetzt sitzen![13]

> [The hopes shoot up, joyful and fresh, / Like air defense artillery! / Hurrah! I'm dead pleased, / Hope is green like the green table, / They're now sitting at in Geneva!]

Allusions to popular national songs make the messages memorable, and pithy endings drive them home, as in the song "Heil Hitler!," addressed to German citizens on 23 April 1933: "Blutige Jahre werden vergehen, / Dann wirst du alles verstehen" (Bloody years will pass, / Then you will understand everything, 179). The last surviving song, "Das Dachaulied" (The Dachau Song, 245–46), was written in the concentration camp of that name where Soyfer was imprisoned from June to September 1938. The ironic motto over the entrance serves as the running theme and refrain of the song: "Arbeit macht frei" (Work makes you free), but the first lines supply the context of violence: "Stacheldraht, mit Tod geladen, / Ist um unsere Welt gespannt" (Barbed wire, loaded with death, / Surrounds our world). In the face of the human toll — "Und so viele sind zerbrochen / Und verloren ihr Gesicht" (And so many are broken / and have lost their face) — stands the hope for "Freiheit" (freedom) and repeated exhortations to the comrade to remain human: "Bleib ein Mensch, Kamerad."

German National Poet from Vienna: Difficulties with Josef Weinheber

The section of Austrian society that greeted the rise of Hitler with enthusiasm found its literary representative in Josef Weinheber (1892–1945). His mission lay within Greater Germany, where he himself would come to the fore as the new national poet. Weinheber worked with the most ambitious forms of the German canon and saw himself following in the footsteps of Goethe and Hölderlin. Weinheber joined the National Socialist Party in 1931 and committed suicide when it became clear that the Third Reich was in its death throes. The cultural deprivation of his early years — he was the son of a Viennese butcher, grew up in an orphanage, and developed his poetic skills as an autodidact — may help explain his drive toward heroic grandeur, high culture, formal sophistication, and technical virtuosity. The feature that distinguishes him from other poets who joined the National Socialist cause is not just formal mastery, but an enduring fascination with language that prompted him to explore both the most elevated registers of the German poetic tradition and the colloquial forms of his native Vienna. He builds on a humanist poetic tradition that modeled itself on the great Greek and Roman poets and was renewed by Klopstock for the "classical" age of German literature in order to develop the German language through poetry so that it might compete successfully with the languages of other cultures past and present.

Weinheber's literary breakthrough came with the collection *Adel und Untergang* (Nobility and Doom, 1934), in which he demonstrates his poetic range and above all his mastery of complex form in a series of classicistic poems, in variations on an ode by Hölderlin, and in a "Heroische Trilogie" prefaced by a quotation from Schopenhauer.[14] Weinheber's poetic credo is encapsulated in the "Hymnus auf die deutsche Sprache" (Hymn to the German Language, 2/98–99), in which he worships the German language as mother, lover, and god, alluding to the Lord's Prayer — "Vater unser" — in the invocation "Sprache unser!" (Our language!). Weinheber uses the most emotive words of the time to convey the splendor of the German language: "Blut," "Volk," "Heimat," "Scholle," "Kampf," "Opfer," "Schicksal" (blood, people, homeland, clod of earth, battle, sacrifice, fate). Hyperbolically, the German language comes to enshrine the expansionist ambitions of National Socialism: "Du nennst die Erde und den Himmel: deutsch!" (You call earth and heaven: German!).

Weinheber's subsequent work is poetically more sophisticated. With his volume *Zwischen Göttern und Dämonen* (Between Gods and Demons, 1938), he seeks to outdo Rilke's *Duineser Elegien*, choosing not the sonnet, but the most elevated and classical of lyric forms, the ode. In a ten-part cycle — each part consisting of four odes — he counters Rilke's searching, sensitive poetic voice with a poetic persona confident of his mission. Projecting himself as the true heir of Hölderlin — who supplies the motto — he places man heroically at the center of the universe: "Nicht das Ding rechtfertigt den Menschen, sondern / er das Ding" (It is not the thing that justifies man, but man who justifies the thing, 2/431). From the postwar perspective, the volume *Kammermusik* (Chamber Music, 1939) is more readily accessible: it treats musical forms and instruments, exploiting the musical qualities of language. Correspondingly, Weinheber's final collection celebrates the word, in what is the culmination of his work: *Hier ist das Wort* (Here is the Word), completed in 1944, and published posthumously in 1947. The collection contains poems on language, classical ode forms, and metrical feet in the tradition of Klopstock, poems dedicated to Hölderlin, translations of Sappho, Horace, and Shakespeare as well as a poem on translating, and a series of occasional poems. Like *Kammermusik*, it is a collection that can — for the most part — be "appreciated without reference to Weinheber's political aberrations."[15] Such an analysis, however, would miss the point of these works: in a wide variety of forms and modes, they celebrate aspects of language and exemplify the power and range of German as a poetic medium — as well as Weinheber's own skill. His poetic aspirations were strengthened by his nationalistic fervor, and nationalism gave the language he loved the highest possible status. Selective readings run the risk of presenting a sanitized view of literary history, one in which literature is severed from its cultural and political context in the name of timeless poetic worth.

The collection that has survived the Third Reich most easily is *Wien wörtlich* (Vienna Word for Word, 1935), which was repeatedly reissued, most recently in 1985. Weinheber here pays linguistic homage to his native city in an overtly popular mode. In the introductory poem, the poet aligns himself with his fellow speakers of Viennese, and concludes by distancing himself emphatically from the German classics that shaped Weinheber's career:

> Des hat ka Goethe gschriebn, des hat ka Schiller dicht',
> is von kan Klassiker, von kan Genie,

des is a Weaner, der mit *unsern* Göscherl spricht,
und segn S', erscht *des* is für uns Poesie. (2/131)

[This wasn't written by Goethe, it wasn't composed by Schiller, / it's not by a classical poet, not by a genius, / it's by one of us Viennese, speaking with *our* tongue, / and you see, *that's* real poetry for us.]

Weinheber was however equally emphatic in designating the collection a "Nebenwerk" (minor work, 4/572) in order not to endanger his reputation as a poet of the Greater Germany and one who was aspiring to become part of the modern canon of poetic "Genien Europas" (geniuses of Europe, 4/573).

In espousing National Socialism, Weinheber placed his work in the service of a political cause now widely judged the most inhumane the world has seen. His enthusiastic allegiance is expressed most overtly in poems such as the "Ode an die Straßen Adolf Hitlers" (Ode to the Roads of Adolf Hitler, 3/473–75) and his "Hymnus auf die Heimkehr" (Hymn to Austria's Return Home, 411–15), which appeared in the *Bekenntnisbuch österreichischer Dichter* (Austrian Writers Confess their Faith) published by the Bund deutscher Schriftsteller Österreichs in June 1938, in response to the *Anschluss*.[16] Remarkably, in contrast to the reputation of other poets in the *Bekenntnisbuch*, Weinheber's fame, or notoriety, survived beyond the era of National Socialism, not only in Austria. Metaphors of battle, conquest, and doom continue into his postwar reception in German literary histories,[17] and he was still given considerable exposure in the 1970s as a poet engaged in a tragic conflict. In the latter decades of the century he was gradually excluded from the narrative as exemplifying a "steriler Klassizismus" (sterile classicism)[18] — a judgment that unwittingly recalls the genealogical criteria propagated by the Nazis and places his work firmly before the origin of truly modern German poetry at the "Stunde Null." By the end of the century he was all but buried among the names of a fortunately distant past.[19]

Weinheber nowhere offers the symbiosis of linguistic subtlety, formal finesse, and rhetorical force that marks out Brecht's best poetry, or the poetic vision and intellectual range that characterize the verse of Franz Baermann Steiner. Yet he is no minor poet. At a time of political upheaval, Weinheber's verse stands as a fascist counterpart to the Marxist poetry of Brecht, representing one political extreme in the spectrum of poetic responses to National Socialism. As such, his work is powerful testimony to the connection between poetry, politics, and morality — a connection German Idealism had sought to sever. It sensitizes us to the important role of moral issues not only in the production of literature, but also in its reception. His poetry is embedded in the German and Austrian poetic tradition, draws on theories of language current at the time — with Karl Kraus being a notable presence — and expresses values espoused by many Austrians at a crucial period in the country's postimperial search for identity. What Weinheber stood for retained credibility in a postwar context that looked to homely traditions, as is evident from a substantial volume published by admirers in 1950 entitled *Bekenntnis zu Josef Weinheber* (Declaration of Commitment to Josef Weinheber).[20] Weinheber's work builds on the classical and the modernist tradition and in some respects points forward to poetic projects of later decades: for example, there is an affinity between his Hölderlin variations and the montage effects created in the variations on famous poems by the leftwing German poet Peter Rühmkorf. Weinheber's work forms part of the poetic matrix that gave rise to the language experiments of the Wiener Gruppe: equally fascinated by language, they developed its local and supra-regional potential in poetry based on a highly creative counter-aesthetic.

A political constellation that is no longer shaped by the parameters of the postwar era has created a context in which it may be possible to read even this most morally compromised of poets, as is evident in *Falsches Futter* (Wrong Fodder, 1997) by the German writer Marcel Beyer (1965–). In the poem "Achter Vierter Fünfundvierzig" (Eighth of the Fourth Forty-Five), which refers to the date of Weinheber's death, Beyer focuses on the "Hymnus auf die deutsche Sprache," situating it historically before the *Anschluss* and interweaving quotations with references to photographs of Weinheber that show the trappings and environment associated with Nazism: black boots, dog, mountain spring and wooden hut, shot through with a sharp voice that contrasts with the poet's own "unscharfe Zunge" (blunt/unfocused tongue).[21] The poem juxtaposes Weinheber's semi-religious elevation of the German language with violent imperatives, images recalling Hitler, and (fictionalized) details of Weinheber's self-destruction. Using techniques of defamiliarization, Beyer's poem engages with a poem that is part of the German — and Austrian — poetic tradition. In the long term, such responses may prove more productive than moral condemnation, selective acceptance, or convenient amnesia. For they indicate that there is need for a differentiated approach to the literature written in the era of National Socialism: an approach that takes account of the many different, complex interactions between moral issues and aesthetic quality both at the time of writing and in the multi-faceted processes of reception.

Poetry in Exile

There is consensus that National Socialism brought an immense loss of literary talent in Austria. Even more than before the war, the landscape of

"Austrian" poetry is henceforth geographically complex, even if one only includes work in German. It includes poets born in German-speaking Austria and those born in the Austro-Hungarian Empire prior to its dissolution; it includes poets who remained in German-speaking Austria during the era of National Socialism and continued their careers there after the war, such as Erika Mitterer; poets who established their careers in the First Republic and were driven into exile, dying there during the war years, like Franz Werfel in 1945, or returning to Austria after the war, like Theodor Kramer, who came back from Britain in 1957 but died in the following year; poets who remained in exile but were nevertheless able to establish themselves in the postwar German literary context, such as Erich Fried and — if one considers him part of "Austrian" literature — Paul Celan; and poets who remained in exile without being able to gain recognition in the postwar context. The loss of talent is clear in the case of poets such as Jura Soyfer, who were murdered. What remains less clear is the loss of poets who were unable to fulfil their literary potential, or who were hindered in the development of their literary careers: because they were unable to transmute trauma into poetry; because they could not return to a German-speaking country for practical or psychological reasons and lacked a German-speaking public arena that would have made a successful literary career possible; because writing outside the German-speaking world, they lacked the contacts and infrastructure to disseminate their work. Rather than attempt a survey here of Austrian poets in exile, I shall focus on two exiled writers who created a significant body of lyric poetry but have remained on the periphery as far as literary historiography are concerned, only now gradually gaining recognition: Franz Baermann Steiner (1909–52) and H. G. Adler (1910–88).

Like his friend Adler, Steiner grew up in an assimilated German-speaking Jewish family in Prague. He moved in literary circles and was steeped in the German intellectual tradition, his poetry being marked by an intense engagement with German poetry in the classical tradition. Like Adler, who became a leading historian of the Shoah, and their mutual friend Elias Canetti, who turned from creative writing to his studies for *Masse und Macht* (Crowds and Power, 1960) when the war broke out, Steiner focused much of his energy in exile on non-literary works in order to analyze and address the experience of the Holocaust: he became an anthropologist in Oxford and turned to writing on slavery as a "sacrifice" in 1939.[22] Steiner's attempts to publish the poetry collection "In Babylons Nischen" (In the Niches of Babylon) in 1950 failed because the German publisher got into financial difficulties, and two posthumous volumes of his poetry edited by H. G. Adler attracted little attention; Steiner's collected poetry only appeared in 2000.[23]

Steiner's varied oeuvre is enriched by his understanding of colonialist processes from the perspective of an anthropologist committed to cultural

diversity, and imbued with the suffering inflicted on his own people —
while himself living in Britain during the war years, he lost his parents in
Treblinka. His poetic vision is enshrined in its most impressive form in a
cycle of poems that remained unfinished but stands as one of the major
poetic statements of the twentieth century: *Eroberungen* (Conquests), written mainly in 1940–45 and published posthumously only in 1964, was projected with thirteen parts, of which two remained unwritten. The work
resonates with allusions to Goethe, Hölderlin, and Trakl, but above all it
responds in structure, thematic scope, and rhythm to the *Duineser Elegien*.
While acknowledging the importance of Rilke for his poetry, Steiner explicitly avoided a ten-part structure for his cycle in order to obliterate any traces
of emulation.[24] This example of a Bloomian "anxiety of influence"[25]
demonstrates the power Rilke continued to exert, while the personal tone
and vision of Steiner's cycle show how fruitful an engagement with Rilke's
work could be, at best, for later poets. The world Steiner depicts is in fact far
removed from the rarefied space evoked by his predecessor: the work voices
a passionate critique of imperialism and pays homage to persecuted peoples
by incorporating their myths. It alludes to foundational texts of various cultures, appropriating figures from *Robinson Crusoe* and integrating textual
elements from the Jewish canon, and it engages emotively with the brutal
destruction wrought by the contemporary war. Steiner's personal commitment is conveyed in the substance and tone; any sentimentality is avoided
by the intertextual fabric of the work, by mythical figures such as "der Ein-
same" (the lonely one), reminiscent of the protagonists in Trakl's verse, and
by the stylized, decentered persona that frames the cycle: "Der Schritt
schwingt hin, / Den abend durcheilt der leib, / Gedehnte brust achtet
nicht der arme" (The step swings away, / The body hurries through the
evening, / The stretched breast does not heed the arms).[26] *Eroberungen* is
a powerful countertext to the *Duineser Elegien*, signaling the transition
from modernism to an era of German poetry in which political events
pressed poetry into an ethically committed response.

   Adler's career testifies to the continuing difficulties exiled writers faced
in the postwar era. His, too, is a subtly individual voice that was forced to
develop its idiom outside the mainstream German-speaking cultures. Having spent the war years in concentration camps — where he lost his wife
and parents — and returned briefly to postwar Czechoslovakia, Adler
finally left Prague in 1947 and settled in London, establishing his reputation primarily with socio-historical works, notably *Theresienstadt
1941–1945* (1955, [2]1960, reprint 2005) and *Der verwaltete Mensch*
(Administered Man, 1974), a study of the deportation of Jews. While he
was eventually able to publish prose works including *Eine Reise* (A Journey, 1962) and *Panorama* (1968) as well as poetry collections including
Viele Jahreszeiten (Many Times of Year, 1975) and *Stimme und Zuruf*
(Voice and Call, 1980), and was elected President of the German-Speaking

Writers Abroad PEN Centre (1973–85), his experience as a writer was marked by a sense of lacking public resonance, and much of his work remains unpublished: in total, the poetry in his estate comprises in excess of 900 poems in seven volumes, written over more than six decades.[27]

A sizeable number of poems are extant from the period 1942–44. In the cycle "Theresienstädter Bilderbogen" of 1942, the titles record the procedures and locations of the concentration camp: "Auf dem Bahnhof," "Ankunft der Greise," "Durchsuchung," "Der Siechenhof," "Abspeisung," "Totenfeier" (At the Station, Arrival of the Old Men, Search, The Hospital Yard, Feeding, Funeral Ceremony).[28] Adler draws on imagery and diction reminiscent of Expressionist poetry to convey daily reality, with similar tensions between themes of dissolution, sickness, and decay, and regular, rhymed forms that here provide a counterweight to the barbaric crimes of the henchmen. In the cycle's final poem "Totentanz" (Dance of Death, 87), apocalyptic vision is anchored in the record of brutal murder:

> Verrucht ragt wüst ein Schädel auf in Schattengröße
> Und gröhlt sein grelles Lied zu tauben Wänden,
> Vermodert dumpf zerschlitzt in ekler Schinderblöße
> Mit ausgerenkten Knorpelhänden,
> Vernebelt zwischen welk gegerbten Leichen,
> Die starr gepeinigt scheppernd schleichen.

> [Heinously, a skull rises, monstrous shadow / And bawls out its shrill song to deaf walls, / Decaying, fusty, slashed in odious knacker's nakedness / With the dislocated cartilage of hands, / Misty between the wilted leather of corpses, / Clattering and creeping in rigid torment.]

Adler's later poetry shows increasing complexity of meaning, density of imagery, and a concentrated language that is sensitive to the phrases and rhythms of everyday speech — he regularly visited German-speaking countries to keep in touch with subtle changes in the language[29] — yet classical in its vocabulary and syntactic structures. At the center is a concern to bear witness and give voice to the truth — a truth that is projected into the future as well as remembering the past. Fear, mourning, and death continue as themes into the late poetry, but their resonance extends beyond immediate history, involving the reader in an endeavor that reaches through language and encompasses its limit and end:

> Die Sprache halten wir nicht mehr, wir
> Halten sie nicht aus, die Worte fallen
> In Ohnmacht dahin, die Lippen brechen
> Bei unseren zerpreßten Lauten[30]

[We can no longer hold language, we / Cannot bear it, the words fall / Away in a powerless faint, the lips break / Under the pressure of our failing sounds.]

It remains a challenge for German studies and Austrian studies alike to integrate work written in exile into a broadly based conception of twentieth-century literature in German, and not limit it to the special categories of "exile studies" and "Holocaust literature." Literary historiography otherwise risks re-enacting the exclusion that prevented writers like Steiner and Adler from developing their work in the context of a German-speaking readership.

The Pressures of the Past and the Claims of the Present

The political constellation of 1945 created a distinctive context for Austrian poetry. Whereas intellectuals in the Federal Republic of Germany were concerned to establish a new beginning in order to separate modern German culture from the National Socialist past, Austrians interpreted the National Socialist years as a period of foreign occupation and sought to establish a continuity of tradition with the period before the *Anschluss*. Lernet-Holenia signaled this continuity as follows: "In der Tat brauchen wir nur dort fortzusetzen, wo uns die Träume eines Irren unterbrochen haben, in der Tat brauchen wir nicht voraus-, sondern nur zurückzublicken" (Indeed we need only continue where the dreams of a madman interrupted us, indeed we do not need to look forwards, only backwards).[31]

For Austrian poetry, this had a number of consequences. It meant that there was a greater affirmation of tradition and of the values of the *Heimat* than in West Germany, and high value was accorded to local features that were distinctively Austrian. Timeless nature poetry — which in fact also offered a refuge for West German poets during and after the war — was here supported by the sense that it would restore Austria to its true self. There was little incentive to rethink and recast the possibilities of poetry, and the traditionalists held sway into the 1960s. Austria brought forth no initiative comparable to the Gruppe 47, a loosely organized group of writers that aimed to set new standards for literature in West Germany. Whereas the Gruppe 47 tended to encourage morally committed literature and in the 1960s became involved in political issues, young Austrian poets generally challenged the establishment in more anarchic ways and looked to language rather than politics to destabilize traditional structures and ways of thinking. The pressure to address the involvement of the older generation in the crimes of National Socialism came much later in Austria than in Germany, and the literary provocations and attacks were generally staged in dramatic form or prose invectives rather than in poetry. The focus before and after the Cold War was less on the stark political divide and subsequent unity between two Germanies than on the complex relationship with West Germany, and to some extent the cultures of the old Empire.

In the immediate aftermath of the war, the poets who had established themselves in the prewar decades continued to dominate the poetic landscape: Weinheber's posthumous *Hier ist das Wort* of 1947 appeared in a second edition two years later; Lernet-Holenia produced the collections *Germanien* (Germania, 1946), *Die Trophäe* (The Trophy, 1946), and *Das Feuer* (The Fire, 1949); Rudolf Henz published *Wort in der Zeit* (Word in Time, 1945, second edition 1947), *Österreichische Trilogie* (Austrian Trilogy, 1950), and *Lobgesang auf unsere Zeit* (Paean to Our Time, 1956); other works included Georg Grabenhorst, *Blätter im Wind* (Leaves in the Wind, 1953) and Karl Heinrich Waggerl, *Heiteres Herbarium: Blumen und Verse* (Humorous Herbarium, Flowers and Verse, 1950, and later editions).

A rather different voice is that of Christine Lavant (1915–73), though her poetry is in many ways typical of the traditionalist tendencies of the time: it is firmly rooted in an Austrian rural setting that remained virtually untouched by the war and its upheavals, the female speaker casts herself in traditional gender roles, incorporating biographical elements, and the prime theme is the poet's relationship with God. Growing up in impoverished, isolated circumstances and suffering from poor health and impaired vision and hearing, Lavant was a self-taught poet who learnt her craft above all from Rilke and Trakl. Her mentor was Ludwig von Ficker, who had gained prominence especially as publisher of *Der Brenner* — one of the key periodicals before the First World War — and had already supported Trakl. Lavant's three main poetry collections were published by the prestigious Otto Müller Verlag, and her remarkable career culminated in the awards of the Georg-Trakl-Preis (1954 and 1964) and the Großer Österreichischer Staatspreis für Literatur (1970).

Lavant's poems enact an ongoing address to God that takes the form of exhortation, accusation, questioning, and expressions of hope, with the "I" of the speaker providing a unifying force in the poems and imparting an authenticity of emotional expression that contributed powerfully to her positive reception. Her imagery is concrete and sensuous, sustained by references to nature, biblical motifs, and an embodied self, as in the following lines from the poem "Vater, du gabst mir ein schwaches Gehör" (Father, you gave me poor hearing) in her first collection *Die Bettlerschale* (The Beggar's Bowl, 1956):[32]

Ich habe dir schon als Kind nie getraut,
weil meine Ohren dich niemals hörten,

und hob meine Herzwärme restlos auf
für die näheren Menschenstimmen.
Eine solltest du mir wohl lassen!
Wenn ich die brennenden Dornen zerkaue,
wenn ich das bittere rote Meer
allein überquere, läßt du mich dann
drüben die Menschen verstehen?

[Even as a child I did not trust you / because my ears never heard
you, / and I preserved all my heart's warmth / for the closer voices
of human beings. / You should allow me to keep one of these! /
When I chew the burning thorns, / when I cross the bitter red sea
/ alone, will you allow me / to understand the people on the other
side?]

The communication processes at the center of the poem are imbued with
tension: the poet's address to God is set against her distrust; and her contact with human voices is threatened by the loss of companionship on the
imminent lonesome journey. The depiction of her (actual) deafness is
saved from sentimentality by the confidence of the poet's disputing voice
and the strength of the images: feeling gains physical reality in the compound "Herzwärme"; the burning thorns recall the bush through which
God spoke to Moses, while negating divine communication; and the
image of the red sea contrasts God's united people with her own isolation.
The persona at the center of Lavant's poems moves between hope and
despair, searching for signs of a time beyond suffering, in a poetic
world that unites traditional religion, the magical qualities of pagan tradition, and personal myth: "Hinter dem Rücken der hiesigen Zeit / hab ich
der andern, der doppeltgehörnten / vogelfüßige Zeichen gemacht / bis
die Glorie herfand" (Behind the back of time here / I made bird-footed
signs to the other, the two-horned time / until glory found its way
here).[33]

The poetic legacy of Hölderlin, Rilke, and Trakl, and the evocative
strength of biblical language and imagery, are important features of continuity in Austrian poetry across the temporal divide of the war. For Paul
Celan (1920–70), these traditions permit a sustained engagement with the
Holocaust against the grain of a beloved mother tongue that had brought
death and untold suffering to his people. His is among the most metaphor-
ically rich, thought-provoking and finely crafted poetry produced in the
second half of the century in the German language. He only published the
first of his collections in Austria: *Der Sand aus den Urnen* (Sand from
the Urns, 1948), which he subsequently withdrew because of printing
errors. He settled in Paris in 1948, but remained in close contact with German writers and published all his later volumes in Germany. He gained

early fame with the poem "Todesfuge" (Fugue of Death), first published in 1948, which is melodious in style, lyrical in its refrains, and emotive in its imagery: "dein goldenes Haar Margarete / dein aschenes Haar Sulamith" (your golden hair Margarete / your ashen hair Shulamith).[34] His later poetry becomes increasingly laconic and densely textured, placing considerable demands on the reader's willingness to respond to semantic clues and the movement of the words.

The enigmatic meaning and concentrated diction in collections with titles such as *Sprachgitter* (Language Mesh, 1957), *Die Niemandsrose* (The No One's Rose, 1963) and *Lichtzwang* (Light Compulsion, 1970) gave rise to the view that his poetry was "hermetic" and his metaphors "absolute." That his aim was communication with his readers is evident in an early statement in which he comments on the first time he recited Schiller's famous poem, "Das Lied von der Glocke" (The Song of the Bell) at the age of six: "Wer weiß, ob nicht der Eindruck, den das auf meine Zuhörer machte, nicht alles Weitere ausgelöst hat . . ." (Who knows whether the impression this made on my listeners didn't motivate everything that followed?).[35] His poems convey loss in piercingly memorable images:

> WIE DU dich ausstirbst in mir:
>
> noch im letzten
> zerschlissenen
> Knoten Atems
> steckst du mit einem
> Splitter
> Leben. (2/261)
>
> [HOW YOU die out in me: // even in the last / worn-out / knot of breath / you are there, with a / splinter / of life.]

The neologism "sich aussterben" is formed along the lines of "sich ausweinen" (to cry oneself out), literally: "How you are dying yourself out in me," transforming the finality of the beloved person's death into an ongoing joint process.

Celan's poems are founded in moral commitment, and in some cases refer explicitly to historical events. An example is the concluding poem in the volume *Fadensonnen* (Thread Suns, 1968), written in 1967 in response to the Six-Day War in Israel and published in the Swiss and Israeli press. The first stanza reads as follows:

> Denk dir:
> der Moorsoldat von Massada
> bringt sich Heimat bei, aufs
> unauslöschlichste,

wider
allen Dorn im Draht. (2/227)

[Think of it: / the peat-bog soldier of Masada / is making a
homeland for himself, most / ineffaceably, / against / every barb
in the wire.]

The words "Denk dir," which are repeated at the start of each of the four
stanzas, exhort the reader to allow the words to penetrate into thought
and reflection. Gradually, the addressee "du" becomes the Jewish people,
as the poet justifies the state of Israel by evoking the past. The poem fuses
different periods of Jewish history, celebrating the new State of Israel as
the home of persecuted Jews. The reference to the bog soldier connects
the death camps, where the protest song "Moorsoldatenlied" (The Peat
Bog Soldiers) had been sung, with Masada, where the last Jewish rebel
soldiers held out against the Romans in order then to commit mass suicide;
the poem identifies these with the soldiers in the current war. Each of the
elements in the image has a historical basis, and the poem connects them
across time in a message for the present. The metaphor "unauslöschlich"
reverses the literal "Auslöschung" (extermination) of Jews in the Holocaust. "Dorn im Draht" evokes the barbed wire — "Stacheldraht" — of
the death camps, but gains added signifying power from the substitution of
the biblical "thorn." This in turn connects with the biblical metaphor
"Dorn im Auge" (thorn in the eye — English: flesh), which is developed in
the following stanza.

Celan sent the first version of the poem to a friend, the poet Franz
Wurm, asking him "ob das, was hier zur Sprache zu kommen versucht,
dahin und auch einigermaßen zu sich kommt"[36] (whether what is here trying to become speech, arrives there and also more or less finds itself). The
meaning is here personified and shown groping for expression in language; it
is "prelinguistic," yet only gains its identity in language. This brief comment
shows a highly analytical approach to language, and yet not a rationalist one.
Celan's poems are not about language, but they reveal an acute sensitivity to
its nuances and communicative force, drawing the reader's attention inexorably to the poem's value as a "Zeugnis" (evidence, 2/31) of the past.

Ingeborg Bachmann (1926–73) grew up in Klagenfurt, but, like
Celan, she made her career in Germany and settled outside the German-
speaking countries — in Italy. Whereas Celan only attended one meeting
of the Gruppe 47, and his reading met with little success, Bachmann was
firmly integrated in the group and awarded the Preis der Gruppe 47 for her
volume *Die gestundete Zeit* (Mortgaged Time, 1953). Her second collection, *Anrufung des Großen Bären* (Invocation to the Great Bear, 1956),
was to be her last volume of poetry; although she wrote a number of
further poems, she subsequently focused on prose. Her poetry is mainly in

free verse, with powerful rhythms and richly evocative imagery in poems such as the hymnic celebration "An die Sonne" (To the Sun).[37] Many of her poems engage with the past in ways that were atypical of the work published at the same time in Austria. An example is the series entitled "Psalm" of 1953, which recalls the cosmic dislocations in Trakl's poem of the same name,[38] but has a specifically political focus: "Wie eitel alles ist. / Wälze eine Stadt heran, / erhebe dich aus dem Staub dieser Stadt, / übernimm ein Amt / und verstelle dich, / um der Bloßstellung zu entgehen" (How vain everything is. / Take a city and roll it here, / rise up from the dust of this city, / take over a public office / and dissimulate / in order to escape being exposed, 55). By recalling the biblical "All is vanity" (Eccles. 1: 1) — a prominent theme in German poetry of the Thirty Years' War — Bachmann establishes an elevated, timeless context that acts as a foil for the satirical portrayal of contemporary society where Nazi criminals were speedily integrated in public life, enabling cities to rise up from the ashes as if nothing had happened. The pun on "sich verstellen" and "bloßstellen" draws on the techniques of satirical wordplay used by Kraus and Brecht. By contrast with Lavant, whose speaker creates the effect of being congruent with her empirical self, Bachmann creates more varied personas. In the poem "Die gestundete Zeit" (37), the speaker projects an active, male identity and observes his beloved being obliterated and silenced by the sand, without turning back to rescue her like Orpheus. In "Dunkles zu sagen" (To Say Dark Things), Orpheus is evoked as the model for the poet: "Wie Orpheus spiel ich / auf den Saiten des Lebens den Tod" (Like Orpheus, I play / death on the strings of life, 32). Such gender tensions are unusual at this time in German literature, and taken much further in Bachmann's prose trilogy *Todesarten* (Ways of Dying, 1971–79).

Political themes become central in the work of Erich Fried (1921–88), whose collection *und VIETNAM und* (and VIETNAM and, 1966) attained cult status for the student movement in West Germany. His early collections *Deutschland* (1944) and *Oesterreich* (1945), published by the Austrian PEN Club and a Zurich publisher respectively, are already characterized by the directness that is typical for his work throughout, and by a range of poetic modes that tend toward the political without being propagandistic. While Brecht is less important overall for Austrian than for East and West German postwar poetry, Fried builds on his clear and forceful diction, thought-provoking word plays, effective punch-lines, and on his use of parody, as in his adaptation of the church hymn "Ein feste Burg" (A Strong Fortress) by Martin Luther for a poem attacking the authorities in connection with the controversial death of the terrorist Ulrike Meinhof (268).

Like Brecht, Fried does not limit himself to political verse. His love poems in the collection *Liebesgedichte* (Love Poems, 1979) are moving by their very simplicity:

Im warmen Bett schlägst du
wirklich du
nackt die Decke zurück
und streckst mir
zum Einzug
zwei lebende Arme entgegen[39]

[In the warm bed you / truly you / naked, fold back the cover /
and stretch out toward me / for entry / two living arms]

Unlike Brecht, who carries on the tradition of emulating classical forms —
for example in his hexameter adaptation of the Communist Manifesto —
Fried tends more toward short, metrically free forms, experimenting
already in the 1950s with the type of permutation that was developed further in concrete poetry (e.g. "Adam und Eva," 1/123–4), creating montage effects with documentary material, or recasting "found" texts in
poetic form (e.g. a newspaper advertisement for police dogs in "Tier-
markt/Ankauf," Animal Market/Buying, 2/26–27). He is a master of the
aphoristic poem, as in the final poem of *und VIETNAM und*, entitled
"Anpassung" (Conforming):

Gestern fing ich an
sprechen zu lernen
Heute lerne ich schweigen
Morgen höre ich
zu lernen auf (1/400)

[Yesterday I began / to learn to speak / Today I am learning to be
silent / Tomorrow I will / stop learning]

Fried here continues an endeavor that had earlier driven the work of
Kraus, Brecht, and Soyfer: commenting on developments in Germany and
Austria over the entire era of the Cold War from his vantage point in London, he uses the power of the poetic word to make the reader aware of the
need to engage with current political events if society is to be humane.
While the past continues to act as a reminder of how conformism destroys
humanity, his concern throughout is with the dangers of the immediate
present.

Language Games

The traditionalist forces that dominated the literary scene in Austria during
the aftermath of the war were initially effective in suppressing younger
writers who looked to avant-garde movements rather than to the classics,

and who were experimenting with new uses of language and form. While the periodicals *Neue Wege* (New Paths) and *Stimmen der Gegenwart* (Voices of the Present) provided important publication opportunities for experimental work by poets such as Ernst Jandl (1925–2000), Friederike Mayröcker (1924–), H. C. Artmann (1921–2000), and Andreas Okopenko (1930–), book publishers were conservative. Okopenko comments in the afterword to his volume *Gesammelte Lyrik* (Collected Poems) published in 1980 that media other than such specialist outlets remained "hermetisch verschlossen" (hermetically sealed)[40] until the late 1950s or early 1960s and that much of his work had had to remain "Tiefkühlware" (frozen goods, 168). Unlike Jandl, Mayröcker, and the poets of the Wiener Gruppe, he only came into his own as a lyric poet in subsequent decades, latterly with inventive collections of "Lockergedichte" (loosening poems) and "Spontangedichte" (spontaneous poems): mainly aphoristic verse based on wordplay, semantic association, and sound correspondence, composed according to varying principles into volumes that invite the reader to browse rather than read systematically, and that key into popular traditions of absurd verse. An example is the couplet entitled "*Mann, realistisch:* Krieg ist zwar sehr was Spannendes, / doch manchmal auch Entmannendes" (*Man, realistic //* War of course is fascinating / but now and then emasculating).[41] By drawing on colloquialisms, dialect, English, and advertising doggerel, he surprises the reader with the creative resources inherent in everyday language. He was awarded the Großer Österreichischer Staatspreis für Literatur in 1998 and the Georg-Trakl-Preis in 2001 — late accolades for a poet who failed to find a way into the public arena in the postwar years.

The strength of the conservative establishment encouraged innovatively inclined poets to find alternative means of developing their aesthetic, not only individually, but also in cooperative ventures. The most prominent group to emerge was the Wiener Gruppe, which consisted mainly of the poets Gerhard Rühm (1930–), Konrad Bayer (1932–64), Oswald Wiener (1935–), and Friedrich Achleitner (1930–), with H. C. Artmann also contributing intermittently. Meeting in bars, they explored the performative dimension of poetry, and they were able to draw on a diversity of talents to develop interdisciplinary forms: Rühm was also a composer, Wiener a jazz musician, and Achleitner an architect. The group constituted itself in the mid 1950s, was most active in the years 1957 to 1959, and finally disintegrated with Konrad Bayer's suicide in 1964. While it was firmly rooted in the cultural scene in Vienna, it connected up with earlier and concurrent projects outside Austria, seeing itself in the tradition of Dada and the *Sturm*-Kreis, and pursuing initiatives with Eugen Gomringer in Switzerland and Helmut Heissenbüttel in Germany.

The Wiener Gruppe responded creatively to a general heightened interest in language, as is emphasized retrospectively by Wiener: "*Sprache* [schien] die nabe aller einsicht und allen umgangs" (*Language* [seemed to be] the hub of all insight and social interaction).[42] An immensely fruitful impetus came from Ludwig Wittgenstein, initially from his *Tractatus* (1921), in which he uses the tools of logic to delineate the boundaries of language, and then especially from the *Philosophische Untersuchungen* (Philosophical Investigations, 1953). Wittgenstein here focuses on the interplay between natural language and thought, highlighting indeterminacies and fuzzy edges through the analogy between language and "Spiel" (play/game). He uses metaphor in order to explore the power of language to structure thought, making the reader conscious of language as a means not of defining, classifying, and fixing ideas as abstract entities, but of exploring, shaping, and modifying them in pragmatic interaction with the world. A number of factors made the Wiener Gruppe particularly receptive to Wittgenstein. Their avant-garde aspirations fostered an intellectual approach to poetry: as Wiener highlights, they strove to eliminate the participation of emotions in poetry in order to develop a systematic "forschungsprogramm" (research program, 49). Wittgenstein was relatively unknown in Austria and offered an innovative angle on language, with the "open" structure of the *Philosophical Investigations* encouraging experimentation. Moreover, he was a man of their time and an Austrian — a "zeitgenosse" (55) and "ein landsmann" (49). As a group, they could play "language games" with several participants and realize the performative aspect of language, and as poets in the specific cultural environment of Vienna, they could play out the possibilities of natural language in a concrete *Heimat* with its own indigenous idiom.

Contrary to Wittgenstein's concern with language in its communicative context, the tendency with poets of the Wiener Gruppe is to explore and move beyond the boundaries of conventional communication, thereby carrying out a programme of poetic investigations. This is evident in Rühm's poem "darum spiel ich" (that's why I play):[43]

> ich bin ein spielball der wellen
> bin ein spielball des geschicks
> bin ein spielball und so weiter
> und so weiter und sonst nix
>
> darum spiel ich öfters fussball
> handball kopfball und ballett
> roll von einem ort zum andern
> nett fett bett adrett

> [i'm a playball of the waves / i'm a playball of fate / i'm a playball and so on / and so on and that's all // that's why i often play football / handball / headball and ballet / roll from one place to another / nice fat bed neat]

In the first stanza, a conventional metaphor involving the word "Spiel" (being tossed about by the waves, being a plaything of fate) is gradually divested of meaning in a series of permutations that culminate in the colloquial negation "nix" (nothing), which rhymes with the elevated "geschicks" (of fate). The connector "darum" (for that reason) suggests a logical connection between the first and second stanza, but only yields a verbal connection through the word "spiel." What starts off as a series of ball games ends with "Kopfball" — a pass using the head in soccer rather than a game in its own right — and the activity of playing ballet, which extends the use of "spielen" beyond the boundaries of conventional idiom. The poem concludes with a series of words that are connected only by their sound, without any logical or grammatical connection. Following its portentous beginning, the poem has thus gradually freed the words from their communicative function and logical context, culminating in an exuberantly meaningless play of words. By projecting himself as the object of a game, then as a player, and finally as a ball, the poet experiments with different roles without taking control of the game. The poem thereby involves the reader in a linguistic process where conventional language games turn into free play.

The poets of the Wiener Gruppe produced a considerable body of dialect poetry, an enterprise which H. C. Artmann initiated with his volume *med ana schwoazzn dintn* (with a black ink, 1958). While this tends to be viewed as entirely distinct from the dialect verse of the "folk" tradition, the binding force of regional identity and the oral nature of dialect contributed to making it an effective medium for performance, including scatological jokes that are more typical of the dialect context than the registers otherwise found even in concrete poetry: "waun s / aun da schenan blaun donau / schdinggd // daun / hod da johann schdrauss / im soag / an schas lossn" (when it / stinks / by the beautiful blue danube // then / johann strauss / in his coffin / has let off a fart).[44] The dialect verse is enormously varied, however, including permutations of stock phrases on the one hand and long ballads such as H. C. Artmann's sensationalist Bluebeard renderings on the other. It permits natural language to be explored through the tension between regionally specific orality and supra-regional script. Whereas the effects of transcription defamiliarize the homely idiom for Austrians, readers in other German-speaking areas are faced with their common language in an unfamiliar guise. The structural techniques of concrete poetry remove the words from the language-specific context of everyday communication and transform them into a potentially universal medium.

During the period when West German writers tended to focus on the need for political commitment, the concept of poetry as a game served as a productive means of broadening the spectrum of literary possibilities. It enabled poetry to act subversively through the language rather than as a rhetorical tool. For Ernst Jandl, playing with language — "das Spiel mit

Sprache" (11/188–89) — is fundamental to all types of poem, while permitting different types of freedom and constraint with respect to the rules. The prime purpose of the game, in his view, is to divest language of its everyday function as a means of communication in order to evolve moves and combinations on the basis of rules that are specifically poetic. Looking back over the twentieth century, he sees invention both as freedom and as constraint:

> [Die] seit Beginn unseres Jahrhunderts [. . .] gewonnene Freiheit für die aktiv Partizipierenden ist groß, aber nicht grenzenlos. Für die Puristen etwa beinhaltet sie die Abstinenz von den meisten der bisher praktizierten Spielregeln. Das führt zu einer neuen Art von Nötigung: die Hervorbringung von Kunst wird weitgehend identisch mit der Erfindung neuer Spielregeln. (11/188–89)

> [[The] freedom won since the start of our century for the active participants is considerable, but not boundless. For the purists, it entails the abstinence from most of the rules that have been used in the past. This leads to a new type of coercion: the production of art becomes largely identical with the invention of new rules.]

Contrary to the Romantic concept of originality, which was invested in the author, this type of invention is focused in the text, with aleatory poems constituting an extreme realization of the principle. For the reader, each text potentially presents itself as a new game, and the act of reading becomes a process of discovering relationships between elements of language that may confound rational expectations and set up connections based on analogy or contrast, or evolve complex patterns of sound and rhythm. While many Austrian poets in the latter decades of the twentieth century have challenged their readers in this way at certain points, purism has tended to give way to more accessible forms of dialogue with the reader.

Jandl himself was never a purist: he engages his reader's interest with a lively mixture of familiar and unfamiliar techniques, word plays and amusing surprise effects, appealing to children as well as to adults: characteristically, his final collection is entitled *peter und die kuh* (peter and the cow, 1996). The synaesthetic experiments and multimedia effects of concrete poetry are played out in a series of poems that include a "kaltes gedicht" (cold poem) and a "desinfiziertes gedicht" (disinfected poem) (10/153–54). In "stummes gedicht" (silent poem), the heavily theorized stimulation of different senses in concrete poetry is connected with the Romantic ideal of originality, with both being subverted in a broken promise: "zum ersten mal / wird ein gedicht / gerochen" (for the first time / a poem can be / smelled, 10/156). In "gewürfeltes gedicht" (poem thrown with the dice, 10/147), the poet utters the numbers one to six to instigate the first six lines of the poem, only to allow his creation to silence him in the seventh: "mit *sechs* entfaltet sich großes gewächs / schnürt mich ein und beendet mein sinnen" (with *six* a large plant burgeons / strangles me and ends my deliberations). The systematic language experiments of earlier decades here become funny and thought-provoking games that play ironically with the concept of poetic creativity while appealing to the imagination, satisfying the reader's expectations to the extent of providing a strong sense of closure. More than any other postwar poet, Jandl was able to move between serious and popular culture and between written and spoken forms of poetry, appealing to a broad readership and attracting large audiences to lively performances. His work is a celebration of the anarchic power of language: "die rache / der sprache / ist das gedicht" (the revenge / of language / is the poem, 10/89).

"Where Are We Now?"

The fascination with language that prompted the language games of the Wiener Gruppe has continued to stimulate younger Austrian poets such as Ferdinand Schmatz (1953–), who sees himself carrying on the avant-garde tradition, and Raoul Schrott (1964–), who builds on the group's theoretical reflections in his theoretical volume *Fragmente einer Sprache der Dichtkunst* (Fragments of a Language of Poetry, 1997). However, toward the end of the century, a broadening of concerns is evident, as poets encompass overtly personal experience in their poetry and develop an increasing interest in the interaction between poetry and the empirical world.

A transition from a language-based world into one that is grounded empirically can be traced in the work of Peter Waterhouse (1956–). His collection *passim* (1986) self-referentially signals a world consisting of text. In a series of eight poems entitled "Sprache 1" (Language 1) etc.,[45] words relating to speech acts foreground language as the prime means of connecting disparate aspects of the world: the clouds, items of clothing, facial features, geographical features. The poem "Sprache 2" consists of one line only, posing the question "Glauben Sie mir das Wort Blume?" (Do you believe me when I say the word flower?, 86). Focusing on the relationship between truth, object, and language, the question situates this key issue in the philosophy of language precariously between speaker and addressee. In other poems, too, language is the central concern. The first poem in the collection, entitled "Wo sind wir jetzt?" (Where Are We Now?, 7), begins with a contradiction: "O ja: O nein" (Oh yes: Oh no). The convergence of present time and present space is enacted in the mouth of a chewing beetle: "Minimales knackendes Geräusch / die Welt knistert winzig" (Tiny crackling sound / the world rustles minutely) — it is a world that is withdrawn in the following section of the poem, which takes the reader into the interstices between statement and negation. In the final lines, a dialogue ensues that moves from repetitious questions into typographically complex references to a thing — "Baum" (tree) — and time. The poem finally merges into language itself: "Es ist ein / Toben um Sprache" (There is a / Raging around/about language). Where Wittgenstein's *Tractatus* ends with human silence at the boundaries of language, Waterhouse centers on language and surrounds it with chaotic, unstructured sound. By contrast with the precise evocation of the world inside the beetle's mouth, however, the final gesture seems unintentionally bathetic, an empty gesture toward a self-sufficient world of language that has ceased to yield more than platitudes.

"Wo sind wir jetzt?" takes the reader to the point where language and world have ceased to interact meaningfully, while neither is capable of constituting meaning on its own. A change of perspective is evident in the volume *Prosperos Land* (2001), where Waterhouse offers the reader a textual landscape that no longer has a center in language, but is grounded multifariously in geographical landscapes, historical time, and personal experience. In a collection of extremely brief poems in the style of the haiku, usually consisting of three lines, the speaker responds to observations made on journeys through Carinthia, Slovenia, and Italy. Three poems are distributed spaciously across each page, inviting the reader to travel with the eye and mind, exploring connections across landscapes and people through the perspective of the poet as traveler. The volume gives a sense of place, but it transcends cultural specificity as words link different poems and parts of the book, and a form belonging to an entirely different time and culture further dispels the continuity of a particular cultural context.

A move into more empirical spheres is evident also in the work of Friederike Mayröcker, whose earlier collections are remarkable for their idiosyncratic use of language and resistance to interpretation. The poems in *Das besessene Alter* (The Possessed Age, 1992) and the poetic diary from 1996–2001 entitled *Mein Arbeitstirol* (My Working Tyrol, 2003) tend to be shorter than those of earlier collections, and make more sparing use of special typographical effects. Recognizable settings ground the stream of associative connections and provide contexts for the characteristic neologisms. The sensuous quality of her language is intensified by comparison with earlier collections, and the poems sustain a sense of active dialogue, many of them beginning or ending with a dedication, addressing a "du" (you), and evoking emotional relationships. Mayröcker's creative use of word elements gives unexpected vibrancy to small details like the pansies in the first lines of "Flugschrift" (Aeroscript):[46]

diese um ihre Köpfe *verstürmten*
Öhrlinge Stiefmütterchen gelb-
ohrig (zerlegt) isabellen-
farben vom brausenden

April, und legten sich vornüber
beetwärts

[*stormed* around their heads / these earlings pansies yellow /
eared (dismantled) isabelline / by blustery / April, and lay
forward / toward the flowerbed]

There are many explicit connections with poetic tradition in Mayröcker's
work: for example, the name of Hölderlin runs through several poems in
Das besessene Alter like a leitmotif (31–34), and her creative handling of
morphology, her use of inversion, and occasional invocations at times recall
the tradition of elevated hymnic verse. However, the resonances from the
Bible, Trakl, and Rilke that were characteristic of so much verse written in
the earlier decades of the century have receded. Her voice is very much her
own, entering into dialogue mainly with contemporaries such as the poets
Oskar Pastior, Thomas Kling, or Peter Waterhouse, and above all — across
the boundary of death — with her partner Ernst Jandl.

Mayröcker's late collections reveal a more overtly personal and emotional dimension than her earlier work, a tendency that accords with a general trend toward personal and autobiographical literature in German and
is evident also in other poetry published by Austrian writers around the
turn of the millennium. Personal memories and reflections on relationships
constitute the focus of the collections by Evelyn Schlag(1952–), whose
volume *Brauchst du den Schlaf dieser Nacht* (Do You Need the Sleep of this
Night, 2002) takes the reader through elegiac poems on love and loss,
evoking recollections of significant moments from the past: a conversation
following an illness, the purchase of a hat with a partner, the imagined life
story of two teddybears.[47] The poem "Mythologie" (Mythology, 92) is
concerned not with the timeless myths of peoples, but with her own empa-
thetic response as a child to the heroic stallion in the 1960s television series
Fury — a memory that is rescued from triviality as the poet renews its personal meaning. While Schlag's work is less obviously motivated by linguistic experimentation than that of many of her colleagues, she sees it as being
specifically Austrian for linguistic reasons, identifying a predilection for
wordplay as a national characteristic: "There is a subversive power in the
way Austrians use language, because very often we have that underdog
feeling vis-à-vis a German German-speaker."[48] The comment suggests that
at the end of the twentieth century, there is still a pronounced need for a
distinct identity among Austrian poets — and a sense that this identity continues to be under threat from the larger German neighbor. Consistent
with this identity is the tradition in which Schlag situates her work: it is
indebted to Rilke, Celan, and the Austrian writer Ilse Aichinger.[49] Schlag's
work thereby testifies to the continuity of a remarkably productive tradition in Austrian poetry.

The empirical world takes on a very different poetic shape in the work of Raoul Schrott, and his poetic ambitions go far beyond the German tradition to encompass a European poetic heritage of over four thousand years. Holder of a professorial qualification in comparative literature, he projects himself as a learned poet in the humanist tradition, connecting language, poetry, and science in intellectually demanding conceits: his collection *Tropen* (1998) provides the reader with a (fictional) dictionary definition of the title word on the dust jacket, including the Greek meanings of the word *tropos* and the two meanings of the German plural noun "Tropen": "tropics" and "tropes."[50] The volume moves through different times and disciplines, combines treatises on scientific topics with historical discourses on script and reflections on the function of tropes, and juxtaposes running prose with poetic texts and pictograms in varying typographical configurations. A poetic history of mountains unites the perspectives of Petrarch, Dante, and Shelley commenting on their historical ascents of peaks such as Mont Ventoux and Mont Blanc with the voice of Schrott commenting on his ascent of the Austrian Wildspitze and Graukogel. Prose is transformed into free verse to bring out the poetic quality of quoted texts, by eliminating capitals, inserting line breaks, and punctuating the sentences with the raised, centered dots that were the hallmark of that most mannered of German poets, Stefan George. In this way, too, scientific explanations by Galileo or Einstein gain new luminance. The subtitle of the collection is *Über das Erhabene* (On the Sublime): Schrott thereby situates his work in the most illustrious tradition of rhetorical and poetic theory (206). However, he avoids the emotive flights of the sublime style, instead reaching out through quotations into the realm of scientific discourse.

Schrott not only moves between different registers, but blurs the boundaries between different types of text as well as "primary" and "secondary" literature. Where Mayröcker resists interpretation by creating texts that are self-sufficient, Schrott provides the explication alongside the poem and offers poetic texts that have their origins in existing discourse. Compilation and translation are as important to his enterprise as the origination of text, as is evident in the anthology *Die Erfindung der Poesie: Gedichte aus den ersten viertausend Jahren* (The Invention of Poetry: Poems from the first four thousand years, 1997), in which he offers a polemical treatise on poetics in order then to introduce the reader to the work of great European poets, ranging from the verse of the first known author, a priestess writing in Sumerian in the twenty-fourth century B.C., to the verse of the Welsh poet Dafydd ap Gwilym from the fourteenth century A.D. Schrott's theoretical criticism of the German tradition is reflected in his omission of poetry in German from a global heritage to which he himself claims to look for inspiration.

Schrott is not alone in seeking to make his mark as a *poeta doctus* in the field of German literature: to date, his work stands in the shadow of the equally learned German poet Durs Grünbein, winner of the coveted

Büchner-Preis in 1995. Schrott sees himself in competition with this German rival, as is evident when he attacks Grünbein in good humanist style without doing him the honour of mentioning his name.[51] Rivalry also motivates Schrott's insistence that Austrian poets like himself benefit from being bilingual — "zweisprachig" — by comparison with the monolingual Germans (*Fragmente*, 115–17). This is ironic insofar as Schrott selects those registers of German for his work that are supra-regional, and indeed presents writing rather than oral performance as the prime medium of poetry: his thematic and visual foregrounding of script in *Tropen* is matched by his emphasis on the primacy of script in his anthology. Making a virtue of the transitoriness of the oral tradition, he designates transmission through script as the criterion for including an author, claiming that it signals an incipient awareness of language as an independent poetic medium.[52]

Schrott's elaborate displays of erudition and his emphasis on the primacy of the written medium can be seen as a means of securing prominence in a cultural context that has given mass culture and literary performance an increasingly important role. The performative potential of poetry has been important in Austria throughout the postwar period: the country has a tradition of literary festivals going back to the 1960s and 1970s, when the arts festival Steirischer Herbst (Styrian Autumn) in Graz and the Klagenfurt literary festival were instituted, and both concrete poetry and dialect poetry favored oral delivery. A newer development has been the emergence of poetry slam in cities such as Vienna, Innsbruck, Salzburg, and Linz, which attracts young audiences to a type of performative poetry event that depends on rule-governed spontaneity and sees itself as part of pop culture. Poetry here once again becomes a game, but one that focuses on entertainment without intellectual aspirations, and it looks for its tradition not to old Europe, but to America. Yet it is significant that the inimitably Viennese poet Jandl is retrospectively seen by Austrian slam enthusiasts as one of them.[53]

The popularity of performative modes is symptomatic of a changing view of poetry across national borders, with a stronger emphasis on its qualities of sound, its affinities with music, and its entertainment value. Austrian poetry is well placed to respond to this development creatively, given its lively heritage of performative verse. However, it seems unlikely that this will significantly weaken written forms. Rather, it is to be anticipated that Austrian poets will continue to draw on the whole range of linguistic possibilities, and exploit the productive interaction between competing traditions.

Notes

[1] See Rainer Maria Rilke, *Werke. Kommentierte Ausgabe*, ed. Manfred Engel et al., 5 vols. (Frankfurt: Insel, 1996–2003), 2: 113. Following first mention of an

edition in the notes, references will be given in the text in the form of the page number; the volume number (followed by a slash) is specified only where there are references to more than one volume of the edition.

[2] The work is dedicated to Wera Ouckama-Knoop (1900–1919), the daughter of friends, whose premature death touched Rilke deeply.

[3] Letter to Katharina Kippenberg, 23.2.1922, in Rilke / Kippenberg, *Briefwechsel* (Wiesbaden: Insel, 1954), 455.

[4] Alexander Lernet-Holenia, *Das lyrische Gesamtwerk*, ed. Roman Roček (Vienna and Darmstadt: Zsolnay, 1989), 95; see also 234–36 and 353–58.

[5] For the epithet "Sterilke" see Karl Kraus, "Notizen," *Die Fackel* 27 (1925–26), nos. 706–11 (Dec. 1925), 54 (in reprint, ed. Heinrich Fischer, 39 vols. [Munich: Kösel, 1968–76], vol. 31). For the remaining quotations, see K. Kraus, "Winke für die Schwangerschaft," *Die Fackel* 28 (1926–27), nos. 743–50 (Dec. 1926), 82 (in reprint, vol. 32).

[6] Erika Mitterer, "Briefwechsel in Gedichten mit Rainer Maria Rilke 1924–1926," in E. Mitterer, *Das gesamte lyrische Werk*, ed. Martin G. Petrowsky and Petra Sela, 3 vols. (Vienna: Edition Doppelpunkt, 2001), 1: 29–117; here: 43. See also Rilke, *Werke*, 1: 333. The two poets only met in November 1925, when Mitterer visited Rilke; his letters are concentrated in the summer of 1924, while her letters continue until December 1926. The correspondence has received little attention to date. The most sensitive discussion of Rilke's contribution is to be found in Ulrich Fülleborn's commentary in Rilke, *Werke*, 2: 769–71, 818–29. See also Katrin Kohl, "Dialogic Transformations: The Poetic Correspondence between Erika Mitterer and Rainer Maria Rilke," in *After Duino. The Later Poetry of Rainer Maria Rilke*, ed. Karen Leeder and Robert Vilain (provisional title, forthcoming, 2007).

[7] See the dismissive discussion of the correspondence by Manfred Engel, "Briefwechsel in Gedichten mit Erika Mitterer," in *Rilke-Handbuch. Leben — Werke — Wirkung* (Stuttgart and Weimar: Metzler, 2004), 432–34.

[8] See especially the poem "Da ich dir schrieb, sprang Saft," Rilke, *Werke*, 2: 372. Rilke did not send this poem to Mitterer.

[9] Mitterer published a number of volumes of poetry after the war, including *Klopfsignale* (Knocking Signals, 1970) and *Das unverhüllte Kreuz* (The Uncovered Cross, 1985), and throughout her career she also wrote novels, including *Alle unsere Spiele* (1977, reissued in 2001, tr. *All Our Games*, 1988).

[10] Franz Werfel, *Das lyrische Werk*, ed. Adolf D. Klarmann (Frankfurt: Fischer, 1967), 448.

[11] Karl Kraus, *Schriften*, ed. Christian Wagenknecht, 20 vols. (Frankfurt: Suhrkamp 1989), 9: 339.

[12] See Erwin Chvojka, "Einleitung," in Theodor Kramer, *Gesammelte Gedichte*, ed. E. Chvojka, 3 vols. (Vienna et al.: Europaverlag 1984), 1: 7–22; here: 14.

[13] Jura Soyfer, *Das Gesamtwerk* (Vienna, Munich et al.: Europa, 1980), 59.

[14] Josef Weinheber, *Sämtliche Werke*, ed. Friedrich Jenaczek (Salzburg: Müller, 1980–), 2: 7–127. In the following discussion of Weinheber's work, I am indebted

to Mark Elliott, "German Poetry beyond the Boundaries of the Nazi Era: The Modernist Legacy" (Diss., University of Oxford, 2006).

[15] *A Companion to Twentieth-Century German Literature*, ed. Raymond Furness and Malcolm Humble (London and New York: Routledge, 1991), 289.

[16] *Bekenntnisbuch österreichischer Dichter*, ed. Bund deutscher Schriftsteller Österreichs (Vienna: Krystall, 1938), 113–16.

[17] See the popular history by Fritz Martini, *Deutsche Literaturgeschichte von den Anfängen bis zur Gegenwart* (Stuttgart: Kröner 1949), 551–53; his stylistic revisions for the 1968 edition (601–2) left the picture of Weinheber unaltered.

[18] Wolfgang Beutin, Klaus Ehlert et al., *Deutsche Literaturgeschichte: Von den Anfängen bis zur Gegenwart* (Stuttgart: Metzler, 1979), 364; similarly in the revised and expanded fourth edition (Stuttgart and Weimar: Metzler, 1992), 453.

[19] In the revised and expanded sixth edition of Beutin, Ehlert et al. (2001), Weinheber is mentioned only once as part of a list of names, erroneously — and ironically — as an author of the "Innere Emigration" (484).

[20] Heinrich Zillich, ed., *Bekenntnis zu Josef Weinheber: Erinnerungen seiner Freunde* (Salzburg: Akademischer Gemeinschaftsverlag, 1950).

[21] Marcel Beyer, *Falsches Futter* (Frankfurt: Suhrkamp, 1997), 16. See Katrin Foldenauer, "A Conception of Lyric Poetry and its Deconstruction — the Austrian Poet Josef Weinheber and his Reception in the Work of Marcel Beyer," in *Austrian Studies* 12 (2004) (*The Austrian Lyric*, ed. Judith Beniston and Robert Vilain), 98–115.

[22] See Jeremy Adler and Richard Fardon, "An Oriental in the West: The Life of Franz Baermann Steiner," in Franz Baermann Steiner, *Selected Writings*, ed. J. A. and R. F., 2 vols. (New York and Oxford: Berghahn, 1999), 1: 16–100; here: 76.

[23] Franz Baermann Steiner, *Am stürzenden Pfad*, ed. Jeremy Adler (Göttingen: Wallstein, 2000).

[24] See Franz Baermann Steiner, *Eroberungen. Ein lyrischer Zyklus*, ed. H. G. Adler (Heidelberg and Darmstadt: Schneider, 1964), 99. On Steiner's reception of Rilke, see Elliott, "German Poetry beyond the Boundaries of the Nazi Era," 191–211.

[25] See Harold Bloom, *The Anxiety of Influence: A Theory of Poetry*, second edition (Oxford: Oxford UP, 1997), in which Bloom argues for a Freudian model of reception, identifying strategies of misreading and avoidance of great precursors as characteristic of the "strong" poet.

[26] Steiner, *Am stürzenden Pfad*, 345; translation see "Conquests I–VII," translated by Jeremy Adler, in Steiner, *Selected Writings*, 2: 249–66; here: 249. See also Part 13, *Am stürzenden Pfad*, 382.

[27] See Franz Hocheneder, "Nachruf und Nachlass bei Lebzeiten. Über die Schaffensbedingungen und Publikationsmöglichkeiten H. G. Adlers zur Zeit des englischen Exils," in *H. G. Adler*, special volume of *Text + Kritik* 163 (July 2004), 86–97; here: 94.

[28] "Gedichte aus den Lagern," in *H. G. Adler: Der Wahrheit verpflichtet. Interviews, Gedichte, Essays*, ed. Jeremy Adler (Gerlingen: Bleicher, 1998), 61–107 ("Theresienstädter Bilderbogen," 63–87).

29 "Zu Hause im Exil," in *H. G. Adler: Der Wahrheit verpflichtet*, 19–31; here: 25.

30 H. G. Adler, *Stimme und Zuruf. Gedichte* (Hamburg: Knaus 1980), 59 (from the poem "Wohin? Was wir uns erwarten," written in 1979).

31 Alexander Lernet-Holenia: "Gruß des Dichters. Brief an den *Turm*," in Petra Nachbaur and Sigurd Paul Scheichl, *Literatur über Literatur: Eine österreichische Anthologie* (Graz: Styria, 1995), 149–50; here: 149.

32 Christine Lavant, *Die Bettlerschale. Gedichte* (Salzburg: Otto Müller, 1956), 127.

33 Christine Lavant, "Hinter dem Rücken der hiesigen Zeit" (1960), in Lavant, *Kunst wie meine ist nur verstümmeltes Leben*, ed. Armin Wigotschnig and Johann Strutz (Salzburg: Müller, 1978), 91.

34 Paul Celan, *Gesammelte Werke*, ed. Beda Allemann and Stefan Reichert, 5 vols., Frankfurt: Suhrkamp, 1983), 1: 42. The poems "Wie du dich ausstirbst" and "Denk dir" (see below) are quoted by kind permission of Suhrkamp Verlag/Insel Verlag. For the translations I have drawn on Paul Celan, *Selected Poems*, tr. with an introduction by Michael Hamburger (Harmondsworth: Penguin, 1996), and John Felstiner, *Paul Celan: Poet, Survivor, Jew* (New Haven and London: Yale UP, 1995).

35 Letter to Hans Bender, November 18, 1954, in Paul Celan, *Briefe an Hans Bender*, ed. Volker Neuhaus (Munich: Hanser 1984), 35.

36 Letter to Franz Wurm, June 8, 1967, in Celan / Wurm, *Briefwechsel*, ed. Barbara Wiedemann (Frankfurt: Suhrkamp, 1995), 71.

37 Ingeborg Bachmann, *Werke*, 4 vols. (Munich: Piper, 1978), 1: 136–37.

38 Georg Trakl, *Dichtungen und Briefe. Historisch-kritische Ausgabe*, ed. Walther Killy and Hans Szklenar, 2 vols. (Salzburg: Müller, 1987), 1: 55–56.

39 Erich Fried, *Gesammelte Werke*, ed. Volker Kaukoreit and Klaus Wagenbach, 4 vols. (Berlin: Wagenbach, 1993), 2: 382 (from the poem "Einer ohne Schwefelhölzer"). These lines and the poem "Anpassung" are quoted by kind permission of Verlag Klaus Wagenbach.

40 Andreas Okopenko, *Gesammelte Lyrik* (Vienna and Munich, 1980), 168.

41 Andreas Okopenko, *Streichelchaos. Spontangedichte* (Klagenfurt and Vienna: Ritter, 2004), 102. See also A. Okopenko, *Immer wenn ich heftig regne. Lockergedichte* (Vienna: Edition Falter/Deuticke, 1992).

42 Oswald Wiener, "Wittgensteins Einfluß auf die 'Wiener Gruppe,'" in *die wiener gruppe*, ed. the Walter-Buchebner-Literaturprojekt (Vienna: Böhlau, 1987), 46–59; here: 46.

43 Gerhard Rühm, "darum spiel ich," in *Die Wiener Gruppe*, ed. G. Rühm (Reinbek bei Hamburg: Rowohlt, ²1985), 48. Quoted by kind permission of Gerhard Rühm.

44 Gerhard Rühm, *Sämtliche Wiener Dialektdichtungen* (Graz and Vienna: Droschl, 1993), 21.

45 Peter Waterhouse, *passim. Gedichte* (Reinbek bei Hamburg: Rowohlt, 1986), 85–92.

46 Friederike Mayröcker, *Das besessene Alter. Gedichte* (Frankfurt: Suhrkamp, 1992), 21.

47 Evelyn Schlag, *Brauchst du den Schlaf dieser Nacht. Gedichte* (Vienna: Zsolnay, 2002), 39, 72, 93.

[48] "A Conversation with Evelyn Schlag," in Evelyn Schlag, *Selected Poems*, translated by Karen Leeder, with an introduction by E. Schlag (Manchester: Carcanet, 2004), 161–68; here: 165.

[49] Evelyn Schlag, "Introduction," in *Selected Poems*, ix–xii (ix).

[50] Raoul Schrott, *Tropen. Über das Erhabene* (Munich and Vienna: Hanser, 1998).

[51] Raoul Schrott, *Fragmente einer Sprache der Dichtkunst: Grazer Poetikvorlesung* (Graz and Vienna: Droschl, 1997), esp. 21–22. Compare Durs Grünbein, *Galilei vermißt Dantes Hölle und bleibt an den Maßen hängen. Aufsätze 1989–1995* (Frankfurt: Suhrkamp, 1996), 20.

[52] Raoul Schrott, *Die Erfindung der Poesie. Gedichte aus den ersten viertausend Jahren* (Frankfurt: Eichborn, 1997), 14.

[53] In 2004, an announcement of a performance of Jandl's verse at the Salzburg Literaturhaus commended him as a "Slam-Poet, bevor es das Wort gab" (slam poet before the word existed) (http://www.br-online.de/kultur/literatur/lesezeichen/20041114/20041114_6.html) (5.12.2005).

7: Writing in Austria after 1945: The Political, Institutional, and Publishing Context

Anthony Bushell

AUSTRIA WAS LIBERATED FROM German occupation in May of 1945. By July of that year, while cities such as Vienna were still struggling with the ravages brought about by the fierce defense of the Reich's eastern borders, and some 34,000 Austrians had been killed in air-raids alone,[1] the debate on the future and the function of literature in postwar Austria was already receiving considerable attention from Austrians of all political persuasions. Immediately after the war Viktor Matejka had become head of Vienna's Department for Culture and Adult Education. He had been interned in Dachau by the National Socialists and was to emerge alongside Ernst Fischer as one of the best known of the Austrian Communists in the early postwar period. On 25 July 1945 Matejka gave a lecture in Vienna entitled "Was ist österreichische Kultur?" (What is Austrian Culture?), in which he rejected as a point of contact any of the many fateful dates in Austria's history, including the emergence of the First Republic following the collapse of the Austro-Hungarian Empire after the First World War, or the Austria immediately before the Nazi occupation:

> Mögen große Teile unseres Volkes Kultur rein sentimental als Erbe auffassen, wir sehen hier eine Aufgabe, die auf einem Ruinenfeld noch dringlicher geworden ist [. . .]. Es gibt daher kein Zurück auf 1789 oder 1848 oder 1918 oder 1934 oder gar 1938. Wir müssen uns unsere Kulturwelt selbst bauen.[2]

> [Even if large parts of the population regard culture in purely emotional terms as something inherited, we see here a challenge that has become more urgent, set, as it is, amidst a sea of destruction . . . For this reason there will be no going back to 1789 or 1848 or 1918 or 1934, let alone 1938. We must be the constructors of our own cultural world.]

Remarkably similar in both content and tone was a speech delivered before the Austrian Parliament by another former inmate of Dachau, Leopold Figl; on 21 December 1945, a day after he had become the conservative chancellor of the first freely elected postwar Austrian government, he declared:

Das Österreich von morgen wird ein neues, ein revolutionäres Österreich sein. Es wird von Grund auf umgestaltet und weder eine Wiederholung von 1918 noch von 1933, noch eine von 1938 werden [. . .] Wir wollen das neue, das junge Österreich![3]

[The Austria of tomorrow will be a new, a revolutionary Austria. It will be reformed from its very roots and there will be no repetition of 1918, or 1933, or 1938 . . . We seek an Austria that is new and young!]

Remolding Austrian Identity

Despite this emphasis upon a new beginning, all sides were soon to realize that the future would also be shaped by what was made of the past, and in literature it was striking how few new, young or revolutionary voices were allowed to be heard in postwar Austria. Matejka's position was contradicted in many ways by the views of Ernst Fischer. As Minister of Education in the first cabinet and provisional government, formed as early as April 1945 under Chancellor and President Karl Renner, Fischer was in a key position to influence the remolding of Austrian identity, yet even the Communist in him recognized that a labor force infected by years of National Socialist propaganda would need some evocation of the concept of Austria's past, drawing on a sense of patriotism and tradition, in order to be cleansed and rehabilitated politically.[4] The Österreichische Volkspartei (Austrian People's Party, ÖVP), to which Chancellor Figl belonged, issued fifteen guiding principles in a policy document released in June 1945 which included the explicit recognition of Austrian culture and Austria's past: "Zielbewußte Pflege des österreichischen Geistes und schärfste Betonung des eigenständigen österreichischen Kulturgutes, das in dem als Vätererbe auf uns überkommenen christlich-abendländischen Ideengut begründet ist."[5] (The conscious cultivation of the Austrian spirit and the most explicit emphasis upon unique Austrian cultural values which are founded in a body of Christian and western ideas inherited from previous generations.) Culture, and especially literature, was thus to be both instrumentalized and in many respects institutionalized by all political parties working in Austria after 1945, and the question of Austria's cultural legacy was to shape much of the debate as Austria re-emerged with its borders of 1938 restored. Now, however, the country was to be occupied for a decade by the four Allied powers that in turn brought their own very different concepts of the function of literature to the task of creating a postwar Austrian state. And while the Allies were keen to turn Austrians into good and safe Europeans, Austrian politicians were conscious that they had the more urgent task of first turning their fellow-citizens into good and self-assured Austrians.

The absence of an Austrian government in exile had had far-reaching implications for the nature of the re-emerging Austrian state and its cultural manifestations. In particular, no unifying philosophy of the "new" Austria had been developed by Austrians in exile during the *Anschluss* and the war years other than the desire to be disassociated from the German Reich. Thus, monarchists, Socialists, conservatives, Communists, Catholics and Jews alike all had reason to despise or extol elements of Austria's cultural history, but not the same elements, and yet each of the political and social groupings accepted that postwar Austrian literature could be pressed into service in the cause of promoting Austrian identity among its citizens.

It has been asserted that no country seized or overrun by the fascists or their allies, not even Germany itself, could show a higher proportion of its writers forced into exile than Austria.[6] Amongst the many who left Austria were those with a claim to being the country's most significant contributors to twentieth-century European literature; they included Robert Musil, Hermann Broch, Franz Werfel, Elias Canetti, Stefan Zweig and Joseph Roth. Their presence was to be denied to the Second Republic in its formative years, often through premature death. Many hundreds of other Austrian writers had been scattered throughout Europe and North and South America. In some instances, as in London, Austrians had been able to form loose associations, with either Socialist or Communist leanings, such as the Austrian Labour Club or the Austrian Centre. Yet the restoration of Austria's independence did not mark the ascendancy of these exile groups in the new Austria. For many artists and writers, temporary exile would turn into a permanent rejection of Austria. One researcher has established that of some one hundred and twenty-one Austrian writers known to have fled into American exile, nearly ninety (some 74%) remained permanently in the United States while less than 17% returned home to Austria.[7] A few had even succeeded in changing language. Robert Neumann, Hermynia zur Mühlen and Anna Gmeyner had moved across to English, the language of their exile, while others, such as Hilde Spiel, remained able to move confidently at both a linguistic and social level between both cultures. Yet others were simply left stranded after 1945, like the poet Theodor Kramer, who worked in England as a librarian but held on resolutely to the language of the country from which he had fled for his life.

In postwar Austria itself there was a noticeable lack of enthusiasm to encourage the return of exiled writers, and certainly little space at an institutional level was made available for them. A number of writers such as Hilde Spiel or Franz Theodor Csokor returned in the uniform of the Allies. But the passionate debate conducted in Germany about the possible return of Thomas Mann was commented upon with derision in Austria, and when Walter von Molo pleaded for Mann's return to Germany, this was greeted by one contributor to a leading Austrian literary journal as "demütiges Gebettel" (humble pleading).[8] Politicians certainly had little incentive to encourage their return. This was partly due to their own biographies: many of the leading political figures such as Renner were not the products of exile but had remained in Austria throughout the *Anschluss* and war years. To acknowledge the hardships and sacrifice of exile would be an admission of their own compromised moral and political position. If denazification of Austria's political ranks remained a half-hearted affair, it was inevitable that the endeavor to purge the ranks of Austrian writers would be equally lackluster. For the postwar political parties the desire not to lose the potential votes of those initially blacklisted by the Allies carried far more weight than meeting the needs and aspirations of Austrians in exile. Cold-war politics also meant that for the western occupying powers, detecting and combating Communism were soon to become far more pressing tasks than exposing writers' former allegiances to non-Communist ideologies. In January 1946 the Austrian Education Ministry issued its "Liste der gesperrten Autoren und Bücher" (list of proscribed authors and books). Writers whose name appeared on the ban were nevertheless read and in demand. The journal *Der Turm* reported in 1947 that according to the head of a public library in Vienna, young people in particular were reading the poetry of Josef Weinheber with pleasure.[9]

Well beyond the immediate postwar period there has been a tenacious belief among Austrians that the country had learned its lesson from its dis-astrous union with Hitler's Germany and had quickly come back to its senses, and so the respected Austrian historian Erika Weinzierl could write:

> Auch wenn viele Österreicher hohe Ränge in der nationalsozialistischen Hierarchie bekleideten und eine nicht geringe Zahl an Kriegsverbrechen beteiligt war, so hat doch in den letzten Kriegsjahren die Mehrheit der österreichischen Bevölkerung dem Nationalsozialismus als deutscher Herrschaft zumindest passiven Widerstand geleistet.[10]

> [Even if many Austrians had held high office in the National Socialist hierarchy and a far from insignificant number had been party to war crimes, nevertheless, in the final years of the war, the majority of the Aus-trian population had offered at least passive resistance to the German dominance of National Socialism.]

The belief that those who had remained in Austria had done enough to put themselves beyond censure or collective guilt was constantly reinforced by selective references to the Allies' Moscow Declaration of 1943, which had described Austria as Hitler's first victim, and this attitude among many Austrians permitted a wide-spread evasion of any act of self-scrutiny at all levels of Austrian society. For literature the situation was complicated fur-ther by the nature of the historical legacy. The conflict in Austria's literary community had not been a clear confrontation between pro-Nazi and anti-Nazi writers. The corporate, one-party state (*Ständestaat*) introduced by Chancellor Dollfuss after the Civil War in the mid 1930s had enlisted the help of many writers in advancing its cause, especially in the task of writing the fiction of an Austrian identity. These authors represented a grey area in the rehabilitation of Austrian literature after 1945. Significantly, the backgrounds of these writers reflected those of many of the key politicians and civil servants from the Dollfuss era who were entrusted after 1945 with the task of restoring — as opposed to creating — an Austrian state. Civil servants and writers alike had gone along with Dollfuss's authoritarian state and had then sat out the years of Austria under German control with greater or lesser degrees of personal compromise.

Representative of these writers were men such as Rudolf Henz. Strongly identifying with the conservative and Catholic stance of Dollfuss's *Ständestaat*, Henz had been head of the cultural section of Austrian Radio (RAVAG) before the war as well as a prominent personality in other organizations close to the governing Vaterländische Front (Fatherland Front).[11] According to one distinguished literary scholar, Klaus Amann, Henz also ingratiated himself with his new Nazi masters in 1938 by uttering anti-Semitic remarks.[12] After 1945, Henz was able to re-establish himself as a leading figure in Austrian literary life. Not only was he able to continue his own writing career but as editor of the journal *Wort in der Zeit*, a publication which can be regarded as the forerunner to one of Austria's most illustrious literary journals, *Literatur und Kritik*, he was in a position to exert considerable influence in promoting certain writers and literary tastes to the detriment of others. The literary scholar Karl Müller sees Henz as the archetypal literary figure in the restored Austrian republic:

> Henzens ideologische und literarische Position nach 1945 qualifizierten ihn als den Mann der Stunde: katholisch, kirchentreu, österreichisch, großkoalitionär, abendländisch, antikommunistisch, pragmatisch, ästhetisch traditionell, ordnungsverbunden, volksverbunden.[13]

> [Henz's ideological and literary position after 1945 qualified him as the man of the moment: Catholic, loyal to the Church, Austrian, favoring the grand coalition, defender of western and Christian values, anti-Communist, pragmatic, aesthetically conservative, non-radical, close to the people.]

Literary Journals

The literary journals that emerged immediately after the Second World War constituted an important rallying point for the literature of the newly formed Second Republic.[14] Some journals were very much the products and mouthpieces of the occupying powers, such as *Die Brücke* in the Soviet Zone, *Europäische Rundschau* in the French zone and *Erziehung* and *Kontinente* in the American zone. But a number of other journals were edited by prominent Austrian writers, such as *PLAN*, edited by Otto Basil, and *Lynkeus*, edited by Hermann Hakel. These early postwar journals brought to a restored Austria voices that were a far cry from the revolutionary and new Austria proclaimed by Figl or Matejka, a fact that is well illustrated by the journal *Der Turm*. The journal itself was a product of the Österreichische Kulturvereinigung, a cultural movement financed by the conservative ÖVP and close to the Catholic Church. The president of the association was Hans Pernter, who had been education minister in Chancellor Schuschnigg's cabinet between 1934 and 1938. The editor of *Der Turm* was Egon Seefehlner, and the journal betrayed a markedly conservative and religious character.[15] Paradigmatic for the literary values advocated by many of the literary organs appearing at the time, *Der Turm* reproduced in its first issue the famous juxtaposition "Preuße und Österreicher" (Prussian and Austrian) by Hugo von Hofmannsthal, a statement on the nature of the Austrian spirit. The fact that journals had recourse to a piece written by Hofmannsthal in 1917 was indicative of the retrogressive stance of many of the journals at this time. It is not surprising that many authors who had come to terms with the Austro-fascism of the 1930s and had served the state at the time by promoting supposedly Austrian values in their works were able to find a home and a continued literary existence in the Second Republic when the Austrian state encouraged writers to extol the specific and special nature of the Austrian character. In particular, through its patronage in the awarding of many literary prizes and stipends, the Austrian state secured the continued allegiance of writers who had been closely identified not only with the *Ständestaat* but also with National Socialist ideology. Henz himself received numerous distinctions after 1945, including Das Große Ehrenzeichen für Verdienste um die Republik Österreich in 1954 — a medal in recognition of his contributions to the Republic of Austria — and the Literaturwürdigungspreis der Stadt Wien in 1956. The well-known and popular writers Max Mell and Gertrud Fussenegger had displayed great enthusiasm towards union with Germany before the war. Mell had served in the 1930s as President of the writers' association Bund der deutschen Schriftsteller Österreichs, which had pronounced anti-Semitic leanings, while Fussenegger had welcomed the annexation and, like Mell, had been a member of the NSDAP.[16] They were representative of a generation of writers who continued their prewar literary careers in the "new" Austria and who were to find in the 1950s institutional recognition and sustenance through numerous state-sponsored literary awards.

The quiet rehabilitation of even the most compromised of Austrian writers was aided and abetted by the institutional guardians of German literature: the professional academics and university teachers working in the field of *Germanistik*. The most prominent of the Austrian Germanists active at the time of Austro-fascism and the *Anschluss* continued to work and publish after 1945. Adalbert Schmidt, Heinz Kindermann, Norbert Langer and, most controversially of all, Josef Nadler (1884–1963), had written in the spirit of the ethnic and racial approach to literature favored by the National Socialists. After the war they abandoned that position and adapted quickly to the state-approved approach of stressing the uniqueness of Austria within the German-speaking community. In their later work they avoided any confrontation with the vexed question of literature under the Nazis. Heinz Kindermann, for instance, in his postwar encyclopedic guide to Austrian writers, *Wegweiser durch die moderne Literatur in Öster-reich* (1954), suppressed all details relating to links with National Socialism. The party membership of Austrian Nazi writers such as Mirko Jelusich, Linus Kefer or Robert Hohlbaum is conveniently forgotten. A veil of silence and discretion is drawn by Kindermann in his entries for those writers who had resigned from the Austrian PEN Club after the Ragusa (Dubrovnik) affair in order to demonstrate their pro-German position. They included Bruno Brehm, Enrica Handel-Mazzetti, Franz Nabl, and Egon Caesar Conte Corti. At the same time Kindermann's entries on significant Austrian writers such as Karl Heinrich Waggerl and Josef Perkonig fail to mention their contributions to the publication calling for Austria's annexation, "Künstler bekennen sich zur Heimkehr ins Reich"[17] (Artists and Writers Speak Out in Favor of Austria's Return to the Reich). This institutional amnesia, paralleled and matched by the state's lethargy in the question of restitution for those disposed following the *Anschluss*, was in keeping with a postwar Austrian society anxious to heal wounds without the trauma of having first to cleanse them.[18]

The conservative writers of postwar Austria were for the most part happy to adhere to a vague Hofmannsthalian view of Austria in their work after 1945. The failure to perform a wholesale scrutiny of the established literary professionals added to the acute problems of younger writers trying to establish themselves. As editors men such as Henz or Ernst Schön-wiese, the latter as editor of the literary journal *das silberboot*, did little to encourage avant-garde writing. Schönwiese's Salzburg publication is especially instructive because it was, strictly speaking, the re-launching of a journal that had existed briefly before the war. And although Schönwiese did not exclude the work of younger writers, including occasional pieces from those who had been in exile, his interests were devoted principally to those writers established before the war. Literary movements such as Surrealism or Dadaism, which had been an anathema to the National Socialists and were largely unknown to the younger generation of Austrians after 1945, as well as the literature associated with some of the younger West German writers seeking a fresh start, found little response in the journal.

A few literary journals, by contrast, did attempt to make space for new voices, notably Otto Basil's *PLAN* (1945–48) and the journal *Neue Wege*, which became one of the few genuine outlets for the first postwar generation of Austrian writers as well being a mouthpiece for Austrian youth in general (*Neue Wege* had begun life in 1945 as *Theater der Jugend*, edited by Hans Zwanziger and Walter Hills. It was renamed *Neue Wege* in 1948).

This journal brought contributions from some of the best of the younger generation, including H. C. Artmann, Christine Busta, Herbert Eisenreich, Erich Fried, Ernst Jandl, Ernst Jirgal, Friederike Mayröcker, Andreas Okopenko, and Walter Toman.[19] For these writers and others, such as Wieland Schmied or Milo Dor, who were striving to revitalize Austrian writing, Austrian postwar society otherwise offered little encouragement: going well beyond the immediate postwar years, Claudio Magris has spoken of the "stagnantly conservative atmosphere of the 1950 and 1960s" with regard to Viennese and Austrian intellectual and social life.[20]

Restoration and Provocation

Ironically, the resistance to the new was not simply the preserve of those who had remained in Austria and in whose firm grip many of the institutional structures were to remain. Exile itself did not guarantee fresh perspectives. Not only was the Austrian state after 1945 willing to promote writers who had supported the annexation of Austria, even those who had been in exile had recourse to their work in order to foster an Austrian identity. For example, the exiled Austrian theater group Laterndl, perhaps the most significant focus of Austrian culture in London during the war, found itself performing works by writers such as Karl Schönherr, despite his open support for the *Anschluss*, because his oeuvre also included work that was considered a vital expression of the specifically Austrian theater tradition.[21] Nor did those returning to Austria from exile always bring a fresh impulse to the country's literary life or its cultural institutions. This is evident in the approach to the radio play in Austria. The *Hörspiel* was to become one of the great literary and innovative achievements of German literature in the early postwar period, especially in the British zone of occupation in Germany, where the BBC gave considerable assistance to the Germans. In Vienna, Hans Nüchtern resumed control of literary broadcasting in 1945 after his enforced exile, and his view of the genre was much more conservative. He saw little need to develop the *Hörspiel* beyond a concept of broadcast theater.[22] Without doubt the most glaring instance of returning exiles succeeding in preventing certain trends emerging in Austrian literature were the efforts of Hans Weigel and Friedrich Torberg, who, together with the director of Vienna's prestigious Burgtheater, Ernst Haeusserman, conducted a successful campaign to keep the plays of Bertolt Brecht off the Austrian stage for a major part of the 1950s and 1960s.

The Austrian state was in a strong position, for it possessed the necessary institutional means to endorse and perpetuate its preferences in literature since all school books and set texts under the Austrian educational system were subject to its approval. Well into the 1960s, those writers from the interwar years who were closely identified with the *Ständestaat* were generously represented in such works as school anthologies at the expense of younger writers.[23]

The difficulty of gaining recognition for new literature was made all the greater by the endeavor also to rescue what might be regarded as established "canonical" writers from their abuse at the hands of National Socialism. For example, in the 11 May 1946 edition of the Communist-orientated *Österreichisches Tagebuch*, Johann Muschik devoted an article to "Grillparzer und das Dritte Reich." At a more elusive level, those returning to work in the Austrian theater after a period of exile noticed that the very diction used on the Viennese stage had been corrupted, giving way to a bombastic and insensitive form of delivery described as "Reichskanzleistil" (the bureaucratic language and articulation of the National Socialist administration).[24]

New literature had also to wait for old accounts to be settled. There may have been no Austrian government in exile but there had been an Austrian PEN Club in London during the war, headed by Robert Neumann. From London attempts were made after 1945 to re-establish the Vienna branch under Csokor's leadership. As Csokor tried to mediate between the views of Austrian writers in exile and those who had remained in Austria, it became clear that resentments and divisions still ran deep among Austrian writers. The divisions were deepened further by a perception that the postwar PEN in Vienna stood too closely allied to the Soviet Union. (Both Ernst Fischer and Viktor Matejka were extremely active in the Club.) The Vienna PEN only gained widespread credibility when disillusioned Austrian Communists left the Party following the Soviet suppression of the Hungarian uprising in 1956. Nevertheless, the Club was to remain for many years subject to intense rivalries and extreme reactions among writers of the old guard. In October 1972 its president, the controversial and conservative writer Alexander Lernet-Holenia resigned as an expression of protest at the awarding of the Nobel Prize for literature to the West German "Bolshevik" Heinrich Böll. There followed an unseemly power struggle within the PEN Club, in which Hilde Spiel's candidature was thwarted by another former Jewish exile writer, Friedrich Torberg.

These wranglings among the older generation of writers reinforced the general impression among younger writers that literary life in Austria was firmly in the hands of those with little interest in promoting the works of the next generation. If Vienna was seen as an unwholesome bed of intrigue, then it is fair to say that provincial Austria offered little alternative encouragement. Postwar Austria, like West Germany, had been constituted as a federal republic in order to decentralize power. The various Austrian provinces also held a measure of patronage in promoting literature but this was usually of a pronounced conservative nature, especially in such provinces as Carinthia, and little structural or institutional support was available for writing of an even vaguely avant-garde nature.

In the late 1950s, Austrian literature witnessed an eruption of provocative literary events intended by the younger writers to challenge and outrage the ossified world of Austrian letters. Five young writers, Friedrich Achleitner, H. C. Artmann, Konrad Bayer, Gerhard Rühm, and Oswald Wiener formed a loose association that subsequently became known as the "Wiener Gruppe." In a series of staged readings, cabarets and "events" between 1957 and 1959 they introduced a spirit of anarchy and subversiveness (they would, for instance, smash a piano on stage); the value of such stunts resided not so much in the integrity of any particular literary statement as in the venting of a feeling of pent-up frustration which challenged the literary establishment that this younger generation found so suffocating.

Provocation was to remain a hallmark of much literary activity from this point on within Austrian literature. Not only did younger writers attack the generation before them, many of whom in their eyes bore a National Socialist taint, they began to assail Vienna's hold on literary production in Austria. Members of the first wholly postwar generation of Austrian writers such as Michael Scharang argued that they could gain nothing from the generation directly above them. Those who might have acted as models had been murdered by the National Socialists while the Austrian state had done little to encourage the return of those living abroad who might have offered a line of tradition.[25] Admittedly, by the standards of Paris and Berlin, Austria's part in the student movements of the 1960s, the ban-the-bomb protests, opposition to the war in Vietnam, and expressions of a nascent feminist movement remained a relatively mild affair. Years of grand coalition government had weakened rather than strengthened parliamentary government in Austria, and unrivalled economic prosperity appeared to confirm the Austrian path of neutrality and the nepotistic practice of distributing posts and offices between the two dominant parties.

Austrian literature entered a long phase of antagonism. The absence in Austria of newspapers of European standing meant that public opinion on literary matters was often formed at a banally superficial level by tabloid newspapers for which the literary developments from the 1960s on were an outrage. The heavily subsidized Austrian theater was a particular target for their invective, yet these attacks only encouraged writers and dramatists to produce more works openly intended to provoke. The works of Peter Handke, Wolfgang Bauer, and Thomas Bernhard were interpreted by the popular press as either degenerative or openly insulting to the Austrian state and its institutions. This hostility culminated most notoriously in the production by the German director Claus Peymann at the Burgtheater in 1988 of Bernhard's play *Heldenplatz*, a work in which every aspect of public life in the Second Republic is pilloried mercilessly.

State-sponsored and alternative literatures have not only run parallel to one another, they have often crossed and merged in a particularly Austrian way. Highly critical works attacking the duplicity and complicity of Austrian society often brought recognition from the state. The novel *Die Wolfshaut* gained its author Hans Lebert the Förderungspreis des Österreichischen Staatspreises in 1962.[26] His work represented an early example of a body of highly critical texts which took up the belated task of treating the almost taboo theme of Austrians' involvement in the Third Reich. This theme showed too the growing number of female writers active in postwar Austrian literature, with important contributions from authors as diverse as Marie-Thérèse Kerschbaumer, Anna Mitgutsch and Elisabeth Reichart. The election of Kurt Waldheim to the Presidency of the Republic in 1986 may have drawn unwelcome attention to the state of Austria in the light of the President's alleged war-time activities, yet for the first time almost since the ending of the Second World War the nation found itself at the centre of world attention, and the response of its writers became something more than a matter of domestic politics.

Other literary movements have also emerged from protests directed at state or civic decisions. The demonstrations surrounding the fate of a building used as part of the Vienna festival in 1976 were an example of attempts to create literary and cultural centers independent of state control. Arena, a house used to host youth cultural events at the festival, was meant to be demolished immediately after the festival. Instead, it was occupied and became a short-lived symbol of the alternative literary community in Austria. An atmosphere of confrontation outside the building, highlighted by the presence of leading younger writers on the one side and large units of police on the other, helped further the image of young Austrian literature as being politically engaged and highly critical of the state.

A profound and lasting challenge to the hegemony of Vienna over literary practice in Austria was represented by the formation in provincial Graz of the Forum Stadtpark and the emergence of the literary journal *manuskripte*. Provincial Styria of the 1950s was by no means a promising setting for the promotion of modern Austrian literature. It was the city fathers' reluctance to consent to the renovation of the disused Stadtpark-Café for use by local artists and writers that prompted a response from Graz's artistic community, culminating in the successful establishment of the building in November 1960 to act as a forum not only for literature but also for art, film, theater and cabaret. Its foundation was also a clear expression of the rejection of the tastes and attitudes associated with Vienna's PEN Club. The journal *manuskripte*, initiated by Alois Hergouth and Alfred Kolleritsch, grew out of this movement and quickly developed into Austria's leading avant-garde journal. Its unmistakable broad page format, the strikingly original art work of its covers, and its generous allotment of space to new writers and to work in progress gave the journal a unique place in Austria's literary life. There are few leading writers in Austria today whose work has not appeared at some stage in their career in the pages of *maunuskripte*. And in the course of the journal's history it has reflected many of the intellectual struggles taking place within Austria's literary community, exposing, as in the late 1960s, the divisions between heavily politicized writers such as Michael Scharang and Elfriede Jelinek on the one hand, and others such as editor Kolleritsch or Handke on the other, who represented a more artistically autonomous approach to literature.[27] Yet not even a vibrant journal such as *manuskripte*, which relies heavily on subsidies from the province of Styria and the city of Graz's cultural department, could hide the structural weakness in Austria's publishing institutions.

The Literary Marketplace

Austria is a small country with a population of a little under eight million. Unlike other small European countries, however, its writers have direct linguistic access to a massive neighboring market — Germany. The German-speaking community has the largest number of native speakers in Europe, and this offers tremendous earning potential for those Austrian writers who are able to market themselves successfully in that wider context. While such a market would not be available to writers working in languages such as Finnish, Hungarian, or Greek, the broader context has brought with it certain disadvantages, since Austrian publishing houses cannot compete with their German rivals. Inevitably, Austrian publishing had been severely disrupted by the Nazi occupation of the country. Characteristic of such disruptions was the fate of the eminent publishing house of Zsolnay. Founded by an energetic Jewish publisher in the 1920s, its owner Paul Zsolnay fled to London to escape persecution and made contact with the British publisher Heinemann. During the German occupation of Austria, Zsolnay was renamed Bischoff-Verlag. The publishing house's original identity was restored in 1945, and while the currency reform of November 1947 had a devastating impact on book and journal production alike, Zsolnay survived and was responsible for publishing a distinguished list of both Austrian and European writers in the postwar years. However, in the 1980s financial difficulties led to Zsolnay being sold to a West German publisher.[28]

For the most part, Austrian publishers have been unable to compete with German publishing houses in terms of remuneration to their authors, and it has been a constant feature of postwar Austrian literature to see, almost without exception, Austria's leading writers appearing under the imprint of (West) German publishing houses. Austrian publishers have also had to rely heavily on state support, which is subject to political decision-making and patronage. In a strictly legal sense, much of Austrian literature is owned by Germany since the copyright for much Austrian literature is in the hands of German publishers; German ownership of Austrian literature is made complete when it is borne in mind that the great canonical figures of Austrian literature, from Arthur Schnitzler to Hofmannsthal, Robert Musil to Hermann Broch, Peter Handke to Thomas Bernhard, are all published by leading German publishing houses. Decisions to launch or relaunch the great Austrian writers through new editions are thus taken outside Austria. This has also led to the curious situation of a network of Austrian cultural institutions — established around the world since 1945 with the intention of promoting Austrian literature and culture — using Austrian taxpayers' money to purchase large numbers of books printed in Germany in order to distribute them to institutions such as universities. Large German media concerns have also had the capital to buy heavily into the Austrian publishing market, including the lucrative book-club business. At the same time a small number of Austrian publishers, frequently sustained by the energy and commitment of individuals, have attempted to retain a well-defined Austrian publishing profile. It was the achievement of the Residenz Verlag under Wolfgang Schaffler to establish a publishing house outside Vienna and, based in Salzburg, achieve a literary standing to equal those of its German neighbors, thereby winning back some of Austria's leading writers.

The strident commercial promotion and exploitation of literary works familiar in the United States and Great Britain, where film and television spin-offs are often built into the writing formula, have begun to make themselves felt in the Austrian literary market place. Formerly the German-speaking world adhered to a more rigid distinction between popular and serious literature than was the case in the English-speaking world. But the Austrian book market has begun to follow practices familiar in New York and London.

Literary competitions and book prizes have been adopted in order to promote literary awareness and book sales. In many respects these are an adjunct to the cultural tourism that is so important for the Austrian economy. In recent years the best known of these competitions has been the "Ingeborg-Bachmann-Wettbewerb," held in Bachmann's native Klagenfurt since 1977. This has become a media event with considerable television exposure, and for the invited competitors it can be a bruising experience as their work is commented upon by a jury of distinguished literary specialists. As with ubiquitous television talent shows, the discomfort of the contestants must, in the opinion of the program makers, form part of the audience attraction of the event, and it is also difficult to escape the impression that the photogenic qualities of the young authors play a part. Naming a prize after this distinguished postwar writer cannot hide the fact that her own international prominence, like that of other Austrian writers such as Ilse Aichinger and Paul Celan, was created outside Austria itself and relied on the encouragement and verdict of the German Gruppe 47.

Klagenfurt also constitutes an important focal point of discussion for contemporary Austrian literature in two other respects. Firstly, it is the home and power base of the right-wing politician and one-time leader of the Freedom Party, Jörg Haider. Haider's high personal profile and the entry of his party into government with the Austrian People's Party after elections in October 1999, shattering years of Grand Coalition rule in Austria, brought the country into the international limelight. Austria found itself isolated within the European Union, and among writers there were expressions of horror at political developments within the country; some authors responded by threatening to leave the country for good. At a structural level, the significance of the Freedom Party's entry into government was that it threatened to endanger the culture of subvention that maintained much of Austrian literary life. Haider had appealed to many young entrepreneurs who objected to the perceived heavy burden of taxation in Austria and the practice of subsidies.

Secondly, there is an aspect to Klagenfurt's literary life that receives little attention yet reveals an added dimension to literature in Austria: few Austrians are conscious of the literary life of a linguistic minority community found scattered in Carinthia close to the old Yugoslav border. The Slovenes are ethnically a Slav people to be found in largely rural settlements, and it is difficult to speak of the existence of that urban intelligentsia which is usually a prerequisite to literary activity in Europe. The fate of the Slovenes in Austria has been harsh. Tensions between Slovenes and German-speakers were heightened in the last century by the attempts of Yugoslavia to make good its territorial claims to Klagenfurt and the border regions after 1918 and again after 1945. Such claims contributed to an intensifying sense of German nationalism among the German-speaking Austrians of Carinthia. The Slovenes were subject to a series of atrocities during the Second World War, and Slovene writers have had to struggle on a number of fronts since 1945. The language faced discriminatory measures within the Austrian school system.[29] Slovenia itself was until its independence a minority regional language in the former Yugoslav Federation, whose Communist structures offered little appeal to Austrian Slovenes while the Federation was still in force. (The existence of an independent Slovenia where the language enjoys all the privileges and status of sovereignty may yet have long-term implications for raising the status of the language within Austria.) Much Slovene literature produced in Carinthia, and usually printed and published in Klagenfurt, had been of a simple, devotional nature with little claim to literary ambition. Indeed the written language was historically often the preserve of the clergy. The frustrations of the younger Carinthian Slovene writers coming to adulthood after the war matched those of their German-speaking compatriots, and in the same year that *manuskripte* first appeared (1960), the Slovene journal *Mladje* (sapwood) was launched, representing as major a development for Slovene literature as *manuskripte* did for Austrian literature in German. *Mladje* was in large measure the work of the most significant of the postwar Slovene writers, Florjan Lipuš, and it was he who achieved something of a rare breakthrough for Slovenian writing into mainstream Austrian literature when his novel *Zmote dijaka Tjaza* appeared in a German version, which was entitled *Der Zögling Tjaz* (Young Tjaz, 1981). Peter Handke — whose mother's family was of part Slovene descent — acted as joint translator of the novel.

Commercial globalization may well diminish the specifically Austrian quality of its literature. Much Austrian literature is indeed not produced in Austria itself for it is not uncommon for Austrian authors to work in Germany or to reside and write for much of the year in Italy. Moreover, exile has once again become a feature of the Austrian literary landscape, but now it is tax exile in Ireland rather than the political exile of the 1930s and 1940s that draws writers out of Austria. The literary market place is also incessantly wishing to discover something fresh and is in that respect no different to today's fashion or popular music industry. Certainly, the German book market rediscovers and markets Austrian literature on a regular basis, as was the case when the Frankfurt Book Fair chose Austria as its main theme in 1995 and introduced to a surprised international public the sheer volume and range of literary activity in this small Alpine republic.

The end of the Grand Coalition government in Vienna between conservatives and Socialists suggests that levels of financial support for literature will no longer continue to the degree that they have in the past. It may be a sign of political maturity and secure identity that the state no longer has to pay its writers to promote Austria by means of prizes and book subventions, as it did in the days of the *Ständestaat* of the 1930s or in the early postwar period. Even in a well-educated nation such as Austria, reading habits among the young are changing. Writers are adapting to these changes by marketing themselves, for instance through their own sophisticated Web sites, and there is no sign of a diminishing will among new writers in Austria to come forward. True, much literature is force-fed by publishers' requirement for a constant source of bestsellers and for new names and faces. Few countries, however, are custodians to such a profound and rich literary tradition as Austria, and changes in institutional structures are unlikely to discourage the urge of Austrians to write and to reproduce their experience of life in a central European state through the medium of the literary work. And as Central Europe opens up, initially since the collapse of the Iron Curtain and, at an accelerated pace, with the accession of new states to the European Union, it is clear that both the Austrian state and Austrian writers may find themselves adapting increasingly to a role of speaking to and for the concerns of this heartland of Europe, a role for which they are uniquely placed both geographically and historically. It is difficult not to agree with the verdict of the Polish

Germanist and Canetti scholar Stefan Kaszynski: "Es gibt viele mitteleuropäische Literaturen und eine gemeinsame semiotische Lesart, mit der man ihnen gerecht wird. Die Lesekultur ist in Mitteleuropa noch verhältnismäßig hoch entwickelt. Das ist der Stolz und die Hoffnung dieses Weltteils." (There are many literatures in Central Europe and there is a common semiotic way of reading to do them justice. Central Europe's reading culture is still relatively highly developed. This is both the pride and the hope of this part of the world.)[30]

Notes

[1] Lonnie Johnson, *Introducing Austria* (Riverside, CA: Ariadne, 1989), 126.

[2] Viktor Matejka, *Was ist österreichische Kultur?* (Vienna: Im Selbstverlag des Verfassers, Vienna, I., Rathaus), 8.

[3] Quoted in Walter Kleindel, *Österreich: Daten zur Geschichte und Kultur*, ed. Isabella Ackerl and Günter K. Kodek (Vienna: Ueberreuter, [4]1995), 383.

[4] See Ernst Fischer, *Das Jahr der Befreiung: Aus Reden und Aufsätzen* (Vienna: Stern, 1946).

[5] Klaus Berchtold, *Österreichische Parteiprogramme 1868–1966* (Munich: Oldenbourg, 1967), 377.

[6] Siglinde Bolbecher and Konstantin Kaiser, *Lexikon der österreichischen Exilliteratur* (Vienna: Deuticke, 2000), 7.

[7] Peter Eppel, "Bemerkungen zur Frage der Rückkehr österreichischer Emigranten aus den USA," in Johann Holzner et al., eds., *Eine schwierige Heimkehr: Österreichische Literatur im Exil 1938–1945* (Innsbruck: Innsbrucker Beiträge zur Kulturwissenschaft, 1991) 111–38; here: 112.

[8] *PLAN* 1, Heft 9 (Sept.-Oct. 1946), 768.

[9] *Der Turm* 2, Heft 8 (1947), 265.

[10] Peter Dusek, Erika Weinzierl, and Anton Pelinka, *Zeitgeschichte im Aufriß: Österreich seit 1918* (Vienna: TR-Verlagsunion, [3]1988), 223.

[11] Herbert Zeman, ed., *Geschichte der Literatur in Österreich: Das 20. Jahrhundert* (Graz: Akademische Druck- und Verlagsanstalt, 1999), 105.

[12] Volker Kaukoreit and Kristina Pfoser, eds., *Die österreichische Literatur seit 1945* (Stuttgart: Reclam, 2000), 30.

[13] Karl Müller, *Zäsuren ohne Folgen: Das lange Leben der literarischen Antimoderne Österreichs seit den 30er Jahren* (Salzburg: Otto Müller, 1990), 229.

[14] For a detailed discussion of the many short-lived journals published in the early postwar period see Rüdiger Wischenbart, *Der literarische Wiederaufbau in Österreich 1945–1949* (Königstein/Ts.: Hain, 1983), and Elisabeth Weber, *Österreichische Kulturzeitschriften der Nachkriegszeit 1945–1950* (Frankfurt am Main: Lang, 1988).

[15] Wischenbart, *Der literarische Wiederaufbau*, 15.

[16] Müller, *Zäsuren ohne Folgen*, 323. Müller reproduces the NSDAP membership numbers for Mell and Fussenegger as for dozens of other Austrian writers.

[17] Reichspropagandahauptamt Wien (Hrsg.), Wien, 1938, quoted in Karl Müller (footnote 13), 315.

[18] See, for example, Robert Knight, ed., *"Ich bin dafür, die Sache in die Länge zu ziehen."* *Wortprotokolle der österreichischen Bundesregierung von 1945–52 über die Entschädigung der Juden* (Frankfurt am Main: Athenäum, 1988).

[19] Zeman, ed., *Geschichte der Literatur in Österreich: Das 20. Jahrhundert*, 557.

[20] Claudio Magris, *Danube* (London: Collins Harvill, 1990), 196.

[21] Richard Dove, "Theatre of War: The Austrian Exile Theatre Laterndl," *Yearbook of the Research Centre for German and Austrian Exile Studies*, 2 (2000), 209–29; here: 225.

[22] Roland Heger, *Das österreichische Hörspiel* (Vienna: Braumüller, 1977), 58–59.

[23] Joseph McVeigh, *Kontinuität und Vergangenheitsbewältigung in der österreichischen Literatur nach 1945* (Vienna: Braumüller, 1988), 78.

[24] Evelyn Deutsch-Schreiner, *Theater im "Wiederaufbau": Zur Kulturpolitik im österreichischen Parteien- und Verbändestaat* (Vienna: Sonderzahl, 2001), 10.

[25] Michael Scharang, *Das Wunder Österreich oder Wie es in einem Land immer besser und dabei immer schlechter wird: Essays, Polemiken, Glossen*, ed. Michael Lewin (Vienna: Europaverlag, 1989), 10.

[26] Anthony Bushell, "A Book Too Soon? Hans Lebert's Novel *Die Wolfshaut* and Austrian *Vergangenheitsbewältigung*," *Trivium: Essays in Germanic Studies* 28 (1993): 93–103.

[27] Kaukoreit and Pfoser, eds., *Die österreichische Literatur seit 1945*, 138.

[28] Zeman, ed., *Geschichte der Literatur in Österreich: Das 20. Jahrhundert*, 575.

[29] Johann Strutz, "Die slowenische Gegenwartsliteratur in Kärnten, Florjan Lipuš und der deutschsprachige Kontext," in Andreas Brandtner and Werner Michler, eds., *Zur Geschichte der österreichischen-slowenischen Literaturbeziehungen* (Vienna: Turia und Kant, 1998), 345–66; here: 346–47.

[30] Stefan Kaszynski, "Die große Hoffnung," in Andreas Pribersky, ed., *Europa und Mitteleuropa? Eine Umschreibung Österreichs* (Vienna: Sonderzahl, 1991), 213–22; here: 221.

Figure 1. *1988 premiere of Thomas Bernhard's* Heldenplatz *at the Burgtheater in Vienna, directed by Claus Peymann — a theater scandal against the background of the Waldheim affair.* © *Erwin Schuh, CONTRAST Foto, Vienna.*

Figure 2. *Cartoon in* Der Morgen, *26 December 1932, lampooning the plethora of contemporary plays and biographies featuring Kaiser Franz Josef I. His comment, which reads "So I am to be spared nothing!," echoes the first words he is supposed to have uttered in response to the telegram announcing the murder of his wife, Empress Elizabeth (Sissy), in Geneva in 1898. ("Mir bleibt doch gar nichts erspart auf dieser Welt.") Courtesy of the Austrian National Library.*

Figure 3. *Veza and Elias Canetti in Vienna-Grinzing, October 1937. From* Elias
Canetti — Bilder aus seinem Leben, *edited by Kristian Wachinger. Munich:
Carl Hanser Verlag, 2005. Used by permission of Carl Hanser Verlag and the
Heirs of Elias Canetti.*

Figure 4. The Burning of the Palace of Justice. *Painting by Hugo Löffler.*

FRANZ WERFEL

VERDI

ROMAN DER OPER

11.—22. TAUSEND

IN MENSCHLICH BEWEGTER HANDLUNG,
IN ERSCHÜTTERNDEN SCHICKSALEN,
IN HUNDERT FIGUREN IST HIER DIE

ILIAS DER MUSIK

MIT DER INTUITIVEN KRAFT DES
GROSSEN DICHTERS GESTALTET. IM
MITTELPUNKT DES GESCHEHENS STEHEN

VERDI UND WAGNER

PAUL ZSOLNAY VERLAG

Figure 5. *Franz Werfel's* Verdi, *the first book published by Paul Zsolnay Verlag (1924). A bestseller.*

Figure 6. *Cover of* Bekenntnisbuch österreichischer Dichter. *Edited by Bund Deutscher Schriftsteller Österreichs. Vienna: Krystall-Verlag, 1938. Courtesy of the Austrian National Library.*

Figure 7. *Scene from the film* Salto in die Seligkeit, *1934.*

Figure 8. *H. G. Adler in his study in London. Photo © Colin Davey/ Camera Press, image courtesy of DLA Marbach.*

Figures 9 and 10. *Otto Basil and the first issue of his literary journal,* PLAN.
Courtesy of Christine Basil and the Austrian National Library.

Figure 11. *Poster for the first "Styrian Autumn" literature festival, 1972. Design: pool-aktion gruppe Industrie, steirischer herbst. Used by permission of steirischer herbst Press Office.*

Figure 12. *Heimito von Doderer (second from left) and Hans Weigel (right) at the Café Sacher, 1966. Courtesy of Bezirksmuseum Alsergrund.*

Figure 13. *Ingeborg Bachmann in her flat in Rome. Photo © Garibaldi Schwarze, courtesy of Dokumentationsstelle für neuere österreichische Literatur / Bildarchiv Wien.*

Figure 14. *Peter Handke challenging the goalie. His novel* Die Angst des Tormanns beim Elfmeter *(The Anxiety of the Goalie at the Penalty Kick, 1970) became a modern classic. Photo © and courtesy of Isolde Ohlbaum.*

Figure 15. *Effigy of Elfriede Jelinek in Frank Castorp's 1995 production of her play* Raststätte, oder, Sie machens alle *(Motorway Services, Or They All Do It, 1994). Photo © and courtesy of Matthias Horn.*

Figure 16. *Helmut Qualtinger as "Herr Karl," satirical embodiment of the Viennese opportunist. Photo © and courtesy of Ingrid Votava, Pressefoto Votava, Vienna.*

kleine reihe lesen

edition exil

alma hadzibeganovic

ilda zuferka
rettet die kunst

Figure 17. *Alma Hadzibeganovic's first book (2000). She came to Austria from
Sarajevo in 1992 and was the first writer to be awarded the literature prize Schreiben
zwischen den Kulturen (Writing between the Cultures), in 1997. Courtesy of
edition exil, Vienna.*

8: Austrian Responses to National Socialism and the Holocaust

Dagmar C. G. Lorenz

IN THE DECADES FOLLOWING the Second World War widespread Austrian support for Austro-fascism and National Socialism as well as Austrian participation in the Nazi military and the actual degree to which Austrians had taken part in the Holocaust gradually came to light. It also became obvious that authoritarian attitudes, intolerance, racism, and chauvinism — the syndrome referred to in the 1970s as "everyday fascism" and described by Ingeborg Bachmann in *Der Fall Franza* (The Franza Case, published posthumously in 1981) and thematized by Elfriede Jelinek in *Die Ausgesperrten* (The Excluded, 1980) — had outlasted the Nazi system.[1] The survival of old attitudes had been obvious since anti-Semitic demonstrations in 1947 in Austrian cities and the founding in 1948 of the Verband für Rückstellungsbetroffene protecting those who had benefited from the deportations that began soon after the Nazi takeover by acquiring under-priced property owned by Jews.[2] In the 1970s and 1980s writers and critics explored lingering proto-fascist and anti-Semitic attitudes among the contemporaries of the Nazi era and realized that these patterns were perpetuated in the following generations in the absence of a legitimate public forum to express them. Latent anti-Semitism also persisted, though Vienna's small postwar Jewish community, consisting primarily of Displaced Persons, was considered only temporary, even by its members.[3] In 1986, in the heat of the Waldheim election campaign, anti-Semitism in conjunction with anti-US sentiments regained a semblance of legitimacy. It was fostered by the invectives directed against the World Jewish Congress by the Austrian media, particularly the *Kronen-Zeitung* and the *Kurier*. Articles in these and other papers alleged or suggested that American Jews were engaging in an anti-Austrian conspiracy to topple the conservative presidential candidate and meddle in internal Austrian affairs.

Even at the end of the twentieth century the trauma of the 1930s and 1940s was impossible to overcome, as the conservative People's Party (ÖVP) formed a coalition government with a successful extreme rightwing movement, the Austrian Freedom Party (FPÖ). Along with the victory of populism, concerned critics continued the process of unraveling the events of the Nazi era. During that time of heightened uncertainty and polemics

Austrian intellectuals were still — or once again — struggling to reach conclusive assessments of the cataclysmic social and political changes of the years between 1938 and 1945. Doron Rabinovici, for example, in *Instanzen der Ohnmacht* (Powerless Authorities, 2000) presented a profound new analysis of the *Judenräte* (Jewish councils in German-imposed ghettoes), arguing that though frequently reviled for complicity with the Germans, their members were mere tools to implement Nazi policy. The extreme experiences — the megalomania of the mainstream population under National Socialism and the humiliation and extermination of the disenfranchised — continued to be revisited in films, fiction, exhibitions, and historical treatises, yet with no consensus on the reasons for or the impact of the unimaginable state-sanctioned crimes.[4] The fates of exiles were also reexamined, for example in the novel *Nachwelt* (Posterity, 1999), in which Marlene Streeruwitz traces the life of the sculptor Anna Mahler in the USA from the perspective of a woman writer at the turn of the millennium. Moreover, current events and phenomena such as the election of 1999, which had brought an openly xenophobic party into the government, and hostility toward so-called foreigners, were often interpreted as a continuation of fascist traditions in Austria or examined in the light of the fascist past.[5]

The Postwar Repression of Memory

The emotional and intellectual impact of the events concentrated in the few years between 1934, the year of the Austro-fascist coup d'état, 1938, the year of the Nazi invasion and the Kristallnacht (Night of Broken Glass), and 1945, the year of Nazi Germany's unconditional surrender, extended well beyond the generations directly involved. With ever more information becoming available and with increasing temporal and emotional distance, the attitudes toward Austrian fascism and National Socialism were adjusted from one decade to the next. Literary and critical writing reveals this process of abandoning and returning to the issues of responsibility, guilt, and understanding in conjunction with the past and one's own personal history. The body of texts devoted to Austro-fascism, National Socialism, and the Holocaust display a wide range of approaches and viewpoints including repression and silence, denial and self-justification, mourning and remembrance, and accusation and incrimination.

From the outset, highly publicized events and controversies thwarted initial attempts to reconfigure or repress the past. It soon became obvious that the patterns characteristic of totalitarian societies had already been present before the 1930s. To understand the rise of extremism in the 1920s, the rejection of the new republic among large segments of the population, including prominent intellectuals such as Stefan Zweig and Hugo von Hofmannsthal, had to be re-examined. At the same time it became clear that a valiant battle for an egalitarian social system had been fought all through the First Republic by individuals and groups that tended to be dismissed by conservatives and elitists.[6] The troubles of the First Republic, founded in the wake of the defeated Empire and marked from the beginning by pervasive pessimism and opposition, had been bemoaned for various reasons by many celebrated authors ranging from Joseph Roth to Heimito von Doderer. Many of the writers who had supported social reform — Socialists, feminists, and Jewish activists — had become subject to persecution, forced into exile, or murdered. After 1945 the majority of them remained forgotten. Among the intellectuals who had been inspired by the social and political changes of the 1920s and who experienced the disasters of the 1930s as a series of defeats were Elias Canetti and Veza Canetti, Friedrich Torberg, Berthold Viertel, Karl Kraus and countless "Kleinkünstler," satirists and cabaretists such as Jura Soyfer, Hermann Leopoldi, Karl Farkas, and actors including Elisabeth Bergner and Leon Askin.

The intellectual movements and art forms supporting the republic as well as the resistance against the erosion of democracy eventually became the topic of scholarly and broader cultural discussion.[7] So did the revelations about the criminal involvement of individuals and corporations in the Holocaust begun by Simon Wiesenthal in the postwar years along with the question as to what happened to the perpetrators. The Eichmann trial, for example, was not only relevant to Germans but had obvious implications for Austria and Austrians as well. Finally, the Waldheim scandal,[8] during which yet another layer of silence and repression was removed, made it impossible for Austrians to uphold the benign interpretations of Austrian interwar history and the years under National Socialism.[9]

The soothing collective memory constructed just after the war became increasingly brittle as the notion that Austrians, resisting the German onslaught, had been the innocent victims of ruthless invaders, was proven false. Generally speaking, the topic of the Holocaust had been unwelcome among Austrians, but during the "Renaissance" of Jewish culture in the 1980s it could no longer be avoided.[10] Neither could the official acknowledgment of Austria's rich Jewish history. The changing attitudes in the dominant culture can be deduced from Austrian institutional history. The Dokumentationsarchiv des österreichischen Widerstandes (DÖW), an archive documenting the Austrian resistance, was founded in 1963 upon the initiative of former freedom fighters. However, it took much longer for the Vienna Jewish Museum to open — until 1993. About that time the remnants of an ancient synagogue were discovered at the site of the medieval ghetto, the Judenplatz, and a heated debate began on how to deal with this reminder of Vienna's Jewish history. In 2000 a monument honoring the victims of the Shoah was erected at the Judenplatz site as well as an archive and a museum. These developments correspond to attitudes in Austrian mainstream culture and in Jewish circles.

Reticence regarding the Jewish heritage had been common even among Austrian Jewish intellectuals, some of whom, like Hans Weigel, had returned from exile and assumed a leading role in the postwar literary establishment. Like other Jews who planned on staying in Vienna, Weigel complied with Austrian Chancellor Leopold Figl's demand that Jews blend into the dominant culture.[11] Even Austria's renowned Jewish Chancellor Bruno Kreisky, who was in office from 1970 to 1983, was careful not to seem partial to Jewish concerns and the State of Israel. If at public events he acknowledged his Jewish heritage at all, he did so only obliquely. At the same time, acquiescence to majority demands must not be taken for integration. The Jewish diplomat Hans Thalberg observed that a deep moat separated Jewish from Gentile memory and the perceptions of Jews and non-Jews in Austria.[12]

Disregarding facts such as the "thousands upon thousands of Austrians cheering Hitler on the Heldenplatz,"[13] Austrian writing suggested a fundamental difference between the Austrian national character and that of the Germans. This distinction was relatively easy to maintain since it conformed to the traditional Austria narrative from Grillparzer to Hofmannsthal.[14] The construct of an autonomous Austrian national identity drew on the traditions of Catholicism, the Baroque, and the multinational Empire,[15] thereby de-emphasizing more recent developments including the modernism and political activism of the First Republic as well as the rise of fascism. Authors such as Heimito von Doderer and Hilde Spiel in their historical fiction and memoirs foregrounded a glorified and sanitized imperial tradition, even though the Empire had ended twenty years before the *Anschluss*, Austria's merging with Nazi Germany.[16] Even critical narratives such as the memoir by the Jewish Socialist Elisabeth Freundlich, *Der Seelenvogel* (The Soul Bird, 1986) begin nostalgically with the "golden" past of the Empire: "Man schrieb neunzehnhundertdreizehn, und es war der letzte Friedenssommer der österreichisch-ungarischen Monarchie."[17] The fact that many Austrians, including Hitler and Eichmann, rather than deploring the golden past had led the Nazi movement and implemented the racial program and the Holocaust, was a non-issue among those eager to restore Austria's standing in the international community.

Characteristic of other attempts to "save" Austria's image are Doderer's monumental novels *Die Strudlhofstiege* (The Strudlhof Steps, 1951) and *Die Dämonen* (The Demons, begun in 1931, published in 1956). The latter, an epic inquiry into the seminal dynamics of the first part of the twentieth century by Doderer, an erstwhile Austrian member of the Nazi Party and a veteran of the German military, is set in 1927, a year of social unrest culminating in the burning of the Palace of Justice. Without examining the ensuing radicalization of the public sphere and the shift

toward the political right, *Die Dämonen* ends on a note of private harmony: several of the major characters finalize their romantic relationships,
and one young couple leaves Austria. For Doderer, as for other authors,
including Elias Canetti, 1927 marked the end of an era.[18] Unlike Canetti,
however, Doderer suggests increased emotional and social stability in the
face of external turmoil rather than impending doom. Thus, Doderer
bypassed the most pressing issues confronting Germans and Austrians in
the 1950s: dealing with the prehistory and history of fascism and National
Socialism and examining the experience of exile, war, and genocide. Even
with a Jewish character, Mary K., Doderer opted for a solution of personal
bliss. Mary marries her working-class lover, who has abandoned his proletarian mentality. Thus, the interwar Socialist experience is also obliterated.
There is no mention of the concentration camps that would have awaited a
disabled Jewish woman and an upstanding Socialist — horrors of which an
intellectual in the 1950s was obviously aware.

Doderer's novels were hailed by Austrian critics, including the prominent postwar author Gerhard Fritsch, a Second World War veteran who
was involved with the most influential Austrian literary journals. Fritsch
declared *Die Dämonen* "the most important novel of the 1950s" (Daviau,
xxv). Moreover, the policy of silence practiced by mainstream authors was
also endorsed by other leading cultural figures such as Rudolf Henz who,
like the celebrated novelist Alexander Lernet-Holenia, had taken "inner
emigration" in Austria, that is, abstained from public involvement after the
Nazi takeover. After the war Henz worked with some of the same journals
as Fritsch (Daviau, xx). The same names appear over and over in conjunction with the papers and journals of the early Second Republic, showing a
small, tightly knit network of critics and authors at work.

Ironically, the deceptive version of Austrian history as one of victimhood dates back to the efforts of Austrian exiles, including Jewish intellectuals, although the latter had been targets of anti-Semitism. The 1943
Moscow Declaration had validated the concept of Austrian victimhood,
which became the basis for postwar historiography and informed the Austrian collective memory. In later years, beyond serving ideological and
emotional purposes, the "Geschichtslüge" (historical lie) protected the
Nazi perpetrators and prevented the victims from claiming restitution.[19]
Austrian refugees resorted to this version of history in order to vindicate
their native country, whether from loyalty or because they hoped to return
after the war to build a democratic society or even to re-establish the
monarchy. Hence pre- and postwar writings of most Austrian exiles draw
clear distinctions between Austrians and Germans, for example Stefan
Zweig, Hilde Spiel, Joseph Roth, Frank Zwillinger, and Friedrich
Torberg.[20] A prominent figure in the Second Republic, Torberg distanced
himself from "dem Deutschen," which, as he disapprovingly maintained,
was all too often the accepted role model of Austrian authors.[21] While many

Austrian authors cast German figures as the real Nazis, pedantic, unfeeling authoritarians and instigators with a slavish sense of hierarchy (recalling Adorno's profile of the authoritarian character), Austrian figures, on the other hand, may appear seducible and corrupt, but come across as more humane. Like the character Wohlbrecht created by Jakov Lind, they were shown to possess a "golden heart," popularly ascribed to the Viennese and later unmasked by Helmut Qualtinger as a sloppy and sentimental form of cruelty.[22]

Moreover, the Second Republic's tourist industry reaped the benefits of portraying Austria as a charming musical nation replete with tradition as in the Hollywood film *The Sound of Music*, or as a nation with a rich imperial heritage fostering grace, culture and beauty as in Ernst Marischka's *Sissi* films. At the same time, scholars and intellectuals took the forthcoming damning historical data into account as well as the negative perceptions of exile authors such as Lind, Canetti, Freundlich, and Erich Fried, of survivors such as Robert Schindel, and of children of survivors — Jelinek, Ruth Beckermann, and Doron Rabinovici. For the members of the prewar generations it became increasingly difficult to maintain the status of innocence, and it was impossible for the postwar generations to avoid questioning the role their forebears had played in the Nazi era.[23] Even though much of the "father" and "mother" literature by the 1960s generation, published in the 1970s and 1980s, barely scratched the surface and showed strong apologetic tendencies, it was nonetheless significant that family secrets and episodes such as the Nazi euthanasia program and the Holocaust were publicly problematized at all.[24]

The places of residence chosen by Austrian authors as well as their publishers also reveal changes in the public climate. Early on, authors whose writings contained an open or implicit indictment of their compatriots, as did Ilse Aichinger's *Die größere Hoffnung* (The Greater Hope, 1948), Ingeborg Bachmann's story "Unter Mördern und Irren" (Among Murderers and Madmen, in *Das dreißigste Jahr*, The Thirtieth Year, 1961), and her *Der Fall Franza*, did not publish in Austria, nor did they have their primary residence there. Likewise, authors who wrote about the Nazi concentration camps, such as Paul Celan in "Todesfuge" (Death Fugue, 1948) or Peter Edel in his novel *Schwester der Nacht* (Sister of Night, 1947), left the country or changed the focus of their writing, as did Benedikt Kautsky, the author of an eloquent early concentration camp memoir, who became involved in party politics and turned to writing about social issues.[25] Exile authors such as Zwillinger, Fried, and Canetti, whose works examined the Nazi past and fascist structures, did not take residence in Austria, although they were frequent and honored visitors in the 1970s and 1980s. On the other hand, many younger authors writing about the Nazi past, the Holocaust, and the coexistence of former victims and perpetrators, for example Jelinek, Schindel, Beckermann, Rabinovici, Josef Haslinger, and Vladimir

Vertlib, live and publish in Austria and have contributed significantly to shaping public debates in and about Austria.

Confronting the Past

In the 1950s and 1960s Austrian editors and publishers steered clear of manuscripts apt to cause controversy because their experimental form or politically sensitive topics might compromise Austria's wholesome image or the dogma of innocent suffering. Yet from the beginning, the Second Republic, because of its neutral status, participated both in Western postwar culture and in the discourses of the Eastern Bloc. The result was a discursive position between the opposing camps. Neither the West German concept of 1945 as the "Stunde Null" (Zero Hour) nor the passionate anti-fascist self-examination characteristic of East German literature took hold in Austria. However, even if implicitly or explicitly rejected, both approaches to the past were accessible in Austria which, under Allied occupation until 1955, was a battleground for the competing eastern Socialist and western capitalist models. A number of Austrian authors, including Aichinger and Bachmann, who had begun their careers in Vienna, were impressed by the call for a new beginning issued by the West German Gruppe 47 as well as by Existentialism. They affiliated themselves with intellectuals in West Germany and other western countries. Neither Aichinger nor Bachmann, however, embraced the concept of "Kahlschlag" (tabula rasa) propagated by the West German writer Wolfgang Weyrauch, but rather expressed the importance of past events and traditions for the present in their style as well as their ideas.

A keen awareness of the past informs Aichinger's call for continued vigilance and distrust after the defeat of the Nazi regime, and her ornate lyrical style is reminiscent of German classical and Romantic literature.[26] On the other hand, Peter Edel, a social realist author, who continued his career in East Germany, addressed in his fiction and autobiographical works the concerns foremost in Socialist countries, the class struggle culminating in National Socialism and re-education in the spirit of Socialism. He emphasized the need for a thorough rethinking of the past, overcoming bourgeois, and according to him, crypto-fascist values. He traced the character development of the proletarian hero as well as individual and collective victory over bourgeois religious and cultural values.

Immediately after the war there were attempts in Austria to revive Marxist and Socialist positions which had played a central role in the prewar era, but without success. Otto Basil's journal *PLAN*, which had been founded in 1937 in opposition to Nazi cultural politics and resumed publication in 1945, validated leftist traditions, but was discontinued in 1948.[27] Similarly, conservative rivals soon eclipsed the Socialist critic

Hermann Hakel, who after the war had assumed an influential role in mentoring young authors. In keeping with its imposed neutrality, postwar Austria resorted to a national narrative of an imperial heritage of ethnic diversity and cultural splendor. This theme, present on every level, be it literature, film or advertisement, contributed to the success of the Second Republic as a center for international diplomacy, trade and tourism. The heritage invoked for this purpose may have been little more than a myth, as suggested by Claudio Magris's term "Habsburg myth," but it was momentous in creating a post-Shoah national identity and a sense of cohesion. At the same time, Austrian authors did not engage in *Vergangenheitsbewältigung* (coping with the past) and *Trauerarbeit* (work of mourning) to the same degree as West German critics and authors.[28]

The larger paradigm of the Austrian imperial heritage also implied the legacy of Jewish Austria, in particular Jewish Vienna.[29] Although Austria's Jewish communities and cultural networks had been destroyed, older Jewish authors adhered to pre-Holocaust attitudes. Though only a few survivors and exile authors actually had returned to Austria or settled there for the first time, they included such prominent personalities such as Weigel, Torberg, Wiesenthal, Hakel, Thalberg, Kreisky, Heinz Sichrovsky, and Franz Weintraub. Another equally diverse group of former Austrians took a significant part in the cultural life of the Second Republic by lecturing and publishing in Austria on a regular basis, including Canetti, Spiel, Lind, Fried, Zwillinger, Jean Améry, and Manès Sperber. The Jewish intellectuals who returned after 1945 reintroduced their traditionalist viewpoints to the literary discourse. For the post-Shoah generations the writings of former exiles formed the basis for their own distinctly Jewish narratives. By mediating their experience of growing up Jewish in post-Shoah Vienna through the works of fin-de-siècle and interwar Jewish texts, they created the impression of a cultural continuity that *de facto* did not exist.[30]

The critic and author Hans Weigel, upon returning from his exile in Switzerland, assumed the role of an aesthetic arbiter. He acted as a defender of traditional high culture and became a proponent of Viennese local patriotism. A highly visible cultural figure, he later spearheaded popular events such as the Vienna Stadtfest and publicized his love for Vienna in articles such as "Ein krasser Fall von Liebe" (A Crass Case of Love, in his *Glückliches Österreich*, Happy Austria, 1978), which in the 1980s was on display in Vienna's streetcars and buses. Weigel's activities extended to numerous literary and cultural journals, and he was instrumental in establishing and editing the series *Junge österreichische Autoren* designed to introduce and promote new talents. Weigel wielded enormous power as a literary critic.[31] In the postwar era he published authors as diverse as Ilse Aichinger, Herbert Eisenreich, and Marlen Haushofer. Since he rejected socially critical literature and objected to works dealing with the Holocaust, Austro-fascism, or Jewish topics, the writers he mentored either conformed to his preferences or had to seek support elsewhere. The verdict of a group of likeminded critics such as Weigel, Wolfgang Kraus, Otto Breicha, Rudolf Henz, and Gerhard Fritsch decided literary success and failure in Austria.

Major authors such as Celan, Aichinger, Bachmann, and Peter Handke were able to publish abroad, but not everyone in disagreement with the cultural establishment found favor with Swiss or German publishers. For decades the authors of the Wiener Gruppe, whose avant-garde texts included Austrian dialect, provocative vulgarisms and attacks on the complacency of the established intellectuals did not, and for many years their works remained unpublished. The dominant pro-Austrian and anti-Leftist position went hand in hand with a strong ideological and stylistic traditionalism and supported Austrian and German premodern aesthetics. Weigel's own interpretations of major Austrian authors, Stifter, Schubert, Raimund, Nestroy, Johann Strauss, and to a lesser extent, Grillparzer, in *Flucht vor der Größe* (Flight from Greatness, 1960) illustrate the avoidance of politically and socially critical debates. In his rejection of literary experiments and his rigorous language purism, Weigel placed himself in the conservative tradition of Karl Kraus, and his vision of Vienna was one of the nineteenth century (Daviau xxxi). Late in his career, at the time of the Waldheim debate, Weigel did articulate serious concerns about rightwing radicalism, racism, and mass manipulation through the media in *Man kann nicht ruhig darüber reden* (You Can't Discuss it Calmly, 1986). Significantly, though, this essay ends on an idealistic note characteristic of much of Weigel's work. Weigel ultimately placed his trust in the younger generation because of his continued confidence in the powers of high culture and education. The post-Shoah generations were unable to share the hopes that Weigel and other Jewish elder statesmen derived from the ideal of humanist "Bildung."

Friedrich Torberg, already an established writer and journalist in the First Republic with extensive connections to prewar Prague and Budapest, had gone into exile in the United States. Supporting the virulent opposition to Communism and Socialism that had emerged among the Western Allies at the beginning of the Cold War, Torberg declared even mildly leftist views to be incompatible with Austrian Jewish tradition. When he returned to Vienna in 1951 he made a name for himself as a decidedly Jewish writer and cultural critic.[32] He wrote about the Holocaust and Jewish topics in *Golems Wiederkehr* (Golem's Return, 1947), "Mein ist die Rache" (Revenge is Mine), and *Süßkind von Trimberg* (1971), thereby breaking the taboo of discussing Jewish suffering and depicting complex, even morally reprehensible Jewish characters at a time when non-Jewish authors refrained from casting Jews other than as victims and virtuous persons.[33] Torberg's satirical cultural history *Die Tante Jolesch oder der Untergang des Abendlandes* (Aunt Jolesch or the Decline of the West, 1975) is devoted to the memory of Viennese and Prague Jewish journalists such as Egon

Erwin Kisch, Anton Kuh, Alfred Polgar, and Egon Friedell. By calling attention to these important authors he constructed a Jewish memory opposing that of the dominant culture, which acknowledged primarily non-Jewish Austrian or German authors. Through his anti-assimilationist stance Torberg won the admiration of younger Jewish intellectuals in search of self-realization outside the limitations of post-Shoah Vienna, even though they did not share his radical anti-leftist views. Positioning himself as heir to the legacy of Habsburg Central Europe, Torberg continued to be passionately opposed to the residues of National Socialism, Communism, and Socialism, and he had nothing but contempt for the readership of what he referred to as the "Hausmeisterblatt" (paper for janitors), the *Kronen-Zeitung*.[34]

The main issue that separated the two Jewish Austrian traditionalists, Weigel and Torberg, was their attitude toward Germany. From the start Weigel had displayed a conciliatory attitude, stressing the cultural and linguistic cohesion between Austrians and Germans.[35] Torberg, for whom Jewish concerns were primary, emphasized Austria's historical and cultural specificity and cast Germans and Austrians as opposites. Setting the tone in postwar literary circles and influencing the next generation of Austrian writers — Herbert Eisenreich, Jeannie Ebner, Marlen Haushofer, and Gerhard Fritsch — the older mentors' and role models' distaste for avant-garde writing and influences that supposedly threatened to downgrade Austrian high culture had ultimately an isolating effect. The most influential journals of the early Second Republic, *Wort in der Zeit* and *Literatur und Kritik* with their pronounced elitist aspirations, remained marginal within the larger German-speaking sphere. Well into the 1960s they sought to validate their "Austrian" viewpoints by attacking West German literary practices, particularly the vulgarity and social criticism ascribed to authors associated with the Gruppe 47 such as Heinrich Böll and Günter Grass.[36]

The aesthetic values proclaimed by the major Austrian critics supported the political and social agenda of the young Second Republic. They prevented the confrontation with fascism and the Holocaust, topics too embarrassing and vulgar for the traditionalist modes of writing and reasoning. While the Austrian literary establishment decried the expression of violence, sexuality, and use of innovative aesthetic forms designed to depict the unprecedented atrocities of the Nazi era, the brutality of the recent past was revealed in an international discourse represented by Bruno Apitz's *Nackt unter Wölfen* (Naked among Wolves, 1958), Edgar Hilsenrath's *Nacht* (Night, 1964), Lind's *Seele aus Holz* (Soul of Wood, 1964), Jerzy Kosinski's *The Painted Bird* (1965), and Peter Weiss's *Die Ermittlung* (The Investigation, 1968). In Austria manuscripts employing a similarly casual, yet revealing and shocking language breaking the taboo of portraying Nazi crimes and the Holocaust had little chance of being.

published. Oswald Wiener's *die verbesserung von mitteleuropa* (the improvement of central europe, 1969), which combines linguistic experiment with a playful approach to taboo subjects, Peter Handke's *Publikumsbeschimpfung* (Insulting the Audience, 1966), a performance in which targeted insults are hurled at an audience of presumed perpetrators and collaborators, and Jelinek's *Die Ausgesperrten*, examining residues of fascism in conjunction with a massacre in a 1950s lower middle class Viennese family, were all published in the Federal Republic.

The cataclysmic effect of learning about the hidden past after having been raised with the myth of victimization is obvious from the work of Austria's most prominent authors, Ingeborg Bachmann and Thomas Bernhard. Whereas other writers who began their careers after 1945, such as Peter Handke in *Wunschloses Unglück* (A Sorrow Beyond Dreams, 1974) and Brigitte Schwaiger in *Lange Abwesenheit* (Long Absence, 1980), perpetuated claims of innocence or partial innocence, these authors, both born in provincial Austria, came to recognize, thematize, and condemn their compatriots' entanglement with National Socialism and the Holocaust. Bachmann's and Bernhard's mature works reveal a keen awareness of the continued, generally unacknowledged legacy of fascism, racism, and corruption in Austria and express the frustration of Austrians born after the fact and yet incapable of liberating themselves from this heritage. While Bachmann left Austria, thus physically distancing herself from her country of origins, Bernhard, whose cutting criticism articulated traumas familiar to his entire generation, became firmly integrated into the Austrian literary establishment of the 1970s and 1980s, even though many considered him an *enfant terrible*. In the 1980s and 1990s new oppositional voices came to the fore, articulating the counter-memory of Jews, the children of exiles and Holocaust survivors. These authors successfully challenged Austria's collective memory by portraying their and their parents' experience from the standpoint of Jews victimized and marginalized by fascists, Nazis and their collaborators and supporters — by average Austrians. Finally, the issues of fascism and National Socialism and the profound impact of totalitarian structures on the social fabric came to be viewed as an integral part of the present. By the 1970s at latest it was obvious that the past could not simply be left behind, because painful and shameful situations in the present had their origin in earlier decades, as Handke showed in *Wunschloses Unglück* and Peter Henisch in *Die kleine Figur meines Vaters* (The Small Figure of my Father, 1975). In the following decades Austrian authors explored the deliberate imitation as well as the subconscious reproduction of Nazi practices, as in Josef Haslinger's *Opernball* (Opera Ball, 1995).

In the 1980s Austrian writers born in the 1940s moved to the forefront of autobiographical writing about the legacy of the Nazi era, whether in political or personal terms, for example Andreas Okopenko in *Kindernazi* (Children's Nazi, 1984), Elisabeth Reichart in *Februarschatten* (February

Shadows, 1984), and Thomas Bernhard in *Auslöschung* (Extinction, 1986). The diverse views expressed at the end of the twentieth and the beginning of the twenty-first century called to mind forgotten debates of the pre-Nazi era and took up earlier unresolved discussions about identity, ethnicity, gender, and race. Even though some of the reactions such as post-Nazi anti-fascism may seem belated, they fulfilled very topical needs. For Austrian intellectuals of the postwar generations it was vital to work through the confusing panorama of the past transmitted by less than forthcoming parents and grandparents and to confront the legacy of the past as it was shaping the future. Especially at critical junctures when history seemed to repeat itself, the authors of the second generation of survivors or perpetrators needed to establish their own positions. The processes of fact-finding and reflection assumed a particular importance in Austria because of the overwhelming presence of historical reminders everywhere. Social structures and practices are still deliberately connected to the past, and Austria's urban landscapes call to mind past centuries. Moreover, red and white markers are attached to buildings of historical significance alerting tourists and reminding residents of people and events of the past.

This carefully constructed spectrum of continuity and connectivity made it easy to ignore the most traumatic historical break, the invasion by Nazi Germany and the erasure of Austria as a sovereign nation for a decade and a half. Only very late were the markers for Gestapo prisons and other incriminating sites added to those commemorating cultural icons such as Mozart and Beethoven. As in other "victim" countries, including France, the Netherlands, the country with the "highest relative Jewish death rate of any Western European country,"[37] and Eastern Europe, sociologists, writers, and historiographers were reluctant to deal with the victims of the so-called victims, the Jews, Roma, the disabled, and the homosexuals oppressed not only by German Nazis but also by common Austrian civilians and soldiers.

Alfred Hrdlicka's controversial monument commissioned for the 1988 commemoration of the German invasion expresses the dimensions and preferences of the collective memory. The imposing set of sculptures at the Albertinaplatz in Vienna represents idealized Austrian fighters in white marble and, almost as an afterthought, the figure of a Jew cast in bronze lying on the pavement. The filmmaker and critic Ruth Beckermann describes her reaction to Hrdlicka's monument as follows:

> Das Mahnmal Alfred Hrdlickas kommt der Meinung aller jener entgegen, die bedenkenlos Opfer gegen Opfer aufrechnen: die Kriegsopfer gegen die Opfer der nationalsozialistischen Gesinnung — Juden, Zigeuner, Homosexuelle, Geisteskranke [. . .] Was immer dieses Denkmal den Wienern sagen will, mir sagt es: Im Staub seid ihr gelegen. Auf dem Bauch seid ihr gerutscht. Und das ist heute unser Bild von euch. Fünfzig

Jahre danach formen wir euch nach diesem Bild. Als frommen Alten. Das rührt ans Herz und rückt die Opfer gleichzeitig in angenehme Distanz; suggeriert es doch, daß die Juden ein seniles, altersschwaches Volk waren, dessen natürlicher Tod kurz bevorstand. (*Unzugehörig*, 13–16)

[Alfred Hrdlicka's monument supports the view of all those who thoughtlessly weigh victims against victims: victims of war against victims of National Socialism — Jews, Gypsies, homosexuals, the mentally ill. [. . .] Whatever this monument may want to tell the Viennese, it tells me: "You lay in the dust. You slipped onto your bellies. And that's how we see you today. Fifty years later, we form you after this image. As devout old people." That moves the heart while removing the victims to a pleasant distance; after all, it suggests that the Jews were a senile and decrepit nation whose natural death would soon have happened anyway.]

Beckermann's statement satirizes the dominant narrative by revealing two opposing historical narratives in post-Shoah Austria, that of the doubtless well-intentioned, leftist-inspired, non-Jewish sculptor, who considers non-Jews, the Austrian workers and anti-fascists, and the German Nazis, as the major historical players, and that of the Jewish children of survivors rejecting narratives that marginalize Jews and Jewish suffering.

Jews at the turn of the millennium developed a markedly different relationship to Austria than the preceding generations. Although earlier Jewish intellectuals contemplated how to coexist with and eventually be accepted by the Catholic majority in an increasingly anti-Semitic climate, the first priority for the second and third post-Shoah generations is to avoid becoming too Austrian. As Beckermann noted, Jews decided to put an end to pointless discussions with anti-Semites. Instead, they assumed the role of self-determined agents in the literary and political arena. Some took leading roles in the anti-Haider movement, helping to establish an Austrian civil society and expanding the international range of their works. At the turn of the millennium the question about how to co-operate with non-Jews was not a pressing issue. Such co-operation, which occurred on all levels, was problematic in view of the past. For many authors Jewish specificity was a desideratum as they engaged in the project of constructing a contemporary Jewish identity.

From Waldheim to Haider

Of the numerous incidents triggering debates about the past the most polemical discourse erupted in the mid-1980s in conjunction with the presidential campaign of the former UN Secretary Kurt Waldheim, whose affiliation with Nazi special military units in the Balkans gave rise to an international political scandal. Even after Waldheim's election victory the criticism did not subside, and the collaboration of oppositional groups such as anti-fascists, anti-racists, Jewish activists, feminists, ecologists, pacifists, and others created a network of dissent. However, at the time of the Waldheim election the political right gained momentum as well. The popularity of the right-of-center Freedom Party (FPÖ) increased dramatically under the leadership of the populist Jörg Haider, a member of the postwar generation and committed to revisionist politics and history. Haider's success was based on a xenophobic platform that appealed to new and old racists and revisionists eager to vindicate the Nazi generation. Increasing economic problems and fears that joining the European Union might jeopardize Austria's autonomy provided further support for the Freedom Party.

The critical public confronting the rightwing movement consisted of writers and intellectuals such as Haslinger, Jelinek, Streeruwitz, Beckermann, Rabinovici, Anton Pelinka, and Robert Menasse. These Jewish and non-Jewish dissenters joined forces and articulated their discontent in the media, on the street, and on the World Wide Web. Indeed, the Waldheim affair provided a strong enough impetus for an oppositional Jewish culture to form denouncing the irresponsible use of the past. Likewise, at the point when the right-wingers launched their offensive the repression of democratic debates in Austria's "social partnership," which for decades had provided stability, came under scrutiny.[38] Haslinger's analysis of Waldheim's campaign strategies, *Die Politik der Gefühle* (The Politics of Emotions, 1987), brought other important issues into the debate, notably the role of the media and the political use of advertising techniques, including agencies and tools of the US advertising industry, to elicit irrational mass responses. Publicizing alternative Austrian experiences was another way to undermine the image of a uniform Austrian culture. Beckermann's essay about Jews in post-Shoah Austria, *Unzugehörig* (Not Belonging, 1989), revealed the repression of Jewish experiences and points of view.[39] In his numerous publications, the political scientist Pelinka traced the history of Austro-fascism and provided new insights into the developments leading to the Waldheim crisis and beyond.[40] The continued attacks on the Waldheim regime resulted in an unprecedented public confrontation with the Nazi era. So did the controversies occasioned by the commemorations of the *Anschluss* and the Kristallnacht in 1988. Films, novels, documentaries, and essays further compromised the narrative of Austrian victimhood and revealed the continued marginalization of victimized groups and persons: Jews, homosexuals, the disabled, the homeless, intellectuals, and so-called "foreigners." Moreover, the persistent gender inequities, already lambasted in the works of Jelinek, were thematized in conjunction with racism and xenophobia by younger feminist authors such as Streeruwitz.[41] In addition, repressed revolutionary cultural memory of the interwar period was recovered in conjunction with new editions and posthumous publications of the literary works of Veza Canetti by her husband Elias Canetti and the belated publication of memoirs such as Freundlich's *Der Seelenvogel* and *weiter leben* (living on, 1992), the autobiography of the Vienna-born Auschwitz survivor Ruth Klüger. These works revealed long-ignored gender-related aspects of the Austrian past.

With the disintegration of the Eastern bloc the political polarization of East and West came to an end. As a result of the delegitimization of Marxist ideology, authors of the Left spectrum repositioned themselves. Some, like Jelinek, Henisch, and Anna Mitgutsch redefined themselves through their Jewish ancestry.[42] Thus, the Holocaust as a historical turning point and a major element in Austrian identity formation came into focus. Jelinek, for example, the child of a near-victim of the Holocaust and intellectually close to the 1960s leftist movement, emphasized her Jewish background after the demise of the Austrian Communist Party. Her earlier work had already shown a keen interest in Holocaust perpetrators and their children and examined contemporary sado-masochistic relationships that mirrored Nazi practices.[43] However, she had not made her biographical connection to these issues as clear as she did later. Jelinek's anti-Haider polemics of the 1990s were clearly informed by Nazi history. In his novel *Steins Paranoia* (1988) Peter Henisch, who had been affiliated with the Austrian Communist Party, examined Vienna urban culture from the viewpoint of an Austrian Jew who had mistakenly had considered himself assimilated. Influenced by the outsider perspective of his girlfriend, an American Jewish exchange student, the protagonist of Henisch's novel becomes aware of the anti-Semitism in his surroundings and begins to realize the ubiquitous reminders of the Holocaust. About the same time, Mitgutsch converted to Judaism to honor the memory of her grandmother, who had survived the Holocaust in hiding. In *Abschied von Jerusalem* (Leaving Jerusalem, 1995) she portrayed an identity as multi-layered and confusing as her own, revealing the difficulty of coming to terms with the dilemma of being involved with perpetrators and victims, past and present alike. The fact that authors who until the mid-1980s had considered themselves participants in the dominant Austrian culture now acknowledged their indebtedness to Central European Jewish culture and history resulted in a mainstreaming of Jewish Austrian writing, which previously had been a marginal phenomenon. Not coincidentally Robert Schindel's *Gebürtig* (Born, 1992) und Doron Rabinovici's *Suche nach M.* (Search for M., 1997) reveal possibilities of interactions and coexistence between Jews and non-Jews that for the characters in Nadja Seelich's film *Kieselsteine* (Pebbles, 1982), seemed doomed to failure.

The inclusion of the FPÖ in the Austrian government in 2000 incited protest from all progressive groups, especially as self-appointed pro-government voices had begun the process of, in Jelinek's words, denazifying those who had voted for the FPÖ. In opposition to the old-new chauvinism, which Beckermann termed Austro-Nazism in opposition to the established concept of Austro-fascism, a broadly based civil society formed in an attempt to destabilize the pro-Haider forces.[44] Indeed, with the Austrian Communist Party invalidated, and the SPÖ excluded from the government as the result of the coalition between the conservatives and the Freedom Party, the dissenters were without political representation. Some authors contemplated in their works the validity of withdrawal into the private sphere as possible responses to overwhelming social and political pressures, for example Mitgutsch in *Abschied von Jerusalem* and Rabinovici in *Suche nach M.* Jelinek went so far as to forbid further performances of her plays on Austrian stages. Her self-exclusion recalls Bernhard's posthumous decision to bar his plays from Austrian theaters. While these reactions call to mind the inner exile of the 1930s and 1940s, the political responses of the authors involved were markedly different. Many of them assumed leading roles in the protests against Jörg Haider and his party. Indeed, for authors who, like Rabinovici, had played a key role as an oppositional activist since the Waldheim campaign, withdrawal is a mere literary potentiality. Similarly, Streeruwitz and Beckermann, despite their skepticism regarding the possibility of effecting political change through literature, theater, and film, were at the forefront of the protest movement.[45]

The single most important factor in the consolidation of a critical public, an Austrian civil society, was the conservative/rightwing coalition. As with the earlier Waldheim scandal, this development called for action and solidarity among dissenting groups. The ensuing debates and protests, including demonstrations and happenings, revealed that despite the skeptical observations and statements of earlier decades Jewish and non-Jewish dissenters could and did work together against the perceived threat of neo-fascism and racism. The experience of the 1990s promoted a widespread political awareness, and progress in communication technology made possible new networking strategies. The rift that opened at the turn of the millennium was no longer one between Jews and non-Jews but between those able to avail themselves of the new technologies and those still relying on the traditional communication channels. Likewise, different levels of education, international experience and the lack thereof, as well as economic privilege play an important role in the formation of consciousness and the willingness to meet the problems of the present with an open, informed mind. Among the politically involved authors of the twenty-first century there seems to be agreement that the ability to recognize the dangers of neo-fascism and other forces threatening personal and social freedom depends largely on the ability to read and interpret the multiplicity of post-modern texts in a historical continuum.

Notes

[1] See Anni Kienast and Gerda Zorn, eds., *Der alltägliche Faschismus* (Berlin: Dietz, 1981).

[2] John Bunzl and Bernd Marin, *Antisemitismus in Österreich* (Innsbruck: Inn-Verlag, 1983), 66.

[3] For example Jean Améry, "Der ehrbare Antisemitismus," *Weiterleben – aber wie?* (Stuttgart: Klett-Cotta, 1982), 151–84.

[4] See Hamburger Institut für Sozialforschung ed. *Vernichtungskrieg: Verbrechen der Wehrmacht 1941 bis 1944. Ausstellungskatalog* (Hamburg: Institut für Sozialforschung, 1996). The *Wehrmacht* exhibit visited Vienna in 1995 at the Alpenmilchzentrale. Beckermann's film *Jenseits des Krieges* (Vienna: filmladen, 1997) was shot at the exhibit. Beckermann also published a companion book, *Jenseits des Krieges* (Vienna: Döcker, 1997). In 2002 an updated and expanded version of the exhibit was the object of demonstrations and protests in Vienna. See Helga Embacher, ed., *Juden in Salzburg: History, Cultures, Fates* (Salzburg: Pustet, 2002); Vladimir Vertlib, *Das besondere Gedächtnis der Rosa Masur* (Munich: dtv, 2003).

[5] See Wilfried Graf, "Das österreichische Faschismussyndrom: Von der nationalen Verdrängung zur Wiederkehr des Massenwahns?" in Robert Misik and Doron Rabinovici, eds., *Republic der Courage: Wider die Verhaiderung* (Berlin: Aufbau Taschenbuch Verlag, 2000), 42–52.

[6] In Hilde Haider-Pregler and Beate Reiterer, eds., *Verspielte Zeit: Österreichisches Theater der dreißiger Jahre* (Vienna: Picus, 1997), for example, the focus is shifted from the traditionally more common discussion of the consequences of the collapse of the Habsburg Empire to the caesura that occurred with the destruction of democracy in 1933 and the Civil War in 1934. See especially Erika Weinzierl, "Österreichische Kulturpolitik in den dreißiger Jahren" in *Verspielte Zeit*, 14–26; here: 23.

[7] Horst Jarka, "Opposition zur ständestaatlichen Literaturpolitik und literarischer Widerstand" in Klaus Amann and Albert Berger, eds., *Österreichische Literatur der dreißiger Jahre* (Vienna: Böhlau, 1985), 13–41; Ruth Beckermann dir., *Wien Retour* (Vienna: filmladen, 1983).

[8] The Waldheim affair is discussed in the introduction to this volume.

[9] The Austrian Jewish author Günther Anders responded to the widespread indignation about the Eichmann trial and the call for an end to the prosecution of perpetrators in an open letter to Eichmann's son Klaus in Günther Anders, *Wir Eichmannssöhne: Offener Brief an Klaus Eichmann* (Munich: Beck, 1964).

[10] See for example Günther Scheidl, "Renaissance des 'jüdischen' Romans nach 1986" in Anne Betten, Konstanze Fliedl, and Volker Kaukoreit, eds., *Judentum und Antisemitismus: Studien zur Literatur und Germanistik in Österreich* (Berlin: Schmidt, 2001), 132–50.

[11] See Ruth Beckermann's account of the formation of a Jewish community and her own growing up Jewish in post-Shoah Vienna, *Unzugehörig* (Vienna: Löcker, 1989), 65.

[12] Hans Thalberg, *Von der Kunst, Österreicher zu sein* (Vienna: Böhlau, 1984). See also Beckermann, *Unzugehörig*, 10.

[13] Donald G. Daviau, "Introduction" in Daviau, ed., *Austrian Writers and the Anschluss: Understanding the Past — Overcoming the Past* (Riverside, CA: Ariadne Press, 1991), viii.

[14] See Dagmar C. G. Lorenz, "The Pluralist Paradigm: The Anti-Idealism of Austrian Literature" in Donald G. Daviau and Herbert Arlt, eds., *Geschichte der österreichischen Literatur I* (St. Ingbert: Röhrig, 1996), 66–76.

[15] Daviau (xxvi) notes that in August 1945 the journal *Der Turm* republished Hugo von Hofmannsthal's "Preuße und Österreicher," an essay revolving on typecasting Northern Germans and Austrians.

[16] For example the "Sissy" films by Austria's star director Ernst Marischka, who had already made a name for himself with escapist films prior to 1945.

[17] Elisabeth Freundlich, *Der Seelenvogel* (Vienna: Zsolnay, 1986), 19.

[18] See especially Elias Canetti, *Masse und Macht* (Hamburg: Claassen, 1960); *Die Fackel im Ohr: Lebensgeschichte 1921–1931* (Munich: Hanser, 1980); Ruth Beckermann, dir., *Wien Beckermann* (Vienna: filmladen, 1983).

[19] Joseph William Moser, "The Portrayal of the Historical Lie of Austria Being the First Victim of Hitler's Aggression in Josef Haslinger's 'Politik der Gefühle' and Ruth Beckermann's 'Unzugehörig': Österreicher und Juden nach 1945," Master's Thesis, Ohio State U, 1999. See also Beckermann, *Unzugehörig*, 91.

[20] Stefan Zweig, *Schachnovelle* (Stockholm: Bermann-Fischer, 1943) contrasts a well-bred Austrian monarchist with brutal Nazi and fascistoid characters. Jakov Lind, *Eine Seele aus Holz* (Neuwied: Luchterhand, 1962) juxtaposes the corruptible lower-middle-class Austrian Wohlbrecht with opportunist German Nazis, and Friedrich Torberg in *Golems Wiederkehr* (Reinbek bei Hamburg: Rowohlt, 1981) reveals homicidal inclinations in the characters of Germans in Prague, who can only be stopped by a quasi supernatural force.

[21] Friedrich Torberg, "Die Deutschen — österreichisch gesehen" in *Apropos: Nachgelassenes, Kritisches, Bleibendes* (Munich: Langen Müller, 1981) 141–60; here: 141.

[22] See Lind, *Seele aus Holz*; Carl Merz and Helmut Qualtinger, *Der Herr Karl* (Munich: Langen Müller, 1962).

[23] "Mein Vater ist '43 zu Hause gestorben [. . .] Die werden heute ja alle als Mörder hingestellt. Das kann ich nicht glauben, das kann ich nicht glauben, und ich weiß von Erzählungen, daß es immer geheißen hat: Wir sind beschossen worden, wir haben uns natürlich gewehrt. [. . .] Ich glaube nicht, daß meine Onkel Mörder sind. Ich glaube auch nicht, daß mein Großvater ein Mörder ist. Das kann ich nicht glauben, denn sonst müßte ich mich selbst aufhängen. [. . .] Aber das hier, das macht uns glauben, daß unsere Onkel unsere Väter Mörder sind," states an approximately forty-five-year-old woman in Beckermann's documentary film: *Jenseits des Krieges* (Companion Book), 71.

[24] See Regina Kecht, "Faschistische Familienidyllen — Schatten der Vergangenheit in Henisch, Schwaiger and Reichart" in Daviau, ed., *Austrian Writers and the Anschluss*, 299–313.

[25] By the time Benedikt Kautsky's *Teufel und Verdammte: Erfahrungen und Erkenntnisse aus sieben Jahren in deutschen Konzentrationslagern* (Zurich: Büchergilde Gutenberg, 1946) appeared in Austria (Vienna: Verlag der Wiener Volksbuchhandlung: 1961), the author was already devoting himself to other topics, including the history of unions in the USA. He edited Engels's correspondence and took an active role in the SPO, Austria's Socialist Party.

[26] Aichinger, "Aufruf zum Mißtrauen" in *PLAN* 1/5 (1946), 588.

[27] See Ruth V. Gross, *PLAN and the Austrian Rebirth: Portrait of a Journal* (Columbia, SC: Camden House, 1982).

[28] See Alexander and Margarete Mitscherlich, *Die Unfähigkeit zu trauern* (Munich: Piper, 1967).

[29] Cf. the title of a collection of essays by Otto Basil, *Das große Erbe* (Vienna: Stiasny, 1962). Vienna's Jewish past is functionalized for the tourist industry: see Ruth Beckermann,"Beyond the Bridges" in Dagmar C. G. Lorenz and Gabriele Weinberger, eds., *Insiders and Outsiders: Jewish and Gentile Culture in Germany and Austria* (Detroit: Wayne State UP, 1994), 301–7; here: 302–4.

[30] See Matti Bunzl, "The City and the Self: Narratives of Spatial Belonging among Austrian Jews" in *City and Society* (1996), 50–81.

[31] As early as 1946 Hans Weigel suggested a resumption of cultural relations between Austria and Germany in the fifth issue of *PLAN* (Gross, *PLAN and the Austrian Rebirth*, 93); see also Weigel, *Die Leiden der jungen Wörter* (Zurich, Munich: Artemis, 1974).

[32] See for instance Torberg's essays in *Österreichische Monatsblätter für kulturelle Freiheit*, 1954–1965.

[33] One such problematic protagonist is the Jewish informer in *Hier bin ich, mein Vater* (Frankfurt am Main: Fischer, 1966), written in 1948.

[34] Friedrich Torberg, *Die Tante Jolesch oder der Untergang des Abendlandes in Anekdoten* (Munich: dtv, 1984), 127.

[35] Weigel, "Das verhängte Fenster," *PLAN* 1/5 (1946), 397–77; also: *Die Leiden der jungen Wörter* (Zurich: Artemis, 1974).

[36] See Dagmar C. G. Lorenz, "Ein Definitionsproblem: Österreichische Literatur" in *Modern Austrian Literature* 12/2 (1979): 1–21; here: 14.

[37] Pascale R. Bos, "Etty Hillesum (1914–1943)" in S. Lillian Kremer, ed., *Holocaust Literature: An Encyclopedia of Writers and Their Work* (New York: Routledge, 2002), 1: 549–53.

[38] Geoffrey C. Howes, "Critical Observers of their Times: Karl Kraus and Robert Menasse" in Ernst Grabovszki and James Hardin, eds., *Literature in Vienna at the Turn of the Centuries: Continuities and Discontinuities around 1900 and 2000* (Rochester, NY: Camden House, 2003), 143. Robert Menasse in *Die sozialpartnerschaftliche Ästhetik: Essays zum österreichischen Geist* (Vienna: Sonderzahl, 1990) discusses the repressive aspects of a system that tried to minimize conflict at all cost.

[39] See Robert Menasse, *Das Land ohne Eigenschaften: Essay zur österreichischen Identität* (Vienna: Sonderzahl, 1992), and Beckermann, *Jenseits des Krieges*.

[40] See Anton Pelinka, *Windstille: Klagen über Österreich* (Vienna: Medusa, 1985) and *Populismus in Österreich* (Vienna: Junius, 1987).

[41] See also Anton Pelinka and Günter Bischof, eds., *Women in Austria* (New Brunswick: Transaction Publishers, 1998).

[42] See *Jelineks Wahl: Literarische Verwandschaften*, ed. Elfriede Jelinek and Brigitte Landes (Munich: Goldmann, 1998). The anthology contains texts by German-speaking authors for whom Jelinek has an affinity, including Jewish writers such as Robert Walser, Paul Celan, and Irene Dische.

[43] Dagmar C. G. Lorenz, "Elfriede Jelinek," *Holocaust Literature: An Encyclopedia of Writers and their Works* (New York: Routledge, 2003), 1: 587–99; here: 590.

[44] Ruth Beckermann, "Ich nenne es 'Austronazismus.'" Homepage des D.I.R. http://www.infolinks.de/dir-ml/99/11029e79b9a5.htm

[45] Ruth Beckermann's film *Homemad(e)* (Vienna: filmladen, 2001) captures the concerns of Austrians, including the Jewish author Elfriede Gerstl, at the time when Haider's party becomes part of the Austrian government. See Marlene Streeruwitz, "Alles, was falsch ist" in Isolde Charim und Doron Rabinovici, eds. *Österreich: Berichte aus Quarantanien* (Frankfurt am Main: Suhrkamp, 2000), 123–33; here: 125; and, in the same volume, Elfriede Jelinek, "Moment! Aufnahme! 5.10.1999," 100–109.

9: Drama in Austria, 1945–2000

Juliane Vogel

THE RECONSTRUCTION OF THE AUSTRIAN THEATER after 1945 had initially to face the traumatic fact that the Staatsoper and the Burgtheater, previously the centers of its tradition, could no longer be used for performances. The great venues of Austrian drama had been destroyed by bombs. Performances were held in "Ronacher," a former popular entertainment hall. This destruction of the national theaters meant the destruction of cultural and political self-respect. "Mit dem Stephansdom hat Wien seinen Glauben, mit der Burg seinen Stolz, mit der Oper die Freude verloren" (Along with St Stephen's, Austria lost its faith; with the Burg, its pride; and with the Opera, its enjoyment), wrote the editor Rudolf Kalmar.[1] The bombs had struck a central medium of Austrian self-presentation. A culture which had always considered "theater" a political category had to manage for over ten years without a national stage.

In this traumatic situation, all efforts were devoted to constructing a continuity that could conceal this break. When the Burgtheater and the Opera reopened on 15 October and 2 November 1955 respectively, it became clear that the renewal of the Austrian stage was not to include any reflection on how and why it had been destroyed. Not only did the restored state theaters open their doors, but on 26 October 1955, later proclaimed a national holiday, the State Treaty was signed. What was being celebrated was not liberation from Nazi rule, nor the establishment of democratic structures, but the quasi-natural return of Old Austria. "Als das Burgtheater zu spielen begann, hat sozusagen das Herz Österreichs wieder den ersten Schlag getan und den ganzen Kreislauf der Empfindungen bewegt, der uns wieder das richtige Bewußtsein von uns selbst und den Glauben an unsere Zukunft gegeben hat" (When the Burgtheater resumed its performances, Austria's heart began to beat anew, sending emotions through our veins, restoring our proper self-awareness and our faith in our future), wrote Friedrich Schreyvogl, who had vigorously promoted Austria's absorption into Nazi Germany and was from 1954 to 1961 deputy director of the Burgtheater.[2] As the ruins of the state theaters were rebuilt, the self-image of an injured theatrical nation was given cosmetic treatment. In relation to the theater, as elsewhere, the past evoked not the period of collaboration with National Socialism, but a fantasy of theatrical culture under the Habsburgs.[3] As early as 1945, Alexander Lernet-Holenia had written: "Wir haben uns nur zu besinnen, daß wir unsere Vergangenheit sind, und sie wird unsere Zukunft werden"[4] (We have only to call to mind that we are our past, and it will become our future).

The politics of continuity were accordingly pursued on all theatrical fronts. The classics were lovingly cultivated. The dramas of Franz Grillparzer, Friedrich Schiller, Johann Wolfgang Goethe, and (especially) Gotthold Ephraim Lessing, providing links to an unsullied past, were placed in the service of political restoration. And no time was lost in re-employing those actors and directors who had been active between 1938 and 1945. Untainted plays could be performed by deeply tainted actors. The theatrical dynasties who had found fame under National Socialism continued to dominate the stage in the postwar period. In 1946 a production of Lessing's *Nathan der Weise* was entrusted to Lothar Müthel, who had held the post of director of the Burgtheater under the Nazis and had entered the limelight with an anti-Semitic production of Shakespeare's *The Merchant of Venice*.[5]

Continuities were also sought in the postwar period by the programs and manifestos which demanded a new theater. A new language had not yet been found, and the old one was only too available. Even the texts that called passionately for a new start obscured their demands by adopting the formulae of the 1930s. Visions of a new theater were expressed in late-Expressionist, neo-Christian diction. Writing in the literary magazine *PLAN*, founded by Otto Basil in 1945, the author Franz Probst demanded a new beginning in high-flown rhetoric. His visionary images evoked the new theater as a timeless ritual, purified of any traces of history:

> Theater ist uns Gewohnheit geworden. Wir rennen ihm nach, wir naschen von allen Tischen. Doch fehlt uns die Ehrfurcht nach neuer Heiligung. [. . .] Das wäre eine Aufgabe unseres Theaters: uns die Quellen zu weisen, aus denen die vor uns geschöpft, aus denen die vor uns Heilung und Stärkung geholt haben. [. . .] Theater ist Notwendigkeit, Schicksal. Aber nicht dann, wenn es Zeitprobleme behandelt.[6]

> [We take theater for granted. We run after it, grabbing titbits from every table. But we lack the reverent desire for new consecration. [. . .] That would be a task for our theater: to show us the sources from which our predecessors drew, in which they found healing and strength. [. . .] Theater is necessity, destiny. But not if it deals with problems of the day.]

Although he also mentioned the names of Bertolt Brecht and Ödön von Horváth, Probst expected renewal to come from mystery plays such as *Jedermann* (Everyman, 1911) by Hugo von Hofmannsthal, the form of drama favored by the *Ständestaat* (corporate state).

The plays written for major stages and performed there also helped to construct a continuity that elided the years 1938 to 1945 with respect both to dramatic form and to their authors' biographies. Dramatists such as Max Mell and Rudolf Henz, who had enjoyed success under the National Socialists, erased the traces of the recent past by presenting themselves in new works as spokesmen of a timeless humanism.[7] But even the plays of the popular dramatist Fritz Hochwälder (1911–86), who returned to Austria from emigration in Switzerland, were remote from the crises of the historical present. In their form and content they followed classicist models of drama, ignoring modernism and adopting the stage techniques of Friedrich Schiller. By this stress on formal, historical, and psychological continuity, and the return to bourgeois aesthetics, the achievements of the theatrical avant-garde in the early twentieth century were once more consigned to oblivion. The focus of the traditional form was on great human crises. The greatest stage success of the postwar period, Hochwälder's *Das heilige Experiment* (The Holy Experiment, written in 1941–42 in his Swiss exile), dramatized the liquidation of the state established on Socialist principles by the Jesuits in eighteenth-century Paraguay, showing great individuals in classical situations of conflict and decision. A self-contained dramatic plot, with responsible figures as protagonists and set in the past, separated events on the stage sharply from the present. The unities of action, time, and place counteracted the process of fragmentation that was central to the experience of modernity and to avant-garde theater. Thus the foundations were laid for a stable and durable Burgtheater culture which saved its audiences from having to confront either theatrical modernism or the war and postwar periods. Not until 1965, in his play *Der Himbeerpflücker* (The Raspberry Picker), would Hochwälder address the theme of the Holocaust.[8]

A new type of drama, independent of formally and politically restorative tendencies, began to develop only in the mid-1950s. Sustained by a new avant-garde, it opposed the myths on which the identity of the Second Republic was founded. The new artistic groups were rebelling on dramatic terrain against the attitude represented by the state's cultural institutions, which regarded the National Socialist occupation as a purely external intervention in Austrian history and denied any complicity in the mass murder of Jews. Aesthetic techniques were their weapons against the forces that based their political mission on a timeless Austrian culture and put forward the pseudo-religious experience of resurrection instead of analyzing Austrian enthusiasm for Hitler. In the avant-garde theater, as elsewhere, the confrontation with the fascist or authoritarian mentality was the starting-point for a new aesthetic exploration.

Critique of Language

The texts and actions that originated in this context did not operate with the techniques of "commitment" or of political theater. Early on, they refrained from dealing explicitly with political tyranny and from issuing explicit accusations — though anti-fascist theater in Austria should not be ignored.[9] Avant-garde drama turned its fire not against beliefs, but against established institutions and dramatic conventions; even when it adopted a political position, its challenge was based not on its political principles but on its aesthetic radicalism. The artists and authors known as the Wiener Gruppe, in particular, challenged bourgeois theatrical culture by making use, in cellars or on the streets, of theatrical forms alien to the bourgeois canon. Their aesthetic horizons were bounded not by the dramatic work and the "fixed theater," but by "spontaneous theater":[10] cabarets, processions, fairs and the like, which turned everyday life into theatrical poetry.

Their texts became political by subjecting the theater's dominant medium of communication to a fundamental critique. Their attacks were aimed at the authority of language, which as the accomplice and agent of power took possession of the individual in order to transform him into a compliant instrument of the ruling powers. They wanted to show in dramatic texts how power was exercised not only through physical force, but also in the laws of grammar and semantics. The members of the Wiener Gruppe and their successors reconstructed the "seizure of power" carried out by language, displaying the totalitarian framework of a medium which organized and manipulated the speakers' thought and action by means of a concealed code. In a political reading of the *Tractatus logico-philosophicus* by Ludwig Wittgenstein, language was seen as a means of limiting experience, not extending it. Recognizing that the limits of language coincided with the limits of a consciousness hemmed in by social conditions, the avant-garde sketched out scenes which were experimental in character. Dramatic experiments and projects demonstrated how language should be seen: not as a transparent medium of self-expression, but as an anonymous, inscrutable authority that assumed power over the speaker and controlled his utterances. This critique of language, which was interested only in the forms of language, not in what was said, probed grammatical rules, and displayed in detail the corruption of socialized discourse. The causes of fascism were sought in the consciousness of manipulated speakers or in the transformation of a dishonest and manipulative language into a perfectly functioning unit of society.

The new beginning after 1945, however, also provided the point of contact with a tradition that had been broken and often disowned. Although the authors of the 1950s and 1960s saw themselves as an avant-garde without allegiance to any literary heritage, their texts, written to resist the past, show many signs of reappropriating this tradition. A critique of language using theatrical techniques could link up with many movements that reached back before 1945 and into the eighteenth and nineteenth centuries. Ever since the Enlightenment, texts written in Austria had analyzed the mechanisms of a linguistic usage shaped by authoritarianism.[11] With particular sensitivity to formulae, clichés, and ecclesiastical and bureaucratic language, they showed how language was stamped by the authorities and channeled into formulaic phrases. Liturgy and officialese, as ossified forms of language, had become indispensable resources for dramatic discourse. The comedies of Johann Nestroy sprang from an awareness that language was not at the free disposal of the bourgeois subject. His plays made it clear that the supposedly autonomous subject was never master of his own speech. This general mistrust of formulaic language hardened when modern mass media put language into circulation in commodified form. In particular, the journalistic cliché was recognized and attacked as a modern, commercialized variant of linguistic stereotyping. The great antagonist of the "set phrase," in drama as elsewhere, was the satirist Karl Kraus: in his apocalyptic play *Die letzten Tage der Menschheit* (The Last Days of Mankind, written between 1915 and 1922) he had dramatized the seizure of power by language and the colonization of dramatic figures by the journalistic cliché.[12] In panoramic scenes from the course of the First World War, this drama put on trial the attempts by warmongers to shape the public's consciousness through language. Each individual scene called the press to account by means of quotations. Kraus's main weapon against cliché was to mount a display of corrupt phrases. By reproducing in detail a discourse that had been subverted by the press, he dissolved the contours of his dramatic figures. Individuality capitulated before the authority and the omnipresence of clichés. Names became allegories, and characters became types that displayed openly their origin as quotations from the press. By his radical assumption that language creates circumstances instead of being created by them, Kraus used drama as language critique. The modern horizon of dramatic discourse was the apocalyptic chatter that permitted neither the development of individual discourse nor the construction of individual characters. This representation of the theater as world and the world as theater, with its alienated and soulless figures, provided a point of contact after 1945 for the dramas of a new literature that was both conscious and critical of language.

Another stimulus that was no less important for dramatic literature after 1945 came from the works of the part Austrian, part Hungarian dramatist Ödön von Horváth, whose plays of the 1920s and 1930s criticized their contemporary world by criticizing its language. His dramas, among which *Geschichten aus dem Wiener Wald* (Tales from the Vienna Woods, 1931) had a particularly durable influence, showed the dramatic figure as helpless before the linguistic stereotype. The protagonists' sole means of expression was a half-educated jargon which, in its incoherence, its helpless groping for a "higher," cultivated language, revealed that the speakers had no language of their own. Horváth's figures have only a dispossessed idiom: this is as true of the victims of circumstances, who can articulate their sufferings only through half-educated clichés, as of those who make them suffer. The latter, when the phony linguistic façade starts to crumble, readily resort to physical violence. This type of drama conveys Horváth's insight that under prevailing circumstances people are incapable of authentic self-revelations; their expressions of feeling are "verkitscht [. . .], verfälscht, verniedlicht und nach masochistischer Manier geil auf Mitleid"[13] (vulgarized, falsified, prettified, with a masochistic craving for compassion). This advanced critique of language was taken further by dramatic works of the 1970s.[14]

The past provided one further counter-force with which to oppose clichés. Resisting the euphemisms of Austrian identity politics, the Wiener Gruppe looked back to the Viennese popular theater of the eighteenth century and reanimated a comic figure who even then had practiced a critique of language through the body. This was Kasperl, who, banished from the stage by bourgeois society, had protested against the increasing sublimation demanded by the advance of civilization and had upheld the rights of the body against a dishonest verbal discourse. Hungry, thirsty, greedy, and lecherous, Kasperl, or Hanswurst — known to the bourgeois public as the comic figure of Papageno from the Mozart-Schikaneder *Magic Flute* — embodied the residual resistance that could not be disciplined by speech. As such, he became the central figure of the Viennese avant-garde and was featured by Konrad Bayer (1932–64), Gerhard Rühm (1930–) and above all H. C. Artmann (1921–2000) in mini-dramas with appropriate titles such as Artmann's *Die mißglückte Luftreise* (The Disastrous Trip through the Air, 1955), *die hochzeit caspars mit gelsomina* (caspar and gelsomina get married, 1960) and *die liebe fee pocahontas oder kasper als schildwache* (the dear fairy pocahontas or kasper as sentry, 1961).[15] Their authors were aware of the dramatically transformed situation that the anarchic revenant Kasperl had to confront in the mid twentieth century. Their texts showed what was in store for the undisciplined, illiterate body in modern society. In their experimental scenes they exposed the comic figure to the grip of a ruthlessly institutionalized society. In most of the Wiener Gruppe's dramas featuring Kasperl or Hanswurst, the central figure, albeit comically, comes to grief.

It is particularly in Konrad Bayer's mini-drama *Kasperl auf dem elektrischen Stuhl* (Kasperl in the Electric Chair, 1968) that the "illiterate" Kasperl falls into the clutches of the law. Claiming to have murdered his wife, Kasperl gives himself up to the authorities, only to undergo police investigation and execution. The official formalities not only stall the development of the dramatic situation, they also impose order on the anarchic bodies of the figures involved in the theatrical action. In addition, the play follows the discursive model of the language exercise. By learning sentences, the illiterate figures become speakers who can say the right thing in social frameworks. While in prison, Kasperl, who has no identity and cannot fill in a form, is trained in model sentences and in repetitive social situations. The Kasperl drama turns out also to be a Wittgenstein drama. It analyses and deconstructs a discourse whose grammatical form imposes radical limitations on the speakers" potential for experience and knowledge. At the same time, the return to the Viennese popular theater was governed by Romantic irony: *Kasperl auf dem elektrischen Stuhl* is theater within theater. The action begins in the auditorium, among spectators who comment on the play in stereotyped phrases. A further homage to Romantic irony occurs when Kasperl, who cannot read or write, finally reveals himself as the author of the entire play.[16]

Sprechstücke

The dramatic texts of the Wiener Gruppe also paved the way for what was called the *Sprechstück* or "speech-play," which undertook a strictly formal analysis of the complicity of language with power, discarding traditional forms of theatrical representation. Peter Handke (1942–) continued the Wiener Gruppe's experiments in his early plays, above all *Kaspar* (1968), at a time when provocative theater was emerging from underground and conquering the public stages. The date 1968 marks the end of aesthetic restoration, in the theater as elsewhere. Hence, Handke's speech-plays do not belong to the short-lived actions of an unofficial theater that kept changing its venues and challenging the police; they attacked the bourgeois theater in its traditional location.

Kaspar, explicitly described by Handke as a *Sprechstück*, deals with a twofold Kaspar-Kasperl figure. At first, the title seems to recall the name of the comic figure from popular theater. Kaspar looks "pudelnärrisch" (daft) and his clothing clearly identifies him as a clown, yet these references are promptly retracted — his name is spelled with "a," not "e," and a stage direction asserts in an openly self-contradictory manner: "Kaspar hat keine Ähnlichkeit mit einem Spaßmacher"[17] (Kaspar bears no resemblance to a clown). For he is simultaneously the famous foundling Kaspar Hauser, who was discovered in 1828 in Ansbach (in northern Bavaria), uncared-for and unable to speak, and until his murder in 1833 underwent a painful course of instruction in language. Handke exploits the similarity between the names Kaspar and Kasperl in order to explore the structural similarity between their destinies in bourgeois society. The comic figure, like the nineteenth-century foundling, is also the guinea pig in a terrorist experiment in language-teaching. In both cases, a person without a written record is introduced into the space of cultural manipulation. Handke not only draws on historical sources but also creates an experimental situation of ideal purity in order to present a person's socialization as a process of linguistic adjustment and repression. The linguistic torture is carried out not by people, but by anonymous voices, further dehumanized by technical means, which equip the awkward Kaspar with senseless but socially appropriate sentences and gradually civilize his body as well. Like Bayer, Handke shows that the speech appropriate to power does not convey any content, nor does it assist communication between people. His Kaspar, too, is put through a linguistic exercise, in which he learns long lists of socially acceptable sentences. The outcome of the experiment can only be judged negatively. The socialized Kaspar is a dead Kaspar, who enters society by asking the question previously uttered by a dying woman: "Warum fliegen da lauter so schwarze Würmer herum?"[18] (Why are there all those black worms flying about?). At the height of pedagogical success, he quotes, albeit not verbatim, the last words spoken in Horváth's *Glaube Liebe Hoffnung* (Faith Love Hope, 1932) by Elisabeth, who is driven into a corner, and ultimately to suicide, by the same society.[19] A society based on this type of socialization would thus be a society of the living dead. At the end of the play, the principle of serial repetition extends to Kaspar himself. Fully socialized, he spontaneously multiplies. Suddenly a large number of identical Kaspars appear on the stage. But they do not behave as one might expect. Rather than exemplars of obedience, Kaspar's doubles are malevolent revenants of the repressed comic figure. Split off by hysterical self-division from the perfectly socialized individual, they respond to the total victory of cliché with shrill, inarticulate shrieks. The uproar of the multiple Kaspars reveals the anarchic side of a language that has been wholly subordinated to society.

Viennese Actionism

The critique of the individual's domination by language was not, however, pursued solely by linguistic means. Expelled from the language-games of the speech-play, the body reconquered the stage by violence. From controversy over the language-oriented work of the Wiener Gruppe there developed a complementary performative tendency that restored the old rights of the body and added some new ones. At the end of the 1960s a group of artists formed under the name of Wiener Aktionismus (Viennese Actionism), calling for the total desublimation of bodily desire in dramatic situations. Following on from the theatrical experiments of the Wiener Gruppe, which had exploited such forms as procession, opera, and cabaret, the Actionists developed radical body scenarios that responded physically to the symbolic order. Otto Mühl (1925–), Hermann Nitsch (1938–), Rudolf Schwarzkogler (1940–69), Günther Brus (1938–), and — mediating between both artistic groupings — Oswald Wiener (1935–), propagated in both theory and practice an art of extravagance, dissipation, spillage and violence, in which repressed instinctual urges were released in spectacular scenes. Actionistic events were intended to be devoid of meaning; the material character of the action's components was to be highlighted. All signs were eliminated: "Weg mit den Symbolen" (Away with symbols), demanded Oswald Wiener, unmistakably rejecting the semiotic function of the sign.[20] For Otto Mühl, likewise, the action represented nothing beyond itself:

> nicht meißeln oder pinseln, sondern den leuten den dreck ins gesicht werfen, den leuten die kunst austreiben. Keine umwege, sondern gleich den menschen angehen, ihm die glieder verrenken, ihn mit anderen materialien vermischen, ihn zum objekt machen. Man kann ihm einen fuß ausreißen, ihn schreien und erbrechen lassen.[21]

> [Not using chisel or paintbrush, but throwing muck in people's faces, driving the art out of them. No roundabout methods, but going right up to someone, dislocating his limbs, mixing him with other materials, making him an object. You can tear off one of his feet, make him scream and vomit.]

Bodily boundaries were overridden, fluids and excretions were spilled in an actionist manner. Releasing the body from the prison-house of language, the theater marked itself out by discarding writing and language, by its polemical rejection of all forms of representation and meaning as a formative impulse of the latest Austrian drama. Viennese Actionism left its stamp on the dramatic texts of recent decades. The plays of Elfriede Jelinek, Wolfgang Bauer (1941–), Marlene Streeruwitz (1950–), and Werner Schwab (1958–94), which explore the tension between speech-play and action, verbal and physical violence, are shaped by actionist tendencies. It was particularly Oswald Wiener who radicalized the relations between language and action, meaning and violence, in his text *purim*, inserted into his experimental novel *die verbesserung von mitteleuropa* (the improvement of central europe, 1969). Based on a ritual, the Jewish Purim festival, he put the violence of language, which pinned down its objects by police methods, in contact with the violence of action, which assaulted and annihilated its object as a body. This aggression is addressed to the theater audience. What essentially happens in the play is that the guests who have paid to attend a theater performance are summoned by name and then massacred with relaxed brutality. Linguistic and physical violence, appeal and action, are cut short and combined. Not only do the spectators perish, so do the conventions of bourgeois theater. Wiener's actors leap over the gap dividing stage from stalls, invading the hitherto sheltered zone in which the bourgeoisie enjoy the arts, and drawing it into their action. The play *purim* is a theater of trespass, eliminating the boundary between art and life.

This destruction of bourgeois theatrical conventions reunited the action with the *Sprechstück*. They converged on a radical negation of the bourgeois role as spectator. Although its attacks were only verbal, Peter Handke's *Publikumsbeschimpfung* (Insulting the Audience, 1966) had already challenged the traditional habits of theatrical consumption, depriving the spectators of their immunity. In a long, iconoclastic speech addressed to the audience, his *Sprechstück* swept away all illusions about illusion: "sie brauchen nicht zu wissen, daß hier eine Bühne ist. Sie brauchen keine Erwartung. Sie brauchen sich nicht erwartungsvoll zurückzulehnen"[22] (You don't need to know that this is a stage. You don't need to expect anything. You don't need to lean back expectantly).

Misanthropic Tirades: From Handke to Bernhard

On the other hand, Handke's linguistic exercise *Publikumsbeschimpfung* pointed far beyond the experimental framework of the *Sprechstück*. Its title already proclaimed it a misanthropic discourse. By privileging a single speech-act, that of the insult, it followed on from a type of drama that even in the past had made rhetorical and theatrical capital from the experience of political impotence. Handke's *Sprechstück* gave systematic and radical form to a drama of denunciation, such as had entered literary history with Ferdinand Raimund, Nestroy or Kraus. When the actors in *Publikumsbeschimpfung* begin their insults, they are continuing a kind of theater which centers on the seemingly endless tirade of the misanthropic speaker:

> [. . .] ihr vaterlandslosen Gesellen, ihr Revoluzzer, ihr Rückständler, ihr Beschmutzer des eigenen Nests, ihr inneren Emigranten, ihr Defätisten, ihr Revisionisten, ihr Revanchisten, ihr Militaristen, ihr Pazifisten, ihr Faschisten, ihr Intellektualisten, ihr Nihilisten, ihr Individualisten, ihr Kollektivisten, ihr Antidemokraten etc.[23]

> [you economic migrants, you would-be revolutionaries, you backwoodsmen, you nest-foulers, you internal emigrants, you defeatists, you revisionists, you revanchists, you militarists, you pacifists, you fascists, you intellectualists, you nihilists, you individualists, you collectivists, you antidemocrats, etc.]

The abstract, distilled, and decontextualized form of attack in Handke's *Publikumsbeschimpfung* is an important link to the dramatic work of Thomas Bernhard (1931–89), which at first glance might seem to restore a realistic backdrop and late-bourgeois characters to the stage. Bernhard's protagonists, like those of Ibsen, Chekhov, or Strindberg, belong to doomed upper-bourgeois families. But his dramas, which taken as a whole again display repeated features, can be understood as "speech-plays," since they formalize the misanthropic speech-act *ad libitum* and *ad nauseam*. As a rule they give vent to the monological energies of powerless patriarchs in tirades which are acts of overwhelming self-assertion, degrading their dependants, especially their wives and daughters, into mute and passive figures. Their uncompromising discourse, always swift to condemn, is uttered in a zone of death.

Yet if Bernhard's drama operates in a region of death, that is also because it is governed by all manner of repetition compulsions.[24] His literary language consists so much in repetition with minor variations that its rigidly formalized structure seems to invite a musical rather than a literary analysis.[25] But on the level of action, too, structures of recurrence dominate those of succession and linearity. Developments, changes, and events are forestalled by repetition. Anything that happens is usually part of a series. Bernhard's plays are often set on anniversaries (*Heldenplatz*, Heroes Square, 1988) or birthdays (*Ein Fest für Boris*, A Party for Boris, 1970; *Vor dem Ruhestand*, Before Retirement, 1979). The "ignoramus" and the "madman" in *Der Ignorant und der Wahnsinnige* (1973) meet at the 222nd repetition of *The Magic Flute*, while *Die Macht der Gewohnheit* (The Force of Habit, 1974), whose very title announces repetitions, combines the form of drama with that of the musical rehearsal. Yet it becomes increasingly clear that this omnipresent repetition compulsion in Bernhard's work results from historical circumstances. For both criminals and victims, it points to the omnipresence of a past that can neither be mastered nor remembered — the period 1938–45, which, as the Waldheim affair made clear, continued to be the subject of collective repression in the Austrian media. Repetition, taking the place of recollection, brings Nazi criminals and Nazism's victims alike under its spell. Thus the play *Vor dem Ruhestand* shows us the rituals of a criminal family. Rudolf, the judge and former SS officer, still attached to National Socialism even after 1945, bases his postwar existence entirely on repetitions. Together with his dependents, who are either devoted or submissive, he celebrates the return of Himmler's birthday every year. These ghostly reenactments are ended only by the patriarch's death.

For the victims, repetition is evidently the consequence of trauma, as is evident from the play *Heldenplatz*, written for the fiftieth anniversary of the *Anschluss*. Here repetition shapes the behavior and experience of the Jewish Schuster family, whom Hitler drove into emigration. Professor Schuster, whose brother, reduced to despair by the *Anschluss* in 1938, committed suicide, repeats his action in 1988 by throwing himself out of the window. As we learn from the survivors' accounts, his life, marked by exile and persecution, was governed by an idiosyncratic system of unremitting, tyrannical rituals. His wife, on the other hand, suffers from another form of repetition. Even fifty years on, she is pursued by the yelling of Hitler's devotees on the Heldenplatz. Over and over again she undergoes the acoustic hallucination of the shouting of the Nazi crowd, till finally this howling, audible to all in its full fury, breaks into the theatrical space and brings about her death.

Yet for Bernhard, repetition can also lead to perfection. In varying experimental structures, his dramas display the fabrication of highly crafted human machines. Misanthropic patriarchs drive rebellious human bodies to artistic perfection through drilling and exercises. Their never completed and ultimately deadly project aims at total control, total precision and simultaneously at total artificiality. In this sense, *Der Ignorant und der Wahnsinnige*, a back-stage or dressing-room drama, deals with a female machine: it centers on the Queen of the Night, who represents Bernhard's radical synthesis of Romantic myths of art, especially those in Offenbach's *Tales of Hoffmann*.[26] The Queen of the Night is a miraculous coloratura performer and a puppet, like Hoffmann's Olimpia: "Es müßte doch | eine ungeheuere Befriedigung sein | die Gewissheit | einen Mechanismus als Tochter zu besitzen | oder eine Tochter als Mechanismus | berühmt | und berühmt und unvergleichlich [. . .]"[27] (It must be enormously satisfying to be certain you have a mechanism as daughter or a daughter as mechanism, famous, famous and incomparable). Yet she is also a consumptive, moribund singer like Hoffmann's Antonia. The perfection of the coloratura and the frailty of the human body are contrasted in one and the same figure. The artistic project to which Bernhard's characters devote themselves demands the suppression of the body and the subjection of the feminine element. Significantly, this always implies the total subjugation of the opposite sex, whose artistic gifts are simultaneously essential to the project. As a rule, it is fathers and patriarchs who rear the perfect virtuoso under laboratory conditions, for example in *Die Macht der Gewohnheit* or *Der Theatermacher* (The Theater-Maker, 1984).

However, the patriarchs who deliver monologues in Bernhard's plays are far from being the acknowledged representatives of social power. For all their domestic authority, they are impoverished, crippled, or otherwise in decline. The autocracy they institute by means of language is merely a sign of impotence. Their misanthropy reveals itself as the obverse of their unsatisfied desire for affirmation. Accordingly, some of Bernhard's plays — *Der Weltverbesserer* (The World-Fixer, 1979), *Über allen Gipfeln ist Ruh* (The Hills are at Peace, 1981), *Einfach kompliziert* (Simply Complicated, 1986), *Minetti* (1976) — have therefore been called *Anerkennungskomödien* (comedies of recognition), since their elderly monomaniacs waver between contempt for the world, megalomania and the lust for fame.[28] In their solitude and their incessant discourse, they owe something to Samuel Beckett's figures. His *Endgame* is always present, even if Bernhard lays less stress on the existential dimension that is so prominent in Beckett's drama.

Elfriede Jelinek

The misanthropic dramaturgy of negation — "Sie haben erkannt, daß wir vornehmlich verneinen"[29] (you've realized that we usually say no), to quote Handke's *Publikumsbeschimpfung* — is not yet exhausted. The principle of negation is radicalized in Elfriede Jelinek's dramatic texts, which follow programmatically from Bernhard's. Creative processes are interpreted as destructive: "I'll swing the axe," runs their dramatic credo. This destructive gesture of creation goes for broke, deliberately disregarding nuances: "Ich vergrößere (oder reduziere) meine Figuren ins Übermenschliche, ich mache also Popanze aus ihnen" (I enlarge [or reduce] my figures to superhuman dimensions, turning them into dummies).[30] Jelinek's theater offers no subtle psychology, any more than Bernhard's. Unlike Bernhard's theatrical figures, however, hers increasingly lose any semblance of humanity. Her method of enlargement, or reduction, dissolves any likeness to a person. Closed and bounded characters are replaced by extended, battered *Sprachflächen* (linguistic surfaces), which reject depth and repel any attempt at deeper analysis. By dissolving the contours of individual discourse, the figures who appear on stage are depersonalized and transpersonalized. What is spoken has no subjective origin and no connection with an individual. Discourse is always that of "several."[31] Utterances are pluralized and embedded in intertextual relationships. The speakers repeat and quote speeches "die es schon gibt"[32] (that already exist). As with Kraus, dramatic speech draws on the quotation, or rather on a vast medley of quotations from literature and the media. Given that all speech is intertextually bound, Jelinek draws a radical inference: the discourse that already exists is the discourse of the dead. Speaking with dead tongues, the speakers are also acting in a zone of death. "I am dead" — the central sentence from Edgar Allan Poe's "The Facts in the Case of M. Valdemar" — formulates the poetic precondition of their appearance, allowing not only the voices of well-known poets but also and especially the voices of the nameless dead of the Holocaust to become audible in dramatic discourse. Jelinek's texts are constructed on the principle of montage, bringing disparate voices together and simultaneously dismantling what is said.

The linguistic surfaces thus produced are at once monological and choric. As they become frequent in Jelinek's plays, these assume a depersonalized and at the same time pluralized form. In *Bambiland* (2003), occasioned by the USA's war on Iraq, there is no longer any recognizable speaker, only a confusion of media voices broadcast through the ether. The introduction of the chorus in *ein sportstück* (a play about sport, 1998) and *Das Lebewohl* (The Farewell, 2000) takes account of this tendency to have many voices within a single voice.[33]

Jelinek's dramaturgy unfolds within the framework of a sharply defined Marxist-feminist model. Both in her prose and her dramatic texts, she unmasks class rule and male rule, disclosing the interplay between economic and sexual exploitation. Her first play, *Was geschah, nachdem Nora ihren Mann verlassen hatte* (What Happened after Nora left her Husband, 1979), used the form of a Brechtian "Lehrstück" (didactic play) to deal with the complicity between bourgeois femininity and big business.[34] Then the "artist drama" *Clara S.* (1981) investigated the material and cultural conditions to which female creativity is subject in bourgeois society. The abbreviation "Clara S." conceals the name of the German pianist Clara Schumann, wife of the composer: as an artist she had no surname of her own, she was forbidden to compose, and her creativity was suppressed by frequent pregnancies. Unlike the parody of Ibsen's *A Doll's House*, the play breaks free from subordination to its literary model. With the help of historical montage, it constructs a laboratory situation in which the myth of male original genius undergoes experimental testing. The house of the sex-obsessed Italian poet Gabriele D'Annunzio provides a meeting-place for women who hope that in return for "submission," that is, sexual self-surrender, the artist will support their own artistic work. Here Clara Schumann, the nineteenth-century female artist, meets dancers and singers from the twentieth century. While subjecting the myth of privileged male creativity to a searching critique, the play also invites us to laugh at stereotyped female roles. Men and women are equally dependent on prepackaged speeches and poses which, by their artificiality, deconstruct the bourgeois notions of authenticity and originality, masculinity and femininity. The dramatic form approaches a revue. The action disintegrates into hysterical individual scenes.

The artificial character of femininity, or rather the rules by which it is constructed in bourgeois society, is also the theme of the plays *Krankheit* (Illness, 1987) and *Moderne Frauen* (Modern Women, 1987). Yet women's suffering is not displayed in a tear-jerking manner. Both male and female persons are artificial dummies made of language, garrulous dolls split off from a mute body that cannot verbalize its pain.

In the later plays, this critique of the sexual politics of bourgeois society gives way to a critique of the dishonesty and repressiveness of the Austrian mass media. Jelinek shows how the press and television try to hush up Austria's complicity in the crimes of National Socialism. Here, too, the newspaper quotation is the appropriate device for exposing and denouncing the political catastrophe of denial and self-deception in Austrian public life. Accordingly, the play *stecken, stab und stangl* (stick, rod and pole, 1996) reveals the full spectrum of lies within a dramaturgy based on the media. It chooses the form of the talk show, which is particularly apt for the unbridled display of linguistic surfaces. The starting-point for discussion is a news item involving crime and the radical Right, a bomb explosion in Oberwart (in Burgenland) on 4 February 1995, in which four Roma (Gypsies) resident there were killed. For Jelinek, this date marked the blackest day in the history of the Second Republic, by showing that racial aggression continued in Austria even after 1945.[35] In her play, she was able to demonstrate that the media, dealing with these murders, resorted to the same strategies of euphemism, denial, and repression that were applied to the Holocaust.[36] The quotations from Austrian newspapers that are worked into the play document how Oberwart and Auschwitz gave rise to the same reactions from the press — that the same butchers were at work. The organizing metaphor for this dramatic text about repression is cro- cheting. The figures produce endless quantities of crochet-work, with which they conceal the gaps in their smug self-image.

The radical line of this drama includes the plays of Streeruwitz, who similarly uses the stage to challenge patriarchy. Her plays *Waikiki Beach* (1992), *Sloane Square* (1992), *New York, New York* (1993) and *Ocean Drive* (1994) are designed to destabilize the pillars of patriarchal theater. She too takes as her dramatic subject the relations between the sexes in the bourgeois world. However, Streeruwitz engages with traditional theatrical models much more than Jelinek does. While Jelinek increasingly replaces dialogue with anonymous linguistic surfaces, Streeruwitz offers escalating plots and sharp dialogue, revealing the inability of her figures to communi- cate. While Bernhard and Jelinek favor lengthy tirades, she prefers to abbreviate. As in her prose, the syntax of her figures' discourse is shattered and shortened by the brutal and untimely intervention of the full stop. Streeruwitz's artistic language arises from the artificial fragmentation of her sentences, cutting the speakers off from themselves and one another. Although the challenging plot lines always remain clear, the stage action is repeatedly interrupted by revue-like interludes that alienate, reflect and distort it. The span of the action, which is realistic despite caricature, is in turn permeated by surreal, allegorical, and mythological elements. Generic or textual quotations develop familiar forms of alienation. All the formal elements are used that the theater has been able to appropriate in the course of its history: "Ready-made components — linguistic, gestic, dra- maturgic — are recycled, forming a texture of acoustic and visual 'second- hand material.' Items of the cultural heritage (Shakespeare or Chekhov), musical quotations (such as Puccini's *Tosca* and Beethoven's *For Elise*), ges- tic quotations (the Pietà, the classical chorus) combined with coffee-table chatter and talk-shows are interwoven to produce an alienating effect. Declamation and song, often choreographed in a stylized fashion, under- line the artificiality of the texture."[37] The variety of forms quoted matches that of the themes that are raised but swiftly used up: health fads and popu- lar ignorance, youth crime and meaningless research, stars and the power of the media, environmental damage and state surveillance — Streeruwitz has no qualms about working media commonplaces into her plays and linking dramatic events to day-to-day political discussion.

New *Volksstücke*

By showing, in grotesquely exaggerated form, the collapse of urban, provincial, and Alpine communities, Streeruwitz participates in one of the most controversial dramatic genres of postwar Austrian literature. Her plays could be called "anti-Volksstücke," polemically directed against a genre which since its origins in the nineteenth century has brought the life of the people onto the stage, whether idealizing it or deploying social criticism. Streeruwitz initially looks to the dramas which, from the late 1960s on, attacked the traditional *Volksstück* with new, negative versions of the genre.[38] Their targets were a theater that used realistic portrayal and sentimental social criticism to expose the "people" to the voyeuristic empathy of a bourgeois audience, and the postwar Austrian rural *Heimat* film, which idealized Austria as the home of a "natural" populace against the Technicolor background of the Alps. For the dramatist Werner Schwab, the "Volksstück" was "jene Form, die mir am widerlichsten war. Und diese Form habe ich zu sprengen versucht"[39] (the form I hated most. And I've tried to blow it apart).

The polemical potential of this anti-form developed in the 1960s in dialogue with the bitterly critical *Volksstücke* of Horváth. The theatrical history of the Second Republic is also the history of the reception of Horváth, which occurred in several phases. He had stripped the enchantment from an already discredited form: whether through idyllic images or socially critical tableaux, the traditional *Volksstück* had sought to obscure the fact that the "people" had long since developed into an aggressive petty-bourgeoisie. In his name, the critique of language could be combined with this genre, and the avant-garde's reflections on language could be exploited for the new and negative *Volksstück*. The reception of Horváth in the 1960s and 1970s was initially associated with Helmut Qualtinger, who, both as an actor and a reciter, had sought to raise the profile of Horváth when he had almost been forgotten. Qualtinger's monologue *Der Herr Karl* (1961), uttered by post-1945 *homo austriacus*, criticizes the language of the Austrian petty-bourgeoisie and reveals the linguistic and psychological tricks of an Austrian fellow-traveler who struggles, mostly in vain, to conceal his true political sympathies behind empty clichés. His authoritarian character cannot be kept down, and the fascist emerges from behind the mask of the hearty Viennese. In 1970, Horváth's reputation gained a further boost when Peter Handke published an essay with the provocative title "Horváth ist besser als Brecht."

Yet the "denunziatorisches Volksstück"[40] was not merely a continuation of Horváth's drama. From the late 1960s and the 1970s down to the present, it has undergone a radicalization that did not stop at unmasking language and the consciousness behind it. The *Volksstück* genre, renewed in Horváth's spirit, continued to diagnose the repression and survival of fascist mentalities in those sections of the population that had in the past been defined by the ideological concept of the *Volk*. But the stress now lay on sensitizing the audience to the development of physical violence. The socially critical impulse behind Horváth's plays, and also their occasional tear-jerking, were downplayed or rejected in favor of actionism. The new plays provided snapshots of a collective consciousness always on the verge of violence and offered exaggerated diagnoses of the social status quo, with no moralistic treatment of the emotions provoked in the spectator. As a rule, they showed latent aggression being released against a scapegoat who was delivered up to collective, sometimes ritual, slaughter. The pessimistic punch line of the post-1945 anti-*Volksstück* was the killing of those who infringed the rule of silence and the taboo on memory by confronting their fellow-citizens with what the latter would rather forget. Those members of society who broke the collective repression were the objects of violence. The stage disclosed the hidden mechanism, with atavistic and ritual over-tones, which organized the Austrian *Volksgemeinschaft* or people's community, in the old Nazi term, as a community of violence.

The linguistic medium of such *Volksstücke* was no longer the half-educated jargon of Horváth's speakers. Instead, dialects and group-specific language were defamiliarized in a way that revealed their real meaning. Dialect was stripped of the phony innocence and naivety ascribed to it in the identity politics of the Second Republic (something to which the Austrian *Heimat* film of the 1950s gives eloquent testimony). It was now the sociolect of a brutalized petty-bourgeoisie, helping its speakers to shed their civilized inhibitions. The language spoken on the stage was no longer simple and folksy, but corrupt and artificial, with a potential for violence that was unleashed in excremental and murderous excess. The new *Volksstück* made good use of the experiments in criticism of language that the avant-garde theater had developed in dialogue with Wittgenstein's philosophy.

It was above all the plays of Peter Turrini (1944–) that tried out linguistic and other "schockstrategien" (shock strategies). In *Rozznjagd* (Rat Hunt, 1967) a couple canoodles on a rubbish-heap. Garbage here makes its first stage appearance, heralding the scrap heaps on which Jelinek's and Werner Schwab's figures will perform. The rendezvous takes place in one of those dilapidated settings that play a significant role throughout present-day Austrian drama. The bankrupt world theater seeks its settings where nobody wants to be. In the dramatic presentation of how modern society generates waste, the Baroque motif of *vanitas* returns to the stage. Amid the rubbish of civilization, the two lovers get rid of the artificial cultural and corporeal signs on which their status and their social identity had been founded: clothes, hanks of hair, dentures, and so forth. Finally, as they stand naked and vulnerable on the rubbish-heap, they are shot by two men hunting rats. A brief moment of authenticity ends with casual brutality. This allegory, both cynical and simple, is followed in Turrini's *Sauschlachten* (Slaughtering Sows, 1972) by a radical exaggeration of the village violence that the sentimental *Volksstück* and the *Heimat* film had concealed behind sugary emotion. Turrini shows the killing of an outsider:

a farmer's son, who cannot speak but only grunts, is slaughtered and devoured. He has to die because his pig-language speaks the truth about conventional language. His grunting is the acoustic mirror of their speech, putting an end to lying and restoring the truth about dishonest communication.

Distaste for the *Volksstück* can extend to rejecting the genre term even in its negative form. Although the Graz dramatist Wolfgang Bauer gives his play *Gespenster* (Ghosts, 1973) the generic label *Volksstück*, he does not want his dramas to be understood as such. Like *Gespenster*, the plays *Party for Six* (1967), *Magic Afternoon* (1968), and *Change* (1969) give an ethnologically precise insight into those "authentic" life-styles with which the young drop-outs of the 1960s and early 1970s distanced themselves from the bourgeois lives of their parents. Bauer subjects his cast to a dramaturgy of disillusion. His figures repeatedly form communes, or rather artists' communes, and these are presented not as the longed-for site of freedom, but as a scene of apathy and loss of identity.[41] The supposed escape into "exotic anarchy" leads first to monotony, then to catastrophe. The dramatic chronicle of uneventful tedium is abruptly shattered by fatal, or at least disastrous, *coups de théâtre*. Action is replaced by a high-risk game of chance among prisoners who try to escape from boredom, raising the stakes until they finally prove fatal. Instead of events, we have the calculation of events, aiming to prevent, at a high cost, the perpetual iteration of the same. Bohemian circles are dominated by the same repression, the same cynicism, and the same potential for violence as the life of the hated parental generation. The behavior patterns of late-capitalist society keep reproducing themselves, even in rebels and dropouts.

In his *Fäkaliendramen* (scatological plays, 1991) the dramatist Werner Schwab also worked with the negative of the *Volksstück*, writing *Volksstücke* without, or against, the people. The title *Volksvernichtung* (Exterminating the People, 1992) is to be taken literally, as the promise given in the title of the collection is ruthlessly fulfilled. Almost like an anatomist, Schwab dissects the corpse of the bourgeoisie in order to expose what is in the guts of a society based on repression and dominated by Catholicism. Excrement signifies the end of Christian transubstantiation.[42] While the Christian Communion transforms matter into spirit, Schwab reduces everything to dung. There is no transformation. The "sausage" is the consummation of a society whose priests have become butchers.

Instead of using an artificial dialect, Schwab develops an impersonal, depersonalized written language, "schwabisch" (Schwabian). His figures speak a barbaric officialese that represents a special case of "constipation" and blockage in the medium of language. At the same time, it represents a form of defecation. The harsh, lifeless discourse of his figures and the abject materiality of the body — sign and matter, one rigid and the other loathsome — are similarly excreted. Speaking, in this presentation, is a bodily function, corresponding to physical evacuation, while the body of discourse is one excrement among others.

In the play *Die Präsidentinnen* (The Female Presidents, 1990), the first of Schwab's "scatological plays," three monstrous Catholic petty-bourgeois women appear. Grete, Erna, and Mariedl are passionately fixated on their kitchens and specialists in repression or psychological and physical constipation. While they solemnly hold pieces of excrement aloft, they can only release their sexuality in perverted, quasi-Catholic forms. That makes the "Präsidentinnen" even less restrained in yielding to their fantasies: Mariedl cleans toilets with enthusiasm, Erna saves money, and Grete lives as a merry widow within the bounds of Catholicism. Their voices are united in a joint delirium of happiness, until the return of the repressed puts an end to their happy illusion. In Mariedl's violent counter-vision, however, Grete's and Erna's violated children return and take revenge on their mothers. Under the psychagogic leadership of the toilet-cleaner, happiness is transformed into nemesis. Bent on revenge for the destruction of their dreams, Erna and Grete kill Mariedl with the cool expertise of professional butchers.

Such a radically pessimistic drama provides the foil for Peter Handke's late dramatic work, which, like his prose, aims to mount a radical opposition to the tendencies of present-day theater. Since his oratorio-like play *Über die Dörfer* (Through the Villages, 1981) Handke has been working on a new, allegorical theater, intended not to radicalize existing reality, but to produce a visionary opening in its midst. Against the negativity of the avant-garde theater in Austria, he wants to set something new and positive, a language of proclamation or preaching against the malevolent discourse of a totalizing misanthropy. His new theater is one of structures with internal motion, configurations of dramatic characters, of pro and contra, and finally of abstraction. His figures derive from literature and maintain explicit intertextual links with their originals. Thus the *Spiel vom Fragen* (Game of Questions, 1989) takes the form of an abstract interchange between *Mauerschauer* (spectator from the wall) and *Spielverderber* (spoilsport), allegorical names concealing Ferdinand Raimund, a dramatist of the Viennese popular theater, and the Russian dramatist Anton Chekhov. The dramatic movement is modeled on a pilgrimage and a scientific expedition, which again brings a dynamic allegory of questioning onto the stage.[43] Against the background of a theater that treats repression and its catastrophic failure on the stage, Handke calls for a theater of questioning. In a society that asks no questions, his play aims to teach questioning, though not in the form of a didactic play, containing a ready-made lesson, but by pressing forward into the unknown.

In his dialogue with Raimund and Chekhov, Handke finally renews a constellation which has shaped the whole of present-day Austrian drama, and indeed points beyond it. It is epitomized in a question Thomas Bernhard repeatedly asked in his texts and that can unfold its aesthetic potential only in the open form of a question: "Is it a tragedy? Is it a comedy?" There is no answer, for in the texts of present-day Austrian drama, horror and humour mutually interrupt and infiltrate each other. The result is not a static picture, but the unstable image of a kaleidoscope.

Notes

[1] Quoted in Hilde Haider-Pregler, "Der Staatsakt der Wiedereröffnung von Burg und Oper," in Kristian Sotriffer, ed., *Das größere Österreich: Geistiges und soziales Leben von 1880 bis zur Gegenwart* (Vienna: Tusch, 1982), 424.

[2] Haider-Pregler, "Der Staatsakt der Wiedereröffnung," 424.

[3] See Klaus Amann, "ich ich sein wer sein? Zum Begriff 'österreichische Literatur,'" in Eijiro Iwasaki, ed., *Begegnung mit dem "Fremden": Akten des VIII. Internationalen Germanistenkongresses Tokyo 1990*, 11 vols. (Munich: Iudicium, 1991), 9: 138–46.

[4] Alexander Lernet-Holenia, letter of 17 October 1945, *Der Turm* 1, nos. 4–5 (1945), 109.

[5] See Peter Roessler, *Studien zur Auseinandersetzung mit Faschismus und Krieg im österreichischen Drama der Nachkriegszeit und der 50er Jahre* (Cologne: Pahl-Rugenstein, 1987), 76.

[6] Franz Probst, "Das Theater ist tot! Es lebe das Theater!" *PLAN* 1, no. 7 (July 1946), 589–92; here: 589.

[7] See Friedbert Aspetsberger, "Versuchte Korrekturen. Ideologie und Politik im Drama nach 1945," in Friedbert Aspetsberger, Norbert Frei, and Hubert Lengauer, eds., *Literatur der Nachkriegszeit und der fünfziger Jahre* (Vienna: Österreichischer Bundesverlag, 1984), 241–70.

[8] In fact, Hochwälder had written *Holokaust* in 1961, but he withdrew it and it was published only in 1998. See Judith Beniston, "Fritz Hochwälder's *Holokaust*: A Choice of Evils," *Austrian Studies* 11 (2003): 65–84.

[9] See Roessler, *Studien zur Auseinandersetzung mit Faschismus und Krieg.*

[10] See Gerhard Rühm, "grundlagen des neuen theaters," in Peter Weibel, ed., *die wiener gruppe: ein moment der moderne 1954–1960* (Vienna and New York: Springer, 1997), 621–25; here: 625.

[11] See Wendelin Schmidt-Dengler, "Writers and the Language of Prayer: Secularisation in the Austrian Literature of the 1970s," *Austrian Studies* 10 (1999): 119–36.

[12] See Edward Timms, *Karl Kraus, Apocalyptic Satirist: Culture and Catastrophe in Habsburg Vienna* (New Haven and London: Yale UP, 1986).

[13] Kurt Bartsch, *Ödön von Horváth*, Sammlung Metzler 326 (Stuttgart: Metzler, 2000), 43–44.

[14] On Horváth's reception in postwar Austrian drama, see Wendelin Schmidt-Dengler, *Bruchlinien: Vorlesungen zur österreichischen Literatur 1945–1990* (Salzburg and Vienna: Residenz, 1995), 269.

[15] See Wendelin Schmidt-Dengler, "Die Einsamkeit Kasperls als Langstreckenläufer. Ein Versuch zu H. C. Artmanns und Konrad Bayers Dramen," in W. Schmidt-Dengler, ed., *verLockerungen: Österreichische Avantgarde im 20. Jahrhundert* (Vienna: Edition Praesens, 1994), 75–95.

[16] See André Bucher, *Die szenischen Texte der Wiener Gruppe* (Bern: Lang, 1992); Ulf Birbaumer, "Die Wiener Gruppe und das Theatralische," in Hilde Haider-Pregler and Peter Roessler, eds., *Zeit der Befreiung: Wiener Theater nach 1945* (Vienna: Picus, 1998), 329–39.

[17] Peter Handke, *Kaspar*, in P. Handke, *Stücke I* (Frankfurt am Main: Suhrkamp, 1977), 103.

[18] Handke, *Kaspar*, 152.

[19] See Ödön von Horváth, *Glaube Liebe Hoffnung*, in Ö. v. Horváth, *Gesammelte Werke: Kommentierte Werkausgabe in Einzelbänden*, ed. Traugott Krischke, 14 vols. (Frankfurt am Main: Suhrkamp, 1986), 6: 68.

[20] Oswald Wiener, *Die verbesserung von mitteleuropa*, XXVII.

[21] Quoted in Kerstin Braun, *Der Wiener Aktionismus: Positionen und Prinzipien* (Vienna, Cologne et al.: Böhlau, 1999), 191–92.

[22] Peter Handke, *Publikumsbeschimpfung*, in Handke, *Stücke I*, 21.

[23] Handke, *Publikumsbeschimpfung*, 46.

[24] See Oliver Jahraus, *Das "monomanische" Werk: Eine strukturale Werkanalyse des Oeuvres von Thomas Bernhard* (Frankfurt am Main: Lang, 1992).

[25] Wendelin Schmidt-Dengler speaks of "Variationen des Identischen": see "Ohnmacht durch Gewohnheit. Zum dramatischen Werk von Thomas Bernhard" in W. Schmidt-Dengler, *Der Übertreibungskünstler: Studien zu Thomas Bernhard* (Vienna: Sonderzahl, [3]1997), 156–74; here: 156.

[26] See Claudia Liebrand, "Obduktionen. Thomas Bernhards *Der Ignorant und der Wahnsinnige*," in Franziska Schössler and Ingeborg Villiger, eds., *Thomas Bernhard und die Medien* (Würzburg: Königshausen & Neumann, 2002), 78–92.

[27] Thomas Bernhard, *Der Ignorant und der Wahnsinnige*, in T. Bernhard, *Stücke I* (Frankfurt am Main: Suhrkamp, 1988), 79–171; here: 126.

[28] See Manfred Mittermayer, *Thomas Bernhard*, Sammlung Metzler 291 (Stuttgart: Metzler, 1995), 159.

[29] Handke, *Publikumsbeschimpfung*, 27.

[30] Elfriede Jelinek, "Ich schlage sozusagen mit der Axt drein," *TheaterZeitSchrift* 7 (1984): 14–16.

[31] See Christine Schmidt, "Sprechen — Sein. Jelineks Theater der Sprachflächen," *Sprache im technischen Zeitalter* 38 (2000): 65–75.

[32] Jelinek, "Ich schlage sozusagen mit der Axt drein," 14.

[33] On the chorus in Jelinek, see Ulrike Hass, " 'Sinn egal. Körper zwecklos.' Anmerkungen zur Figur des Chores bei Elfriede Jelinek anläßlich Einar Schleefs Inszenierung von *Ein Sportstück*," *Text und Kritik* 117 (1999): 51–62.

[34] See Allyson Fiddler, "Jelinek's Ibsen: Noras Past and Present," *Austrian Studies* 4 (1993): 126–39.

[35] See "Ich bin im Grunde ständig tobsüchtig über die Verharmlosung. Ein Gespräch mit Elfriede Jelinek," www.elfriedejelinek.com

[36] On Jelinek's materials, see Daniela Bartens, "Das Häkeln und die Avantgarde. Zu Elfriede Jelineks *Stecken, Stab und Stangl*. Eine Handarbeit," in Kurt Bartsch, ed., *Avantgarde und Traditionalismus: Kein Widerspruch in der Postmoderne?* (Innsbruck: Studien, 2000), 153–77.

[37] See Elin Nesje Vestli, "Ein akustisches Setting: Überlegungen zur Dramaturgie von Marlene Streeruwitz," in *Trans: Internetzeitschrift für Kulturwissenschaften* 9 (2001): 4.

[38] See Hugo Aust, Peter Haida, and Jürgen Hein, *Volksstück: Vom Hanswurstspiel zum sozialen Drama der Gegenwart* (Munich: Beck, 1989).

[39] See Helmut Schneider, "Vom Schrottwert der Dinge: Das Allergewöhnlichste im Blick," *Salzburger Nachrichten*, 5 Jan. 1991; Jutta Landa, "Königskomödien oder Fäkaliendramen?" *Modern Austrian Literature* 26, 3/4 (1993): 217–29; here: 229.

[40] Jutta Landa, *Bürgerliches Schocktheater. Entwicklungen im österreichischen Drama der sechziger und siebziger Jahre* (Frankfurt am Main: Athenäum, 1988), 23.

[41] See Schmidt-Dengler, *Bruchlinien*, 275–76.

[42] See Herbert Herzmann, "Volksstückvernichtung oder mein Körper ist sinnlos. Anmerkungen zu den Fäkaliendramen von Werner Schwab," in Gerhard Fuchs and Paul Pechmann, eds., *Werner Schwab* (Graz: Droschl, 2000), 106–26.

[43] See Karl Wagner, "Ohne Warum. Peter Handkes Spiel vom Fragen," in Gerhard Fuchs and Gerhard Melzer, eds., *Peter Handke: Die Langsamkeit der Welt* (Graz: Droschl, 1993), 201–14.

10: Austrian Prose Fiction, 1945–2000

J. J. Long

GERMANY'S ANNEXATION OF AUSTRIA in 1938 destroyed the flourishing literary culture of interwar Austria almost overnight. Among the émigrés from Nazism were many of the most eminent literary figures of the age, and remarkably few of the exiled Austrian writers returned after 1945. This offered, as film-maker and writer Ruth Beckermann puts it, "an opportunity for the mediocre, those who stayed behind, to attain honor and glory."[1] The charge of mediocrity, though apposite, conceals another characteristic of those who stayed behind, namely the fact that many of them had co-operated to a greater or lesser degree with the National Socialists. The opportunity for such writers to attain "honor and glory" depended not solely on the absence of returning exiles but on a favorable cultural climate arising from developments within the wider fields of politics and cultural politics.

Austrian self-understanding in the postwar decades was characterized by what has been aptly dubbed double-talk. The thesis that Austria had been the first victim of Hitlerite aggression insisted that Germans, not Austrians, were responsible for the War and the Holocaust, while domestic politics both tacitly acknowledged the fact that Nazi sympathies and willing participation in the *Wehrmacht* were widespread phenomena, and rehabilitated the vast majority of those who had been involved. A similar phenomenon can be seen at a microcosmic level in the re-emergence of literary culture. Although the PEN Club had enshrined anti-fascism as one of its humanitarian principles, the Vienna PEN Center — re-established in 1947 — largely failed to exclude writers who had collaborated with the Nazis. A *Literaturreinigungsgesetz* (Purification of Literature Act) was passed by parliament but never implemented, while the Education Ministry's list of banned authors contained, in 1948, just six names. The institution of literary prizes tended to further the rehabilitation of those who had remained in Austria between 1938 and 1945. Throughout the 1950s, numerous prominent writers of a nationalist bent, who had begun their careers under the *Ständestaat* (corporate state) received Austria's major literary awards. The situation was exacerbated by continuities in cultural policy and the cultural bureaucracy, which ensured that the state support available to writers tended to go to the same names as had benefited before and during Nazi rule. In Germany, the Gruppe 47 provided both a forum and a powerful voice for left-liberal writers who, in the immediate postwar period, were seeking to re-establish Germany's literary credibility and undertake a reckoning with the older generation of authors discredited by their complicity in Nazism. No such organization existed in Austria.

It would be a misrepresentation, however, to suggest that the literary scene of the late 1940s was purely restorative. Two novels published in 1948 illustrate respectively the restorative tendencies of the establishment and the beginnings of a new literary culture: *Der Graf von Saint-Germain* (The Count of Saint-Germain) by Alexander Lernet-Holenia (1897–1976), and *Die größere Hoffnung* (Herod's Children) by Ilse Aichinger (1921–).

In the late 1940s, Lernet-Holenia enjoyed a reputation as the "grand old man" of Austrian literature. Though he had been a member of the Reichsschrifttumskammer (Reich Chamber of Literature) during the war, he afterwards claimed rather spurious anti-fascist credentials. But his outlook remained fundamentally nationalist, conservative, and aristocratic. His vast oeuvre is of uneven quality, but *Der Graf von Saint-Germain* is symptomatic of the conservative and restorative impulses in Austrian fiction of the immediate postwar period. One night in 1918, the novel's narrator, Philipp Branis, kills his fiancée's lover, Karl des Esseintes, the last living member of the des Esseintes family. In 1760, it had been predicted by the Count of Saint-Germain that the des Esseintes clan would endure beyond the dissolution of Austria, yet Branis appears to have proved this prophecy wrong. Branis marries his fiancée immediately after the murder, but she soon dies, having given birth to a son. Twenty years later, in early 1938, the son reveals the capacity to remember events that happened before his birth and are clearly "inherited" from his real father, des Esseintes. Saint Germain's prophecy is thus fulfilled. It is this realization that leads Branis to write his memoirs. He completes them as the German annexation of Austria begins, and is killed while fleeing to Switzerland. Within this skeletal narrative, there are numerous flashbacks and digressions, written in leisurely, mildly archaic German and dealing with Austria's political development between the First World War and the *Anschluss*, and Branis's earlier life. There are also long essayistic reflections devoted to the philosophy of history, the theory of the state, the existence of God, the nature of religion, the ethics of murder, and the ontology of death. Although ostensibly dealing with contemporary politics, there is a pronounced irrationalist, supernatural thread running through the novel, which is explicitly articulated in the following passage: "Die Geschichte der Welt [folgt] dem Mythos [. . .] und nicht der Logik! Die Logik erfindet immer nur mehr oder weniger vernünftige Vorwände für das, was blindlings geschieht, der Mythos ist aber längst am Werke und läßt das Unbegreifliche geschehen" (The history of the world is based on myth, not logic! Logic always merely invents more or less rational pretexts for events that happen without rhyme or reason, but myth has always been at work all along, causing the inconceivable to happen).[2] With its mystification of history, its nostalgia for the Habsburg era, and its refusal to confront Austria's recent, post-*Anschluss* past, Lernet-Holenia's novel is a fascinating attempt to establish continuity with the cultural values and quasi-feudal traditions of a mythical pre-1918 Austria.

Ilse Aichinger's *Die größere Hoffnung*, on the other hand, is one of the few Austrian novels of the immediate postwar period that take Nazism as their subject. Though the words "Nazi," "Jew," and "Vienna" do not occur in the novel at all, contextual factors and textual clues establish the novel's subject unequivocally as the Nazi persecution of Viennese Jews between the *Anschluss* and the liberation. The protagonist of *Die größere Hoffnung*, Ellen, lives with her maternal grandmother, her Jewish mother having been forced to emigrate, and her father having abandoned the family and joined the *Wehrmacht*. After failing to secure a visa for her own emigration, Ellen joins a group of Jewish children and experiences the progressive shrinkage of the freedoms available to her friends, the introduction of ration cards, the compulsory wearing of the Star of David, Allied bomb attacks on the city, and the suicide of her grandmother. The "great hope," the hope that flight or emigration might be possible, is repeatedly thwarted, leading to a nebulous "greater hope," the possibility of reconciliation or redemption beyond earthly existence. Such redemption appears to be offered in the closing pages of the novel. At the moment she is killed by an exploding shell, Ellen experiences an epiphanic vision of the morning star, symbol of the "greater hope" that forms the novel's title.

In formal terms, *Die größere Hoffnung* is a novel of considerable ambition. Its time structure, though broadly linear, is episodic and begins *in medias res*, and the third-person narrator focalizes events largely through the eyes and consciousness of Ellen herself. The representation of the world though the limited spatial and conceptual horizons of a child means that the reader has to supply much of the wider context to make the narrated events intelligible. The discrepancy between Ellen's understanding of her environment and that of the reader is capable of generating considerable pathos, but this is undercut by additional narratological complications. For Ellen is not the only focalizer: there are passages observed through other characters or the collective consciousness of the children, but in some passages the viewpoint becomes utterly ambiguous, not localizable with any certainty within a single identifiable consciousness. This technique has a profoundly disorientating effect, which prevents the novel from degenerating into sentimentality, and calls into question the validity of the redemption promised by the ending. The implication of the narrative form of *Die größere Hoffnung* is that linearity and omniscience are inadequate to the task of representing the traumas of recent Austrian history; indeed, that narrative after Auschwitz cannot be other than difficult, fractured, and indeterminate.

Lernet-Holenia's work is aristocratic, nostalgic, stylistically traditional, and evasive about Nazism, while Aichinger's tackles Nazism directly, and in formal terms employs devices that situate her novel firmly within the high-modernist tradition. Despite the continuing public success of conservative writers in the 1950s and beyond, the postwar Austrian novels that have established themselves in the canon tend to follow Aichinger in their espousal of a modernist aesthetic and a critical stance towards recent Austrian history. Nothing illustrates this better than the postwar anti-*Heimatroman*.

The Anti-*Heimatroman*

Heimat means home, the place in which one is born and grows up, and to which one feels a particular affinity, a sense of belonging. Over the course of the nineteenth century, it became a politically charged term. The Austrian *Heimatroman* or rural novel, as exemplified in the work of the nineteenth-century writers Ludwig Anzengruber and Peter Rosegger, celebrated rural and agricultural life, community, rootedness, and tradition. It is thus a largely conservative genre that responded to urbanization, industrialization, and other aspects of modernity by upholding the illusion of an unspoiled, unchanging landscape in which peasants tilled the soil and lived according to the rhythms of nature. The potentially reactionary ideology of the *Heimatroman*, with its antimodern parochialism, rejection of the cosmopolitan, and a naïve sense of community grounded in continuity of the bloodline and an intimate connection to place, made it ripe for appropriation by the National Socialists. Despite the postwar popularity of authors such as Karl Heinrich Waggerl, the most notorious representative of proto-Nazi *Blut und Boden* (blood and soil) literature, and the continued success of Austrian *Heimat* films, the *Heimatroman* was perceived by many serious writers as a compromised genre that could be resurrected only in the form of the critical or anti-*Heimatroman*.

Die *Wolfshaut* (The Wolf's Fell, 1960) by Hans Lebert (1919–93) is generally seen as the first anti-*Heimatroman*. It narrates events that happen in the winter of 1952 to 1953 in the fictional Styrian village of Schweigen. The protagonist, Johann Unfreund, is a sailor who returns to Schweigen in 1946 after an absence of thirty years.[3] He lives opposite the ruins of a brick factory, and at the beginning of the novel, he finds the corpse of Hans Höller, a young villager, leaning against the window frame of the factory with his eyes wide open and a look of terror on his face. This is the first of several mysterious deaths that take place, and Unfreund becomes drawn into an investigation that uncovers the causes of both the current fatalities and the unexplained suicide of his own father in 1945. It finally comes to light that a group of villagers, the so-called "Ortswacht," had executed six "Fremdarbeiter" (forced laborers from Nazi-occupied Eastern Europe) in the brick factory in the spring of 1945. Unfreund's father had been a member of the firing squad, as had those villagers who die during the course of the novel. The opening pages of the novel convey a sense of the untroubled restoration of normal life after the interruption of the war, aided by rising economic prosperity. At the same time, however, there is a suggestion that the rhythm of the seasons and agricultural life is no longer part of the rural idyll of the traditional *Heimatroman*, but has given way to a stultifying boredom.[4] The persistence of the fascist mentality is most tellingly embodied in two of the novel's characters, Vinzenz Rotschädel and Ilse Jakobi. Rotschädel repeatedly gives the Hitler salute, continues to refer to Habergeier by his wartime rank of *Ortsgruppenleiter*, and drunkenly urinates a swastika on the grave of a man he has recently murdered. Ilse, the village teacher, is a caricature of the tall, blond-haired, blue-eyed, "Aryan" woman. She is an enthusiastic gymnast who declares proudly that she has learned to obey, to give orders, and to march in all weathers. When a schoolboy dies because she takes her pupils on an ill-fated ski-trip in adverse weather, she uses the rhetoric of Social Darwinism to justify her behavior. This characterization is decidedly lacking in subtlety, and its intention is clearly polemic rather than mimesis. But behind their grotesque caricatures lies a serious point: Jakobi and Rotschädel hold attitudes and assumptions that are tacitly held by large swathes of the rural populace. In particular, their behavior is still motivated by a belief in the tenets of National Socialism and a continued faith in the Führer as a legitimating authority.

Lebert's technique, which he described as "Transparentismus" (Transparentism), allows mythic and transcendent forces to be perceived behind or beyond the concrete realism of the fictional world. This has led to an oft-voiced suspicion[5] that Lebert represents Nazism as an epiphenomenon of an all-pervasive metaphysical evil, which diminishes his status as an antifascist writer because his concern is with evil per se rather than with the political realities of the Third Reich. But the mythological scheme of *Die Wolfshaut* is in fact the work of an unreliable first-person narrator who is himself a member of the village community. The novel thus dramatizes a process of myth-formation within the represented world, showing that the discourse of transcendent forces can easily be enlisted in the service of a narrative that seeks to exculpate those responsible for wartime atrocities. Over and against this, the investigations of Unfreund demonstrate that moral responsibility for the murders of the *Fremdarbeiter* can be located unambiguously in the actions of the *Ortswacht*.

Numerous *Heimatromane* were produced in Austria in subsequent decades. In his self-consciously modernist novel *Fasching* (Shrovetide, 1967) Gerhard Fritsch (1924–69) follows in Lebert's footsteps and uses the genre to expose the persistence of the Nazi past in postwar Austria. A more whimsical anti-*Heimatroman* is Gert F. Jonke's *Geometrischer Heimatroman* (Geometrical *Heimatroman*; 1969). Jonke (1961–) belonged to a group of avant-garde writers who constituted themselves as Forum Stadtpark in Graz in 1960, and were rechristened "Grazer Gruppe" six years later. Members of the Forum Stadtpark were heavily indebted to the earlier avant-garde movement, the Wiener Gruppe, whose experiments with language, concrete poetry, and dialect went hand in hand with aggressive but often humorous anti-bourgeois actionism. The legacy of the Wiener Gruppe is clearly evident in Jonke's "geometric novel," which abandons any claim to represent reality, and instead emphasizes the materiality of language and its role in creating (rather than representing) the fictional world. Although the novel is full of incident, there is no logical plot development, nor is there a single narrative consciousness that would guarantee the ultimate coherence of what is narrated. The text is made up of unattributed fragments of dialogue and narrative, extracts from various pseudo-documents such as the Parish Chronicle, a newspaper report on the death of an itinerant entertainer, the laws governing the conduct of bridge wardens, the treble score of a folksong, and various maps of the village.

Jonke's novel does not, however, exhaust itself in formal game playing; it is also sharply satirical. Indeed, Jonke's target is the authoritarian mentality not only of the rural populace, but the Austrian state and its cumbersome bureaucracy. A good example of this mechanism is provided by the introduction of the following regulation towards the end of the text: "Aus Sicherheitsgründen wird es hinkünftig verboten sein, durch Wälder und Alleen zu gehen, um die Bevölkerung vor den *schwarzen Männern*, die sich hinter Bäumen verstecken, zu schützen" (For security reasons, it is henceforth illegal to walk through woods and avenues. This is to protect the population from the *black men* who hide behind trees).[6] The regulation is generated by literalizing a metaphor, for "Wer fürchtet sich vor dem schwarzen Mann?" is a game played by Austrian (and German) schoolchildren. But it develops a life of its own, and leads to a series of paranoid security measures that culminate in the deforestation of the entire country. The suggestion is that ludicrous bureaucracy and pointless security measures can be generated by purely imaginary anxieties and produce decisions that are incommensurable with the perceived threat.

A *Heimatroman* that is often seen as occupying the opposite pole of narrative realism is *Schöne Tage* (Beautiful Days, 1974), the first in a trilogy of autobiographical novels by Franz Innerhofer (1944–). *Schöne Tage* was followed by *Schattseite* (Shadow Side, 1975) and *Die großen Wörter* (The Big Words, 1977). *Schöne Tage* is a third-person narrative focalized through the consciousness of Holl, the illegitimate son of a farm hand who is sent, at the age of six, to live on his real father's farm. For the next eleven years he endures a life of what is effectively serfdom — in the 1950s! Like the other agricultural laborers, Holl is subjected to repeated beatings, unreasonable demands, and backbreaking work, all of which reduce human beings to the level of animals and rob them of dignity and individuality. But history begins to catch up with this anachronistic backwater: the first tractor is purchased towards the end of the decade, and Holl's ability to drive it gains him a certain degree of respect. Literature provides an escape from the brutal conditions on the farm. Eventually, Holl rebels, becoming an apprentice to the local blacksmith. *Schattseite* and *Die großen Wörter* continue the story of Holl's slow and difficult progress toward a fully self-conscious subjectivity though the stages of the apprenticeship, military service, factory labor, the *Abitur* (graduation from gymnasium), and university study, though his career is beset by repeated patterns of optimism and disillusionment. *Schöne Tage* remains the most powerful novel of Innerhofer's trilogy. In its existential immediacy and quasi-documentary portrayal of agricultural existence, it demolishes the central assumptions of *Heimat* ideology, exposing as an illusion the notion that life on the land is or ever was harmonious and idyllic.

Dealing critically with the legacy of the *Heimatroman* has allowed Austrian novelists to address a wide range of thematic concerns beyond those discussed so far. In his novels *Menschenkind* (Human Being, 1979), *Der Ackermann aus Kärnten* (The Peasant from Carinthia, 1980) and *Muttersprache* (Mother Tongue, 1982), Josef Winkler (1953–) deals with subjects such as suicide and homosexuality, and in so doing aggressively breaks the taboos that determine what can and cannot be mentioned in Austria's rural communities. Norbert Gstrein (1961–) has responded to the transformations in the economy and the landscape brought about by the postwar expansion of Austria's tourist industry. In *Einer* (One, 1988) and *Das Register* (1992), he depicts life in Alpine ski resorts, exploring the effects on individuals of the seasonal economy and the continued dominance of a regressive, provincial mentality.

No discussion of the postwar Austrian *Heimatroman* would be complete without a mention of *Schlafes Bruder* (Brother of Sleep, 1992), an idiosyncratic novel by Robert Schneider (1961–) that is legendary for being rejected by twenty-three publishers before becoming a worldwide best seller. It tells the story of Johannes Elias Alder, who is born into an early nineteenth-century peasant family in a remote Vorarlberg hamlet and soon shows signs of extraordinary musical talent. Schneider includes numerous metafictional asides drawing attention to his subversion of the traditional conventions of the *Heimatroman*. He portrays a dystopian rural landscape that appears not only indifferent but inimical to the peasants who work the land, while the peasants themselves are characterized by deformity resulting from centuries of endogamy, sexual deviance such as bestiality and incest, religious fervor, and hostility to change.

In *Der stille Ozean* (The Pacific Ocean, 1980), the second book in his seven-volume cycle of novels and reportage entitled *Die Archive des*

Schweigens (The Archives of Silence), Gerhard Roth (1942–) makes a notable attempt to salvage something useful from the *Heimatroman*. Roth's early work evinces the radical formalism of the Grazer Gruppe, of which he was a member. *Der stille Ozean*, by contrast, is a sober chronological account of the experiences of Ascher, a surgeon who leaves Vienna to live in a Styrian village after a fatal blunder in the operating room. He starts to observe the village community, his language betraying the stereotyping of the anthropological gaze: he speaks of "the farmer," "the baker," and so on, rather than introducing them by name. He also witnesses the persistence of anachronistic ways of life, including the almost hysterical annihilation of local fauna to control a rabies epidemic. Rather than rejecting this rural mode of existence, Ascher gradually accommodates himself to its rhythms, resigns from his job permanently, and starts a new life as a country doctor. Though by no means uncritical, *Der stille Ozean* is unusual among postwar Austrian novels for having a protagonist who turns his back on metropolitan life and settles in the country.

In the wake of the publication of *Schlafes Bruder*, one critic complained that the anti-*Heimatroman* was itself now degenerating into precisely the conventionalized kitsch it had sought to oppose.[7] But it remains one of the most significant and distinctive trends of postwar Austrian literature. Indeed, its influence can be found in the work of three of Austria's finest postwar novelists: Thomas Bernhard, Peter Handke, and Elfriede Jelinek.

Three Individualists: Bernhard, Handke, Jelinek

Thomas Bernhard (1931–89) published four volumes of poetry in the late 1950s, but it was his early novels *Frost* (1963), *Verstörung* (translated as Gargoyles, 1967), *Das Kalkwerk* (The Lime Works, 1970), and *Korrektur* (Correction, 1975) that established his literary reputation. These early novels are dark and intense portrayals of pathological mental states, intellectual hubris, and the overwhelming oppressiveness of Austrian history. *Frost* is a diary novel that recounts the experiences of a medical student who has been sent to the village of Weng, a kind of Alpine anti-idyll, to observe and report on the reclusive painter Strauch. The narrator offers a vivid description of Weng and its inhabitants: the avaricious and sexually rapacious landlady, the unscrupulous gravedigger, the generally morbid population. But this empirical world is counterbalanced and eventually overwhelmed by Strauch's fantastic and potentially insane view of the universe. The narrator "quotes" Strauch's monologues at great length, drawing himself and the reader into the painter's strange mental world. It is a world in which the landscape is saturated with indexical traces of war, crime, and atrocity; in which parts of the body are secretly connected with each other; in which chance meetings become uncanny harbingers of death; in which the slaughter of cows by cattle thieves hints at human sacrifice. Strauch's fragmentary utterances are abundant in non sequiturs, and disintegrate the narrative fabric that attempts to form around them. This finally subverts the narrator's enterprise. He succumbs to the pull of Strauch's language, losing all sense of himself as an autonomous agent, and becoming thoroughly permeated with Strauch's thoughts. The medical gaze is ill equipped to deal with the personal charisma of Strauch, and medical discourse seems unable to offer a diagnosis or a solution. The narrator expresses anxiety that he has produced nothing but nonsense, and returns to Vienna where he learns about Strauch's probable suicide from a newspaper report.

While *Frost* offers no clinical diagnosis of Strauch's condition, the figure's language implies schizophrenia. *Verstörung*, too, has a quasi-schizophrenic central character, Prince Saurau, a relic of the Habsburg Empire struggling to manage his vast country estate as a feudal anachronism within the capitalist democracy of the Second Republic. His monologue, which occupies two-thirds of the novel, circles around themes of tradition, property, inheritance, and their relationship to the changed social and economic conditions of the postwar era. The estate of Hochgobernitz, we learn, is doomed, for Saurau's son and heir is certain to liquidate it. Similar thematic issues are addressed in *Korrektur*, whose protagonist, Roithamer, experiences Austrian history as an inescapable burden. Roithamer flees Austria to take up an academic post in Cambridge, divests himself of his ancestral estate, and yet can escape the influence of his family and homeland only by taking his own life.

In *Frost*, *Verstörung*, and *Korrektur*, the words of the central protagonist are relayed to the reader by a separate narrator figure. Bernhard takes this technique of quotation to its probable extreme in *Gehen* (Walking, 1971), but uses it most tellingly in *Das Kalkwerk*. *Das Kalkwerk* begins with the murder, by Konrad, of his wife. The killing, it transpires, was the last of many acts of violence that Konrad had perpetrated against her. Most notably, he had used her as an object of experimentation, carrying out hearing experiments supposedly derived from the methods of the nineteenth-century otologist Viktor Urbantschitsch. Konrad perverts Urbantschitsch's techniques, torturing his wife for hours on end by repeating the same sentences and words to her, and demanding an immediate response as to their effects. Being crippled and wheelchair-bound, she is unable to escape. The structure of narrative transmission in *Das Kalkwerk* is complex: the anonymous first-person narrator relates what has been told to him by two property managers named Fro and Wieser concerning their conversations with Konrad. The text is narrated almost exclusively in that peculiarly German yet literarily very useful mode: the subjunctive of indirect discourse. This feature of the German grammar signals the reader that what is being narrated represents the words, or thoughts, of another, or that the narrator does not take full responsibility for the accuracy of what is stated. The following example is typical: "Er habe von Natur aus die schärfsten und die angestrengtesten Augen, soll er zu Wieser gesagt haben" (He is supposed to have told Wieser that nature had endowed him with the sharpest and most alert eyes).[8] The use of the subjunctive within a structure of embedded perspective distances the reader from the events that are being reported, but there are also elements that work against this distancing, most notably the verbatim rendering of Konrad's monologues. With few exceptions, Konrad is ultimately the source of everything that is narrated about him; thus, the represented world is effectively perceived through his consciousness. By reporting his words without comment, Fro, Wieser and the narrator align themselves with his point of view in a tacit gesture of collusion. Consequently, the reader is effectively coerced into seeing the world of the text from Konrad's perspective. These techniques lead the reader into an unsettling and claustrophobic world of intellectual obsession, sadomasochistic cruelty, and existential despair.

In the late 1970s, Bernhard abandoned novel writing and turned his attention to stage plays and a five-volume autobiography. His fiction of the 1980s is markedly less pessimistic than his early work. Whereas comedy and humor are present but peripheral in the early novels, they become central in *Holzfällen* (Cutting Timber, 1984) and *Alte Meister* (Old Masters, 1984). *Holzfällen* is an invective against the Austrian cultural establishment that viciously lampoons the writers Friederike Mayröcker, Ernst Jandl, and Jeannie Ebner, and the composer Gerhard Lampersberg.[9] *Alte Meister* is a reckoning with the cultural past in general and the Habsburg legacy in particular, in which the comedy is sustained by exuberant metaphorical creativity and bizarre neologisms.

Of Bernhard's late novels, *Auslöschung* (Extinction, 1986) is the most rewarding. On the opening page, a telegram arrives at the home of Franz-Josef Murau (the novel's narrator) informing him of the death of his parents and elder brother in a car accident. This places him in the unexpected position of being the sole heir of Wolfsegg, an expansive estate in Upper Austria. The text is an attempt to come to terms not only with the political, cultural, and familial heritage that Wolfsegg represents, but also with the problem of taking on and disposing of such an inheritance. The action of *Auslöschung* is reduced to a minimum: during the first 300-page chapter, Murau looks at family photographs in his flat in Rome, while the second, equally long chapter, deals with the twenty or so hours during which he arrives at Wolfsegg and oversees the preparations for the funeral. Within this minimal sequence of events, however, Murau takes numerous narrative excursions into the past, stimulated by the photographs and the physical environment of his ancestral home. Wolfsegg is a spatial representation of inherited traditions and, ultimately, Austrian history itself. Although it is tainted by associations with Nazism (it served as a hideout for the local Gauleiter after the War), old feudal customs from the Habsburg era continue to structure social and economic relationships. But the death of Murau's father and brother betokens the end of the family line, and *Auslöschung* ends with the donation of the estate to the Jewish Community in Vienna, and Murau's subsequent death. Murau's refusal to take over Wolfsegg has been read as a refusal to bear the burden of Austria's recent history and an attempt to bring about a spurious historical reconciliation.[10] While Murau can be seen as indulging in an illegitimate identification with the victims of fascism, *Auslöschung* presents a sustained and serious engagement with the consequences of Murau's parents' unacknowledged involvement in Nazism. They react aggressively whenever the attempt is made to draw attention to their post-*Anschluss* collusion, signaling the return of a past that has been inadequately worked through, while Murau himself finds his access to the past blocked by his knowledge that local *Gauleiter* were given refuge on the estate after the war. His inability to take over the property is thus a function of this compelling narrative logic.

The 1960s also saw the rise to prominence of Peter Handke (1942–). Handke is the best-known member of the Grazer Gruppe, and a concern with language and representational convention forms the cornerstone of his work. Many of his early narratives are now recognized as contemporary classics, among them *Die Angst des Tormanns beim Elfmeter* (The Goalie's Fear of the Penalty, 1970) and *Wunschloses Unglück* (Unhappy Beyond Dreams, 1972). *Die Angst des Tormanns* tells the story of ex-goalkeeper Josef Bloch, who, believing that he has been sacked from his job as a fitter, wanders the streets of Vienna and murders a cinema cashier with whom he has spent the night. Fleeing to a village on Austria's southern border, he checks into a guesthouse, and follows newspaper accounts of the police's efforts to track him down. Handke uses the framework of a murder mystery to create expectations of genre that are then systematically subverted, and at the end of the novel the crime remains unsolved. The text is narrated in the third-person in an unemotional style and events are focalized through the distorted consciousness of the murderer Bloch. He inhabits a world saturated with signs, but his paranoid condition turns interpretation into a hazardous and error-prone activity in which even a piece of blotting paper or a birthday telegram dictated by the village postmistress become bearers of secret meaning. Bloch's dislocated sensibility is signaled by a series of linguistic malfunctions, as the relationship between language and its referents becomes inverted, human beings are reduced metonymically to their most conspicuous attributes, and conversation grinds to a standstill because Bloch feels unable to rely on any semantic competence on the part of his interlocutors. Handke's narrative is informed by his knowledge of structural linguistics, on the one hand, and by his reading of Claus Conrad's study of early schizophrenia, on the other, and dramatizes the collapse of personal identity resulting from the breakdown of structures of signification that we ordinarily take for granted.

Wunschloses Unglück was written shortly after the suicide of Maria, Handke's mother, and is an attempt to narrate her life in a way that avoids the depersonalization inherent in, for example, the newspaper announcement of her death with which the text begins. However, the narrator discovers that such depersonalization is not easily evaded. His mother was born into a peasant community in which women had little room for self-realization or self-expression. Language here becomes a powerful force that imposes normative conduct and values upon human subjects from earliest childhood. One children's game is based on the enumeration of social ranks: "Kaiser — König — Edelmann / Bürger — Bauer — Leinenweber / Tischler — Bettler — Totengräber" (Emperor — King — Nobleman / Bourgeois — Farmer — Weaver / Joiner — Beggar — Gravedigger), while another maps out the stations of a typical woman's life: "Müde / Matt / Krank / Schwerkrank / Tot" (Tired / Shattered / Ill / Dying / Dead). "Als Frau in diese Umstände geboren zu werden, ist von vornherein schon tödlich gewesen," the narrator adds (To be born a woman into these conditions was fatal from the very start).[11] While Maria makes various attempts to escape, including a short period as a cook in the Black Forest and an affair with a German army paymaster, she ends up marrying a local drunkard and being absorbed into a village community that privileges the collective over the individual.

Conventional verbal formulations, however, do not only restrict how Maria Handke can live, they also restrict what can be written about her. Handke's narrator includes frequent metatextual reflections on the possibility of biographical writing, and finds that in order to make his mother's life narratable at all, he is reliant on pre-existent cultural forms and formulae. This undermines his initial project of capturing his mother's irreducible individuality, with the result that her life becomes a case study exemplifying the reality of many women's lives in interwar and post-1945 rural Austria. Biography emerges as a balancing act in which individuality has to be accommodated within and communicated through shared conventions of meaning. While Handke's negative representation of rural life situates *Wunschloses Unglück* within the anti-*Heimat* tradition, the text has much broader implications for our understanding of language, narrative, and the role of both in the production of social values and individual subjectivity.

Handke remains a prolific author of novels, stories, essays, and plays. Of his numerous works, *Die Wiederholung* (Repetition, 1986) is perhaps the pre-eminent achievement. The narrator, Filip Kobal, leaves his Carinthian home in the first of the novel's three sections, and travels to Slovenia in search of his brother, who failed to return from the war. This journey is interspersed with reminiscences of Kobal's childhood, his hybrid Carinthian-Slovenian identity, and his sense of being an outsider both in his native village of Rinkenheim and at boarding school. In the second section of the novel, Kobal settles in the Slovenian village from which his family originates, and concerns himself with two books: his brother's horticultural notes on the cultivation of fruit trees, and a German-Slovenian dictionary of 1895. As a result of the brother's horticultural studies, an orchard had been set up in Rinkenheim. It is now slowly dying, but Kobal realizes that he can transform this monument to his brother's life into a sign-system of a different order: writing. His reading of the dictionary returns to Handke's earlier obsession with language. Kobal discovers, for example, that Slovenian has only loan words for war and authority, which leads him to reflect on the fact that different languages construct different worlds. In the final section, Kobal walks through the Isonzo valley and arrives in the karst above the Gulf of Trieste. Here, he encounters various traces of his brother in the face of a young Slovenian, in the glimpse of a basement bedroom, and finally in the name Gregor Kobal engraved in the rendering of a chapel in Maribor. The closing pages contain a paean to the power of narrative. *Die Wiederholung* thus thematizes the positive potential of language, and combines this with travel writing, meditations on memory and cultural identity, the enumeration of physical detail, and a redemptive metaphysics to produce the richest and most intriguing of Handke's novels.

Austria's most recent Nobel laureate, Elfriede Jelinek (1946–, Nobel Prize 2004) has also been Austria's most controversial postwar writer. Her first novel, *wir sind lockvögel baby!* (we're decoys baby! 1970) is an omnivorous montage of fragments that parody the genres of popular culture: science fiction, horror films, advertisements, comics, and so on. While there are three recurrent characters, they give the text narrative coherence only in the loosest sense. Indeed, the first page commands the reader to change the book at will, thereby implying that the structural principles of the text are not those of organic plot development. *lockvögel* has much in common with the work of Austria' postwar avant-garde movements and the interwar movements from which they took their inspiration.

From *Die Liebhaberinnen* (The Lovers, 1975) onwards, Jelinek's work has been much more directly satirical and politically hard-hitting. Jelinek engages critically with the *Heimatroman*, satirizing its clichés and conventions in *Oh Wildnis, oh Schutz vor ihr* (O Wilderness, O Protection from it, 1985), and using it as a vehicle to explore the legacy of fascism in *Die Kinder der Toten* (The Children of the Dead, 1995). Her most characteristic work contains a devastating critique of the family as an institution that perpetuates capitalist property relations and the oppression of women. Combining Marxism and feminism with remarkable stylistic flamboyance, her novels and plays show economic and sexual exploitation to be inextricably linked. This is particularly evident in the notorious novel *Lust* (Pleasure, 1989) in which the director of a paper factory subjects his wife Gerti to repeated and grotesque sexual violence. This brutality goes hand in hand with a ruthless attitude to his employees, and yet both his wife and employees are economically dependent on him and are thus powerless to escape. Except that Gerti does escape, and flees into the arms of a student. This new relationship, however, is structurally identical to the one she has left behind, and she finally returns to her husband. There seems to be no way out of the cycle of male violence and female masochism. *Lust* draws on the conventions of pornography, in which men are always aroused, women always compliant, and all are anonymous (the woman is almost always "die Frau," and the man "der Direktor"). But the violence implicit in pornography becomes explicit in Jelinek's novel, as the director repeatedly strikes the woman, bends her body into painful contortions, and penetrates every orifice even if his wife is still asleep. We are spared no details of smells and stains, and the text is further de-eroticized through the deployment of a wide range of metaphors — particularly automotive metaphors — that emphasize the links between consumerism, socio-economic status, and the objectification of women.

In *Die Ausgesperrten* (The Excluded, 1980), a novel in which overt Nazism continues to manifest itself in domestic violence, the outward espousal of high-cultural values such as classical music is shown to conceal criminality and self-loathing. This theme is further explored in Jelinek's best-known novel *Die Klavierspielerin* (The Piano Player, 1983), whose protagonist, Erika Kohut, is a piano teacher in Vienna. Erika lives with her mother, to whom she remains bound in a relationship of sado-masochistic dependency. Her mother has inculcated strict discipline into her daughter, and Erika repeats this process in her treatment of her pupils. Her outward poise and icy self-control, however, belie self-harm and regular visits to Vienna's Prater, where she observes the activities of prostitutes and frequents pornographic video-booths. The mother-daughter dyad is thrown into turmoil by the arrival of Walter Klemmer. Despite the strong mutual attraction between Klemmer and Erika, however, she cannot function within a relationship that is not governed by structures of sado-masochistic subjection. The novel ends after Klemmer has performed a series of humiliating acts on Erika, which she had ritualistically demanded of him in a letter that he takes at face value. *Die Klavierspielerin* shows how the internalization of petit-bourgeois conformism leads to a damaged self and dysfunctional relationships. The harrowing portrayal of denatured female sexuality, the unmasking of the clichés of romantic love, and the mockery of high-cultural aspiration constitute powerful social critique. It is little wonder that Jelinek, like Bernhard, has frequently been denigrated as a "Nestbeschmutzer," that is, "one who fouls her own nest." Bernhard's cultural critique, however, is less extreme, for he often holds up the Austro-Germanic musical tradition as an enduring and positive cultural value. This cannot be said of Jelinek, for whom the only value that is never questioned is that of style itself. This nihilistic streak means that her novels can provide trenchant diagnoses of cultural malaise, but are incapable of offering solutions beyond the realm of aesthetics.

Women's Writing

Alongside Jelinek, the postwar era has witnessed the emergence of number of distinguished women writers in Austria, foremost among them Ingeborg Bachmann (1926–73). Bachmann was awarded the Gruppe 47 Prize in 1953, and was soon widely recognized as one of the most important poets writing in German. Her novel *Malina* (1971) is so germane to the development of both women's writing and feminist criticism that it is in this context that it is most productively discussed.[12]

At the time of her premature death in a fire in her flat in Rome, Bachmann had been planning a cycle of novels entitled *Todesarten* (Modes of Death), of which only *Malina* was published in her lifetime, the fragmentary drafts of *Der Fall Franza* (The Franza Case) and *Requiem für Fanny Goldmann* being edited posthumously. *Malina* is narrated by a woman who only ever appears as "Ich." The first section of the novel narrates her love affair with Ivan, a Hungarian who has recently moved to the area, and her domestic life with the eponymous Malina, a military historian. This triangular relationship, however, cannot be read in straightforward mimetic terms, for Malina is less a real person than a projection of Ich. Malina possesses all the qualities that Ich appears to lack: he is the embodiment of rationality, financial competence, and conformity to social norms, while Ich, though a respected writer and vastly erudite, struggles to overcome the rupture between the outside world and her own inner world of desire, imagination, and creativity. This is symbolized by a series of unsent or unsigned letters and an interview with a journalist that Ich sabotages by refusing to reply to his questions in the conventional way. Ich, as a representative of one particular mode of female subjectivity, is contrasted with her secretary, Fräulein Jellinek, and with Antoinette Altenwyl, both of whom have made "good marriages," and have become absorbed by the patriarchal structures that Ich finds so oppressive. The second section of the novel consists of dream-like sequences that play through fantasies of violence and sexual abuse carried out by a father against his daughter, often with the assistance or acquiescence of a mother. The father appears to symbolize the violence done to women by patriarchy as it perpetuates itself through the structures of the bourgeois family and the state, and links are drawn between contemporary society and the atrocities of fascism. Four terse lines conclude the section: "Es ist immer Krieg. / Hier ist immer Gewalt. / Hier ist immer Kampf. / Es ist der ewige Krieg." (It is always war. Here there is always violence. Here there is always struggle. It is the eternal war.)[13] In the final section of the novel, Ich's relationship with Ivan has ended, and a series of dialogues with Malina dramatize the failure to reconcile public and private worlds. Ich is finally murdered by Malina and disappears into a crack in the wall, suggesting that the development of a full female subjectivity is impossible under patriarchy.

With its uncompromising modernism, and its oscillation between social satire and anti-mimetic psychological allegory, *Malina* baffled critics when it was first published. Only as feminism gathered strength both inside and outside the academy in the latter half of the 1970s was the text re-evaluated. In particular, the realization by feminist critics that language and the symbolic order are the means by which patriarchy is maintained and are therefore the proper site of political struggle opened up new ways of understanding *Malina*. At the level of Ich's day-to-day life, the novel demonstrates the difficulty of articulating a specifically female mode of subjectivity, of saying "I" as a woman. At the level of form, on the other hand, the text fragments the narrative discourse, eludes both a fully realist and a fully symbolic recuperation, and constructs an irredeemably fractured textual subjectivity, all of which disturbs the stability of the symbolic order, and lends the novel its radical and subversive force.

While *Malina* is widely regarded as one of the finest Austrian novels of the postwar era, the best-selling autobiographical novel *Wie kommt das Salz ins Meer* (Why Is There Salt in the Sea, 1977) by Brigitte Schwaiger (1949–) has been denigrated by feminist and non-feminist critics alike as a work that robs feminism of its radical force and makes it palatable to a comfortable middle-class readership. Schwaiger's novel deals with the marriage of the narrator to an engineer, Rolf, and her affair with their friend Albert, a doctor. She becomes pregnant by Albert, who performs an abortion on her. Finally, the narrator and Rolf get divorced. This slight plot, narrated largely in the present tense and in deceptively simple language, becomes a vehicle for the exploration of patriarchal structures within Austria's Catholic bourgeoisie. Women, in the form of the narrator's mother and grandmother, emerge as the agents through which patriarchal values are perpetuated and illustrate the collusion of women in their own oppression. Furthermore, language is repeatedly exposed as an insidious means by which gender inequality is maintained. When Rolf discovers that the narrator is keeping a diary, for example, he gives his approval, saying that it's good that she should have secrets and promising to buy her a lockable notebook. He thereby regains control over her linguistic freedom while ostensibly encouraging it. He then adds, "Ich finde es rührend, wie du so sitzt und aussiehst, als dächtest du über etwas Wichtiges nach" (I find it touching the way you sit there and look as though you were reflecting on something important).[14] What appears to be a tender compliment is transformed, by the subjunctive, into a snide devaluation of the narrator's intellect. Schwaiger's narrator often appears to have internalized the values of her society to such an extent that she can do nothing but reproduce them. There is, however, an uneasy irony pervading the text that makes it impossible to say whether a given statement is supposed to be taken seriously or is being offered up for critique. This instability of textual meaning possesses the capacity to threaten the symbolic, which makes *Wie kommt das Salz ins Meer* a considerably more subtle, valuable, and politically astute text than Schwaiger's detractors realize.

The other outstanding Austrian women writers of Schwaiger's generation are Elisabeth Reichart (1953–), Lilian Faschinger (1950–), and Anna Mitgutsch (1948–). Reichart's *Februarschatten* (February Shadows, 1984) is a contribution to the ongoing process of Austrian *Vergangenheitsbewältigung* or dealing with the Nazi past. In February 1945, 500 of the 570 inmates of the Mauthausen concentration camp escaped, and all but seventeen were tracked down and murdered not only by Nazi forces but by the local civilian population. This became known as the "Mühlviertler Hasenjagd" (Mühlviertel hare-hunt) and forms the background to Reichart's text, in which the recently-widowed Hilde is confronted by her daughter Erika and, in a series of conversations, is forced to dredge up her fragmentary and buried memories of the manhunt. The mother-daughter dynamic illustrates the tortuous process of remembering and the pain involved in confronting a shameful past, while also adding a new gender perspective to the project of *Vergangenheitsbewältigung* by showing women as perpetrators rather than victims.

As the title of Faschinger's first novel *Die neue Scheherezade* (The New Sheherazade, 1986) suggests, her work is characterized by a delight in fantastic fabulation. Like Bernhard and Jelinek, Faschinger is scathingly critical of Austria. In *Magdalena Sünderin* (Magdalena the Sinner, 1995), the protagonist remarks that as a country Austria has nothing to recommend it beyond its cakes and pastries. And yet this denunciation goes hand in hand with an obsession with her homeland and compatriots, suggesting that even if the physical place has been left behind, affective — albeit negative — bonds remain. This ambivalence not only finds expression on a thematic level, but determines the structure of *Magdalena Sünderin*. In a highly influential essay written in 1980 but published only in 1990, Robert Menasse pointed out that countries like Austria, which define themselves culturally and politically in terms of Catholicism, differ from Protestant countries in the influence exerted by ritualized confession on forms of social discourse. He identifies the confessional situation as a central pillar of the political culture of the Second Republic, and seeks to demonstrate that the prevalence of such situations in postwar Austrian writing leads to an aesthetics which, however critical of Austria it may be on a thematic level, proves at the level of form to be complicit with the political culture it denigrates.[15] *Magdalena Sünderin* reads like a simultaneous illustration and subversion of this very thesis.

The heroine, Magdalena Leitner, abducts a priest at gunpoint at the beginning of the novel, forcing him into the sidecar of her Puch 800 motorcycle and driving to a remote clearing in a Tyrolean forest. Bound and gagged, the priest is forced to hear her confession. Magdalena's confession deals primarily with her travels through Europe, during which she meets seven men, all of whom seem to embody the promise of paradise. And yet the very concept of paradise, as Magdalena remarks, contains within it the concept of expulsion. Needless to say, the idyll proves in each case to be short-lived. Despite their various erotic talents and attractions, Magdalena, like a modern-day female Bluebeard, murders all seven of them. She drowns a melancholic Friesian in the Gulf of Genoa, sets fire to a pathologically jealous Ukrainian, and poisons a philandering Spanish dance instructor in Paris. In London she stabs a Scottish tramp who turns out to be a vampire, and shoots a Jehovah's Witness who turns out to be homosexual. Fleeing southwards, she asphyxiates an elderly sado-maoschist who had employed her to eat with him, read to him, and flagellate him in the cellar of his Baden-Baden villa. Finally, she pushes a serial divorcee from a precipice in the mountains above Garmisch-Partenkirchen. Faschinger adds petty theft to this implausible catalog of misdemeanors: Magdalena sometimes supports herself by swapping her biker's leather cat-suit for a Discalced Carmelite habit and picking the pockets of unsuspecting urbanites or pilfering valuables from churches and cathedrals.

It is clear that this confession is designed to provoke the priest, for Magdalena remains unrepentant. And yet the real scandal of the novel is that the confession simultaneously functions as a seduction. Indeed, since Magdalena admits at the very beginning that her story is a fairytale, it may well be that this was the sole intention all along. As Magdalena realizes that the absolution she had initially demanded is irrelevant, the priest becomes increasingly indulgent towards her, increasingly intrigued and excited by her sexual escapades and, indeed, by her face, figure, and flowing auburn hair. The novel culminates not in a *te absolvo*, but in a night of shared erotic pleasure, and by the time the priest is rescued by his sister and housekeeper Maria, he has given up any intention of returning to his pastoral duties. The novel ends with his vow to preserve the seal of the confessional and not to betray Magdalena's secrets. At this moment, however, the text appears to subvert its own project, for the entire confession that we have just read has been narrated by the priest himself, who quotes Magdalena's confession at great length. As such, the ending forms part of a long chain of ambivalences that can be witnessed throughout the novel, for example in Magdalena's continued thraldom to the rhetoric of sin, guilt, and absolution despite her professedly anti-Catholic views and at times sacrilegious behavior, in the soteriological expectations that accord ill with her secular carnality, or in her claim to be a strong and independent woman even though she spends her time moving from one monogamous heterosexual relationship to the next. Just as the novel both installs and subverts its confessional structure and theological framework, so it both reproduces and ironizes religious, patriarchal, and national stereotypes. The main characters bear names whose Biblical resonances are all too clear: the priest is called Christian, his spinster sister Maria, and the protagonist Magdalena. Magdalena's changing attire oscillates between poles of the saintly and the whorish, and she peddles the crassest of stereotypes, referring repeatedly to the putative national characteristics of various European countries, or to the innate qualities of men and women (as though these were somehow immutable). Yet the Biblical names and hackneyed judgments are offered in such a way as to foreground their stereotypical nature. Taken together, all these features of the text suspend the reader in a moral, theological, and gender-political vacuum. The enormous appeal of Faschinger's sensuous style and fast-moving, picaresque plot is unsettled by the impossibility of determining the novel's value system with any degree of certainty. .

Mitgutsch's novel *Abschied von Jerusalem* (Farewell to Jerusalem, 1995) is set in Jerusalem, a city that the narrator, Dvorah, has visited many times before. While there, she has an affair with an Armenian, but a series of events leads her to the conclusion that he is in fact an Arab terrorist. His photograph in the newspaper several days later confirms this suspicion, and the novel ends as Dvorah, returning to Austria, is detained at Jerusalem's airport. The novel contains frequent and lengthy flashbacks dealing with Dvorah's past life, including her upbringing as a half-Jewish girl in Vienna, where she is subjected to cryptic insults by members of her non-Jewish father's family that she only later learns to decipher. *Abschied von Jerusalem* explores the post-Shoah identity of Austrian Jews. The fact that the narrator calls herself Dvorah even though the name in her passport is Hildegard is a symptom of her increasing discomfort with her grandmother's and mother's attempts at assimilation. But Jerusalem offers no valid alternative. It is divided along religious and ethnic lines, full of latent violence, and perilous for strangers unused to its impossibly labyrinthine topography and the arcane signs by which one can distinguish hostile from benign encounters. Dvorah's stay in Jerusalem is complicated further by gender questions, in particular the clash of liberal Western attitudes and the more codified expectations in orthodox-Jewish and Arab communities. Walking through Jerusalem as a Western woman renders Dvorah vulnerable and disempowered, a target of sexual aggression, confidence tricks, and extortion. Hybridity, often celebrated by postmodern theorists as a liberating state of contemporary subjectivity, is here shown to be a fraught and unsettling condition.

Recent Developments

Several other major Jewish writers have emerged in Austria in recent decades. *Gebürtig* (Born, 1992) by Robert Schindel (1944–) met with wide public and critical acclaim on first publication. It is a structurally complex investigation of Jewish-Austrian identity. The novel's three narrative strands are organized around Danny Demant, an editor at a publishing house. He is currently reading a manuscript by his friend, Emanuel Katz, which contains the novel's second narrative strand: the story of Susanne Ressel, the daughter of a concentration-camp survivor who seeks to bring her father's torturer, Anton Egger, to justice. In order to do this, she is reliant on the testimony of the exiled writer Hermann Gebirtig, who is eventually persuaded to return to Austria but flees again as soon as Egger is acquitted. The third narrative strand concerns Katz's relationship with Konrad Sachs, the son of a notorious Nazi criminal. Sachs seeks redemption in Katz, and is persuaded by Demant to publish his autobiography as an act of exorcism. Schindel's novel presents a highly differentiated view of post-Holocaust identity in German-speaking countries, effectively denying the validity of the Jewish-Austrian binary and dealing instead with a variety of identity positions in which Jewishness ultimately seems the most stable. In *Die Vertreibung aus der Hölle* (The Expulsion from Hell, 2001) Robert Menasse (1954–) takes a different approach to the question of Jewish identity. The novel contains two plot-strands. One narrates the life-story of the half-Jewish historian Viktor Abravanel. Memories of his youth in 1960s and 1970s Vienna are triggered by a school reunion, at which the middle-aged Abravanel accuses his teachers of being ex-Nazis. Though this revelation proves to be untrue, it raises difficult questions concerning the constructed nature of history and the way in which these constructions primarily serve current interests. The second narrative strand is a biographical account of Manasseh ben Israel (1607–57), a Portuguese Marrano (that is, a Jew who has been forced to convert to Christianity) who emigrated to Holland and became a central figure in the Amsterdam Jewish community. The parallels between the two narrative strands expose the banality of Abravanel's problems in comparison with those of Manasseh, and draw attention to the historiographic sleight of hand that manages to yoke their stories together. But they also foreground a disturbing tendency for history to repeat itself. This is manifested less in national or global events than in human behavior, in which subjugation, domination, and willing conformism function, across times and places, to preserve the integrity of some notional or imagined community and to deny difference. Catholicism, Judaism, and Communism are not excluded from these processes, which explains the controversy generated by this deeply pessimistic novel on first publication.

Austria's past has continued to fascinate contemporary authors, though they often approach it in fresh ways. Christoph Ransmayr (1954–), for example, satirizes the Habsburg past and the enduring obsession with it in *Die Schrecken des Eises und der Finsternis* (The Terrors of Ice and Darkness, 1984). The main character, Josef Mazzini, is fascinated by the polar expedition undertaken in 1873 by the Austro-Hungarian Navy. He decides to follow in the footsteps of the explorers, making his way up through Norway and onto the island of Spitzbergen, where he disappears. The parallel action in the novel concerns the 1873 expedition, which is reconstructed with the help of extensive quotations from the account published by expedition leader Julius Payer and the diaries and letters of key members of the team. Mazzini is the subject of considerable narratorial irony: he is portrayed as a naïve dilettante in comparison with the modern-day researchers who work year-round in the waters of the Arctic Circle, while modern transport renders absurd his romantic desire to relive the past. The narrator also ironizes the members of the Payer expedition, particularly the fact that they were willing to endure so much physical hardship out of loyalty to Emperor Franz Joseph. Indeed, such is their sense of duty that they even indulge in some muted mallemaroking to celebrate the Emperor's birthday. Polar exploration emerges as nothing more than a vanity project undertaken to symbolically confirm the legitimacy of the nineteenth-century nation state or the self-esteem of an inadequate individual.

An intriguing response to the legacy of Nazism is Norbert Gstrein's *Die englischen Jahre* (The Years in England, 1998), which deals with an Austrian-Jewish writer called Hirschfelder. Hirschfelder flees Vienna in 1938 on the insistence of his gentile father, and at the outbreak of war is interned on the Isle of Man. After the war, he remains in England, becomes a cult writer, and takes a job as a librarian in Southend on Sea, repairing to a room in the Palace Hotel every afternoon to write. Shortly after Hirschfelder's death, the narrator conducts a series of interviews with his three wives in an effort to piece together the story of his life. These interviews are interspersed with chapters written in the second person and narrating what we take to be Hirschfelder's biography. In the final chapters of the novel, it emerges that Hirschfelder had perished when the ship taking him and other internees to Canada had been torpedoed by a U-boat. The man who goes on to lead Hirschfelder's life was in fact a non-Jewish Austrian who slips into the legal identity that Hirschfelder had vacated and lives off the cultural and emotional capital of being an Jewish émigré intellectual. This allows Gstrein to address issues of Allied internment policy, ethnic impersonation, and legal and performative conceptions of identity, while also opening up highly original perspectives on the more familiar questions of writing and exile.

Austrian fiction of the postwar period has frequently been accused of being apolitical, of turning away from questions of history, with writers preferring, it is argued, to retreat into linguistic exploration and experiment, or dehistoricized, mythical spatio-temporal settings. It may well be true that an intensive preoccupation with language is one of the defining formal features of Austrian fiction, and it is certainly true that the likes of Bernhard, Jelinek, Handke, and Faschinger are among the most distinctive German-language stylists of the past sixty years. And yet the foregoing account of the Austrian novel from 1945–2000 shows that even at their most ludic and experimental, Austrian writers are deeply concerned with the cultural heritage, with problems of the modern world, its technology, industry, economy, its bureaucracy and sexual politics — and with the legacy of both the Habsburg and the Nazi past.

Notes

[1] Ruth Beckermann, "During the *Anschluß* to the Third Reich, Friedrich Torberg escapes from Prague, first to Zürich and then to Paris," in Sander Gilman and Jack Zipes, eds., *Yale Companion to Jewish Writing and Thought in German Culture, 1096–1996* (New Haven: Yale UP, 1997), 551–57; here: 555.

[2] Alexander Lernet-Holenia, *Der Graf von Saint-Germain* (Zurich: Conzett & Huber, 1948), 135.

[3] The place-name Schweigen, which means not merely silence but the conscious act of remaining silent, is part of an elaborate scheme of symbolic names that exist in a quasi-adjectival relationship to the person or place they denote. In the case of the preternaturally sensitive hairdresser Zitter (from "zittern," to tremble), the brutal and short-tempered Rotschädel (red face), the outsider Unfreund (non-friend) and the cattle dealer Ukrutnik (a Czech insult that has no English equivalent, but which corresponds to the German "Schweinehund"), the link between the name and character is especially clear. In other cases, the names are suggestive rather than descriptive: the local politician and ex-*Ortsgruppenleiter* is called Habergeier ("Geier" means "vulture"), the first person to die in the text is Höller (reminiscent of "Hölle," hell), and the village policeman is Habicht (hawk). Several critics have mentioned this aspect of the text in passing. See, for example, Maria Luise Caputo-Mayr, "Hans Leberts Romane: Realismus und Dämonie, Zeitkritik und Gerichtstag," *Modern Austrian Literature* 7, i/ii (1974), 79–98, here: 84; and Konstanze Fliedl and Karl Wagner, "Tote Zeit: Zum Problem der Darstellung von Geschichtserfahrung in den Romanen Erich Frieds und Hans Leberts," in Friedbert Aspetsberger, Norbert Frei, and Hubert Lengauer, eds., *Literatur der Nachkriegszeit und der fünfziger Jahre in Österreich* (Vienna: Österreichischer Buchverlag, 1984), 303–19; here: 310.

[4] Hans Lebert, *Die Wolfshaut* (Frankfurt am Main: Fischer, 1993), 8.

[5] See, for example, Konstanze Fliedl and Karl Wagner, "Tote Zeit: Zum Problem der Darstellung von Geschichtserfahrung in den Romanen Erich Frieds und Hans Leberts," in Friedbert Aspetsberger et al., eds., *Literatur der Nachkriegszeit und der fünfziger Jahre in Österreich* (Vienna: Österreichischer Buchverlag, 1984), 303–19, here: 313; and Jürgen Egyptien, *Der "Anschluß" als Sündenfall: Hans Leberts literarisches Werk und intellektuelle Gestalt* (Vienna: Europaverlag, 1998), 144–45.

[6] Gert F. Jonke, *Geometrischer Heimatroman* (Frankfurt am Main: Suhrkamp, 1969), 123.

[7] Karl-Markus Gauss, "Provincialism, Anti-Provincialism, and Beyond," *The Magazine* [*zur Frankfurter Buch-Messe*] (1995), 31.

[8] *Das Kalkwerk* (Frankfurt am Main: Suhrkamp, 1973), 94. English, which uses tense-shifts rather than the subjunctive to signal reported speech, cannot reproduce the original with any degree of accuracy or power.

[9] Lampersberg was so upset by Bernhard's portrayal of him as an obnoxious and drunken buffoon that he sued Bernhard for libel and succeeded in getting all copies of the novel temporarily confiscated from Austrian bookshops.

[10] Irene Heidelberger-Leonard, "Auschwitz als Pflichtfach für Schriftsteller," in Irene Heidelberger-Leonard and Hans Höller, eds., *Antiautobiografie: Thomas Bernhards Auslöschung* (Frankfurt am Main: Suhrkamp, 1995), 181–96.

[11] Peter Handke, *Wunschloses Unglück* (Frankfurt am Main: Suhrkamp, 1974), 25, 17.

[12] Sigrid Weigel's influential article "Der schielende Blick," for example, is an attempt to formulate a feminist poetics on the basis of *Malina*. S. Weigel, "Der schielende Blick," in S. Weigel and Inge Stephan, eds., *Die verborgene Frau: Sechs Beiträge zu einer feministischen Literaturwissenschaft* (Berlin: Argument, 1988), 83–137.

[13] Ingeborg Bachmann, *Malina* (Frankfurt am Main: Suhrkamp, 1971), 247.

[14] Brigitte Schwaiger, *Wie kommt das Salz ins Meer* (Reinbek: Rowohlt, 1979), 50.

[15] Robert Menasse, *Überbau und Underground: Essays zum österreichischen Geist* (Frankfurt am Main: Suhrkamp, 1997); first published in Vienna by Sonderzahl, 1990.

11: Popular Culture in Austria, 1945–2000

Joseph McVeigh

AUSTRIA'S UNIQUE POLITICAL SITUATION in the first postwar decade did much to shape its popular culture of subsequent decades.[1] The Moscow Declaration of the Allies (1943) viewed Austria as both a victim of Nazi aggression as well as a co-combatant with the Third Reich. As a result, Austria was occupied by the victorious Allies until 1955, but was nevertheless granted a large degree of autonomy through a federal government elected in November of 1945. In the first postwar decade this situation set the stage for a vibrant competition between indigenous cultural traditions and impulses from the foreign cultures represented by the Allied occupation forces. Officially absent from the Austrian cultural landscape at that time was a visible German presence, which was politically — and to a significant degree, culturally — "quarantined" from the land it had annexed in 1938. The Austrian writer Milo Dor spoke of a "paper curtain" between the two lands after 1945 that prevented the free flow of cultural information and artists.[2] Despite censorship and travel restrictions, cultural contact between the two occupied nations slowly resumed to the extent that those Austrians who viewed their culture as distinct from that of Germany, saw cultural impulses from that nation as just one more foreign influence assaulting their beleaguered culture.

Of all the foreign impulses affecting Austrian culture during the occupation, American and British influence had arguably the greatest impact, especially through the programming of the Allied radio networks — such as the American Red-White-Red and the British Alpenland networks — whose contemporary music and entertainment programming became immensely popular among Austrian youth. Although the Allies and Austrians shared many of the same traditions of high culture, they nevertheless diverged significantly with respect to popular culture. American cultural policies in Austria, for example, aimed at "reorienting" Austrian institutions such as radio and the press toward a more "democratic" approach to culture, that is, one more responsive to public taste and allowing for maximal public input and participation. By contrast, Austrian cultural policy of the postwar era, largely promulgated by the conservative Ministry of Education, saw culture as an edifying force that should shape public tastes rather than reflect them.

Austrian efforts to combat a cultural "Überfremdung" (foreign domination) by Allied influences — and eventually German influences as well —
were aided by moral arguments, in particular against the allegedly deleteri-
ous effect on young Austrians of American films and music. The Austrian
laws against "Schmutz und Schund" (Filth and Trash) of 1950, for example, targeted reading materials that exposed young readers to violence, such
as paperback novels with American cowboy and gangster themes, which
were deemed inappropriate for their supposed effect on the behavior and
mores of young Austrians. The *Wiener Zeitung* reported in 1951 that some
21,000 such pulp novels were confiscated and destroyed that year in Vienna
alone. In addition to lists of forbidden titles for young people, the Ministry
of Education also published lists of recommended books that were dominated, not surprisingly, by Austrian authors of the prewar generation.

This defensive stance of the Austrian government vis-à-vis Western and
(some) German popular culture oftentimes produced strange bedfellows.
The conservative Ministry of Education, for example, found the Austrian
Communist Party supportive of its efforts to limit the impact of American
popular culture, although the latter's motivation certainly had as much to
do with Cold War politics as with the protection of Austria's youth.

The political and cultural struggle between Austria and the Allies over
the shaping of popular culture was especially pronounced in the area of
radio, the most important mass medium before the spread of television in
the late 1950s. The Austrian national radio network (initially still called by
its prewar name, RAVAG) was in direct competition with Allied networks:
the German-language radio network of the Americans, Red-White-Red,
and, to a lesser degree, the English-language broadcasts of Blue Danube
Radio, the American Armed Forces station in Austria, as well as Radio
Alpenland in the British sector of occupation.

With the signing of the Austrian State Treaty in July 1955 and the
withdrawal of the Allies later that year, Austrian popular culture entered a
period of relative autonomy in the absence of the visible influences of the
Allied occupation authorities. The first postoccupation years witnessed the
advent of Austria's first television broadcasts as well as the expansion of
radio programming and film production. However, if government officials
thought the absence of foreign troops and their cultural apparatus would
strengthen the effect of their own cultural identity-building policies, they
were greatly mistaken. With the Allies gone and the "paper curtain" to
Germany lifted, popular cultural influences from West Germany began to
play a greater role in Austria, while the effect of American — and, increasingly, British — popular culture among young Austrians became even
stronger through the media of music, film, and television.

Historically bracketed by the period of Allied occupation (1945–55)
and the ongoing process of consolidating a European identity in the present, Austria consistently had to ask itself after 1945 to what extent it could

boast of an indigenous popular culture to stand alongside its renowned high cultural achievements, in view of the increasingly prominent derivatives of foreign cultures. At each stage of its evolution after 1945, Austrian popular culture absorbed impulses from sources outside its borders, but it also spread its own distinctive popular culture — as it had done historically for centuries — to other German-speaking lands. The process of Austrianizing foreign cultural impulses since 1945 has had varied success: some forms have simply been transplanted with little change into the Austrian cultural context (many German and American television programs and films, for example), while others have taken on a more distinctly Austrian character, such as Austropop music.

This essay examines salient features which best reflect the larger evolution of the nation's cultural identity among its populace. Foregoing various categories such as domestic culture, fashion, sports, and the popular stage, this essay will focus on the evolving face of Austrian popular culture as it has been shaped by radio, television, film, and music in the Second Republic.

Radio

Despite the destruction of the main radio transmitter on the Bisamberg outside Vienna by the retreating Nazis in 1945, radio programming in Vienna returned almost immediately after the start of the Allied occupation. In the Soviet zone in Eastern Austria and Vienna the prewar Austrian radio network, RAVAG (Radio-Verkehrs-AG) was reconstituted under its founder Oskar Czieja and prewar Program Director Rudolf Henz. Although exercising certain censorship and veto rights, Soviet influence on RAVAG was primarily exerted through a daily "Russian Hour" propaganda program. However, ongoing tensions between Soviet and Austrian authorities at RAVAG concerning the content of broadcast materials came to a head during the election campaign of 1949, when the RAVAG news department took the unusual step of broadcasting a disclaimer that it could not vouch for the accuracy of its own news broadcasts.[3]

The other three Allies (U.S., Great Britain, and France) set up radio stations in their own respective zones of occupation, with the American network Red-White-Red representing the largest of the three, having studios in Salzburg, Linz and Vienna. In the area of popular entertainment, the competition between RAVAG (renamed Österreichischer Rundfunk — Austrian Radio — in 1953) and RWR produced creative programming on both sides that — for a short time at least — placed Austria in the forefront of popular radio in Europe. The German-language RWR-network, which captured some 65% of listeners in Vienna by the early 1950s, introduced a number of programming and technological firsts to Austrian radio, including commercial advertising, Austria's first disc jockeys, soap operas, and quiz shows before live audiences with listener participation and prizes. RWR's sister-station, the Blue Danube Network, although broadcasting only in English, attracted many young Austrian listeners because of its steady offering of American popular music, including jazz and rock-and-roll.

The American policy of "democratizing" Austrian radio by targeting popular tastes instead of gearing its programming primarily toward cultural elites, as had been the case historically with Austrian radio, meant an explosion of popular entertainment programming on RWR. Efforts by RAVAG to emulate some of these innovations met with opposition from Program Director Rudolf Henz and others who saw the popular culture broadcasts of RWR as the product of "Fanatiker, die im Rundfunk alleine eine Unterhaltungsmaschine, eine musikalische Wasserleitung sehen" (fanatics who view radio as nothing more than an entertainment machine with an unlimited supply of music).[4] According to Henz, such broadcasts drew their popularity "aus der Sensationsgier und aus den niederen Bezirken des Lebens" (from an insatiable sensationalism and from the less respectable side of life).[5] Henz's opinion carried the day in Austrian radio of the early 1950s by appealing to the patriotism of the Austrian public to reject the seductive and supposedly socially corrosive influences of programming that arose out of "irgendeinem ausländischen Geschmack" (some foreign standard of taste).[6]

After the signing of the Austrian State Treaty in 1955, the Allies turned over their radio networks to Austrian Radio, which dismantled its main competitor RWR and most of its programming, continuing only a few programs that conformed to the new guidelines for Austrian radio which Rudolf Henz helped shape in 1955–56. Although a number of successful programs were introduced by Österreichischer Rundfunk after 1955 (for example, the travel guide *Autofahrer unterwegs*, which began in 1957), or continued from the period of occupation (the soap opera *Die Radiofamilie*, which began in 1952 at Red-White-Red, or Heinz Conrad's Sunday-morning broadcast, which began in 1946 and continued for some forty years), political infighting between the Socialists (SPÖ) and the conservative People's Party (ÖVP), on top of growing financial difficulties, made Austrian radio lose some of its vibrancy and innovative tendencies from the 1950s. This was due in no small part to the new programming guidelines established by Austrian Radio in 1956: it sought to avoid polemics of any kind, to cultivate "die Grundsätze des guten Geschmacks" (the principles of good taste), and refrain from offending "die natürliche Moral" (natural morality); similarly, the listener should not be burdened with "eine allzu aufdringliche Werbung" (overly forceful advertising).[7] As a result of this aversion to the commercialization of the mass media, ORF was faced with recurrent fiscal difficulties. From its introduction in the late 1950s until the early 1990s, advertising was strictly limited on Austrian radio and television. In the early 1990s, advertising could be broadcast no more than twenty minutes per day on television and 120 minutes per week on radio. Despite these limits, commercial advertising generated almost half of ORF's income by 1992, whereas subscription fees by listeners and viewers amounted to slightly less (46%). With the passage of the Regional Broadcasting Law of 1993, which permitted the licensing of private radio stations in Austria for the first time, concessions were made allowing up to 90 minutes of advertising per day on the radio.

Because of political infighting between the two main political parties, the SPÖ and the ÖVP, Austrian radio entered a period of malaise in the late 1950s. Reforms were negotiated and put into effect in 1967, providing the system with financial and political stability, and, most importantly, the inspired leadership of a new general director, Gerd Bacher (1925–), in the years 1967 to 1974, 1978 to 1986, and 1990 to 1994. Bacher reorganized Austrian radio and introduced a number of technical and programming innovations that restored Austria's role as one of the more progressive radio systems in Western Europe. Among the first programming changes introduced by Bacher was the reinstatement of the program *Der Watschenmann* (The Whipping Boy), an outspoken forum for the critique of public figures and policies. The program had been so successful on the Red-White-Red network in the early 1950s that its cancellation by Henz after the network's takeover by Austrian Radio in 1955 caused a major public uproar, with a public petition drive conducted by the newspaper *Wiener Kurier* collecting hundreds of thousands of signatures, all to no avail. The reinstatement of this program some twelve years after its cancellation sent a signal to the radio community that Austrian radio had entered a new phase of popular broadcasting. Bacher emulated other innovations of RWR and the BBC in establishing more fixed starting times for programs and a better integration of music and spoken programming, which were not traditional features of Austrian radio.

Reorganization under Gerd Bacher expanded the reach of Austrian Radio into some 94% of Austrian homes by 1971, while offering a wider selection of programming, distributed over three main stations within the system: Ö1, ÖR (Regional Radio), and Ö3. The introduction of Ö3 had a major impact on popular culture in Austria, especially among younger listeners, as it was here that Austropop first found a home in the 1970s. The station was modeled after the popular European stations Radio Luxembourg, France Inter, and Europa I, and soon became the highest rated popular music station in Europe. This lasted until the 1990s, when a new radio landscape emerged not only in Europe, but around the world, through the introduction of Internet-based broadcasting.

The mid-1990s saw some seismic shifts in the radio landscape in Austria. The Regional Broadcasting Law of 1993 broke the monopoly of ORF, by permitting private radio stations. ORF reacted to this new competition by introducing the station FM4 in 1995, targeting a new generation of young listeners with a combined German and English-language program of music (especially the so-called "Wiener Elektronik"), news and comedy. A short time later, Ö3 was re-christened Hitradio and given its own studios and headquarters. The first two private stations, Antenne Steiermark and Salzburg Radio Melody, went on the air in 1995, and by 1998 twelve other private stations followed. In 1999 Austrian radio made the leap into the Internet with Ö1 leading the way, and in 2003 ORF introduced its first Web-radio broadcasts. By May of 2004 there were some 65 commercial and private radio stations in Austria, although public radio still enjoyed a healthy share of listeners: ORF's twelve stations with their national reach still commanded over 82% of listeners in 2001, while commercial stations, whose licenses only permitted regional broadcasting, garnered about 16% of the total.

As a popular medium Austrian radio has managed to thrive in the era of television. To do so, it has had to embrace the very influences that Rudolf Henz had fought so hard to hold at bay in the 1950s, namely popular music from the English-speaking world, commercial radio, and programming shaped by listener tastes. Although television replaced radio as the most popular of the mass media, the process was not immediate, or complete. For example, the radio program *Traummännlein* (Little Dream Man), a five-minute broadcast at 7:00 P.M. each evening that had helped put generations of young children to bed since 1955, was replaced by its television counterpart *Betthupferl* (Bedtime Treat) only in 2000. Similarly, the popular radio program *Autofahrer unterwegs* (Automobile Drivers on the Road) enjoyed over 10,000 broadcasts between 1957 and 1985. Yet, in the area of music broadcasting — of all types — radio remained the dominant force among the mass media, despite the inroads of television.

Television

Apart from the print media, radio and film were the most popular vehicles of mass culture in the first postwar decade. However, the new technology of television that slowly emerged in Austria in the latter half of the 1950s would profoundly affect these and other forms of popular media. Although the first television broadcast in Austria was transmitted on August 1, 1955, it took another sixteen months before regular programming could begin on January 1, 1957. And regular *daily* programming did not become a staple until later in 1959. Nevertheless, after this slow beginning the medium grew quickly: by December 1959 there were already some 127,000 television sets in Austria. This number more than doubled to over 257,000 sets (about 12% of households) in less than two years. And by February 1968 over one million television sets were registered.

Color television was only introduced officially to Austria in September of 1967, with some 25,000 sets in use within two years, despite an initially prohibitive price of over 20,000 Schillings.

In its first decade, television emulated radio and largely reflected the prevailing tastes of the times. For example, the popular radio show *Die Radiofamilie*, which ran from 1952 until 1960, gave birth to the early television series *Unsere Nachbarn: Die Familie Leitner* (Our Neighbors: The Leitner Family), which itself had a long and successful run from 1958 to 1967. Such family shows have always been a mainstay of radio and television as a reflection of society at a particular point in time, and Austria was no different. Moving beyond the middle-class world of the Leitner family of the 1960s, Austrian television of the Kreisky era offered a look into the life of the working-class with the series *Ein echter Wiener geht nicht unter* (A True Viennese Never Gives Up, 1975–79), with Karl Merkatz in the main role as the central character "Mundl." Frequent reruns of *Ein echter Wiener* attest to the sustained interest of the viewing public in the everyday life of the "common man," a focus that underlies the later hit series *Kaisermühlen Blues* (1992–99) as well.

One of the more significant developments in television programming was the rise of the docudrama, which ranged from a dramatized documentary to a blend of history and fiction. Although the first productions of this type at ORF occurred in the late 1960s with films addressing the question of Austria's role in the Second World War, such as *Die Himbeerpflücker* (The Raspberry Pickers, 1965) or *Der Fall Regine Krause* (The Regine Krause Case, 1970), this genre came into its own in the 1970s and 1980s under the direction of ORF Section Chief Gerald Szyszkowitz from 1973 to 1987. During that time ORF produced dozens of made-for-television movies that mixed elements of the documentary film and feature films. Among the most notable of these were the three-part series *Alpensaga* (Alpine Saga, 1976–77), and *Das Dorf an der Grenze* (The Village at the Border, 1979–82). Throughout the 1980s, however, fewer films of this type were produced each year, being replaced in large part by cinematic feature films, which, by the late 1990s, represented almost a quarter of total broadcast time. ORF's purchase of Wien-Film in 2003 placed a rich supply of feature films at its disposal, indicating that this trend will continue.

Although a latecomer to the field of popular media since 1945, television was not immune to the "scandals" that seemed a regular part of the cultural landscape of Austria. Like radio, which had engendered heated discussions in the early 1950s with *Der Watschenmann*, the new visual medium soon developed the power to excite the viewers' emotions with social commentary, as was evident from the furor caused in 1961 by the satirical monologue *Der Herr Karl*, performed by Helmut Qualtinger.

A scandal of a different type, which resulted in parliamentary discussions, was the question of whether the new genre of "reality television" was appropriate for public television. A phenomenon of the early 2000s, Austrian reality shows such as *Taxi Orange* (2000–2001) and *Expedition Österreich* (2004) have participants compete against one another at certain tasks or challenges. Programs such as these represent an attempt to "Austrianize" general international trends in television programming, while other recent popular broadcasts follow a foreign template more directly, like the current hit quiz show *Die Millionenshow* (Who Wants to Be a Millionaire?), or the music competition *Starmania NG*, whose structures closely parallel those of similar shows in other countries, albeit with an Austrian accent.

Despite efforts to provide "Austrian" programming, a significant part of today's television offerings either originate abroad or are co-productions with other countries. Indeed, from its very beginning in the mid-1950s, Austrian television has relied heavily on programs from abroad, especially American productions. Children's series such as *Fury* or *Lassie* were mainstays of early Austrian programming for young people in the 1950s and 1960s, while *Bonanza, Dallas, Tatort* (Scene of the Crime), *Aktenzeichen XY-ungelöst* (File Reference XY Unsolved) and countless other American and German television series shared the airwaves with Austrian hits, such as the long-running detective series *Kottan* (1976–83) or the more recent spoof of Austrian bureaucracy *MA 2412* (1998–2002). By the late 1950s, fully half of all prime-time programs on Austrian television were imported from abroad, and by the late 1960s some two-thirds of such programs originated outside of Austria. A look at the June 2005 programming of ORF1 and ORF2 indicates that this trend continues unabated.[8]

The precarious financial and production situation of early Austrian television was exacerbated by the reticence of the Austrian film industry to allow the use of its facilities and equipment for the production of television programs. This prompted ORF to seek cooperative arrangements with other national television stations beginning in the early 1960s, most notably with the channel Zweites Deutsches Fernsehen of West Germany. A reform law of 1974, however, recognized the potentially damaging effect on Austrian cultural identity that a reliance on foreign programming could entail and put forth as part of its goal a strengthening of an "Österreich-Bewusstsein" (Austria awareness) in the viewing public, as well as increased focus on Austrian authors. By and large, such concerns have proven as ineffective as similar calls to combat foreign cultural influences during the Allied occupation.

Technological advances since the 1970s, such as videocassette recorders, DVDs, satellite and cable television, and Web broadcasts on the Internet have increasingly blurred the boundary between television and the movie industry, whereby the television or computer screen can serve as a personal cinema with a vast array of both broadcast and recorded products at the command of the viewer.

Film

Much like the radio industry after 1945, Austria's popular film industry largely reflected a continuity of personnel, forms, and style through the 1950s and into the early 1960s. Not a few popular film stars of the postwar era had been active on stage and screen throughout the "German interlude." In the initial phase of the occupation, the Allies put together lists of films from the Third Reich that could not be shown in public. Nevertheless, there were many others that could be shown, including a number of so-called "Überläufer"-films, which began shooting or were completed, but never shown, during the Nazi years.[9] Many such films, typically of the entertainment variety, were eventually released after 1945, thus maintaining for their actors and director an uninterrupted continuity with the 1930s and 1940s, and at the same time fulfilling audience demand for familiar personalities on the big screen, such as Hans Moser, Paula Wessely, Paul Hörbiger, Maria Andergast, and many others.

The cultural war being fought by the Austrian government during the Allied occupation against the inroads of foreign popular culture had prompted passage of the "Filth and Trash Laws" in 1950, which aimed to establish standards of public morality for the mass media. However, this did not prevent films such as *Die Sünderin* (The Sinner, 1951) by Willy Forst, starring Hildegard Knef, from causing a scandal, which in turn often helped them become a box office hit. A decade later, in March of 1960, the fight against indecency in the mass media took on a new gravity when a Board of Governors Conference sought to reinforce the 1950 laws with a proposal to allow only those above eighteen years of age to attend public cinema. The same Board reviewed some 276 films and forbade the showing of 141 of them, while restricting an additional 54 to viewers over the age of fourteen. These efforts in 1960 mark the end of the conservative postwar era and its efforts to establish standards of public taste for popular media. The socially turbulent years of the 1960s and 1970s brought not only a retreat from such centralized efforts at shoring up public morality, but an increasingly critical eye toward Austrian society and history.

In the restorative cultural atmosphere in Austria in the 1950s, critical representations of the Second World War and Austria's role therein were neither popular, nor common. To be sure, there were films that dealt with the war period and its aftermath. The pressing issue of returning prisoners of war, for example, was topical in the late 1940s in such films as *Der weite Weg* (The Long Way, 1946), *Arlberg-Express* (1948) or *An klingenden Ufern* (On Ringing Shores, 1948). And there were other films set in the war years, such as *Sturmjahre: Der Leidensweg Österreichs* (Storm Years. Austria's Passage of Suffering, 1946) and *Duell mit dem Tod* (Duel with Death, 1949) both of which portrayed Austria's underground resistance to the Nazis during the Second World War, or the film *Das andere Leben* (The

Other Life, 1948) which shows the efforts of a Nazi officer's wife to save a young Jewish woman by exchanging identities with her. There was even the film *Der letzte Akt* (The Last Act, 1955) directed by Georg Wilhelm Pabst (1885–1967), which portrayed Hitler's last days, and which enjoyed modest box-office success in the U.S. However, in general, postwar Austrian films looked at the rubble and ruin of the war years as the product of German aggression visited upon them as a conquered land. After the signing of the State Treaty in 1955 and the withdrawal of occupation forces, such cinematic arguments for Austrian innocence vis-à-vis Germany faded to the margins of the industry and were replaced by a different type of historical film that looked to a more positive Austrian past.

The most popular genre of films between 1945 and 1960 by far were those of the entertainment variety, such as Emile Reinert's *Wien tanzt* (Vienna Is Dancing, 1951), in which a contemporary Viennese antiquities dealer is transported in a daydream from his still-damaged postwar Vienna to the time of Johann Strauss. Similar escapes into the past often centered around the Habsburg dynasty, with films such as *Maria Theresia* (1951), the *Sissi* trilogy (1955–57), *Die Deutschmeister* (The German Masters, 1955), *Kronprinz Rudolfs letzte Liebe* (Crown Prince Rudolf's Last Love, 1956), and others. The general tenor of these films was that of optimism, and they often highlighted those aspects of Austrian history, culture, and landscape which were the source of particular pride. During the years of occupation, when the Austrian government was preoccupied with wresting full political sovereignty back from the Allies, it came as no surprise that the Austrian Ministry of Education would support the production of films that cast Austria in a favorable light. Indeed, the ministry even commissioned a film that would plead Austria's case for absolution from the sins of the recent past, a bizarre science fiction piece that has aliens from the future holding court over Austria's history, replete with the testimony of historical figures from Austria's past. The film, *1. April 2000* (1952) was supposed to further Austria's public image among the Allies, thus expediting the granting of a State Treaty. The film had only modest success at home, and flopped outside of Austria. Nevertheless, there were any number of films which took the same general approach toward portraying Austria in a positive light for political purposes, among them *Der Engel mit der Posaune* (The Angel with the Trumpet, 1948), based on a novel by the Austrian émigré author Ernst Lothar, who returned to Vienna as a member of the American Armed Forces. Indeed, even the Americans, facing Cold War competition with the Soviets in Central Europe, tried their hand at pro-Austrian propaganda with the film *Die Stimme Österreichs* (The Voice of Austria, 1953), produced by the U.S. Information Service.

In contrast to these less successful official efforts at shaping Austria's historical and cultural identity for mass consumption, the genre of the *Heimatfilm* proved much more effective in projecting a positive and wholesome image of Austria both within and outside its borders. The surprising success of the film *Echo der Berge* (Echo of the Mountains) in 1954 started a wave of similar films set in Austria's beautiful Alpine landscape, which also had a positive impact on the reconstruction of the nation's postwar tourism industry. Titles such as *Die Sennerin von St. Kathrein* (The Dairymaid of St Kathrein, 1955) or *Die Lindenwirtin vom Donaustrand* (The Landlady at the Limetree Inn on the Shores of the Danube, 1957) were especially popular in the Federal Republic of Germany, the major source of tourists vacationing in Austria. The success of the *Heimatfilm* in this period contributed to a boom in Austrian film production between 1955 and 1960, fed by audiences in Germany, which accounted for some 75% of all profit generated by Austrian films in that period. By contrast, ticket sales in Austria accounted for only 7% of the total take for these films. After 1960, however, the wave of the *Heimatfilm* — and movie-going in general — slowly receded before the spread of television. But not before a sub-genre of the *Heimatfilm* had its day: the vacation film. Often set at an Austrian lake resort, such films as *Vier Mädel aus der Wachau* (Four Girls from the Wachau, 1957), *Im singenden Rössel am Königsee* (In the Singing Horse Inn on the Königsee, 1963), or *00-Sex am Wolfgangsee* (00-Sex on Lake Wolfgang, 1966) extolled the virtues of a particular vacation resort as the backdrop for a romantic comedy, according to the recipe: water, hotel, sun, comedy, music, and attractive women. The master of this genre was the director Franz Antel, whose prolific production of light entertainment films also included many popular representations of "das süsse Mädel" (the sweet girl) — the timeless embodiment of the Viennese woman — in such films as *Im Prater blühen wieder die Bäume* (The Trees are in Blossom in the Prater, 1958), *Die ganze Welt ist himmelblau* (The Whole World Is Blue as the Sky, 1964) and *Ruf der Wälder* (The Call of the Forest, 1965). The actress Johanna Matz was perhaps best-known for such roles, although Romy Schneider had also represented this female type as early as 1949 in her film *Wiener Mädeln* (Viennese Girls).

As the conservative political climate in Austria changed during the era of Chancellor Bruno Kreisky in the 1970s, filmmakers took a much more sober — and critical — approach to Austria's history and society. Films such as the made-for-television series *Alpensaga* (1976–77), starring Helmut Qualtinger, caused an uproar with its unvarnished portrayal of Austrian farming society, including institutions such as the Catholic Church. The Waldheim affair of 1985 focused this critical eye more specifically on Austria's role in the Second World War, questioning the depiction of the nation as the victim of Nazi aggression so prevalent in the first postwar decades. Documentaries such as *Deckname Schlier* (Code Name Schlier, 1985) typify this trend: the diary of a young girl who witnessed the treatment of the victims of forced labor at a nearby arms plant during the war provides the basis for a reconstruction of events. The later film *Hasenjagd — Vor lauter Feigheit gibt es kein Erbarmen* (Hare Hunt — So Much Cowardice That There Is No Mercy, 1994) by Andreas Gruber (1954–) similarly reconstructs a harrowing event from the war known as the "Mühlviertler Hasenjagd" (Mühlviertel hare-hunt), when some 500 Russian prisoners of war broke out of the Mauthausen camp, only to be hunted down by nearby residents. More recently, the feature film *Gebürtig* (Born, 2002), directed by Lukas Stepanik and Robert Schindel and based on a novel of the same title by the latter, looked at the past from the perspective of a Jew returning to Vienna during the "Waldheim period" of the mid-1980s. These and many other cinematic reflections on the war years, although common among filmmakers at that time, did not enjoy a wide public audience when compared with the popular cinema of those years. While socially critical films were being produced by the dozen, their combined audience in Austria was but a fraction of that for international cinematic blockbusters such as *Jaws* (1975), *Rocky* (1976) or *Star Wars* (1978).

It is perhaps an irony of Austrian postwar culture that the highpoint of film production in Austria coincided with the advent of the television era in the late 1950s. However, the first to be adversely affected by competition with the new visual medium was not the film industry, but rather the live stage, which not only suffered a drop in attendance, but also saw the conversion of a number of theaters to movie houses in the late 1950s, for example the Neues Schauspielhaus, the Insel-Theater, and the Exl-Bühne. The cinema industry at first appeared unaffected by television's steady growth to ever more households in Austria, as the movie-going public purchased a record 122 million tickets at over 1,200 cinemas in 1958, at a time when there were only some 46,000 television sets in all of Austria. By October 1961, however, the number of television receivers had swollen to over 250,000, and concurrent with this phenomenal growth throughout the 1960s and 1970s, movie attendance steadily sank, until by 1974 the number of cinemas in Austria was down to some 640 (and by 1994 to fewer than 400). In those two decades alone, attendance at the movies declined by millions of viewers annually. If the initial decline in cinema attendance was largely brought about by the introduction of television, the spread of the automobile played its part by providing more mobility to the public in seeking out entertainment. The downward spiral was accelerated by the proliferation of the videocassette recorder, DVD, cable and satellite television systems in the 1980s and 1990s, which enabled movie fans to enjoy films at home.

Another significant factor in the evolution of the Austrian film industry after 1945 was foreign competition. Within a few years after the end of the Second World War, Austrian cinemas were awash in foreign films, primarily from the U.S. and Western Europe, and the Austrian film industry was often forced to look to cooperative efforts with filmmakers of other nations as a way of remaining viable in the cinematic marketplace. Films such as *Die letzte Brücke* (The Last Bridge, 1954), a joint Austrian-Yugoslavian production, were not unusual even in the first postwar decade, although joint efforts of this sort typically sought out German or Swiss cooperation, a trend which became especially pronounced after 1970 in the production of made-for-television movies. As the competition from — and budgets of — foreign films grew exponentially from the 1970s on, Austrian filmmakers increasingly had to rely on joint productions with companies of other nations in addition to their subsidies from the Austrian government. Films like the 1993 American remake of the classic *The Three Musketeers*, for example, were produced with Austrian financing, and some of the film's scenes were shot outside Vienna. In more recent years, such cooperation has become even more critical for filmmakers, since federal support for Austrian film production fell by over 40% after the new center-right government took power in 2000.

As the Austrian entertainment film has retreated before its more popular competitors from Germany and America in recent decades, there have been few commercial successes for Austrian filmmakers. A notable exception was the Austrian-French film *La Pianiste* (The Piano Teacher, 2001) by Michael Haneke, based on Elfriede Jelinek's novel *Die Klavierspielerin* (The Piano Teacher, 1988), which achieved considerable international acclaim as well as some commercial success abroad. Since the 1970s, the Austrian film industry has moved steadily in the direction of the more experimental art film, with a focus on a hyperrealism which strives "to observe Austrian and Western society minutely and to create [. . .] worlds where its members are put on the screen without pity,"[10] thus largely surrendering the popular film market to foreign sources. Directors such as Franz Novotny (*Die Ausgesperrten*, 1982), Paulus Manker (*Der Kopf des Mohren*, 1995) and Ulrich Seidl (*Hundstage*, 2001) are but a few representatives of this cinematic style, which remains one of the salient features of Austrian filmmaking into the present.

Music

The evolution of popular music in Austria after 1945 was no less significantly affected by developments in the mass media — above all radio and television — as well as technological innovations, such as the Wurlitzer jukebox in the 1950s and, more recently, various hand-held devices, such as MP3 players and "iPods," that permit the sharing and personal transporting of large quantities of music. From the very outset of the postwar era, Austrian radio served up a wide variety of popular styles, from the folksy *Schrammelmusik* popular on RAVAG to the jazz, big band and later rock-and-roll music of the competing Allied radio systems. Here, as in other areas of popular culture, the indigenous musical tradition, although still popular through the 1950s, soon began its retreat before an influx of pop music from America, Britain, and Germany. RAVAG's program director, Rudolf Henz, tried to stem the spread of what he termed the "Gedudel und Geheul" (drone and howl) of the music increasingly favored by many young people in Austria, but without success. By the time RAVAG's main competitor Rot-Weiss-Rot ceased broadcasting in July 1955 (along with the U.S. Armed Forces radio station Blue Danube) public taste among many young people had long since accepted this new style of music as its own. With the appearance of the German youth culture magazine *Bravo* in 1957, the popular music of Germany, America, and Western Europe was clearly in its ascendancy. Popular musical artists of the 1950s, such as Freddy Quinn, Conny Froboess or Ted Herold came mainly from the German *Schlager*-industry, although Austrian artists such as Peter Kraus had their audience as well. Austrian officialdom viewed this new music, and especially the new sounds coming from American artists Elvis Presley, Bill Haley and others, with pronounced suspicion, and when a new wave of rock-and-roll swept in from abroad in the 1960s, its potentially negative effect on young fans appeared confirmed when a series of mass arrests at rock concerts followed. In 1966, for example, the Beach Boys appeared in the Wiener Stadthalle under heavy police protection, while that same year, at a Kinks concert in Vienna, 197 young people are arrested, with another 160 arrested the following April at a Rolling Stones concert in Vienna.

The founding of station Ö3 by ORF in 1968 marked a milestone for popular music in the mass media, for here for the first time in a German-speaking country a radio station devoted a large portion of its broadcasting to the international pop scene. However, it wasn't until the 1970s that a truly Austrian version of rock music, — dubbed "Austropop" — established itself, led by the singer Wolfgang Ambros. After his performance of the controversial song "Da Hofa" — a song indicting Austrian society for its prejudice against outsiders — on television in 1971, Austria could stake its claim — albeit a modest one — to a role in the increasingly international pop music market. Although this Austrian variant of international rock never captured more than a token niche of the German-language record market (in Austria: 8% in 1992; down from 12% in 1987), it legitimized Austrian dialect lyrics as an idiom of modern pop music and liberate them from the hitherto exclusive domain of folk music. So too, Austropop maintained an Austrian presence in the German-language pop music sector, and opened the door for later Austrian artists such as Rainhard Fendrich and the group Erste Allgemeine Verunsicherung (First General Insecurity). Austropop's niche as an indigenous alternative to English-language pop music was solidified through Ö3's radio program *Austroparade*, which featured only Austrian artists, and *Musicbox*, hosted by Eva Maria Kaiser, whose support of this music earned her the title "Mother of Austropop." The show *Spotlight* by Peter Rapp, one of the few television music programs to highlight rock and pop music in the 1970s, added to Austropop's cachet when it featured songs by Austrian artists next to international hits.

Apart from Austropop's modest success in Central Europe, Austria did produce one truly international pop star in the 1980s. Falco (born Hans Hölzl) achieved something no other modern Austrian pop artist has been able to repeat, namely to have a #1 hit on the American pop charts. His 1983 song "Der Kommissar" (The Inspector) had reached #5 in an English-language version performed by the group After the Fire, but his greatest success came three years later with his tune "Rock Me, Amadeus" which claimed the #1 spot. Although he would not be able to recreate this success again before his untimely death in a car accident in 1998, Falco did for a short time place Austria in the front ranks of the international pop scene.

If Austrian popular culture after 1970 appeared inexorably headed down a path toward internationalization and away from the more indigenous identity of earlier years, the sudden rise and success of the televised music show *Musikantenstadl* (Musicians' Barn) proved such an analysis to be an illusion. The fading popularity of the Austrian *Heimatfilm* after the early 1960s appeared to have signaled the death-knell of traditional folk culture as a visible part of popular culture in Austria. Yet when the folk-music broadcast *Musikantenstadl* first aired in 1981, no one could have predicted that it would become the longest running music program in Austrian television history, and one that is still in production today. The success of this show and its director, Karl Moik, suggests not only a reassertion of Austrian cultural identity in the face of the international and predominantly English-language amalgam that pop music had become, but perhaps also a challenge to Austropop's use of dialect as a vehicle for socially critical messages. Whatever its political subtext, traditional music and its less problematic view of society and life had survived almost unnoticed by the mass media as a viable, albeit modest part of Austrian popular culture through the 1970s.

Considering the inroads made by non-indigenous popular culture within Austria since the 1970s, particularly in the area of the visual media (film and television) and music — and here Austria is certainly not alone — a continuing trend toward internationalizing mass culture might appear inevitable, especially with the continued efforts toward European political and economic unification. With its relatively small domestic market, Austria has always relied on a lively cultural and economic exchange with other German-speaking lands. Little has changed in this respect since 1945. However, what has changed is the degree to which popular culture from outside Central Europe — primarily from the English-speaking world — has penetrated Austrian culture and consciousness during that time.

Nevertheless, the search for ever-larger markets, which drives the internationalization of popular culture, is limited by the very same leveling effect that makes it marketable around the world. The removal of national or local idiosyncrasies from the international product that could alienate potential consumers abroad leaves a distinct market niche for cultural products with which local populations can identify more closely. This might explain the *Musikantenstadl* phenomenon, or the surprising resilience of Austropop. Moreover, it certainly holds true in the area of sports, which by virtue of popular competitions organized around national teams (Olympics, Soccer World Cup), consistently reinforces national identification with this activity and its personalities.

Popular culture is by its very definition the manifestation of those aspects of life and culture in the broadest sense with which the masses identify, either within a particular nation, or across political borders in some larger entity, such as "Europe" or "Western society." And the vehicles by which popular culture is typically represented to target populations are of necessity the mass media. However, at different points in Austrian history, different media have been more or less dominant as the primary means of disseminating popular culture: radio and film in the 1950s and early 1960s, and television from the mid-1960s to the present. Music occupies a unique position in Austrian popular culture since 1945, as it has always been a major part of the nation's identity through more traditional forms from the nineteenth and early twentieth centuries, and because it can be carried by all of the mass media discussed above, thus always having a presence in the dominant media of a given period. Yet, the maintenance of the traditional forms after 1945 in film and television, and the addition of newer forms of indigenous popular music disseminated through radio and television, cast legitimate doubt on any prognosis of a future "de-Austrianized" popular culture in Austria.

Notes

[1] For full documentation concerning the cultural processes discussed below, see Joseph McVeigh, *Kontinuität und Vergangenheitsbewältigung in der österreichischen Literatur nach 1945* (Vienna: Braumüller, 1988).

[2] Milo Dor, "Der papierene Vorhang," *Die Weltpresse*, May 22, 1951.

[3] See Joseph McVeigh, "'Nicht auf Schlachtfeldern allein wird der Sieg der Demokratie entschieden.' Culture Wars in Postwar Austrian Radio," in John A. McCarthy, Walter Grünzweig, and Thomas Koebner, eds., *The Many Faces of Germany. Transformations in the Study of German Culture and History* (New York, Oxford: Berghahn, 2004).

[4] Rudolf Henz, "Dreißig Jahre Rundfunk in Österreich," unpublished manuscript, *Literaturhaus Wien*, Henz-Nachlaß 30/XII, 5.

[5] Rudolf Henz, "Dreißig Jahre Rundfunk in Österreich," 5.

[6] Rudolf Henz, "Die Grundlagen eines Radioprogramms," unpublished manuscript, *Literaturhaus Wien*, Henz-Nachlaß, 30/XII, 3.

[7] Rudolf Henz, "Richtlinien für die Programmgestaltung im Österreichischen Rundfunk" (July 5, 1956), unpublished manuscript, *Literaturhaus Wien*, Henz-Nachlaß, 30/XI.

[8] For June 21, 2005, no fewer than six American series were scheduled between the two main ORF channels: *Dawson's Creek, Charmed, Malcolm in the Middle, Smallville, The Simpsons,* and *The Fresh Prince of Bel-Air.*

[9] "Überläufer-films" here has the double meaning of: "films that switched sides/switched allegiances" (i.e. they were begon during the Nazi period, but completed or premiered in the postwar years) or "films tht straddle two periods (i.e. the Third Reich and the postwar era) in their production."

[10] Herbert Krill, "A High between Two Lows? The 2002 Diagonale Festival," in *Kinoeye: New Perspectives on European Film*, Vol. 2, Issue 10 (27 May 2002): 4 (http://www.kinoeye.org/02/10/krill10.php).

12: Shifting Boundaries: Responses to Multiculturalism at the Turn of the Twenty-First Century

Allyson Fiddler

THE PHYSICAL AND TERRITORIAL BOUNDARIES of Austria may not have changed since the end of the Second World War and the founding of the Second Republic, but Austria's geopolitical significance, its demographic makeup, and its citizens' understanding of Austrian nationhood have all changed significantly over the last few decades.[1] Austria's internal social and political fabric is altering too, with a move away from the old consensus-based social partnership model towards a pattern of non-interventionist free-market capitalism, modern technologies, international cooperation, and global financial interventions. Rudolf Burger posited that the entry of Austria into the European Union in 1995 brought to near completion Austria's status as a modern European nation. Furthermore, it canceled out both the "Ausschlußtrauma" and the "Anschlußtrauma" that characterized its relationship with Germany (exclusion from the German Reich formed in 1871, and annexation by Hitler's Germany in 1938). According to Burger, only Austria's obligation to remain militarily neutral stands in its way of obtaining full sovereignty as a nation.[2]

The shock occasioned by the meteoric rise in popularity and election success of the extreme right-wing party the Freiheitliche Partei Österreichs (Liberal Party of Austria, FPÖ) in 1999 produced a huge wave of political self-reflection in Austria, both among the general population and in the books, interviews, essays, and works of literature of many of Austria's most high-profile writers and intellectuals.[3] Most of these have been active in countering the nationalism propounded by some FPÖ politicians and like-minded Austrians. This nationalism is at best merely anti-immigrationist and at worst inherently racist, and it is a tendency that has been further fueled by the fear of increased migration to Austria from the EU's most recently added members.[4] The European Union was so concerned about the FPÖ becoming a partner in the new ruling coalition of February 2000 that it placed diplomatic sanctions on Austria and commissioned a report on its government. Although a clean bill of health was finally returned, this was only based on an inspection of the theoretical position — the protection of minorities *in law* — and not on a detailed investigation of the realities of Austria's policies regarding ethnic minorities (*Minderheitenpolitik*).[5]

At the beginning of the twentieth century, the dissolution of the Habsburg Monarchy left Austria with a number of "indigenous" ethnic minorities, or "Völkergruppen" (Croatians, Slovenes, Slovaks, Czechs, Hungarians, Roma, and Sinti), groups that continue to play a vital role in the culture of contemporary Austria. Some, if by no means all, of the art and literature of these minorities reflects on the difficulties and challenges of living between two cultures or of making minority voices heard in a majority German-language culture and society. There is not space in the present chapter to discuss Austria's regional literatures or to consider works written in the Slovene or Croat languages (which are accepted as official in certain administrative and judicial districts of Carinthia, Styria, and Burgenland). Nor is there space here to consider the area of Jewish Austrian identities and literatures.[6]

The following discussion considers instead a number of works of literature and film from the late 1990s and early 2000s that thematize issues of social and racial integration and thus both grapple with and perform stories of multicultural or multi-ethnic reality, shifting psychological boundaries and perceptions of contemporary Austrian identity. The works chosen for detailed discussion here are grouped as follows. First, there are literary works that adopt black protagonists as a focus for stories about racial integration and reflections on contemporary Austrian (and German) society, and these include three by "mainstream" Austrian writers Lilian Faschinger (1950–), Peter Henisch (1943–), and Peter Turrini (1944–), as well as a novel by Stanislav Struhar, a migrant from the Czech Republic (1964–). Second, two films by Austrian directors are discussed: a feature film by Florian Flicker (1965–) that presents a journey through Austria as seen by an illegal immigrant, and a documentary film that responds to the challenge of depicting and demythologizing aspects of everyday racism in contemporary Austria (the collaborative work of Barbara Albert, 1970–, Michael Glawogger, 1969–, Ulrich Seidl, 1952–, and Michael Sturminger, 1963–). Finally, this chapter looks at "Migrant Voices and Interactions," considering works by Denis Mikan (1974–) and Alma Hadzibeganovic (1972–), both émigré writers from Bosnia-Herzogovina, and by Kundeyt Şurdum (1937–) from Turkey. These writers offer reflections on the psychological and material difficulties of belonging to their new *Heimat*. To conclude, a detective-style novel by mainstream Austrian writer Barbara Frischmuth (born 1941) will be discussed, a novel that develops an intriguing plot of intercultural interaction and confusion. Throughout this chapter, it will emerge that contemporary writers are increasingly questioning a homogeneous Austrian identity as they voice a commitment to a more plural understanding of twenty-first century Austrian society.

Writing Black Experiences

Lilian Faschinger's *Wiener Passion* (1999; *Vienna Passion*, 2000) is a fin-de-siècle novel of great richness and humor.[7] It narrates a present-day story about the African-American actress Magnolia Brown and her developing love both for her singing teacher and for Vienna, the city of her ancestors. Into this story, the author inserts a further, more capacious, late-nineteenth-century plot about the adventures of Rosa Havelka, a young woman of Czech (Bohemian) origin, who, after the death of her mother and a brief period in a convent school, runs away to Vienna to make her own way as a maid in the Habsburg capital. Magnolia unearths a blue book at her aunt's house, in which Rosa has documented the story of how she has come to be awaiting execution for the murder of her husband, a crime for which she feels no remorse. Each of the stages in Rosa's journey towards her execution in April 1900 tells of initial good fortune as Rosa is offered a job, or finds a good man or companion, but is inevitably followed by degradation or suffering. The catalogue of her confessions is most varied — including sexual abuse by her employer, an abortion, contracting syphilis, being coerced into self-flagellation, a suicide attempt, periods in a mental asylum and in jail; being mistress to both a budding writer (who likes to use her skin to write on) and then to Crown Prince Rudolf himself. The increasingly unlikely coincidences and the speed with which Rosa stumbles from situation to situation contribute to the humor of Faschinger's novel, as do her encounters with figures such as the Crown Prince, but also with a doctor whose theories on the human soul Sigmund Freud is plagiarizing for his work on the interpretation of dreams.

If Rosa initially views Vienna as a city of opportunity, the capital in which people from all corners of the Habsburg Empire can come together to make their way, her experiences bring her to see it increasingly negatively. However, unlike her Slovene friend Ljuba, she refuses to rebel against any of the injustices she meets. Ljuba is involved in writing a "Dienstbotenfanal" (Maidservants' Clarion) to try to raise the awareness of oppression among her class. Meanwhile Milan, who is also from the Bohemian Forest, is active in trying to establish links with other oppressed Czechs and taking the anti-German message of the Young Czechs to the capital city of what was for them the hated dual monarchy of Austria-Hungary.[8] The capital is resistant even to those from other regions of Austria. Consequently the Tyrolean dairyman who travels to Vienna to seek work is also subjected to "dem in sämtlichen Kronländern bekannten Wiener Fremdenhaß" (379; "the Viennese xenophobia notorious in all the crown territories," 294) and ends up sleeping rough with Rosa and others under the canal bridges.

Faschinger's novel reveals the Habsburg model of multinational understanding as less than perfect. The comical thought processes of one elder Austrian resident clearly show the continuation into the present day of distrustful and racist attitudes both towards those who hail from former Habsburg member states, and towards those who look physically different, such as black people. A number of sexually motivated crimes have been committed in Vienna, and the attacker is believed to be a right-wing extremist. The reaction of Magnolia's aunt is emblematic of much of the covert racism Magnolia encounters in contemporary Vienna. For Magnolia's aunt, the huge numbers of "foreigners" arriving to settle in Vienna present a constant threat:

> man müsse ständig damit rechnen, [. . .] von einem Montenegriner, einem Slowaken, einem Rumänen oder gar einem Schwarzen niedergeschlagen und seiner Ersparnisse beraubt zu werden, auch dem geldgierigen Mann der bosnischen Hausmeisterin sei nicht zu trauen. (389)

> [you always had to reckon with being mugged by a Montenegrin, a Slovakian, a Romanian or even a black man and robbed of your savings, and there was no trusting the Bosnian caretaker's grasping husband either. (302)]

Magnolia is occasionally subjected to racist remarks and is initially full of disdain for her unworldly, hypochondriac singing teacher Josef Horvath. Josef's own first-person story tells how he finally breaks away from his dead mother's influence and from the influence of other ersatz-mothers around him, such as the women in the pharmacy and tobacco shop ("Apothekerin," "Trafikantin"). He gradually discards his medicine, sickly ways, lotions and potions, and he becomes physically fit and much more positive in outlook. Magnolia in turn comes to love Josef and Vienna, despite her previous disaffection with both. She begins to feel more rooted in the city, having discovered the story of the person who turns out to have been her great-grandmother, Rosa Havelka. Faschinger constructs parallels and analogies between the late-nineteenth-century narrative and its late-twentieth-century counterpart such that the strands move closer and closer together, but they have markedly different outcomes. If Rosa's development is a negative one, then Magnolia's is positive, making Faschinger's novel both Bildungsroman and anti-Bildungsroman. It is also a commentary on ethnicity and racial tolerance. Ultimately, Magnolia's accommodation with Vienna, her forthcoming mixed-race marriage to Joseph, and the child they are looking forward to together might be read as symbols of a more optimistic, multicultural Austrian future.

Schwarzer Peter (Black Peter, 2000) by Peter Henisch has a number of points in common with Faschinger's novel.[9] It too is a kind of "Viennese Passion," charting the stages in the mixed-race protagonist's Viennese downfall. Even though happiness and multicultural harmony are ultimately found not in Vienna but in New Orleans, the detailed evocation of Austria's postwar history and the strength of the protagonist's identification with Vienna show that Henisch's novel is also "passionate" about Austria. Hans Christian Kosler points out that although Henisch rails against the picture-postcard image of Vienna (a characteristic also of Faschinger's novel), he nevertheless writes about the city with great affection.[10] But the metaphor describing the protagonist's development in Henisch's *Entwick-lungsroman* is not a biblical one; it derives rather from the children's card game alluded to in the title, in which players try to avoid being left with "Black Peter" (a card with a chimney-sweep on it, and the only one that does not form part of a pair). Like the events of *Wiener Passion*, those in Henisch's novel are told by a first-person narrator. However, the perspective here is unitary by contrast with Faschinger's three narrators. The narrated time ranges over roughly half a century, the life span to date of Peter Jarosch (born 1946), who addresses his unknown listeners as he reminisces from the piano stool of the bar in New Orleans where he works as a jazz musician. Whereas Faschinger's US-born protagonist decides to stay in Vienna, the city of her ancestors, Henisch's Viennese-born protagonist finally opts for the USA.

Much of the novel deals with the conflict between Peter's sense of himself as Austrian and the way he is treated: as an outsider who cannot possibly belong to Austrian society due to his color. The Jewish bookshop keeper who employs Peter in the 1960s, one of a number of father figures to him in the novel, points out that skin color is not always a necessary prerequisite for racism. Herr Jericha's reminiscences provide a device for glossing another period of Austrian history, that of the Nazi era, and his analysis warns against the dangers of racism in the present day. He reflects that an ignorant attitude of "wir sind wir" (we are who we are) can turn into dangerous aggression if given the chance to develop (377).[11]

In fact, despite his different color, Peter only rarely encounters overt, malicious racism, but these form part of a historical pattern. For example, in an episode in the 1970s, a waiter comments that twenty-five years ago, they would have gassed people like him. Similarly, Peter's previously liberal wife Natasha, a trained psychologist, adopts the racist arguments of his childhood friend Robert and decides to divorce Peter when she learns of his previous infidelities.[12] Natasha's rationale sounds as though it comes straight out of the "Kleine Rassenkunde" (Short Guide to Race) Peter found wedged inside her notebook. She had come to understand that people of her kind do better to keep well away from those of his "species" (535). From a prison cell some years later, Peter recounts the events surrounding the final collapse of his marriage. His nostalgia and curiosity for Vienna having proved overwhelming, he has decided to visit Austria, but loses his passport and papers and is imprisoned on suspicion of being an illegal immigrant. Thus Henisch — like Faschinger — narrates parallel dénouements: that of the ending of the Viennese narrative concerning Peter's life in Vienna, and that of the events leading up to the present-day narratorial standpoint. After official identification by his much younger stepsister, Peter returns to New Orleans, a city that Joe, a university historian friend, extols as being not simply a city, but rather an idea (245). Joe describes the process of racial integration and mixing there as one of creolization, with both black and white, old and new mutually influencing each other. Peter seems to agree with the slightly more cynical friend, Mister Griffiths, that New Orleans is perhaps not the Promised Land (283), but still represents a progressively multicultural society. When Joe is asked whether Vienna is not also multicultural, he replies: "Ich weiß nicht [. . .] so war es vielleicht einmal" (I don't know, it may have been like that once, 245), a faint echo of Herr Jericha's opinions that Habsburg Austria represented at least a promising model for an ethnically harmonious multicultural state (376).

Henisch's novel addresses an Austrian readership, but he uses a number of devices to generate a distanced perspective on his homeland. For example, in the course of his performance as jazz singer and storyteller, the narrator explains the Austrian roots of words he uses to his mostly American audience, such as "Schmäh" (trickery, kidding), "Hetz" (fun) or "Beuschel" (lungs, offal dish). In using a protagonist who was fathered by a black American GI but who grows up in Vienna and even speaks Viennese dialect, Henisch develops the perspective of somebody who has no choice but to be seen as "other," and who can occupy the curious position of being both an insider and an outsider. Eva Schobel explains Henisch's rationale as emanating from the desire to retell the story of the Second Republic from a totally different perspective.[13] She refutes the accusations of political correctness that have been leveled at Henisch by critics such as Kosler, who sees his black protagonist as an aptly timed, artificial construct with which to express solidarity with "Andersseiende" (people who are different) at a time of the "(leer)laufende Erregung um Haider" (current [ineffectual] excitement about [Jörg] Haider).[14] Schobel further clarifies the origins of Henisch's novel as having nothing to do with the death in 1999 of Marcus Omofuma, the Nigerian refugee who died of asphyxiation in police custody after being bound and gagged. Nevertheless, critics are right to see with skepticism Henisch's claim that his protagonist Peter Jarosch is "ein Schwarzer wie du und ich" (a Black like you or I). " 'Anderssein' may have its generic features," Maria-Regina Kecht points out, but Henisch's "sweeping statement universalizing the experience of a discriminated ethnic group does not suggest much understanding of racially constructed identity."[15]

Underpinning *Schwarzer Peter* is the main character's attempt to find or to forge his own identity, rather than merely being defined by his position in other people's maps of ethnic or national identity. His sexual identity is also subject to experimentation, and a number of homosexual overtures are initiated by him as an adolescent and young adult. The most

conscious quest undertaken by Peter, however, is his search for his bio-
logical father, and this is the reason he initially travels to New Orleans. The
search ultimately proves fruitless, but it no longer seems relevant, as Peter
seems to have found peace with himself after completing his journey from
the Danube to the banks of the Mississippi.

Czech émigré Stanislav Struhar also chooses the device of a black first-
person narrator (Ben Marchera) in his novel *Das Manuskript* (2002) in
order to make observations on the subject of belonging and not belonging
to Austria and Austrian culture.[16] Like Henisch, Struhar has been criticized
for this inauthenticity, with one reviewer complaining that he does not
focus on the difficulties he must surely have encountered himself as a
refugee.[17] With its sometimes rather contrived style, *Das Manuskript*
received little critical attention on publication. The novel is nevertheless
important in bringing to the fore an immigrant's perspective on the literary business, with all its constraints and expectations. Ben's diary entries
are filled with the minutiae of daily life and with the frustration he experiences at not being able to find a publisher for a novel dealing with the subject of homosexuality. Like Struhar, who wrote his novel in Czech, the
fictional author-protagonist also writes his originals in another language
(in Ben's case, French), and struggles to persuade an Austrian publisher
that his work needs to be translated into German before it is published
(40).

Ben maintains a rather naive, utopian faith in ethnic harmony, expressing his view that the whole of humanity is simply one people (28) despite
his father's traumatic murder by racist youths and despite himself being the
victim of racist attacks. Although Ben fights back, he is loath to admit this
to his girlfriend Ulrike, and explains his injuries away as the result of a
drunken accident. Ben remains philosophical about intercultural violence,
preferring to believe that no country is without its problems and that
home is where the heart is (115). His friend Georg feels that he will not
get far with such optimism in Vienna — that is, in a fundamentally intolerant society where not even the locals are disposed to be tolerant towards
each other (28).

The novel is framed by a short introductory section and a longer concluding part. The first explains how Ben's father had been kicked to death
by four men outside the local tobacconist's in 1983 when Ben was a young
teenager. The concluding part to *Das Manuskript* is dated "Abidjan, im
Jänner 1999" (Abidjan, in January 1999) and tells of the events after Ben's
sudden death of a heart attack and after the birth of his and Ulrike's son,
Ben junior. It is narrated in the first person by Ulrike, who has never
shared Ben's optimistic view on racial tension: she has decided to move to
Abidjan (Côte d'Ivoire) in order to allow their son to experience "eine
wirkliche Heimat" (a real home, 158). If this turn of events represents a
pessimistic slant on the possibility of multicultural harmony, the news that

Ben's work has found a publisher in Austria provides a more hopeful perspective. It suggests that Ben has at last been accepted as an Austrian author (172) and thus holds out the promise of a more ethnically integrated Austria for the future.

Peter Turrini's play *Ich liebe dieses Land* (I Love This Country, 2001) is not set in Austria, but the central concerns are similar to those in the novels by Henisch, Faschinger, and Struhar. The play foregrounds issues such as the racist prejudices and tensions of a modern, multi-racial, but prescriptively monolingual society, filtered here through the experiences of Beni Jaja, a black African illegal immigrant.[18] The Berlin setting of Turrini's play may have been chosen simply because the piece was commissioned by Claus Peymann at the Berliner Ensemble,[19] or perhaps in order to utilize the ironic background noise of Berlin's famous gay Love Parade. At the end of act 1, the chief of police and his wife stumble into the illegal immigrant's prison cell in their fancy dress and makeup from the Love Parade in order to marvel at the phenomenon everyone is talking about — the black man who only says one phrase in answer to anything he is asked: "ich liebe dieses Land." The wife of the chief of police commits an act of physical violation that mirrors a similar act committed earlier on by a doctor: while the latter inspected Beni's rectum for drugs, the woman inserts her finger for sexual thrills. Beni lashes out at her in agony and she falls to the ground. The chief of police wrongly believes his wife to be dead and gives the prisoner an electronic passcard to escape. He is frightened but also grateful to Beni for committing a murder he confesses to have been contemplating for years.

On his escape, Beni makes for the flat of the prison's Polish-German cleaning lady, Janina, who had been allowed to leave Poland in 1981 after presenting to the authorities an invitation by a German doctor to come and clean for him, an invitation that proved fictitious. Janina had befriended Beni in prison, and, it now appears, has designs to marry him. At the close of act 2, the police axe down Janina's door at the very point when, despite a number of rejected physical advances on her part, Janina is lying on the bed with Beni and a moment of tenderness has been reached. In a play full of deliberately pointed ironies, the moment before the police hack down the door and re-arrest Beni (this time for the attempted murder of the wife of the chief of police) presents a parodic tableau of a true "German" family. There is Janina, the Polish-German citizen, Beni, the Black-African would-be German citizen, and finally, between them, a doll with a large, blonde wig. Beni's face has been smeared white with moisturizing cream, in what must be seen as an act of love by Janina, whose arms and hands have until this point in the play been covered by huge gloves to hide her dry, disfigured skin (see stage directions to both acts). It is also, of course, a symbolic sign of his becoming white and German, as Janina's much-prized German Nivea cream — and not the poor Polish imitation she had been used to — is used for the purpose. "Jetzt sind wir echte deutsche Familie," Janina triumphs, "Niemand mehr kann sagen, weg, wird's bald, Tempo, Beeilung" (Now we are real German family. Nobody now say chop chop, hurry up, look lively, 49), but even the symbolic child between them is but a simulacrum of an Aryan, right down to her false blond hair. In her zeal to assimilate, Janina's dreams for the future are marked by stereotypically western consumerism. At their most Germanic, these aspirations are symbolized by Janina's grotesquely enthusiastic "Kaffee und Kuchen" excesses as she lists the types of cake she has bought for Beni: "Schwarzwälder Kirsch, Berliner, Buttercremetorte, Negerküsse, Bienenstich. [. . .] alles für Beni" (Black Forest gateau, doughnuts, butter cream cake, chocolate marshmallows, almond-covered cake. [. . .] all for Beni, 39). Moreover, she demonstrates her assimilation by her mastery of the brand names of cleaning substances: "Meister Proper" are the first words she tries in all ernest to teach Beni, in Turrini's comedic exaggeration of the stereotypical German preoccupation with hygiene ("Der Arzt: Es lebe die Hygiene"; The Doctor: Long live hygiene, 15).

In the second and third acts of the play we learn something more of Beni's story, as he recounts this in English to Janina in her flat, and then to his prison cellmate, a talkative dwarf with a Hungarian accent. The protagonist's missing father functions as a sign or precursor of his displaced nationality. After the oil company in his native Nigeria polluted the rivers and thus took away the fishing community's livelihood, Beni's father blew up the pipeline in his rage and went on the run.[20] Beni was imprisoned in Nigeria, and constantly asked about his father's whereabouts. After his six years behind bars, Beni worked in a harbor, where a German sailor advised him to go to Germany. The sailor countered Beni's concerns about not knowing the German language with the advice that "if anyone wants something from you, then simply say 'I love this country. Ich liebe dieses Land' and they will also love you" (57).

It is the journalist character, in his brief visit to Beni's cell in Act 1, who articulates one of the play's main criticisms of contemporary society, expressed here as a particular feature of modern German living: he bemoans the emotional sterility of the Germans. Their lack of humanity, the journalist explains, is concealed behind their linguistic eloquence and perfection. Thus, if the black man is held prisoner by his lack of language, the Germans are hemmed in by an excess of language; they are "perfekt vernagelt, man sieht sie nicht mehr, sie sind hinter ihren Sätzen verschwunden" (totally hemmed in, you can't see them any more. They've disappeared behind their sentences, 32). In another of the play's ironic flourishes, the journalist himself performs the cold, intellectual verbosity he apparently condemns. Rather than rushing to attend to the injured prisoner, whose face has been kicked in by the racist prison guard, the journalist discourses at length and remarks: "Das Stöhnen dieses Schwarzen ist berührender als jeder Satz, den er sagen könnte" (This black man's moans are more moving than any sentence he could say, 31).

The few brief mentions of actual politicians in Turrini's play reveal a barbed critique of the German Left and in particular the then-contemporary government under Chancellor Gerhard Schröder. The journalist criticizes the chancellor for betraying the working class, and the racist prison guard praises Schröder, Foreign Minister Joschka Fischer, and Home Secretary Otto Schily, who have "den ganzen linken Scheiß hinter sich" (that whole lefty shit behind them, 29). But Turrini's play is not primarily about a disillusionment with the Left. Insofar as it is an exploration of contemporary issues of immigration and multiculturalism, *Ich liebe dieses Land* should be seen rather as a response to the kind of populist racism which has been touted in Austria in particular by the Freiheitliche Partei Österreichs but which has more generally been a feature of anti-immigrationist rhetoric in many European countries, including France and Great Britain. *Ich liebe dieses Land* is published together with "Materialien" that include an interview foregrounding Turrini's reactions to the electoral success of the FPÖ and a letter to the leader of the party at that time, Jörg Haider. As in Henisch's *Schwarzer Peter*, the imprisonment of Turrini's black protagonist echoes the case of the Nigerian immigrant Marcus Omofuma (see above). Given the profile and media coverage of Omofuma's death and the trial of the three policemen charged with his killing in 2002, Austrian readers and audiences cannot fail to have this particular case in mind when Turrini's Nigerian protagonist has his mouth taped over at the end of act 2. In the next work to be discussed here, the collaborative documentary film *Zur Lage* (2002), the Austrian couple who speak to the camera in the concluding section also remember the Omofuma case, but think that taping the foreigner's mouth shut is probably the right thing to have done in the circumstances, given that the detainee had bitten someone previously.

Filmic Responses to the New Austria

Zur Lage is the first full-length film to use Austria's dramatic change of government as its point of departure. The film is a documentary collaboration between four different Austrian filmmakers — Barbara Albert, Michael Glawogger, Ulrich Seidl, and Michael Sturminger — and bears the subtitle "Österreich in sechs Kapiteln" (Austria in Six Chapters). Each of the four directors has a different concept and style, but the overall principle has clearly been to keep interview questions to a minimum and simply allow people to talk. The first of the "chapters" consists of interviews with the drivers who picked up the hitch-hiking Glawogger as he made his way around Austria. They talk about their private lives and problems, and they talk, too, about Austrian history and politics. One long-haired young man, at turns plagued by and wallowing in his apparent resemblance to a pop star, thinks that Hitler's policies were actually quite right, if only he could have got the foreigners out peacefully. Another interviewee is indiscriminate in his condemnation of contemporary politicians: Wolfgang Schüssel (ÖVP politician and chancellor since the ÖVP-FPÖ government of 2000) is a "bow-tie wearing idiot" and Haider (who resigned as leader of the FPÖ in February 2000, continues to be the governor of Carinthia, but has since formed his own breakaway liberal party, Bündnis Zukunft Österreichs), is a "clown." The same driver offers an analogy between the *Vielvölkerstaat* of Austria-Hungary, a state uniting a multitude of peoples, and the contemporary move towards a "Europe of the Regions." In his explanation of the dissolution of the Habsburg Empire, the driver says that everybody had wanted to get out of the "Vielvölkerkerker" (prison for a multitude of peoples) but that it had in fact not been a prison. Indeed, he points out that the European Union, which everyone is now striving to be part of, is not dissimilar given its single currency, its members which are individual nations, and its policy of freedom of movement. Austria's credentials as the center of a previously successful supra-state entity are indeed mobilized by many pro-European Austrians who argue that Austria can have a special role to play in the reconfigured European Union.

The style of *Zur Lage* is deliberately disjointed, with editing for continuity kept to a minimum, but the material engages the viewer through the sheer honesty of the people in it and their almost total lack of compunction that what they are saying is in any way problematic. The most shocking parts are undoubtedly the man and woman talking to camera in the prologue and epilogue of the film (these are some of Seidl's contributions). In one of the epilogue takes, the woman is on the brink of describing her attitudes as Nazi. In a bizarre, near-comic reversal, she notes that there are people who are more Nazi or who think about these issues more emphatically than do she and her partner, but she laments that these people do not dare open their mouths. In another of Seidl's sections, a notorious sender of letters to the editor is interviewed at his home. The film captures the man's furious jogging around the inner perimeter of his garden, and displays his rigid sense of order and tidiness. He brushes vigorously at the leaves on the pavement outside his house, and shows the camera his neatly labeled piles of shirts, a system that his mother devised for him. Where a writer such as Elfriede Jelinek has lampooned a kind of fascistic hygiene and worldview in her novels and dramas, the documentary material of *Zur Lage* makes xenophobic and racist attitudes all the more disturbing because they are presented without critical comment or satirical exaggeration. The sender of readers' letters complains of the "Muslimization" of Austria, and remarks that all these people need to do is to keep having children and soon Austrians will be in the minority and have no say in their own country.[21]

A number of clever cuts bring out thought-provoking juxtapositions and ironies. Barbara Albert cross-cuts between a smug middle-class woman, possibly a housewife, complaining from her armchair that the foreigners should be forced to work, and shots of a Turkish-Austrian woman working at a factory conveyor belt, assembling computers. Moreover, as the latter points out, she is a native of Vienna, having been born there, whereas many have flocked to Vienna from the other Austrian *Länder*. These are the real "Einwanderer" (immigrants). Although Albert's original question is not heard, she has clearly asked her interviewees what they would wish for. The middle-class woman is unhappy in her marriage, but explains that she would not leave her husband after seven years of marriage and all the work they have put into their house. Her wish — to get the house better insulated and thus reduce their bills — is in stark contrast to that of a physically handicapped woman interviewee whose disability does not feature on her list of three wishes. She answers immediately: "sofort eine neue Regierung." Her second wish would be to live with her boyfriend, and the third would be a better future together. A memorable and suggestive piece of editing comes in one of Sturminger's house visits, where the TV presenter Dieter Chmelar first hears from the younger generation (the grandson of the family being interviewed) that Haider's ideas are quite good. The film cuts to the kitchen table, where the three generations of the family sit together and the grandson — as well as the film viewer — hears the grandmother's tale of her persecution at the hands of the Nazis for having a Polish lover.

The strategy for *Zur Lage* was to allow ordinary people to expose their own unwitting xenophobia or at best dubious attitudes towards the immigrant community. By contrast, the German artist Christoph Schlingensief's installation work "Bitte liebt Österreich" for the 2000 Viennese Festwochen confronted the Austrian public with the very real issue of the expulsion of foreign workers and asylum seekers. Schlingensief's ludic, artistic imitation of the *Big Brother* reality television game show was situated right next to the Vienna opera house, one of the primary symbols of high Austrian culture and Viennese tourism, and passers-by were invited to vote on which foreigner should be thrown out of the container next.[22] The installation was seen by its many critics as a tasteless and unnecessary provocation, but it was one of the most concentrated and talked-about artistic critiques of the new FPÖ-ÖVP regime, together with Elfriede Jelinek's refusal, in protest, to allow her plays to be staged on Austrian public stages.[23]

Like Schlingensief, Florian Flicker also explores the interface between recognizable icons of Austria identity (in this case touristic landscape images) and issues of illegal immigration. The protagonist of *Suzie Washington* (1998) is an illegal immigrant (as in Turrini's play above); only Nana Iaschwili (her real name) is not in prison, but on the run after Vienna airport customs discover her forged visa. The viewer learns little of the central character's previous identity, merely that she had been a teacher of French and Russian in her home country of Georgia and that she is en route to Los Angeles to see an uncle. She refuses to accept the reassurance of immigration control that she will come to no harm at home if she returns there, and takes an opportunity to escape from the airport.

Suzie journeys through some of the archetypal tourist scenery of Austria, by coach on scenic roads,[24] by boat over a lake, and on a ski-lift up a mountainside, where she stays for a while in the mountain refuge cum Gasthaus on Austria's border with Germany as the police come ever closer to finding her. In the course of her journey, Suzie's inner voice reads the occasional postcards she may or may not truly be sending to her uncle. But whether the uncle is real or not, Suzie strives towards a far-away, utopian space, as symbolized here by the USA. Postcards normally function to narrate tourist experiences and not generally the experiences of a hounded illegal immigrant, and Flicker and Sturminger — who co-wrote the screenplay — achieve a brilliant and understated deconstruction of Austrian identity by overlaying the traditional tourist image of the country with a more political, contemporary reading of it as being like any other European Union country in its skepticism towards strangers and indeed hostility towards outsiders who do not fit into the tourist category.[25] Austria is a transit land for goods being transported along its motorways and over its mountain passes; it doubtless also functions as a transit state for illegal immigrants moving on to other countries. By the end of the film, the gentle-mannered protagonist has committed a catalogue of crimes, and the film presents an ironic analogy between her situation and that of the armed bank robber who also visits the mountain hut because the police are after him. Suzie — or Jacqueline, as she becomes on finally reaching German soil with her stolen French passport — is criminalized though not actually dangerous like her fellow fugitive. The film ends with a sense of both melancholy and hope as the plane ascends into the skies towards America and possibly towards realization of the protagonist's dreams of a new life.

Migrant Voices and Interactions

As Peter Stuiber has noted, works by authors who have migrated to Austria in the last two decades have to date received very little acknowledgment.[26] Alma Hadzibeganovic and Denis Mikan are both from Bosnia-Herzegovina and are just two examples of a younger generation of migrant writers whose works are written in German and have been published by the Viennese publisher Edition Exil. Both have been awarded prizes instigated by the publisher under the title of "Schreiben zwischen den Kulturen" (Writing between Cultures). The texts discussed here provide insights into intercultural realities and thematize issues surrounding integration and belonging.

Hadzibeganovic's collection *Ilda Zuferka rettet die Kunst* (Ilda Zuferka Saves Art, 2000) contains poetry, two short stories, a short play, the title story or "Reportage," and a performance text.[27] The fictional editor of the title story "Ilda Zuferka rettet die Kunst" presents his theoretical observations on hybridity and modern culture. The text montage of this story consists of a report that the editor has apparently assembled from film material, from Microsoft Word documents, and from the handwritten notes of an art historian, Ilda Zuferka, who returned to Bosnia to try to construct a shelter over a medieval burial site and thereby save it from war damage. This hybrid form prompts the editor to muse that "die hybride Sprache ist die Sprache von verknoteten, gespaltenen Subjekten in hybriden, heterotopischen Kulturen, gekennzeichnet durch Migration" (hybrid language is the language of split subjects, knotted together in hybrid, heterotopic cultures, characterized by migration, 32). The comment on cultural displacement might arguably refer not just to the countries from which migrants are leaving but also to those with growing migrant communities, and the argument that novels no longer function as a means of cementing national unity (32) must also be seen as a positive cultural development.

The war is clearly a theme for Hadzibeganovic, and it serves as an occasional reference point for the stories of her Bosnian women protagonists. In "Etwas läuft," the protagonist Nella is traveling on the U6 underground line and imagines that the secret police might be using her as a kind of human bug. "Doch was könnten sie Brauchbares herausfischen?," she wonders, "das Befinden der Exiljugend, regimeuntreu? Ist sie faschistisch, ist sie kommunistisch, sind die Zustände putschreif, et cetera?" (But what might they fish out that could be of any use? The mood of young people in exile, anti-regime? Are they fascist or Communist, are the conditions ripe for a putsch, et cetera? 20). Her conversations with the friend who gets on a few stops later consist mostly of small talk and gossip about mutual friends, and the narrator explains that their shared childhood experiences are what makes these ostensibly so different-looking Muslim women so close (one of them is covered from top to toe and the other is dressed quite glamorously). But the subject turns obliquely to the war and to what the Serbs and Croats did to them in shutting the borders and leaving them without bread or water (23). But, as the quieter protagonist replies, she and her fellow Bosnians in Vienna are not much better. Instead of pulling together and helping each other to find work and living accommodation, jealousy and competition is the order of the day (24).

In the poem "Sprung vor und -ung," the "-ung" suffix provides Hadzibeganovic with the main rhyming device in a poem in which she playfully exposes the apparent liberation provided to an immigrant woman in the form of a cleaning job: "die nie-der-lass-ung / eine beschäftig-ung / bewillig-ung / mit der verlaut-ung der neuen / volksgruppengesetzgeb-ung / fu kung — kung fu / hole mir den schein der befrei-ung / über eine firma reinig-ung" (residen-tial registra-tion / an occupa-tion / a permis-sion / with the declara-tion of the new / laws on ethnic minority classifica-tion / fu kung — kung fu / get my apparent qualifica-tion of libera-tion / via a cleaning organiza-tion, 11).[28] This is also the main theme of Hadzi-beganovic's short play "Putzköniginnen" (Queen Cleaners), in which two migrant workers, mother and daughter Nada and Wila, work as cleaners for "die Chefin" (the boss) in her plush, middle-class appartment. The two comment on how disgustingly filthy the Austrian woman's flat and car are, how low they have sunk since having to leave their spacious houses in Yugoslavia. When the two are sacked and lose the accommodation they had been renting from their boss, the daughter's yearnings are to go some-where completely different, to a warmer, freer, happier country. "Willst du, daß ich verrotte wie verschimmeltes Schlagobers?," she jibes to her mother, "Wien ist wie eine alte Witwe, die ihren Schmuck zur Schau stellt. Hinter faustdicken Wänden schauen wir taub, wie unser Leben an uns vor-beigeht [. . .] im Fiakertempo der Metropole der Selbstverachtung" (Do you want me to rot here like moldy cream? Vienna is like an old widow showing off her jewels. Deaf behind our thick walls, we watch as our lives pass us by at the slow pace of this metropolis of self-contempt, 90). Like the father in *Jugofilm* (1997) by Serbian-born Austrian director Goran Rebić (1968–), the mother sees her future in the past. She clings onto a dream of going back to their family house and to her former way of life, but as the radio announces NATO air attacks on Serbia, we know — as the daughter does — that Nada's plans are naive.

Denis Mikan's short novel *Emil* (2002) describes the thoughts, experi-ences and everyday actions of Emil, a Bosnian émigré who works as a computer network technician but whose main interests are clearly literary, engaged as he is in writing a screenplay and pieces for a literary magazine.[29] Mostly written in the third person, Mikan's short novel also has a small number of chapters that use a first-person narrator. The identity of the occasional first-person narrator is blurred, and the temptation to confuse him with his friend "Denis" is a deliberate authorial strategy. Talking over apple strudel and beer, Emil tells the narrator (that is, possibly his friend Denis) that his father Mikan Zdravko had made an inventory of his flat before they fled their hometown. By using the author's surname (Mikan) and naming the protagonist's friend "Denis," the author presents us with a fictionalized and distorted biographical projection of himself (like Struhar in *Das Manuskript*). "E.," as Emil is elliptically referred to in places, is of the opinion that it is impossible to tell one's own story without deceiving oneself (21). The title of the chapter is "bestandsverzeichnis" (inventory), suggesting that a list of physical objects may be the most reliable insight into the facts of a person's life. There are countless moments in the novel where Emil reflects on how things seem to be happening to him without any willed action on his part. He sees his actions as those of somebody in a film, his own life seems alien, and he finds himself doing things and going places without any recollection of how.

Emil befriends a Nigerian student called François after the train they are traveling on breaks down. When Emil goes to visit François later in the novel, he is told that François has been arrested along with twenty other Nigerians on suspicion of possessing drugs, and his attempts to find François remain futile. It is tempting to see the amplification of the single Nigerian into a mass arrest of Nigerian students as a parody of a stereotype, but the style of the narration is economically factual here and does not suggest such an interpretation. In *Emil* (as in the texts by Struhar, Turrini, and Henisch) there are moments when black men are either searched or arrested for drug possession. As with the Henisch and Struhar texts, the protagonist's sexual identity is also a site of tension and uncertainty. Emil rants against modern Viennese career women and expounds to an uncomprehending Romanian friend in an unreconstructed macho style that "ihre George-Clooney-Bildschirmschoner, [. . .] werden es wohl kaum schaffen, das einzig Richtige zu tun, um sie vor völliger Nutzlosigkeit zu bewahren, nämlich sie zu befruchten" (their George Clooney screen savers will hardly manage to get them pregnant — the one and only thing that'll save them from being totally useless, 61). But this is a man who, when his girlfriend left him, watched silently and did not act and who seems both attracted to and repulsed by the women he meets. Equally, Emil is vocally homophobic: he fears the priest he thinks is gay, and feels physically sick when a gay student touches him on the shoulder. Interestingly, the people he imagines blowing up in the final scene are all men, drinking beer and talking about sex. "Er wird sich vorstellen, eine Art Superman zu sein, eine Art Beschützer," the reader is informed (He will imagine he's some kind of Superman, a sort of Protector, 99). It is not clear what or whom Emil will think he is protecting. Men, perhaps, or Bosnians? Emil had previously been musing on the bravery of Gavrilo Princip (whose assassination of Archduke Ferdinand and his wife in Sarajevo famously contributed to the outbreak of the First World War). Should we understand Emil's murderous fantasy as an outlet for or negative sublimation of a frustrated, "normal," male sexuality? The novel invites psychoanalytic speculation, and its projected dénouement could, on the contrary, be some kind of purging of the protagonist's repressed homosexuality.

Although Emil is embarrassed and disappointed with himself for immediately asking François where he comes from, their first meeting soon moves on to a discovery of their shared love of French literature, and Camus in particular. Emil cannot bring himself to ask François which of

Camus's books is his favorite (71), but his sense of being a stranger to himself is reminiscent of the philosophical reflections of Albert Camus's protagonist in his classic existentialist novel *L'Étranger* (The Stranger, 1942). Unlike Camus's protagonist Meursault, Emil does not kill anyone, but he does contemplate or at least imagine himself carrying out surreal, murderous actions. The final scene of the novel is projected into the immediate future, in a dreamlike vision of what the narrator tells us will happen. During his holiday to Sarajevo, his first trip "home" since fleeing, Emil will find a hand grenade in his pocket, having previously merely dreamed about taking a grenade away from two children playing in the street. He will throw the grenade onto the floor of a pub, run outside and then wonder why it does not explode: "Nach zehn, elf, zwanzig, fünfundvierzig Sekunden wird er sich wundern, wieso sie nicht hochgegangen ist. Trotzdem wird er zufrieden sein und in die Fremde heimkehren" (After ten, eleven, twenty, forty-five seconds he'll wonder why it hasn't gone off. He'll still be pleased, however, and will return to his foreign home, 99).

Emil's complex relationship with his country of origin and his former compatriots is one of the intriguing dimensions of Mikan's novel. The protagonist's feelings of belonging towards his new home and new language feature alongside the simultaneous existence of both a rejection of his previous, or other, identity and sadness as its primacy diminishes. Emil is on the one hand disappointed that he is losing his mother tongue as his first language, and on the other insistent on using German and eager to dissociate himself from his unintegrated compatriots who hang about outside the Südbahnhof, reminiscing about Yugoslavia before the war. The oxymoron of the novel's final phrase "in die Fremde heimkehren" encapsulates his feelings and suggests that "home" will continue to be not a physical place but a feeling or psychological state of being in between cultures and being a stranger to himself.

The number of Turkish immigrants or Austrian citizens of Turkish origin in Austria is naturally much smaller than those living in Germany (approximately two hundred thousand compared to two and a half million). However, like Germany, Austria recruited large numbers of foreign workers in the 1960s and early 1970s, and Turkish migrants and their families consitute an important minority in Austria's increasingly multicultural demography. In Vorarlberg, where the poet Kundeyt Şurdum has lived since 1971, Turks represent at least 10% of the population, and the lives of Turkish *Gastarbeiter* in Austria formed the basis for a volume of Şurdum's poetry entitled *Landlos: Türken in Vorarlberg* (1991).[30] His later volume *Kein Tag geht spurlos vorbei* (2002) is more wide-ranging. It contains poems about poetry and about the process of writing, poems about relationships and people, poems that make observations about cultural difference, and poems that offer a satirical and sometimes political perspective on Turkish-Austrian interculturalism.[31] The poem "Was dort nicht erlaubt ist" (What is not permitted there, 43) makes comparisons between a "dort" which is possibly Turkish, and a "hier" which is possibly Austrian: "Was dort nicht erlaubt ist / begrüßt man hier mit Anerkennung" (What is not permitted there / is greeted with approval here), or "Was hier heiter herumläuft / Steckt man dort / ins Gefängnis" (People who are here allowed to run around with impunity / are there put / in prison). However, as Sigurd Paul Scheichl points out, the conclusion of this short poem can hardly be read as a political judgment: "Aber was wir vermissen / ist nicht zu finden / weder dort noch hier" (But what we still miss / cannot be found / either here or there).[32] It is, rather, a philosophical reflection on happiness and the human condition, delivered in Şurdum's densely constructed style. The title poem, "kein tag geht spurlos" (no day goes without a trace, 80) tells of the banalities that can inspire the poetic imagination: "kein tag geht spurlos vorbei / oft merke ich es nicht / man sieht zwei mädchen sprechen / und glaubt es sei alltäglich" (No day goes by without a trace / often I don't notice it / you see two girls talking / and believe this might be an everyday occurrence), and the loneliness of the speaker seems less that of the cultural outsider than that of the poetic consciousness: "tief im glas glänzt / diese meine einsamkeit / weder grundlose freude noch sorge" (deep in the glass shines / this loneliness of mine / neither unfounded happiness nor worry). In addition to his own poetry in the German language, Şurdum has been active as a teacher and has written for a *Gastarbeiter* newspaper and for Turkish radio programs in Austria. Şurdum has also translated German-language works into Turkish (for example poetry by Ingeborg Bachmann and Paul Celan and essays by Georg Lukács).

The novelist Barbara Frischmuth is an Austrian writer for whom Islamic culture, and Turkish topoi in particular, have proved a frequent source of inspiration. She studied Turkish and Hungarian at university and was to have written her doctoral thesis on the Bektashi order. As Jennifer E. Michaels explains, "Frischmuth's fluency in Turkish, her familiarity with Arabic and Persian, and her broad knowledge of Turkish and other Islamic cultures have given her the background to become an important and informed mediator of these cultures.[33] Frischmuth has published countless reviews of and articles on literary works by authors from Islamic cultures, and her essays argue for a "genuine interest and a readiness to become spiritually and emotionally involved with the other."[34] She notes with regret that contemporary German literature has fallen way below the standards of the nineteenth century in terms of its interest in and knowledge of oriental subjects.[35]

Critics agree that Frischmuth's autobiographically inspired *Das Verschwinden des Schattens in der Sonne* (The Disappearance of the Shadow in the Sun, 1973) is the novel in which her exploration of Turkey and of the boundaries between the self and the other is at its most extensive. The dissolution of the self in the other — an idea inspired by Islamic mysticism, to which the title of Frischmuth's novel alludes — cannot be achieved, and the protagonist is unable to cast off her own background and cultural identity.[36] The final text the present chapter will discuss, however, is one of Frischmuth's recent works, *Die Schrift des Freundes* (The Friend's Writing, 1998), a novel that explores Turkish-Austrian relationships in a Viennese setting. *Die Schrift des Freundes* has been criticized as lacking the aesthetic and linguistic polish of Frischmuth's other works, but it is an accomplished novel and a highly compelling read, fusing as it does elements of a love story and a story of contemporary multicultural Vienna into a plot reminiscent of a detective novel.[37]

Anna, a computer programmer working on a government-financed program for recording and analyzing data on immigrants in Austria, had previously been a naive and apolitical, if very skilled and intelligent woman. On meeting and falling in love with Hikmet Ayverdi, the protagonist's interest in his life and culture and in his studies of Ottoman calligraphy cause her to wish to bring to an end her highly organized and somewhat ritualized relationship with Haugsdorff, a civil servant from the home office (which has commissioned the "Pacidius" computer program Anna works on). Her line-manager explains their role: "unsere Aufgabe [. . .] ist es, die Daten so miteinander zu verknüpfen, daß mögliche Allianzen sichtbar werden, Vernetzungen und Verknüpfungen, mafiose Strukturen, mit einem Wort, die Daten so aufzubereiten, daß die potentiellen Eiterherde unter den Migranten sichtbar werden" (our task is to link the various data so as to make potential alliances visible, networks and associations, mafia organizations. In short, to process the data in such a way as to show where unrest might be festering among immigrants, 24).[38] As Anna struggles to work out the reasons for Hikmet's sudden disappearance, her knowledge of the Turkish immigrant community increases and the novel takes on dimensions of a political *Entwicklungsroman*. Frischmuth's critique of Austrian (and by extension Western European) racism and of anti-immigrationist sentiments and practices comes to the fore through the humanity of her fictional love story.[39] In fact, Frischmuth only rarely underscores the political point. Anna's colleague and mentor, the Lebanese-Austrian Jussuf, is anxious that his Chinese dissident boyfriend may be sent back when his residence permit runs out, and he reads out some verbatim passages from rejected residency applications that reveal the random nature or sheer inhumanity of some of the decisions. The asylum application of an Afghan woman whose mother and daughter had both been killed by the mujaheddin is rejected, for example, on the grounds that the state could only recognize as legitimate grounds for asylum any actions affecting the asylum seeker directly and not members of her family (256).

Frischmuth's novel subtly foregrounds the issues facing immigrants and the complexities of their own communities. The narration is focalized through Anna, who blushes when Jussuf notes her political awakening. "Hat sie in einem Kokon gelebt? Oder ist es sie bloß nichts angegangen?," she wonders (Had she been living in a cocoon? Or was it just that it had been none of her business? 257). But as Frischmuth, through her narrator, pragmatically suggests: "Aber wer interessiert sich schon wirklich für etwas, was ihn nicht unmittelbar betrifft?" (Who's really interested in something that doesn't immediately concern them?, 257). Arguably, although the reader makes connections and senses developments long before the novel's protagonist, he or she nevertheless identifies with Anna and her search for her lover, and is thus also interested in or awakened to the ethnic and cultural information Anna needs to help her solve the riddle of Hikmet's disappearance and to understand the animosities between the more liberal Alevite Turkish community and their traditionalist Sunni compatriots that form part of the novel's context.[40]

In an address to an Alevite cultural gathering, Haugsdorff appeals to the assembled audience after a bomb attack prevents his boss from attending it in person, not to let the work of integration be destroyed by a few extremists' "brutalen Sinnlosigkeiten" (brutal and senseless actions, 186),[41] but his words point forward ironically to the brutally senseless murder of Hikmet in a house-raid in the last pages of the novel (Hikmet is deliberately dropped out of a high window, and his death passed off as an accident). Hikmet's crime had been to lend his legitimate, Austrian identification papers to those who did not possess them. Failing any progress in finding the perpetrators of the bomb attack, the government has turned its attention to rounding up any illegals in the country, or so the newspapers report (310). The actions of the ministry reveal the ironic and hollow nature of Haugsdorff's party politics, as his Turkish-Austrian fellow citizens are asked to reflect at the next elections "wer in diesem Land für Integration sorge und wer nicht" (who's seeing to integration in this country and who isn't, 186). Frischmuth did not shy from voicing her dissatisfaction with the coalition ÖVP-FPÖ regime of 2000, and expressed her doubts as to the nature of the new government's apparent interest in integration and in preventing xenophobia. She said that she would be persuaded that the government was serious about integration when integrative measures were a reality — for example when "new," that is immigrant, Austrians were put up as candidates or when some kind of voting entitlement for immigrant Austrians was put on the political agenda.[42]

As the author hints in her "Nachbemerkung" (Afterword), the metaphor of the "Schrift des Freundes" can be seen in many ways. It is the calligraphy Hikmet is studying, itself a metonym for learning more about his own cultural heritage and identity (71), and it is an Islamic expression meaning "fate" (213, 347, 352). The "friend" is a synonym for "Ali," or the physical reincarnation of Allah. "In der Schrift aber ist die Welt enthalten," the author further explains, "wer sie zu Bildern gestaltet, formt sie. So lautet meine Schlußfolgerung" (But the world is contained in writing. Whoever makes images out of writing is fashioning the world. That's my conclusion, 352). An analogy might suggest itself, then, between Frischmuth's "Schrift" and the images the reader makes from it, perceptions which themselves might help to form or influence the world. The novel is quite clearly itself the writing of a "friend" of Islam, or of someone who is making a positive literary statement against the demonization of Islamic culture. Anna solves her own mystery and frees herself from a meaningless, automatic, and unengaged life by allowing emotion and some kind of faith (if not necessarily a religious one) into her manner of inquiring about life. It is precisely *not* through the all-too-addictive, solitary, hi-tech world of cyber-knowledge, computer programming, and mobile telecommunications that she acquires her knowledge of Hikmet's life and a new way of living her own.

Barbara Frischmuth describes modern literary techniques as being "ein adäquates Instrument, multikulturelle Aspekte zur allgemeinen und doch differenzierten Debatte zu stellen" (an adequate means of presenting multicultural aspects for general and yet differentiated debate).[43] She praises authors who are "Grenzgänger und Vermittler" (border crossers and mediators) and who, either out of curiosity or out of necessity, are driven into another culture. The writers and filmmakers discussed in this chapter represent both of these groups, even if their motivation to write is not necessarily a conscious, political decision to provide such mediation. There are those who have migrated or fled to Austria and who write about their new home and ways of living or gain a different perspective on their old ones, and for whom the sense of displacement plays a varyingly important role. On the other hand, there are those writers whose curiosity or whose political convictions have led them to create works that explore different Austrian or German identities and challenge a monolithic representation of contemporary Austrian culture and history.

A major question that must remain undeveloped here is whether the appearance of literature *in German* by Austrians originally from other countries or with different mother tongues or ethnicities does not simply lead to a "melting pot" approach to culture, that is, whether it does not diminish the sense of individual *cultures* that exist side by side but all contribute to the multicultural whole. It could rather be argued that the works discussed here, by "old" or "new" Austrians alike, invite the German-language majority readership or audience to expand their understanding of different subject positions and thus subscribe to a more pluralist and inclusive conception of Austria and of the people who live within its geographical boundaries.

Notes

I am grateful to the Arts and Humanities Research Council for a research-leave grant enabling me to undertake research towards this chapter.

[1] For an analysis of many of the factors involved in postwar Austrian nation-building, see Peter Thaler, *The Ambivalence of Identity: The Austrian Experience of Nation-Building in a Modern Society* (West Lafayette, IN: Purdue UP, 2001).

[2] Rudolf Burger, "Die Zeit der Reife: Zum Abschluß der österreichischen Nationsbildung," *Transit: Europäische Revue* 10 (1995): 59–67. For an evaluation of the first years of Austria's membership of the European Union, see *Austria in the European Union*, ed. Günter Bischof, Anton Pelinka, and Michael Gehler, Contemporary Austrian Studies 10 (New Brunswick, NJ: Transaction Publishers, 2002).

[3] For a useful overview of critical responses, see *Österreich: Berichte aus Quarantanien*, ed. Isolde Charim and Doron Rabinovici (Frankfurt am Main: Suhrkamp, 2000).

[4] Of the ten new member states who join the European Union on 1 May 2004, four share a border with Austria: Slovenia, Slovakia, the Czech Republic, and Hungary.

[5] See Vida Obid, Mirko Messner, and Andrej Leben, *Haiders Exerzierfeld: Kärntens SlowenInnen in der deutschen Volksgemeinschaft* (Vienna: Promedia, 2002), 49–50.

[6] See Matthias Konzett's insightful discussion on "The Emergence of Recent Austrian Jewish Writing," in Matthias Konzett, *The Rhetoric of National Dissent in Thomas Bernhard, Peter Handke, and Elfriede Jelinek* (Rochester, NY: Camden House, 2000), 131–50.

[7] Lilian Faschinger, *Wiener Passion* (Cologne: Kiepenheuer & Witsch, 1999); *Vienna Passion*, tr. Anthea Bell (London: Headline, 2000).

[8] For a brief outline of the Czech nationality conflict, see Barbara Jelavich, *Modern Austria: Empire and Republic 1918–1986* (Cambridge: Cambridge UP, 1989), 89–92.

[9] Peter Henisch, *Schwarzer Peter* (Salzburg: Residenz, 2000).

[10] Hans Christian Kosler calls it a "declaration of love" for Vienna, in "Spiel dein Spiel, Negerl! Peter Henisch schreibt den Roman der Zweiten Republik," *Neue Zürcher Zeitung* (14 June 2000).

[11] Duden glosses this Austrian phrase as the expression of a common Austrian attitude of parochial ignorance, self-confidence, and perceived superiority. See *Wie sagt man in Österreich? Wörterbuch der österreichischen Besonderheiten* (Mannheim: Dudenverlag, 1980), 126 (see "mir san mir").

[12] Jennifer E. Michaels details some of the numerous more minor insensitivities and racist stereotypes to which Peter is also subjected. See "The Jambalaya Principle: Otherness and Multiculturalism in *Schwarzer Peter*," in *Balancing Acts: Textual Strategies of Peter Henisch*, ed. Craig Decker (Riverside, CA: Ariadne, 2002), 242–66.

[13] Eva Schobel, "Facts and Fiction: On the Process of Development in *Schwarzer Peter*," in *Balancing Acts*, ed. Decker, 228–41.

[14] See Kosler, "Spiel dein Spiel, Negerl!" 35.

[15] Maria-Regina Kecht, "Wo ist Daheim? America in Narrative Identity Constructions of Contemporary Austrian Literature," in *The Americanization/Westernization of Austria*, ed. Günther Bischof and Anton Pelinka, Contemporary Austrian Studies 12 (New Brunswick, NJ: Transaction Publishers, 2004), 153–169; here: 157.

[16] Stanislav Struhar, *Das Manuskript*, tr. Andrej Leben (Klagenfurt: Drava, 2002). Although written in Czech, the novel was first published in the German translation. Struhar — who fled Czechoslovakia in 1988 — now also writes in German.

[17] Peter Landerl, "[Review:] Stanislav Struhar, *Das Manuskript*" (7 November 2002), at www.literaturhaus.at/buch/buch/rez/struhar/ (29 April 2004).

[18] Peter Turrini, *Ich liebe dieses Land: Stück und Materialien* (Frankfurt am Main: Suhrkamp, 2001).

[19] Claus Peymann famously championed some of the high-profile, controversial Austrian writers at the Burgtheater when he was director there (1986–99). He has continued to stage works by playwrights such as Bernhard, Jelinek, and Turrini since his return to Germany in 1999 as director of the Berliner Ensemble.

[20] Environmental groups were outraged by the pollution of the Niger Delta caused by oil companies, notably Shell, in 1995. The public boycott of Shell petrol was probably strongest in Germany.

[21] The number of Muslims in Austria is in fact extremely small. The 2001 census puts the proportion of Muslims at 4.2% (compared to 2% in 1991). Martin Reisigl and Ruth Wodak, *Discourse and Discrimination* (Oxford: Routledge, 2001) show that without immigration, the Austrian population would have decreased, thus putting the social welfare system in jeopardy.

[22] See www.schlingensief.com (23 September 2005).

[23] See also Elfriede Jelinek's lampoon of Jörg Haider, "Das Lebewohl (Les Adieux)," in *Das Lebewohl, 3 kl. Dramen* (Berlin: Berlin Verlag, 2000), 9–35.

[24] Nana's tourist bus runs under the banner of "The Sound of Music." Flicker talks of Robert Wise's 1965 film as a precursor to *Suzie Washington*, pointing out that the location of the film is still today an escape route to the "New World"; see "Gespräch mit Florian Flicker," in Florian Flicker, *Suzie Washington. Drehbuch und Notizen zum Film* (Weitra: Bibliothek der Provinz, 1999), 101–3; here: 102.

[25] Gundolf Graml made these points in his paper "Tourism as Contact Zone: Gender and Ethnicity in Florian Flicker's Film *Suzie Washington* (1998)," presented to the Modern Austrian Literature and Culture Association at the University of Vermont in April 2003.

[26] See Peter Stuiber, "[Review:] Dimitré Dinev, *Engelszungen*" (29 September 2003), at: www.literaturhaus.at/buch/buch/rez/dinev_engelszungen (29 April 2004). Like Dinev's collection of short stories *Die Inschrift* (2000), the narrative of *Engelszungen* (2003) combines Bulgarian history with densely woven character stories. The stories are prompted by the retrospective gaze of two despairing

migrants at a graveside in Vienna, but the majority of the narrative takes place in Bulgaria.

[27] Alma Hadzibeganovic, *Ilda Zuferka rettet die Kunst* (Vienna: edition exil, 2001).

[28] The law governing ethnic groups — the *Volksgruppengesetz* — dates from 1976, but in 2000 the protection of ethnic minorities was officially incorporated into the Austrian Federal Constitution.

[29] Denis Mikan, *Emil* (Vienna: edition exil, 2002).

[30] Kundeyt Şurdum, *Landlos: Türken in* Vorarlberg, with photographs by Nikolaus Walter (Salzburg: Otto Müller Verlag, 1991). According to Sami Kohen, 180,000 Turks live in Austria and 40,000 of these people are dual citizens (www.hri.org/news/turkey/trkpr/1999/99-10-06.trkpr.html, 14 April 2004).

[31] See Sigurd Paul Scheichl, "Zu Kundeyt Şurdums drittem Gedichtband," in Kundeyt Şurdum, *Kein Tag geht spurlos vorbei* (Eggingen: Edition Isele, 2002), 99–105; here: 103.

[32] Scheichl, "Zu Kundeyt Şurdums drittem Gedichtband," 101.

[33] Jennifer E. Michaels, "Multiculturalism in Barbara Frischmuth's Works: The Representation and Mediation of Turkish and Other Islamic Cultures in *Das Verschwinden des Schattens in der Sonne* and in Various Short Pieces," in *Barbara Frischmuth in Contemporary Context*, ed. Renate S. Posthofen (Riverside: Ariadne, 1999), 67–86; here: 68.

[34] Frischmuth quoted in Michaels, "Multiculturalism in Barbara Frischmuth's Works" (67).

[35] Christoph Gellner summarizes Frischmuth's arguments from *Das Heimliche und das Unheimliche. Drei Reden* (Berlin: Aufbau, 1999) in his article "Grenzüberschreitungen zwischen Orient und Okzident: Literatur, Multikulturalität und Religionsdialog," in *Barbara Frischmuth. Fremdgänge. Ein illustrierter Streifzug durch einen literarischen Kosmos*, ed. Daniela Bartens and Ingrid Spörk (Salzburg: Residenz, 2001), 211–39; here: 211–13.

[36] See Gellner, "Grenzüberschreitungen zwischen Orient und Okzident" (225) for an explanation of the title metaphor and its relevance.

[37] Paul Michael Lützeler describes it as a "Multikultur-, High-Tech-, Wien-, Liebes-, Gesellschafts- und Kriminalroman, voll von neuer Alltagsrealität, ihrer intellektuellen Durchdringung und traumhaften Verarbeitung" (a multicultural, high-tech, Viennese society detective novel cum love story, full of contemporary everyday realities, shot through with intellectual understanding and dreamlike transformations; Lützeler, "Ein Derwisch verschwindet. Barbara Frischmuths Roman *Die Schrift des Freundes*," *Die Zeit*, 27 August 1998).

[38] See also Hadzibeganovic, "Etwas läuft." I do not know whether Frischmuth bases this organization on a real model. I note, however, that the information center Österreichisches Forum für Migrationsstudien (ÖFM) was initiated in 1997 with the aim of fostering cooperation between the various agencies researching migration in the German-speaking countries. It is co-financed by the Austrian Ministry of Interior and the Swiss foundation for population, migration, and ecology.

[39] Jennifer E. Michaels points out that many Austrian writers have voiced their objections to Austria's restrictive asylum laws and that these laws have been criticized by human rights groups (Michaels, "The Jambalaya Principle," 251). More recently, the United Nations High Commissioner for Refugees objected to new regulations barring some asylum-seekers from government-run shelters and rebuked Austrian officials for implying that the UNHCR had given its support for what was effectively a "hardening of reception conditions for asylum seekers in Austria." www.europaworld.org/week99/unrefugee41002.htm (14 April 2004).

[40] See Gellner, "Grenzüberschreitungen zwischen Orient und Okzident" and Frischmuth's own "Nachbemerkung" (Afterword) to *Die Schrift des Freundes* (Salzburg: Residenz, 2002), 349–52.

[41] There was a series of letter bomb attacks in Austria in the 1990s. In 1995 the Mayor of Vienna, Helmut Zilk, was injured by one, and in 1996 a letter bomb was delivered to a relative of Caspar Einem, the Home Office minister at the time and thus responsible for immigration and refugees. Four members of the Roma community were murdered in Oberwart by a bomb attached to a racist sign they were attempting to remove. The Bajuwarische Befreiungsarmee (Bavarian Liberation Army) claimed responsibility for many of these acts. Elfriede Jelinek exposes the conspiracy of public silence surrounding these murders in her play *Stecken, Stab und Stangl* (1997).

[42] Barbara Frischmuth, "Irgendwann ist man es leid . . . ," *Der Standard* (5 February 2000).

[43] Barbara Frischmuth, "Der Blick über den Kulturzaun," in *Schreiben zwischen den Kulturen. Beiträge zur deutschsprachigen Gegenwartsliteratur*, ed. Paul Michael Lützeler (Frankfurt am Main: Fischer, 1996), 19–27; here: 27.

Further Reading

General: Literary History

Arnold, Heinz Ludwig, ed. *Kritisches Lexikon zur deutschsprachigen Gegenwartsliteratur (KLG)*. Munich: Edition Text + Kritik, 1978–. (Also as online resource).

Bartsch, Kurt, Dietmar Goltschnigg, et al., eds. *Für und wider eine österreichische Literatur*. Königstein/Ts.: Athenäum, 1982.

Haas, Franz, et al. *Blicke von außen: Österreichische Literatur im internationalen Kontext*. Innsbruck: Haymon, 2003.

Nachbaur, Petra, and Sigurd Paul Scheichl, eds. *Literatur über Literatur: Eine österreichische Anthologie*. Graz: Styria, 1995.

Neuwirth, Barbara, ed. *Schriftstellerinnen sehen ihr Land: Österreich aus dem Blick seiner Autorinnen*. Vienna: Wiener Frauenverlag, 1995.

Schmidt-Dengler, Wendelin. *Bruchlinien: Vorlesungen zur österreichischen Literatur 1945–1990*. Salzburg and Vienna: Residenz, 1995.

———. *Ohne Nostalgie: Zur österreichischen Literatur der Zwischenkriegszeit*. Vienna, Cologne, Weimar: Böhlau, 2002.

Schmidt-Dengler, Wendelin, Johann Sonnleitner, et al., eds. *Literaturgeschichte: Österreich. Prolegomena und Fallstudien*. Berlin: Schmidt, 1995.

———, eds. *Konflikte, Skandale, Dichterfehden in der österreichischen Literatur*. Berlin: Schmidt, 1995.

Sebald, W. G. *Die Beschreibung des Unglücks: Zur österreichischen Literatur von Stifter bis Handke*. Salzburg: Residenz, 1985.

———. *Unheimliche Heimat: Essays zur österreichischen Literatur*. Salzburg and Vienna: Residenz, 1991.

Spiel, Hilde, ed. *Die zeitgenössische Literatur Österreichs*. Zurich and Vienna: Kindler, 1976. (= *Kindlers Literaturgeschichte der Gegenwart. Autoren — Werke — Themen — Tendenzen seit 1945*. 5 vols. Zurich and Vienna: Kindler, 1971–76.)

Zeman, Herbert, ed. *Das 20. Jahrhundert*. Graz: Akademische Druck- und Verlagsanstalt, 1999. (= Herbert Zeman, ed. *Geschichte der Literatur in Österreich von den Anfängen bis zur Gegenwart*. 7 vols. Graz: Akademische Druck- und Verlagsanstalt, 1994–. Vol. 7.)

———, ed. *Die österreichische Literatur: Ihr Profil von der Jahrhundertwende bis zur Gegenwart (1880–1980)*. 2 vols. Graz: Akademische Druck und Verlagsanstalt, 1989.

Zeyringer, Klaus, ed. *Österreichische Literatur 1945–1998: Überblicke, Einschnitte, Wegmarken.* 2nd ed. Innsbruck: Haymon, 1999, 2001.

History, Society, Culture: 1918–45

Amann, Klaus. *Der Anschluß österreichischer Schriftsteller an das Dritte Reich: Institutionelle und bewußtseinsgeschichtliche Aspekte.* Vienna, Cologne, Weimar: Böhlau, 1988.

Aspetsberger, Friedbert. *Literarisches Leben im Austrofaschismus.* Königstein/Ts: Hain, 1980.

Beniston, Judith, and Robert Vilain, eds. *Austrian Studies,* 14: *Culture and Politics in "Red Vienna"* (2006).

Daviau, Donald G., ed. *Major Figures of Austrian Literature: The Interwar Years 1918–1938.* Riverside: Ariadne, 1995.

———, ed. *Austrian Writers and the Anschluss: Understanding the Past, Overcoming the Past.* Riverside: Ariadne, 1991.

Decloedt, Leopold R. G. *Imago Imperatoris: Franz Joseph I. in der österreichischen Belletristik der Zwischenkriegszeit.* Vienna, Cologne, Weimar: Böhlau, 1995.

Gruber, Helmut. *Red Vienna: Experiment in Working-Class Culture 1919–1934.* New York and Oxford: Oxford UP, 1991.

Kadrnoska, Franz, ed. *Aufbruch und Untergang: Österreichische Kultur zwischen 1918 und 1938.* Vienna: Europaverlag, 1981.

Magris, Claudio, *Der habsburgische Mythos in der modernen österreichischen Literatur.* Revised ed. Vienna: Zsolnay, 2000.

Müller, Karl. *Zäsuren ohne Folgen: Das lange Leben der literarischen Antimoderne Österreichs seit den 30er Jahren.* Salzburg: Müller, 1990.

Pfoser, Alfred. *Literatur und Austromarxismus.* Vienna: Löcker, 1980.

Stieg, Gerald. *Frucht des Feuers: Canetti, Doderer, Kraus und der Justizpalastbrand.* Vienna: Falter, 1990.

Drama 1918–45

General

Beniston, Judith. "Cultural Politics in the First Republic: Hans Brečka and the 'Kunststelle für christliche Volksbildung.'" *Austrian Studies,* 10: *Catholicism and Austrian Culture* (1999), 101–18.

Brückl-Zehetner, Heidemarie. "Theater in der Krise. Sozialgeschichtliche Untersuchungen zum Wiener Theater der ersten Republik." Diss. University of Vienna, 1988.

Colvin, Sarah. *Women and German Drama: Playwrights and Their Texts, 1860–1945.* Rochester, NY: Camden House, 2003.

Deutsch-Schreiner, Evelyn. "Nationalsozialistische Kulturpolitik in Wien 1938–1945 unter spezieller Berücksichtigung der Wiener Theaterszene." Diss. University of Vienna, 1980.

Haider-Pregler, Hilde, and Beate Reiterer, eds. *Verspielte Zeit: Österreichisches Theater der dreißiger Jahre.* Vienna: Picus, 1997.

Pyrah, Robert. "Viennese Theatre and Constructions of Austrian Identity 1918–1938." Doctoral Diss., University of Oxford, 2004.

Steinberg, Michael P. *Austria as Theater and Ideology: The Meaning of the Salzburg Festival.* Ithaca and London: Cornell UP, 1990.

Stürzer, Anne, *Dramatikerinnen und Zeitstücke: Ein vergessenes Kapitel der Theatergeschichte von der Weimarer Republik bis zur Nachkriegszeit.* Stuttgart and Weimar: Metzler, 1993.

Warren, John. "Austrian Theatre and the Corporate State." In *Austria in the Thirties: Culture and Politics,* ed. Kenneth Segar and John Warren, 267–91. Riverside: Ariadne, 1991.

Yates, W. E. *Theatre in Vienna: A Critical History, 1776–1995.* Cambridge: Cambridge UP, 1996.

Richard Billinger

Rabenstein, Edith. *Dichtung zwischen Tradition und Moderne: Richard Billinger. Untersuchungen zur Rezeptionsgeschichte und zum Werk.* Frankfurt am Main: Lang, 1988.

Scheit, Gerhard. "Die Zerstörung des Volksstücks. Richard Billinger und die Tradition des Volkstheaters." *Wespennest* 56 (1984): 4–12. Reprinted in his *Theater und revolutionärer Humanismus: Eine Studie zu Jura Soyfer,* 115–32. Vienna: Verlag für Gesellschaftskritik, 1988.

Felix Braun

Danielczyk, Julia and Hermann Böhm. "Verzicht aufs Burgtheater. Akzeptanz und Verweigerung am Beispiel Felix Brauns (1885–1973)." *Maske und Kothurn* 50/ii (2004): 71–86.

Ferdinand Bruckner

Reul, Ingrid. *Aktualität und Tradition: Studien zu Ferdinand Bruckners Werk bis 1930.* Hamburg: Verlag Dr Kovač, 1999.

Franz Theodor Csokor

Kucher, Primus-Heinz. " 'Die Wollust der Kreatur [. . .] gemenget mit Bitterkeit.' Versuch über den vergessenen Expressionisten Franz Theodor Csokor." In *Expressionismus in Österreich: Die Literatur und die Künste,* ed. Klaus Amann and Armin A. Wallas, 417–36. Vienna, Cologne, Weimar: Böhlau, 1994.

Mitchell, Michael R. " 'Aus der hellen Wohnung zurück in den Zuchtstall': An Examination of F. T. Csokor's *3. November 1918.*" *Modern Austrian Literature* 16/i (1983): 37–52.

Fritz Hochwälder

Baker, R. Paul. *A Question of Conscience: The Dramas of Fritz Hochwälder.* Dunedin: University of Otago, 2001.

Hugo von Hofmannsthal

König, Christoph. *Hofmannsthal: Ein moderner Dichter unter den Philologen.* Göttingen: Wallstein, 2001.

Kovach, Thomas A., ed. *A Companion to the Works of Hugo von Hofmannsthal.* Rochester, NY: Camden House, 2002.

Ödön von Horváth

Balme, Christopher B. *The Reformation of Comedy: Genre Critique in the Comedies of Ödön von Horváth.* Dunedin: University of Otago, 1985.

Bance, Alan. "The Significance of the Irrational in Horváth's *Geschichten aus dem Wiener Wald.*" *Austrian Studies 9: The Austrian Comic Tradition* (1998), 202–17.

Bartsch, Kurt. *Ödön von Horváth.* Stuttgart and Weimar: Metzler, 2000.

Hans Kaltneker

Frei, Norbert. " 'Wir sind nicht gut genug zueinander.' Zum Werk von Hans Kaltneker." In *Expressionismus in Österreich: Die Literatur und die Künste,* ed. Klaus Amann and Armin A. Wallas, 499–514. Vienna, Cologne, Weimar: Böhlau, 1994.

Karl Kraus

Fischer, Jens Malte. *Karl Kraus: Studien zum Theater der Dichtung und Kulturkonservatismus.* Kronberg: Scriptor, 1973.

Timms, Edward. *Karl Kraus: Apocalyptic Satirist,* vol. 1: *Culture and Catastrophe in Habsburg Vienna.* New Haven and London: Yale UP, 1986; Vol. 2: *The Post-War Crisis and the Rise of the Swastika.* New Haven and London: Yale UP, 2005.

Max Mell

Beniston, Judith. "Max Mell in the First Republic: The Acceptable Face of Catholic Drama?" In *From Perinet to Jelinek: Viennese Theatre in its Political and Intellectual Context,* ed. W. E. Yates, Allyson Fiddler, and John Warren, 179–90. Bern: Lang, 2001.

Binder, Christoph Heinrich. *Max Mell: Beiträge zu seinem Leben und Werk.* Graz: Steiermärkische Landesregierung, 1978.

Hermann Heinz Ortner

Danielczyk, Julia. *Selbstinszenierung: Vermarktungsstrategien des österreichischen Erfolgsdramatikers Hermann Heinz Ortner.* Vienna: Braumüller, 2003.

Hanns Sassmann

Peck, Clemens. "Literarische Österreich-Konstruktionen der dreißiger Jahre. Am Beispiel Hanns Saßmann." Diplomarbeit: University of Vienna, 2003.

Arthur Schnitzler

Beniston, Judith. "Schnitzler in Red Vienna." In *Arthur Schnitzler: Zeitgenossenschaften / Contemporaneities*, ed. Ian Foster and Florian Krobb, 217–31. Bern: Lang, 2002.

Weinberger, G. J. *Arthur Schnitzler's Late Plays: A Critical Study.* New York: Lang, 1997.

Jura Soyfer

Doll, Jürgen. *Theater im Roten Wien: Vom sozialdemokratischen Agitprop zum dialektischen Theater Jura Soyfers.* Vienna, Cologne, Weimar: Böhlau, 1997.

Scheit, Gerhard. *Theater und revolutionärer Humanismus: Eine Studie zu Jura Soyfer.* Vienna: Verlag für Gesellschaftskritik, 1988.

Ernst Weiss

Hinze, Klaus-Peter. "Ernst Weiss: The Novelist as Dramatist." *Austrian Studies*, 4: *Theatre and Performance in Austria* (1993), 93–101.

Franz Werfel

Auckenthaler, Karlheinz, ed. *Franz Werfel: Neue Aspekte seines Werkes.* Szeged: Jate, 1992.

Huber, Lothar, ed. *Franz Werfel: An Austrian Writer Reassessed.* Oxford: Berg, 1989.

Jungk, Peter Stephan. *Franz Werfel: Eine Lebensgeschichte.* Frankfurt am Main: Fischer, 1987.

Anton Wildgans

Schmidt-Dengler, Wendelin. "Das langsame Verschwinden des Anton Wildgans aus der Literaturgeschichte." In *Die einen raus — die anderen rein. Kanon und Literatur: Vorüberlegungen zu einer Literaturgeschichte Österreichs*, ed. Wendelin Schmidt-Dengler, Johann Sonnleitner, and Klaus Zeyringer, 71–84. Berlin: Schmidt, 1994.

Prose Fiction 1918–45

Hermann Bahr

Daviau, Donald G. *Der Mann von Übermorgen: Hermann Bahr 1863–1934.* Vienna: Österreichischer Bundesverlag, 1984.

Hermann Broch

Lützeler, Paul Michael, ed. *Hermann Broch, Visionary in Exile: The Yale 2001 Broch Symposium.* Rochester, NY: Camden House, 2003.

Ritzer, Monika. *Hermann Broch und die Kulturkrise des frühen 20. Jahrhunderts.* Stuttgart: Metzler, 1988.

Elias Canetti

Donahue, William Collins. *The End of Modernism: Elias Canetti"s "Auto-da-Fé."* Chapel Hill, NC: U of North Carolina P, 2001.

Lorenz, Dagmar C. G., ed. *A Companion to the Works of Elias Canetti.* Rochester, NY: Camden House, 2004.

Roberts, David. *Kopf und Welt: Elias Canettis Roman "Die Blendung."* Munich: Hanser, 1975.

Veza Canetti

Lühe, Irmela von der. " 'Zum Andenken an die fröhlichste Stadt Zentraleuropas.' Veza Canettis *Die Schildkröten* im Kontext der deutschsprachigen Exilliteratur." *Text + Kritik* 156 (2002): 65–81.

Schedel, Angelika, *Sozialismus und Psychoanalyse: Quellen von Veza Canettis literarischen Utopien.* Würzburg: Könighausen & Neumann, 2002.

Heimito von Doderer

Fleischer, Wolfgang. *Das verleugnete Leben: Die Biographie des Heimito von Doderer.* Vienna: Kremayr & Scheriau, 1996.

Hesson, Elizabeth C. *Twentieth Century Odyssey: A Study of Heimito von Doderer's "Die Dämonen."* Columbia, SC: Camden House, 1982.

Hugo von Hofmannsthal

Alewyn, Richard. *Über Hugo von Hofmannsthal.* 4th ed. Göttingen: Vandenhoeck & Ruprecht, 1967.

Miles, David H. *Hofmannsthal's Novel "Andreas": Memory and Self.* Princeton: Princeton UP, 1972.

Robert Musil

Luft, David. *Robert Musil and the Crisis of European Culture, 1880–1942.* Berkeley and Los Angeles: U of California P, 1980.

Payne, Philip. *Robert Musil's "The Man without Qualities": A Critical Study.* Cambridge: Cambridge UP, 1988.

Joseph Roth

Bronsen, David. *Joseph Roth: Eine Biographie.* Cologne: Kiepenheuer & Witsch, 1974.

Eggers, Frank Joachim. *"Ich bin ein Katholik mit jüdischem Gehirn" — Modernitätskritik und Religion bei Joseph Roth und Franz Werfel: Untersuchungen zu den erzählerischen Werken.* Frankfurt: Lang, 1996.

Hackert, Fritz. *Kulturpessimismus und Erzählform: Studien zu Joseph Roths Leben und Werk.* Bern: Lang, 1967.

George Saiko

Strelka, Joseph, ed. *George Saikos magischer Realismus: Zum Werk eines unbekannten großen Autors.* Bern: Lang, 1990.

Arthur Schnitzler

Rey, William H. *Arthur Schnitzler: Die späte Prosa als Gipfel seines Schaffens.* Berlin: Schmidt, 1968.

Swales, Martin. *Arthur Schnitzler: A Critical Study.* Oxford: Clarendon, 1971.

Weinzierl, Ulrich. *Arthur Schnitzler: Lieben Träumen Sterben.* Frankfurt am Main: Fischer, 1994.

Stefan Zweig

Prater, D. A. *European of Yesterday: A Biography of Stefan Zweig.* Oxford: Clarendon, 1972.

Turner, David. *Moral Values and the Human Zoo: The "Novellen" of Stefan Zweig.* Hull: Hull UP, 1988.

Popular Culture 1918–45

Balázs, Béla. *Der sichtbare Mensch oder die Kultur des Films.* Vienna: Deutsch-Österreichischer Verlag, 1924.

Beckermann, Ruth, and Christa Blümlinger, eds. *Ohne Untertitel: Fragmente einer Geschichte des österreichischen Kinos.* Vienna: Sonderzahl, 1996.

Blau, Eve. *The Architecture of Red Vienna 1919–1934.* Cambridge, MA: MIT Press, 1999.

Büttner, Elisabeth, and Christian Dewald. *Das tägliche Brennen: Eine Geschichte des österreichischen Films von den Anfängen bis 1945.* Salzburg: Residenz, 2002.

Bukey, Evan Burr. *Hitler's Austria: Popular Sentiment in the Nazi Era, 1938–1945.* Chapel Hill and London: U of North Carolina P, 2000.

Klösch, Christian, and Regina Thumser. *"From Vienna": Exilkabarett in New York, 1938–1950.* Vienna: Picus, 2002.

Knepler, Georg. *Karl Kraus liest Offenbach.* Vienna: Löcker, 1984.

Loacker, Armin. *Anschluß im 3/4 Takt: Filmproduktion und Filmpolitik in Österreich 1930–38.* Trier: Wissenschaftlicher Verlag, 1999.

Loacker, Armin, and Martin Prucha, eds. *Unerwünschtes Kino: Der deutschsprachige Emigrantenfilm 1934–1937.* Vienna: Filmarchiv, 2000.

Loacker, Armin, and Innes Steiner, eds. *Imaginierte Antike: Österreichische Monumental-Stummfilme. Historienbilder und Geschichtskonstruktion in Sodom und Gomorrha, Samson und Delila, Die Sklavenkönigin und Salammbô.* Vienna: Filmarchiv 2002.

Rössler, Walter, ed. *Gehn ma halt a bisserl unter: Kabarett in Wien von den Anfängen bis heute.* Berlin, 1991.

Salten, Felix. *Wurstelprater.* Vienna and Leipzig: Graphische Kunstanstalt Brüder Rosenbaum, 1911.

Segel, Harold B. *Turn-of-the-Century Cabaret.* New York: Columbia UP, 1987.

Schwarz, Werner Michael. *Kino und Kinos in Wien: Eine Entwicklungsgeschichte bis 1934.* Vienna: Turia & Kant, 1992.

Veigl, Hans. *Lachen im Keller von den Budapestern zum Wiener Werkel: Kabarett und Kleinkunst in Wien.* Vienna: Löcker, 1986.

———, ed. *Luftmenschen spielen Theater: Jüdisches Kabarett in Wien 1890–1918.* Vienna: Kremayr & Scheriau, 1992.

———, ed. *Weit von wo: Kabarett im Exil.* Vienna: Kremayr & Scheriau, 1994.

Poetry 1918–2000

General

Beniston, Judith, and Robert Vilain, eds. *Austrian Studies,* 12: *The Austrian Lyric* (2004).

Berger, Albert. "Schwieriges Erwachen. Zur Lyrik der jungen Generation in den ersten Nachkriegsjahren." In *Literatur der Nachkriegszeit und der fünfziger Jahre in Österreich,* ed. Friedbert Aspetsberger, Norbert Frei, et al., 190–206. Vienna: Österreichischer Bundesverlag, 1984.

Elliott, Mark. "German Poetry beyond the Boundaries of the Nazi Era: The Modernist Legacy." Diss., University of Oxford, 2006. [Includes discussion of the reception of Rilke in the work of Weinheber and Steiner].

Holton, Milne, and Herbert Kuhner, eds. and trs. *Austrian Poetry Today / Österreichische Lyrik heute.* New York: Schocken, 1985.

Klinger, Kurt. "Lyrik in Österreich seit 1945." In *Kindlers Literaturgeschichte der Gegenwart: Autoren, Werke, Themen, Tendenzen seit 1945,* ed. Hilde Spiel, 291–476. Zurich and Munich: Kindler, 1976.

H. G. Adler

Adler, Jeremy. "Der Wahrheit verpflichtet." In H. G. Adler, *Der Wahrheit verpflichtet: Interviews, Gedichte, Essays*, 205–34. Gerlingen: Bleicher, 1998.

Kohl, Katrin. " 'Zur Bestimmung der Lyrik.' H. G. Adlers Poetik zwischen den Zeiten." *Text + Kritik* 163: *H. G. Adler* (2004): 60–70.

Schmatz, Ferdinand. "Wahres anders gesagt. Dichtung und Wirklichkeit bei H. G. Adler." *Text + Kritik* 163: *H. G. Adler* (2004): 31–41.

H. C. Artmann

Donnenberg, Josef, ed. *Pose, Possen und Poesie: Zum Werk Hans Carl Artmanns*. Stuttgart: Akademischer Verlag Heinz, 1981.

Fuchs, Gerhard, and Rüdiger Wischenbart, eds. *H. C. Artmann*. (Dossier, vol. 3.) Graz: Droschl, 1992.

Ingeborg Bachmann

Albrecht, Monika, and Dirk Göttsche, eds. *Bachmann-Handbuch: Leben — Werk — Wirkung*. Stuttgart and Weimar: Metzler, 2002.

Böschenstein, Bernhard, and Sigrid Weigel, eds. *Ingeborg Bachmann und Paul Celan: Poetische Korrespondenzen. Vierzehn Beiträge*. Frankfurt am Main: Suhrkamp, 1997.

Höller, Hans. *Ingeborg Bachmann, das Werk: Von den frühesten Gedichten bis zum "Todesarten"-Zyklus*. Frankfurt am Main: Athenäum, 1987.

Leeder, Karen. " 'Dunkles zu sagen' ": Die Sprache der Liebe in der Lyrik Ingeborg Bachmanns. In *Ingeborg Bachmann: Kritische Wege der Landnahme*, ed. Robert Pichl and Alexander Stillmark, 11–20. Vienna: Hora, 1994.

Paul Celan

Del Caro, Adrian. *The Early Poetry of Paul Celan: In the Beginning Was the Word*. Baton Rouge: Lousiana State UP, 1997.

Emmerich, Wolfgang. *Paul Celan*. 2nd ed. Reinbek bei Hamburg: Rowohlt, 1999.

Felstiner, John. *Paul Celan: Poet, Survivor, Jew*. New Haven and London: Yale UP, 1995.

Erich Fried

Bormann, Alexander von. " 'Ein Dichter, den Worte zusammenfügen.' Versöhnung von Rhetorik und Poesie bei Erich Fried." *Text + Kritik* 91: *Erich Fried* (1997), rev. ed., 5–23.

Kane, Martin. "From Solipsism to Engagement. The Development of Erich Fried as a Political Poet." *Forum for Modern Language Studies* 21 (1985): 151–69.

Lawrie, Steven W. *Erich Fried: A Writer Without a Country*. Bern and Frankfurt am Main: Lang, 1996.

Ernst Jandl

Schmidt-Dengler, Wendelin, ed. *Ernst Jandl: Materialienbuch.* Darmstadt and Neuwied: Luchterhand, 1982.

Vogt, Michael, ed. *"stehn JANDL gross hinten drauf": Interpretationen zu Texten Erich Jandls.* Bielefeld: Aisthesis, 2000.

Theodor Kramer

Staud, Herbert, and Jörg Thunecke, eds. *Chronist seiner Zeit: Theodor Kramer.* Klagenfurt: Drava, 2000.

Christine Lavant

Rußegger, Arno, and Johann Strutz, eds. *Profile einer Dichterin: Beiträge des 2. Internationalen Christine-Lavant-Symposions Wolfsberg 1998.* Salzburg: Müller, 1999.

Strutz, Johann. *Poetik und Existenzproblematik: Zur Lyrik Christine Lavants.* Salzburg: Müller, 1979.

Friederike Mayröcker

Melzer, Gerhard, and Stefan Schwar, eds. *Friederike Mayröcker.* (Dossier, vol. 14.) Graz and Vienna: Droschl, 1999.

Schmidt, Siegfried J., ed. *Friederike Mayröcker.* (suhrkamp taschenbuch materialien.) Frankfurt am Main: Suhrkamp, 1984.

Erika Mitterer

Petrowsky, Martin, ed. *Eine Dichterin — ein Jahrhundert: Erika Mitterers Lebenswerk.* Vienna: Edition Doppelpunkt, 2002.

Andreas Okopenko

Fliedl, Konstanze, and Christa Gürtler, eds. *Andreas Okopenko.* (Dossier, vol. 23.) Graz: Droschl, 2004.

Rainer Maria Rilke

Fülleborn, Ulrich, and Manfred Engel, eds. *Rilkes Duineser Elegien.* 3 vols. (suhrkamp taschenbuch materialien.) Frankfurt am Main: Suhrkamp, 1980–82.

Komar, Kathleen L. *Transcending Angels: Rainer Maria Rilke's Duino Elegies.* Lincoln and London: U of Nebraska P, 1987.

Reich-Ranicki, Marcel, ed. *Rainer Maria Rilke: Und ist ein Fest geworden. 33 Gedichte mit Interpretationen.* Frankfurt am Main and Leipzig: Insel, 1996.

Ryan, Judith. *Rilke, Modernism and Poetic Tradition.* Cambridge: Cambridge UP, 1999.

Evelyn Schlag

Leeder, Karen, " 'Time, love and literature!' The Work of Elegy in the Poetry of Evelyn Schlag." *Austrian Studies,* 12: *The Austrian Lyric* (2004): 231–48.

Raoul Schrott

Leeder, Karen. "The *Poeta Doctus* and the New German Poetry: Raoul Schrott"s *Tropen.*" *Germanic Review* 77 (2002): 51–67.

Jura Soyfer

Heydrich, Harald. "Jura Soyfers Dachau-Lied und die Tradition der KZ-Lagerlieder. Eine wirkungsästhetische Untersuchung." In *Jura Soyfer (1912–1939) zum Gedenken,* ed. Herbert Arlt and Klaus Manger, 78–91. St. Ingbert: Röhrig, 1999.

Franz Baermann Steiner

Adler, Jeremy. "Franz Baermann Steiner: A Prague Poet in England." In *England? Aber wo liegt es?" Deutsche und österreichische Emigranten in Großbritannien 1933–1945,* ed. Charmian Brinson et al., 125–40. Munich: Iudicium, 1996.

———. "Nachwort." In Franz Baermann Steiner, *Am stürzenden Pfad: Gesammelte Gedichte,* ed. Jeremy Adler, 440–62. Göttingen: Wallstein, 2000.

Kohl, Katrin. "Guarding the Myths. Franz Baermann Steiner's *Conquests.*" In *From Prague Poet to Oxford Anthropologist: Franz Baermann Steiner Celebrated. Essays and Translations,* ed. Jeremy Adler, Richard Fardon, et al., 162–86. Munich: Iudicium; London: University of London School of Advanced Study, 2003.

Peter Waterhouse

Pirro, Maurizio. " 'Glauben Sie mir das Wort Blume?' Productive Language Scepticism and Skilful Questioning in the Work of Peter Waterhouse." *Austrian Studies,* 12: *The Austrian Lyric* (2004): 196–213.

Josef Weinheber

Berger, Albert. *Josef Weinheber (1892–1945): Leben und Werk, Leben im Werk.* Salzburg: Müller, 1999.

Jenaczek, Friedrich. "Josef Weinheber: "Im Grase." Zur Ästhetik der Lyrik Weinhebers und zu ihrem Zusammenhang mit dem Sprachdenken von Karl Kraus." In *Die Österreichische Literatur: Ihr Profil von der Jahrhundertwende bis zur Gegenwart (1880–1980),* ed. Herbert Zeman. 2 vols. Graz: Akademische Druck und Verlagsanstalt, 1989. 2: 1263–1279.

Pongs, Hermann. "Josef Weinheber, 'Zwischen Göttern und Dämonen.' " *Dichtung und Volkstum* 40 (1939): 77–84.

Franz Werfel

Steiman, Lionel B. *Franz Werfel, the Faith of an Exile: From Prague to Beverly Hills.* Waterloo, ON: W. Laurier UP, 1985.

Wagner, Fred. "'Das herrliche Verhängnis' — the Poetry of Franz Werfel." In *Franz Werfel: An Austrian Writer*, ed. Lothar Huber, 37–54. Oxford: Berg, 1989.

Wiener Gruppe

Rühm, Gerhard, ed. *Die Wiener Gruppe.* 2nd, expanded ed. Reinbek bei Hamburg: Rowohlt, 1985.

Walter-Buchebner-Literaturprojekt, ed. *die wiener gruppe.* Vienna, Cologne, Weimar: Böhlau, 1987.

History, Society, Culture: 1945–2000

Aspetsberger, Friedbert, et al., eds. *Literatur der Nachkriegszeit und der fünfziger Jahre in Österreich.* Vienna: Österreichischer Bundesverlag, 1984.

Best, Alan, and Hans Wolfschütz, eds. *Modern Austrian Writing: Literature and Society after 1945.* London: Wolff, 1980.

Bischof, Günter, and Anton Pelinka. *Austrian Historical Memory and National Identity.* New Brunswick: Transaction, 1996.

Bushell, Anthony, ed. *Austria 1945–1955: Studies in Political and Cultural Re-emergence.* Cardiff: U of Wales P, 1996.

Deutsch-Schreiner, Evelyn. *Theater im "Wiederaufbau": Zur Kulturpolitik im österreichischen Parteien- und Verbändestaat.* Vienna: Sonderzahl, 2001.

Fitzmaurice, John. *Austrian Politics and Society Today.* Basingstoke: Macmillan, 1990.

Good, David, and Ruth Wodak, eds. *From World War to Waldheim: Culture and Politics in Austria and the United States.* New York and Oxford: Berghahn, 1999.

Hanisch, Ernst. *Der lange Schatten des Staates: Österreichische Gesellschaftsgeschichte im 20. Jahrhundert.* Vienna: Ueberreuter, 1994.

Kaukoreit, Volker, and Kristina Pfoser. *Die österreichische Literatur seit 1945.* Stuttgart: Reclam, 2000.

Markolin, Caroline. *Modern Austrian Writing: A Study Guide for Austrian Literature 1945–1990.* New York: Lang, 1995.

Mantl, Wolfgang, ed. *Politik in Österreich: Die Zweite Republik: Bestand und Wandel.* Vienna, Cologne, Weimar: Böhlau, 1992.

McVeigh, Joseph. *Kontinuität und Vergangenheitsbewältigung in der österreichischen Literatur nach 1945.* Vienna: Braumüller, 1988.

Schmidt-Dengler, Wendelin. "Zäsuren? Probleme einer österreichischen Literaturgeschichte nach 1945." *Stimulus*, Beiheft 1 (1997): 77–84.

Sieder, Reinhart, et al., eds. *Österreich 1945–1955: Gesellschaft, Politik, Kultur.* Vienna: Verlag für Gesellschaftskritik, 1995.

Steininger, Rolf, and Michael Gehler, eds. *Österreich im 20. Jahrhundert,* vol. 2, *Vom Zweiten Weltkrieg bis zur Gegenwart.* Vienna, Cologne, Weimar: Böhlau, 1997.

Zeman, Herbert, ed. *Geschichte der Literatur in Österreich: Das 20. Jahrhundert.* Graz: Akademische Druck- u. Verlagsanstalt, 1999.

Zeyringer, Klaus, *Österreichische Literatur 1945–1998.* Innsbruck: Haymon, 1999.

Drama 1945–2000

General

Aspetsberger, Friedbert. "Versuchte Korrekturen. Ideologie und Politik im Drama nach 1945." In *Literatur der Nachkriegszeit und der fünfziger Jahre,* ed. F.A., et al., 241–70. Vienna: Österreichischer Bundesverlag, 1984.

Aust, Hugo, et al. *Volksstück: Vom Hanswurstspiel zum sozialen Drama der Gegenwart.* Munich: Beck, 1989.

Haider-Pregler, Hilde, and Peter Roessler, eds. *Zeit der Befreiung: Wiener Theater nach 1945.* Vienna: Picus, 1998.

Landa, Jutta. *Bürgerliches Schocktheater: Entwicklungen im österreichischen Drama der sechziger und siebziger Jahre.* Frankfurt am Main: Athenäum, 1988.

Roessler, Peter. *Studien zur Auseinandersetzung mit Faschismus und Krieg im österreichischen Drama der Nachkriegszeit und der 50er Jahre.* Cologne: Pahl-Rugenstein, 1987.

Aktionismus

Braun, Kerstin. *Der Wiener Aktionismus: Positionen und Prinzipien.* Vienna, Cologne, Weimar: Böhlau, 1999.

Jahraus, Oliver. *Die Aktion des Wiener Aktionismus: Subversion der Kultur und Dispositionierung des Bewusstseins.* Munich: Fink, 2001.

Wolfgang Bauer

Grond, Walter, and Gerhard Melzer, eds. *Wolfgang Bauer.* Graz: Droschl, 1994.

Melzer, Gerhard. *Wolfgang Bauer: Eine Einführung in das Gesamtwerk.* Königsstein/Ts.: Athenäum, 1981.

Thomas Bernhard

Dronske, Ulrich. "Sprach-Dramen. Zu den Theaterstücken Thomas Bernhards." In *Thomas Bernhard: Die Zurichtung des Menschen,* ed. Alexander Honold and Markus Joch. Würzburg: Königshausen & Neumann, 1999.

Jahraus, Oliver. *Das "monomanische" Werk: Eine strukturale Werkanalyse des Oeuvres von Thomas Bernhard.* Frankfurt: Lang, 1992.

Klug, Christian. *Thomas Bernhards Theaterstücke.* Stuttgart: Metzler, 1991.

Schmidt-Dengler, Wendelin. "Ohnmacht durch Gewohnheit. Zum dramatischen Werk von Thomas Bernhard." In W. S.-D. *Der Übertreibungskünstler: Studien zu Thomas Bernhard,* 156–74. Vienna: Sonderzahl, 1997.

Elfriede Jelinek

Caduff, Corinna. *Ich gedeihe inmitten von Seuchen: Elfriede Jelinek — Theatertexte.* Bern: Lang, 1991.

Hass, Ulrike. "'Sinn egal. Körper zwecklos.' Anmerkungen zur Figur des Chores bei Elfriede Jelinek anläßlich Einar Schleefs Inszenierung von *Ein Sportstück.*" *Text und Kritik* 117: *Elfriede Jelinek* (1999), rev. ed., 51–62.

Hoff, Dagmar von. "Stücke für das Theater. Überlegungen zu Elfriede Jelineks Methode der Destruktion." In *Gegen den schönen Schein,* ed. Christa Gürtler, 112–20. Frankfurt am Main: Neue Kritik, 1990.

Janz, Marlies. *Elfriede Jelinek.* Stuttgart: Metzler, 1995.

Schmidt, Christine. "Sprechen — Sein. Jelineks Theater der Sprachflächen." *Sprache im technischen Zeitalter* 38 (2000): 65–75.

Werner Schwab

Fuchs, Gerhard, ed. *Werner Schwab.* Graz: Droschl, 2000.

Landa, Jutta. "Königskomödien oder 'Fäkaliendramen'?" *Modern Austrian Literature* 26 (1993) 3/4: 217–29.

Miesbacher, Harald. *Die Anatomie des Schwabischen: Werner Schwabs Bühnensprache.* Graz: Droschl. 2003.

Marlene Streeruwitz

Fliedl, Konstanze. "Marlene Streeruwitz." In *Deutsche Dramatiker des 20. Jahrhunderts,* eds. Alo Allkemper and Norbert Otto Eke, 835–50. Berlin: Schmidt, 2000.

Hempel, Nele. *Marlene Streeruwitz — Gewalt und Humor im dramatischen Werk.* Tübingen: Stauffenburg. 2001.

Vestli, Elin Nesje. "Ein akustisches Setting. Überlegungen zur Dramaturgie von Marlene Streeruwitz." *Trans. Internetzeitschrift für Kulturwissenschaften,* 9 (2001).

Wiener Gruppe

Bucher, André. *Die szenischen Texte der Wiener Gruppe.* Bern: Lang, 1992.

Schmidt-Dengler, Wendelin. "Die Einsamkeit Kasperls als Langstreckenläufer. Ein Versuch zu H. C. Artmanns und Konrad Bayers Dramen." In *verLockerungen: Österreichische Avantgarde im 20. Jahrhundert. Studien zu Walter Serner u.a.,* ed. W. S.-D., 75–95. Vienna: Edition Praesens, 1994.

Schmidt-Dengler, Wendelin. "Parodie und Reduktion. Die Wiener Volkskomödie und das Theater der Wiener Gruppe." In *Schluß mit dem Abendland: Der lange Atem der österreichischen Avantgarde*, ed. Thomas Eder and Klaus Kastberger, 27–41. Vienna: Zsolnay. 2000.

Prose Fiction 1945–2000

General

Bartsch, Kurt. "Die österreichische Gegenwartsliteratur." In *Die Geschichte der deutschen Literatur*, ed. Viktor Žmegač, vol. 3, 697–825. Königstein/Ts: Athenäum, 1984.

Fiddler, Allyson, ed. *"Other" Austrians: Post-1945 Austrian Women's Writing*. Bern: Lang, 1998.

Greiner, Ulrich. *Der Tod des Nachsommers: Aufsätze, Porträts, Kritiken zur österreichischen Gegenwartsliteratur*. Munich and Vienna: Hanser, 1979.

Hussong, Marion. *Der Nationalsozialismus im österreichischen Roman 1945–1969*. Tübingen: Stauffenberg, 2000.

Kunne, Andrea. *Heimat im Roman: Last oder Lust? Transformationen in der österreichischen Nachkriegsliteratur*. Amsterdam: Rodopi, 1991.

Menasse, Robert. *Überbau und Underground: Essays zum österreichischen Geist*. Frankfurt: Suhrkamp, 1997.

Zeyringer, Klaus. *Innerlichkeit und Öffentlichkeit: Österreichische Literatur der 80er Jahre*. Tübingen: Francke, 1992.

Ingeborg Bachmann

Albrecht, Monika, and Dirk Göttsche, eds. *Bachmann-Handbuch. Leben — Werk — Wirkung*. Stuttgart and Weimar: Metzler, 2002.

———, eds. *"Über die Zeit schreiben": Literatur und kulturwissenschaftliche Essays zum Werk Ingeborg Bachmanns*. Würzburg: Königshausen & Neumann, 1998.

Mayer, Mathias, ed. *Werke von Ingeborg Bachmann: Interpretationen*. Stuttgart: Reclam, 2001.

Stoll, Andrea, ed. *Ingeborg Bachmanns "Malina."* Frankfurt am Main: Suhrkamp, 1992.

Thomas Bernhard

Höller, Hans, and Irene Heidelberger-Leonard, eds. *Antiautobiografie: Zu Thomas Bernhards "Auslöschung."* Frankfurt am Main: Suhrkamp, 1995.

Huntemann, Willi. *Artistik und Rollenspiel: Das System Thomas Bernhard*. Würzburg: Königshausen & Neumann, 1990.

Long, J. J. *The Novels of Thomas Bernhard.* Rochester, NY: Camden House, 2001.

Pfabigan, Alfred. *Thomas Bernhard: Ein österreichisches Weltexperiment.* Vienna: Zsolnay, 1999.

Peter Handke

Fellinger, Raymond, ed. *Peter Handke.* Frankfurt am Main: Suhrkamp, 1985.

Henning, Thomas. *Intertextualität als ethische Dimension: Peter Handkes Ästhetik "nach Auschwitz."* Würzburg: Königshausen & Neumann, 1996.

Michel, Volker. *Peter Handkes Poetik der Erinnerung.* Würzburg: Königshausen & Neumann, 1998.

Elfriede Jelinek

Fiddler, Allyson. *Rewriting Reality: An Introduction to Elfriede Jelinek.* Oxford and Providence: Berg, 1994.

Johns, Jorun B., and Katherine Arens, eds. *Elfriede Jelinek: Framed by Language.* Riverside, CA: Ariadne, 1994.

Gerhard Roth

Schütte, Uwe. *Auf der Spur der Vergessenen: Gerhard Roth und seine Archive des Schweigens.* Vienna, Cologne, Weimar: Böhlau, 1999.

Popular Culture, 1945–2000

Büttner, Elisabeth, and Christian Dewald. *Anschluß an Morgen: Eine Geschichte des österreichischen Films von 1945 bis zur Gegenwart.* Salzburg: Residenz, 1997.

Ergert, Viktor. *Fünfzig Jahre Rundfunk in Österreich.* 4 vols. Salzburg: Residenz, 1974.

Fabris, Hans Heinz, and Kurt Luger, eds. *Medienkultur in Österreich: Film, Fotografie, Fernsehen und Video in der Zweiten Republik.* Vienna, Cologne, Graz: Böhlau, 1988.

Godler, Haimo, et al. *Vom Dampfradio zur Klangtapete: Beiträge zu achtzig Jahren Hörfunk in Österreich.* Vienna, Cologne, Weimar: Böhlau, 2004.

Grissemann, Ernst, and Hans Veigl, eds. *Testbild, Twen und Nierentisch: Unser Lebensgefühl in den 50er Jahren.* Vienna, Cologne, Weimar: Böhlau, 2002.

Jagschitz, Gerhard, and Klaus-Dieter Mulley, eds. *Die "wilden" fünfziger Jahre: Gesellschaft, Formen und Gefühle eines Jahrzehnts in Österreich.* St. Pölten and Vienna: Verlag Niederösterreichisches Pressehaus, 1986.

Kudrnofsky, Wolfgang. *Vom Dritten Reich zum Dritten Mann: Helmut Qualtingers Welt der vierziger Jahre.* Vienna, Munich, Zurich: Molden, 1973.

Larkey, Edward. *Pungent Sounds: Constructing Identity with Popular Music in Austria.* New York: Lang, 1993.

Luger, Kurt. *Die konsumierte Rebellion: Aufwachsen mit der Kulturindustrie 1945–1990.* Vienna and St. Johann: Österreichischer Kunst- und Kulturverlag, 1991.

Pauser, Susanne, et al., eds. *Faserschmeichler, Fönfrisuren und die Ölkrise: Das Bilderbuch der siebziger Jahre.* Vienna, Cologne, Weimar: Böhlau, 2000.

———, eds. *Neon, Pacman und die Yuppies: Das Bilderbuch der achtziger Jahre.* Vienna, Cologne, Weimar: Böhlau, 2001.

Resetarits, Willi, and Hans Veigl, eds. *Beatles, Bond und Blumenkinder: Unser Lebensgefühl in den 60er Jahren.* Vienna, Cologne, Weimar: Böhlau, 2003.

Tozzer, Kurt, and Martin Majnaric. *Achtung Sendung: Höhepunkte, Stars und exklusive Bilder aus 50 Jahren Fernsehen.* Vienna: Ueberreuter, 2005.

Wagnleiter, Reinhold. *Coca-Colonisation und Kalter Krieg: Die Kulturmission der USA in Österreich nach dem Zweiten Weltkrieg.* Vienna: Verlag für Gesellschaftskritik, 1991.

Responses to Multiculturalism around 2000

Bartsch, Kurt, ed. *Barbara Frischmuth.* Dossier, no. 4. Graz: Droschl, 1992.

Decker, Craig, ed. *Balancing Acts: Textual Strategies of Peter Henisch.* Riverside, CA: Ariadne, 2002.

Grünzweig, Walter, and Gerhard Fuchs, eds. *Peter Henisch.* Dossier, no. 21. Graz: Droschl, 2003.

Lamb-Faffelberger, Margarete, ed. *Literature, Film and the Culture Industry in Contemporary Austria.* New York: Peter Lang, 2002.

Landa, Jutta, ed. *"I am too many people." Peter Turrini: Playwright, Poet, Essayist.* Riverside, CA: Ariadne, 1998.

Posthofen, Renate S., ed. *Barbara Frischmuth in Contemporary Context.* Riverside, CA: Ariadne, 1999.

———. "Of Inclusions and Exclusions: Austrian Identity Reconsidered." In *Transforming the Center, Eroding the Margins: Essays on Ethnic and Cultural Boundaries in German-Speaking Countries,* ed. Dagmar Lorenz and Renate S. Posthofen. Columbia, SC: Camden House, 1998.

Roethke, Gisela. "Lilian Faschinger im Gespräch." *Modern Austrian Literature* 33.1 (2000): 85–103.

Contributors

ANDREW BARKER is Professor of Austrian Studies, University of Edinburgh, Co-director of the Centre for Austrian Studies at the Universities of Aberdeen and Edinburgh, and Senior Research Fellow, Institute of Germanic and Romance Studies, University of London. His books include *Telegrams from the Soul: Peter Altenberg and the Culture of fin-de-siecle Vienna*, and most recently the edited volume (with Leo A. Lensing) *Peter Altenberg, "Semmering 1912" / Semmering 1912: Ein altbekanntes Buch und ein neuentdecktes Photoalbum*.

JUDITH BENISTON is Senior Lecturer in German at University College London. She is the author of *"Welttheater": Hofmannsthal, Richard von Kralik, and the Revival of Catholic Drama in Austria, 1890–1934* and of a number of articles on Austrian drama and cultural history, especially of the interwar period. Together with Professor Robert Vilain, she co-edits the journal *Austrian Studies*. She is currently working on a study of historical drama in Austria since the Enlightenment.

ANTHONY BUSHELL is Professor of German at the University of Wales, Bangor, where he served as Head of the School of Modern Languages from 1998 to 2005. His principal area of research is German and Austrian literature of the early postwar period, with a particular emphasis on lyric poetry. He is author of *The Emergence of West German Poetry from the Second World War into the Early Post War Period: A Study in Poetic Response*. He has written extensively on Austrian literature, including articles on Hans Lebert, Peter Henisch, Anna Mitgutsch, and post-1945 Austrian poetry. For a number of years he was the English language editor of the journal *Aussenpolitik: German Foreign Affairs Review* and he is editor of the series Austrian Studies in Context. He is chairman of a joint British-Slovakian research group working on contemporary Austrian literature.

ALLYSON FIDDLER is Professor of German and Austrian Studies at Lancaster University. She is the author of *Rewriting Reality: an Introduction to Elfriede Jelinek* and editor (with W. E. Yates and John Warren) of *From Perinet to Jelinek: Viennese Theatre in its Political and Intellectual Context*. Her recent publications include articles on Carinthia and interculturalism, sport and national identity in contemporary Austria drama, and on Jelinek's plays *Das Lebewohl* and *Burgtheater*. She is a member of the international advisory boards of the journals *Austrian Studies* and *Modern*

Austrian Literature, as well as of the Elfriede-Jelinek Forschungszentrum at the University of Vienna.

MURRAY G. HALL is Professor of German at the University of Vienna. His publications include *Der Fall Bettauer*; *Österreichische Verlagsgeschichte 1918–1938* (2 vols.); *Der Paul Zsolnay Verlag: Von der Gründung bis zur Rückkehr aus dem Exil;* (as editor) *Robert Musil. Briefe 1901–1942*; (as editor with Gerhard Renner) *Handbuch der Nachlässe und Sammlungen österreichischer Autoren*; (as editor with Herbert Ohrlinger) *Der Paul Zsolnay Verlag 1924–1999: Dokumente und Zeugnisse.* He edited Hugo Bettauer's *Gesammelte Werke in sechs Bänden*; Carl Junker, *Zum Buchwesen in Österreich: Gesammelte Schriften (1896–1927)*; and (with Christina Köstner and Margot Werner) *Geraubte Bücher: Die Österreichische Nationalbibliothek stellt sich ihrer NS-Vergangenheit.* In 2002 he was awarded the Goldenes Ehrenzeichen für Verdienste um das Land Wien.

KATRIN KOHL is a Lecturer in German at Oxford University and a Fellow and Tutor of Jesus College, Oxford. Her books include *Friedrich Gottlieb Klopstock* and *Rhetoric, the Bible, and the Origins of Free Verse: The Early "Hymns" of Friedrich Gottlieb Klopstock.* She has published articles on aspects of poetry and poetics in the eighteenth and twentieth centuries, including Rilke, Bachmann, Rühmkorf, Lavant, Pastior, Okopenko and Jandl. She is currently completing a monograph on the role of metaphor in German poetics from the Middle Ages to the present, entitled *Poetologische Metaphern: Formen und Funktionen in der deutschen Literatur.*

J. J. LONG is Professor of German at Durham University, UK. He is author of *The Novels of Thomas Bernhard*, co-editor of *W. G. Sebald: A Critical Companion*, and has published widely on twentieth-century German and Austrian writers, including Wolfgang Hildesheimer, Gerhard Fritsch, Hans Lebert, Bernhard Schlink, Norbert Gstrein, W. G. Sebald, and Monika Maron.

DAGMAR C. G. LORENZ, Professor of Germanic Studies at the University of Illinois at Chicago, focuses in her research on Austrian and nineteenth- and twentieth-century German and German-Jewish literary and cultural issues and Holocaust Studies, with an emphasis on history and social thought and minority discourses. She was the editor of *The German Quarterly* (1997–2003) and held offices in MLA, GSA, MALCA, and AATG. Recent book publications include *Keepers of the Motherland: German Texts by Jewish Women Writers*, and *Verfolgung bis zum Massenmord: Diskurse zum Holocaust in deutscher Sprache.* Edited volumes include *A Companion to the Works of Elias Canetti*; *A Companion to the Works of Arthur Schnitzler*; *Contemporary Jewish Writing in Austria*; *Transforming the Center, Eroding the Margins: Essays on Ethnic and Cultural Boundaries in German-Speaking*

Countries (with Renate S. Posthofen); *Insiders and Outsiders: Jewish and Gentile Culture in Germany and Austria*.

JOSEPH MCVEIGH is Professor of German Studies at Smith College in Northampton, Massachusetts. He is the author of the study *Kontinuität und Vergangenheitsbewältigung in der österreichischen Literatur nach 1945*; co-editor of the two-volume collection of essays *America and the Germans*; and translator of Georg von Welling's *Opus Mago-Cabbalisticum* (1721). He has also published numerous articles on Austrian literary culture since 1918, most recently focusing on Ingeborg Bachmann and her work for the American occupation radio network Rot-Weiß-Rot, after having discovered fifteen previously unknown radio scripts of the comedy series *Die Radiofamilie* which she penned for the network in 1952 and 1953.

RITCHIE ROBERTSON is a Professor of German at Oxford University and a Fellow and Tutor of St John's College, Oxford. Since 2004 he has been a Fellow of the British Academy. His books include *Kafka: Judaism, Politics, and Literature*; *Heine*, in the series Jewish Thinkers; *The "Jewish Question" in German Literature, 1749–1939: Emancipation and Its Discontents*; and *Kafka: A Very Short Introduction* (2004). He has edited *The German-Jewish Dialogue: An Anthology of Literary texts, 1749–1993*, and *The Cambridge Companion to Thomas Mann*. He was co-editor of the yearbook *Austrian Studies* from 1990 to 1999 and has since 2000 been Germanic Editor of the *Modern Language Review*. He is currently working on a study of the Austrian Enlightenment.

JANET STEWART is Lecturer in German at the University of Aberdeen, where she also contributes to the Cultural History program and has recently developed a postgraduate degree in Visual Culture. She is a Director of the Centre for Austrian Studies, a collaborative venture with the University of Edinburgh. She is the author of *Fashioning Vienna: Adolf Loos's Cultural Criticism* as well as a number of articles on twentieth-century Austrian and German literature and on cultural and urban history. Together with Simon Ward, she has edited a volume of essays on contemporary Austrian culture, *Blueprints for No-Man's Land: Connections in Contemporary Austrian Culture*. She is currently preparing a cultural history of public speaking and public space, entitled *Talking of Modernity: The Sites and Subjects of Urban Discourse in Berlin and Vienna*.

JULIANE VOGEL is Professor of Modern German Literature at the University of Vienna; she is currently a visiting professor at Princeton. Her publications include *Elisabeth von Österreich: Momente aus dem Leben einer Kunstfigur*; *Die Furie und das Gesetz: Die große Szene in der Tragödie des 19. Jahrhunderts*; and many articles on recent Austrian literature.

Index